ALL AUTHORS ARE EQUAL

By the same author

AN OCCUPATION FOR GENTLEMEN

FRONTISPIECE: The Author

ALL AUTHORS ARE EQUAL

The Publishing Life of FREDRIC WARBURG 1936–1971

*

'There can be no good literature
without praise.' W. B. YEATS

HUTCHINSON OF LONDON

HUTCHINSON & CO (Publishers) LTD
3 Fitzroy Square, London W 1

—

London Melbourne Sydney Auckland
Wellington Johannesburg Cape Town
and agencies throughout the world

—

First published 1973

Set in Monotype Baskerville

—

Printed in Great Britain by
Hazell Watson & Viney Ltd, Aylesbury, Bucks

ISBN 0 09 117610 7

W8
$5.00

To

GEORGE ORWELL

and

THOMAS MANN

and

*all those writers, dead and still living,
who have made my publishing business
worthy of respect*

Contents

Acknowledgements

IN the writing of this book I have obtained much interesting material and useful criticism, not only from authors I have published but a number of others. Most are named in the text, especially where I have quoted from their letters to me. But I would like to thank all of them here for their help. Their names are listed in the order of their appearance.

F. D. Sanders (for information on publishing in wartime); Rayner Heppenstall; Sebastian Haffner; T. R. Fyvel; Charles Roth (my London traveller); Claire Lawson-Dick (for information about her brother, Oliver); Lionel Trilling; Thomas D. Burns (about his brother, John Horne Burns); Maurice Goudeket (third husband of Colette); Gore Vidal; Pierre Boulle; C. H. Rolph (on the legal aspects of obscenity); Harold Strauss (on the Japanese translation project); Francis King (for permission to quote from Joe Ackerley's letters); Cyrus Brooks (agent for the alleged lama); Eithne Wilkins (widow of Ernst Kaiser, Musil's translator); John Prebble; Melvyn Bragg; Veronica Wedgwood; Julian Gloag; Dennis Bloodworth; and any others whom I may regrettably have overlooked. Without their assistance this book would have fallen short of my hopes.

David Farrer, a director of and my colleague in Secker & Warburg since 1947, has successfully jogged my memory of several important incidents. My thanks to him, and to John Blackwell, a Secker & Warburg editor, for useful editorial assistance, and to William Neill-Hall, Blackwell's assistant, for help in research among our files. I must also thank *The New Yorker* magazine for permission to use in Chapter 12 material from the piece they printed for me in their issue of April 20, 1957, under the title of 'A Slight Case of Obscenity'.

Finally I owe a big debt of gratitude to my wife for her unflagging devotion to my well-being during the two years it has taken to write the book. In particular, she has willingly abandoned her own work as a painter for almost a year to make conditions easier for me, a sacrifice which I know was not easy for her to make.

Preface

SINCE I published *An Occupation for Gentlemen* in 1959, the book to which this is a sequel, there has been quite a number of books written by publishers on publishing. To some extent I had set a fashion, or perhaps showed that the task was not impossible. Two of these books are outstanding, Michael Howard's *Jonathan Cape* and Philip Unwin's *The Publishing Unwins*, but they differ considerably from my book. Howard's is a history of his firm, while Unwin's consists largely of a bitter-sweet portrait of Sir Stanley Unwin, his famous uncle.

The reason why the number of books on publishing is scanty, and why few of them are worth reading except by those professionally involved, seems clear. There is only a limited number of top or near top executives in those branches of the book trade which appeal to a wide public, and from such a limited number it is obvious that few will have the necessary time or ability to write. It is clear too that much of the information available to a writer-publisher is confidential. A special example of this is that of a publisher's opinion of his own authors. While I am clearly at liberty to say what I like about a George Orwell, a Thomas Mann or a Colette without damaging either their sales or their reputation or their feelings, let alone libelling them – since you cannot libel the dead – I cannot speak as freely about those among the living. It follows that it is difficult for a publisher to write an interesting book about his publishing life at least till after he has retired. By then he may well be exhausted or disillusioned or he may feel that he can write freely only about the distant past which may seem to him less interesting than it appeared at the time. From these dangers I hope I have escaped. If so, it is partly because the calibre of the authors I have published and the books I have issued was high enough to give them a long-lasting value.

All Authors Are Equal is arranged as far as possible in chronological order, though this has presented difficulties. But, since such talent as I have as a writer is for the telling of tales, it was inevitable. The book as a whole may be seen as the story of my publishing life, the chapters and sections of chapters are in the main stories within the story. So it is that the book is a hybrid not an autobiography, not a history of a publishing house, not a philosophy of publishing, not a series of critical studies, but a bit of all these. I have delved into the past, racked my memory, read files, consulted colleagues, written to authors and others for information. What I have chosen to salvage and relate is the more interesting, the more amusing, the more exciting, the more unusual and the more absurd episodes of a long career.

Between 1936 when the firm was founded, and 1971 when I resigned as its executive head, I must have published over 2,000 titles written by many hundred different authors. Only a tiny proportion of these books and authors are mentioned in the text, and these not always the most important or distinguished or saleable. The books I do refer to are those which have an interest for readers today because of what happened before, during or after they were published. The writers who appear are chosen for the same reason, or sometimes because I knew them well, and occasionally because they gave me so much pleasure . . . or pain.

To the many authors who do not figure in these pages I must appeal for understanding. Most, though not all, of them have written excellent novels or useful general books, sometimes superior to those I have included. But they are omitted, often because my relationship with them was so smooth that nothing remarkable happened between us or because their books are now so well-known that I, no literary critic, can add little to what has already been said about them.

British books reflect the national character more directly and more lastingly than any other cultural product. British books can and do influence our opinion of ourselves, and as exports they reveal the nature of the British character wherever the English language is read, that is, in almost every country in the world.

No one book can give a comprehensive picture of the publishing trade and its intricate relationships with printers, binders, papermakers, booksellers, libraries, newspapers, to say nothing of writers and their agents. No one book can reveal all the elements in even one man's publishing life. But I have attempted to paint an impressionist study of publishing in my time, more candid and in some ways more complete than any that has appeared till now. Publishing is still an occupation for gentlemen, as it has always been, and remains also a real business, as it has always been. Whatever I may have written in these pages, I have never quite forgotten its double face. If I had, my career would have been quite a bit briefer.

ALL AUTHORS ARE EQUAL

I

Searchlight

On September 3, 1939 my wife and I sat down at 11 a.m. to listen to the long-awaited broadcast of Neville Chamberlain. Immediately afterwards, the air-raid sirens screamed. 'That,' said Pamela, 'is the most *real* sound I've heard for years.' She stood up and looked out of the window at the sky. It was no doubt a day for the long horizon and an end to double talk. 'This,' said Pamela quietly, 'is the end of my youth. I shall never be young again.' To this I could find no adequate answer. 'Don't you think,' I asked prosaically, 'that we should go down to the air-raid shelter?'

* * *

There are three important goals at which a publisher should aim at the beginning of a major war. The first is to stay alive and if possible unhurt. The second is to keep his office and his stock of books undamaged. The third is to prevent the destruction of his paper supply, since it is a platitude in the publishing trade that paper is short in wartime. Of these three objectives I succeeded only in the first.

In September 1939 Secker & Warburg was exactly three-and-a-half years old, a midget firm, fragile as bone china. As readers of *An Occupation* will remember, we had made a jerky and consistently unprofitable start, but by no means an inglorious one. H. G. Wells, Thomas Mann, André Gide, Lewis Mumford and George Orwell adorned the list, and quite a few other authors of distinction. Insolvent we might be, but we were bursting with vitality. The staff was small. Our premises consisted of four flimsy rooms on the mezzanine of 22 Essex Street, Strand, ill-suited to stand up to a direct hit from any bomb larger than a hand-grenade. Yet, although many publishing houses were evacuated from London, I never considered following in their footsteps, and for an excellent reason – we hadn't the money.

Nor, indeed, had I personally the faintest desire to go. The war, I felt strongly, was my war, my personal crusade as an Englishman and a Jew. The least I could do was to stay in London at the nerve-centre of events and take my chance as a target for the Luftwaffe. In this matter my co-director, Roger Senhouse, patriot, gambler by temperament and physically courageous, was certainly at one with me.

Senhouse was a man of about my own age, the last of a long line of Senhouses from Maryport in Cumberland. A good-looking bachelor, he had been educated at Eton and Magdalen College, Oxford.

Senhouse was to remain with me till November 1962 when he resigned. Some three years later he died. Although we had many differences of opinion and a number of fierce quarrels on matters of policy, I believe he accepted that I was always acting in the best interests of the firm as I estimated them. At times he seemed larger than life, buoyant, audacious and hyper-active. His rages, when he was roused, were uninhibitedly magnificent. Though he seemed to bear no grudges, I fear that at times his friends thought my treatment of him was harsh. Yet the fact remained that he stayed with the firm and me for nearly thirty years. During the first fifteen years there were long periods when he had financial control of the firm, either on his own or with the support of one of his closest friends, yet never did he make any move to throw me out.

Physically brave as a lion, he was something of a moral coward. Yet he had many excellent and some unusual qualities. He was a boon companion when the occasion pleased him. He was a hard worker, though he spent rather too much time on inessentials. He had a real appreciation of literature, coupled with a fabulous memory. He was a connoisseur of modern paintings and of rare books, frequently dealing in them. He was one of the best copy editors and proof readers I have ever known. Above all, he had the important ability to convince many that Secker & Warburg was a distinguished firm with a future. This enabled him, and me, jointly and severally as it were, to acquire many new authors impressed by his magniloquence and my knowledge of publishing practice and theory.

Senhouse, though a bachelor, was very much of a family man and took a great interest in his nephews. He was a first-rate gardener, and once built for me with his own hands a fine rockery in the garden of our country cottage. His clothes were shabby. His office and his London flat were unparalleled miracles of disorder. He might truly be described as one of the last of the distinguished line of English eccentrics.

Throughout this book I have tried to paint a portrait of this baffling character as objectively as possible. His successes and his blunders are alike part of the story. He was perhaps too individualistic (and so too secretive) to fit even into a team so loosely organized as mine. As a patron of literature in the eighteenth century, doing what he liked and to hell with the rest, he would have been in his element. But he was hardly cut out to be an efficient modern publisher in a profit-making system.

In the summer of 1939 Senhouse and his friends had raised a further £5,000 to finance the firm's gaping deficit. This was our provision for war, and temporarily at any rate we were in funds. Though the losses in 1939 were to turn out even larger than usual, I had hopes that the tide might turn. War, I knew, increased the demand for books. At least the 1914–18 war had done so, and it seemed likely the new one would do as much.

Sensibly enough, therefore, I invested as much as I dared of our new capital in paper. Our entire stocks were sent to the great printing establishment of William Brendon at Plymouth. William Brendon was an old friend of mine from my thirteen years at the publishing house of Routledge, and a strong supporter of the firm. We gave Brendons 80% of our printing and binding. In return we received lower rates than we could obtain elsewhere, and still more valuable a longer period in which to pay. My policy of putting all our eggs into one basket seemed at the time sound strategy, but it turned out to have grave tactical defects.

The problem of paper supplies dominated publishing during the war. It influenced nearly every decision made by an active publisher from March 31, 1940 when rationing was first imposed, till as late as the middle of 1948, three years after the end of the war, when it was withdrawn. It had an effect on our own policy and post-war position which can hardly be exaggerated. The rationing scheme worked out by the Board of Trade in the final year of peace made *no provision whatever* for the supply of paper to book publishers. The interests of newspaper owners and magazine proprietors, manufacturers of wrapping-paper for shops, suppliers of toilet-paper, almanacs and a thousand other necessities were thoughtfully considered, but the publishers of books somehow escaped attention. Yet before the war was over, publishers had been granted a higher percentage of their pre-war supplies than any other user. Without books, it might have been said, the people shall perish, if only from boredom.

At the onset of the war the Council of the Publishers Association was concerned about three matters in particular: the possible call-up of vital executives for the armed services, insurance against war-damage, and the supply of paper. To stop the call-up of executives was naturally a forlorn hope almost from the beginning, and insurance against war damage turned out to be a curiously controversial measure. But negotiations between the Board of Trade and the Council led without delay to the inclusion of book publishers among those eligible to receive paper supplies, and individual firms were required to fill in the actual tonnage of paper they had used in the three years 1936–7–8. This period was known as the reference period. The average annual consumption of each firm was computed from these figures, and this average became a quota of 100%. Scrupulously I filled in the forms with figures as exact as I could make them. For us a 100% quota meant about twenty tons of paper a year. Little did I know then what a millstone I was tying round our necks. Before rationing was over, it had nearly suffocated us.*

* * *

On November 9, 1939 we published a novel of undoubted distinction, Rayner Heppenstall's first, *The Blaze of Noon*. Now in our fourth year, we had a good list of European novelists, including Arnold Zweig, author of the famous *The Case of Sergeant Grischa*, Thomas and Heinrich Mann, Gabriel Chevallier, author of *Clochemerle*, Carl Zuckmayer, and Ludwig Renn, but so far as English writers were concerned, the harvest had been unrewarding, certainly in terms of profit, probably in terms of readers' enjoyment. There were, however, some exceptions. Frank Tilsley's first novel, *I'd Do It Again* (1936), the story of a thief, had a harsh brilliance, and he was to become a good popular novelist, but after his second novel he deserted us for one of the larger publishers. Then there was Ralph Fox, with his second novel, *This Was Their Youth* (1937), in which he recreated the atmosphere and character of a typical Northern industrial city in the years before 1914. Fox was the most likeable communist and one of the most likeable men I ever knew. He died

*It is a tribute to the basic honesty of publishers that, with at most three exceptions, we all filled in this horrible form with a good deal of precision.

fighting with the International Brigade in the defence of Madrid against the armies of General Franco. There was James Stern's first book of short stories, *Something Wrong* (1938), which was the work of a master craftsman. But Stern to my great regret has not so far published the fine novel he has it in him to write.

But with Heppenstall's *Blaze of Noon* a potential writer of the first order had manifested himself. Elizabeth Bowen recognized its power and wrote a preface, singling it out from the ruck of indifferent novels which then as now choked the bookshops and libraries. 'It is a story told in the first person,' she wrote, 'by a man in whom one sense is suppressed. The "I" is a blind man, in fact, a young blind masseur who goes to visit a middle-aged woman friend and patient in Cornwall. The impact on him of his new surroundings, the meeting with a new group of people lead the blind man into a complex love affair, both sensual and spiritual, with his old friend's niece . . . this novel, by knocking away devices, looks like – and I think it is – the beginning of something new, unprovincial, in advance of its time.' It was enthusiastically reviewed by other distinguished writers, Edwin Muir, J. C. Powys and V. S. Pritchett who wrote 'his sensuality will shock, but readers will realize that they are being shocked by a writer with one foot in the first rank.' Certainly the *Evening Standard* reviewer was shocked, indeed outraged. His article was headlined by some such words as

BOOK AN AFFRONT TO PUBLIC DECENCY

with the story to follow, including the sentence 'Since *Lady Chatterley's Lover* no novel has been published in this country so boldly challenging as this.' As a matter of face, an *uncensored* Lady Chatterley had certainly not appeared in 1939 in Britain.

In those far-off days permissiveness was not even a dirty word, it was an unknown one. 'Shocking' books simply did not get published. So *Blaze* excited by its unexpectedness. Though the first printing was a mere 1,280 copies, it went into four impressions, and over 6,000 copies were sold by the end of the year. Recently I re-read it. I could not find a single sentence or paragraph which would shock even the puritan publicists of 1972. What it did contain was a moving account of a man and a woman passionately in love by a writer who understood that sex is part of love, though love is frequently not part of sex. *The Blaze of Noon* was not prosecuted, nor was I. For that I had to wait another 15 years.

My young manager, John Pattisson, now a director of Barrie &

Rockliffe, was lunching on *Blaze*'s publication day with a young man then working in the British Museum Library. They had been at Westminster School together a few years before. Pattison had read the midday *Standard* and, apologizing to his friend, rushed back to the office to order an immediate binding of all the unbound stocks, a most sensible decision. The friend's name was Angus Wilson. He was not to appear in my life till ten years later.

* * *

On June 14, 1940, the day on which Paris fell to the German armies, we published a remarkable volume, *Germany Jekyll-and-Hyde*, by Sebastian Haffner. On publication it made a great stir, was specially recommended by the Ministry of Information, praised on the B.B.C., twice mentioned in the House of Commons and once in the Lords, and was referred to editorially in papers ranging from the *Evening Standard* to the *New Statesman*. J. B. Priestley wrote 'I hope it sells a million copies'.

Haffner had come from a civil service family in Prussia, of good, solid Aryan stock. However, even at an early age, he had diverged somewhat from the family image. Essayist and reviewer, he was particularly a music critic. Indeed, his pseudonym, Haffner, had been chosen from Mozart's symphony of that name. In 1938, hating Nazism, he managed to escape and arrived in England a few weeks before the betrayal of the Czechs in September. With him had come his Jewish fiancée, whom he married two days after landing. Married life costs money and soon Haffner had spent the small amount he had managed to bring out of Germany. By the spring of 1939 he was almost at his wits' end, and in desperation had written to me, sending the synopsis of a book he planned to write. He had sent it to my firm because, as he wrote to me, 'you were the publisher of Thomas Mann and generally the leading firm in England for contemporary German literature.' What Haffner could not realize, and what I did not dare tell him, was that the firm was in desperate financial straits.

Haffner's book was to be a political autobiography. I remember it as the most brilliant synopsis ever put before me. Recently Haffner wrote to me, 'I could hardly believe my luck when you reacted in an interested and friendly manner, invited me to see you, and after I had done a first chapter made a contract for the book. How well I remember it! You actually contracted to pay me an advance of £2 a week for half a year. Never in my life, before or after, did I feel such a relief.' This book was never completed. When Haffner was halfway through it, the war broke out, and he felt he must write something less private and more directly political.

In the late autumn of 1939, he sent me several chapters of *A Survey of Germany*. 'You accepted the surprise with much patience and good grace, and continued to pay me my weekly two pounds. This was money in those times!' he wrote. I also suggested the change of title to *Germany Jekyll-and-Hyde,* which suited the book to perfection. We sent the book to the printers at the end of January 1940 . . . and two weeks later Haffner was interned. The Aliens Tribunal decided that Haffner, not being Jewish and not having a job, had not made out a convincing case for going free in war-time England. To say that I was enraged is putting it mildly. It seemed to be all of a piece with what I thought of as the feeble and traitorous policies of the Chamberlain Government.

Haffner had disappeared, but I had no idea where to. My author and his book were in jeopardy. In a fury I rang the Home Office, out of the blue, demanding to speak to a girl I knew who worked there. I talked of the wickedness and folly of interning a strong anti-Nazi at a time when anti-Nazi Germans, if they were Aryans, were not too thick on the ground. I told her that Haffner had written an important book, that it would be of great benefit to Britain in its struggle with Germany to have an original analysis of our enemies' character. If Haffner were left in an internment camp, how the hell, I asked her, could we publish the book? My anger and eloquence brought success. Strange things happened in those days, and ministries perhaps feared the wrath of the public more than they do now. Two months later Haffner rang up. He had been released.

'It was then you actually saved my life,' he wrote in October 1970, 'it was entirely owing to your unsolicited intervention with the Home Office that I was released. How you did it I don't know to this day. Normally it took at least six months for the case of an internee to be heard by an appeals tribunal. If I had been in Seaton camp* in May, I should have been shipped with all the other inmates to Canada in the *Arandora Star,* which was torpedoed and sunk with great loss of life. I am pretty sure I should not have been among the survivors, as I was in no very robust physical condition at that time.' Saving your author's life is an unusual publishing achievement. During the war and after Haffner worked on the *Observer,* but in 1954 went back to Berlin as its German correspondent.

Germany Jekyll-and-Hyde sold moderately well, about 2,300 copies

*An internment camp for aliens of enemy countries in Devon.

out of 3,000 in the first year. Then, even though it was out-of-date, it sold out. Perhaps it was as much as could have been expected, considering that it was published on the day Paris fell. The middle of 1940 to the middle of 1941, the year of supreme crisis for Britain, did not encourage the sale of books like *Germany Jekyll-and-Hyde*.

It is interesting to recall today Haffner's prophecy about the fall of Hitler. 'His end is not a matter for speculation. There is a most genuine-sounding declaration of December, 1932. After walking up and down gloomily brooding, Hitler burst out: "When the party falls to pieces . . . I shall end it all in five minutes with a pistol." It is conceivable that he will do that when the game is up. He has the exact kind of courage and cowardice for suicide in despair.' In his final chapter Haffner suggests certain proposals for Germany after its defeat which nearly approach what has actually happened – 'the dismemberment of the Reich, the creation of new German states like Lower Saxony and the Rhineland, and the integration of Germany into some sort of federal Europe.'

To have known during the war a German who combined sense, vision and morality with a genuine love of his own country gave me some measure of objectivity when the war ended. He had done great work for Britain and for Germany.

* * *

Of all the writers with whom I was concerned as a publisher during the late thirties, by far the most important was George Orwell. But this was not apparent at the time. In 1939 he was 36 years old, he had published four novels and four non-fiction books. His name was known in London literary circles and to a modest public, commensurate with the modest sales he had so far achieved. None could have foreseen then, and none did foresee, the world reputation he was to acquire. For me personally he was a friend who strongly influenced my political thinking. For my publishing house he was to be, though I did not suspect it then, a central figure and financially our salvation.

My first meeting with Orwell had taken place in December, 1936. My firm was then nine months old, the Spanish revolution had begun five months before. It could be said that we had started in a revolutionary age, and certainly I had felt myself to be a revolutionary, though I had hardly thought with any precision about means or ends, bloody or bloodless, socialist or communist or anarchist. But of one thing I had been utterly convinced, that the Tory government of Neville Chamberlain was a most evil government.

My revolutionary urges were to be expressed in the publishing sphere, for I never joined any political group or party. It was my purpose to find and support those writers who wished to put forward a programme for Utopia and outline the road to it. But which programme and what road were the ones that led to the promised land I was far from certain, and this should be counted in my favour, though much was owed by me to my wife's infuriating realism.

Of French and Irish descent, though brought up in England since the age of six, Pamela was clearly blessed with a revolutionary heritage of the highest intensity. With a fluency of speech and a tongue sometimes dipped in vitriol, she might well have become one of the greatest agitators of our time, and has sometimes regretted not doing so. But she was held back by lethargy, lack of ambition, an enjoyment of art and civilization, a horror of publicity, but perhaps most of all the thought that she was linked through her English husband to a people who were in her view sheepishly passive and profoundly non-revolutionary. Anarchism best suited her temperament, and she was profoundly moved by the struggle of the Spanish people. But communism also made some appeal to the all-or-nothing side of her nature, though as she said to me many times, 'communism is a good thing for Russia, but in England it's absurd.'

So my wife had kept me safe from the communist influenza that ravaged so many households between 1936 and 1946. The germs of that dread disease had been spread about by the publishing house of Victor Gollancz, founder of the Left Book Club with a membership of 40,000 subscribers. It was against this powerful organization that I had assembled my own forces, a miscellaneous collection of socialists, anarchists, radicals, independent socialists (the Independent Labour Party), pacifists and eccentrics. Among them was Orwell, introduced to me by Fenner (now Lord) Brockway, then secretary of the I.L.P. Orwell was on the eve of his departure for Spain, in theory to report the war and to write a book, in practice to fight.

Orwell had already delivered *The Road to Wigan Pier* to Gollancz, who had been his publisher from the start, but politically the two men had drifted apart – Orwell did not accept that the way ahead ran through Moscow, Gollancz most certainly did. There were passages in *Wigan Pier* to make a fellow traveller blind with rage, as Orwell knew, and he knew also that the book on Spain he hoped to write on his return from Barcelona could never be published by Gollancz, however skilfully his publisher might try to emasculate the book, as he had tried to emasculate *Wigan Pier* by his preface. Communists and anarchists were drifting to a confrontation in Barcelona, and Orwell could hardly fail to take a line against the former, which is why he had come to see me before he left England, for already I had a reputation for distrust of Stalinism. But there could be no contract before his return, his option to Gollancz still stood. Orwell had come back from Spain in July 1937, his agent had offered the unwritten book to Gollancz who had declined it – he had read Orwell's reports on Spain in the press and these had clearly been too much for him – and on September 1 I had signed a contract with him. We published *Homage to Catalonia* on April 18, 1938, the reviews were few and mainly hostile, the sales negligible (about 500 copies). This major work, perhaps unique in the autobiography of revolution, never started to sell until after the author's death twelve years later.*

* * *

A month before publication Orwell had become ill with a tubercular lesion in one lung and had been forced to go into a sanatorium in Kent which he had left on September 1, but only to travel the next day with his wife to Marrakech, since his doctor had insisted on a warm climate for the winter. The trip had been made possible through the generosity of L. H. Myers, the novelist. Orwell was back at home by April 11, 1939 with the completed MS of his novel *Coming Up For Air*, still under option to Gollancz. The war was only five months away, a war which was to Orwell still anathema. War, or even preparation for war, seemed to him to lead inevitably to a 'fascisising' process, 'with wage reductions, suppression of free speech, brutalities in the colonies, etc.,' as he wrote to Herbert Read on March 5, 1939. It was this concept of fascism as the enemy, perhaps to be allied to the 'pluto-democracy' of Chamberlain, which led Orwell astray. Ideology, which had bemused political minds both of left and right since 1933, was nearing the end of its havoc-strewn reign and was about to give way to nationalism, a healthy transition on the whole – the enemy was not 'fascism', but Hitlerism or, still more simply, Hitler. By September 3, 1939 this fact had become abundantly clear.

My talks with Orwell during the five months before the war often led to argument. I knew by then who the enemy was, and so did my wife. The fact of being born a Jew had saved me from any doubts on the matter.

The period of the phoney war was a time of bitter frustration for Orwell. On September 3, 1939 he put his ideology into cold storage. It was never to emerge again. From then on it was 'my country right

*A discussion of Orwell and *Homage to Catalonia* can be found in my book, *An Occupation for Gentlemen*, 1959.

or wrong' or even 'left or right'. But he could find no way of serving it, as he longed to do, since he'd been rejected for any form of military service. His finances too were at a low ebb, and he could get little work except trivial journalism. It was about this period that I came to know him with some degree of intimacy. This was post-Catalonia and post-ideology Orwell, not the brilliant young novelist in his mid-twenties, not the lively, almost knock-about, controversialist in his early thirties who wrote *Wigan Pier*, but a desperate man whose experiences had marked him irremediably and transformed him into the pessimistic genius of *Animal Farm* and *1984*. This was the man I came to know and admire, the man whose work obsessed me, the man I tried to help and cherish, the man I could not succeed in keeping alive. Yet, of all those who knew him, I was perhaps the one most likely to succeed, because as his publisher, with my wife, I had a close and lasting relationship to him which enabled me to cajole, to persuade, to warn, and even to bully him. And yet I did not succeed. His wounds had gone too deep, though I did not know it then, and the wounds or most of them were inflicted by destiny in Catalonia.

It was not merely the physical wound of a bullet through his throat or the cold and wearisome nights on the Teruel front. These were serious enough and surely led to his collapse with the lung lesion eight months later. But the spiritual and intellectual damage was as great or greater. In Catalonia Orwell learned at first hand in his own person that what he had feared and had somewhat tentatively sketched in *Wigan Pier* was irrefutably true. Workers could be and were shot down by communist police agents – the reputations of the enemies of the Communist Party were deliberately blackened by false accusations – political opponents were arrested and often murdered without trial – the true history of the past was falsified. The tentative and liberal socialist crusader, the pre-Catalonia Orwell who had regarded 'monopoly capitalism' as the chief enemy of the working class, was transformed into the most powerful cold-war fighter of his day. So tremendous a re-formation in the personality of an intellectually sensitive artist demanded an effort almost too great to be borne. It is no surprise that within eight months the ardent volunteer who had gone to Spain to fight for the workers and against the fascists had suffered the first of the tubercular attacks which were to destroy him.

Homage to Catalonia was the first book of Orwell's to deal with a wholly political theme, the life-and-death struggle of ordinary men and women to overthrow a dictatorship and to establish the anarchists' dream of freedom, a dream shared by the writer himself. The dream was shattered. The enemies of freedom prevailed. This intense experience reverberated through Orwell's mind and emotions. It was the central theme of his book. To embody it must have cost Orwell a formidable expenditure of creative energy. *Homage* was in my view the first of his three great, his most truly Orwellian, masterpieces. Followed inevitably his collapse, that of a man whose body was not strong enough to endure the strains Orwell was forced to lay upon it. The pattern was to be repeated with *1984* – first the idea, then the torture of expressing it in a book, finally the collapse. With *1984* it was to prove fatal. Only in *Animal Farm* did Orwell somehow succeed in rising above the physical and psychological horrors of his imagination, and constructing almost effortlessly (he wrote it in three months) a fairy story so simple and so comic that it had and has a universal appeal.

* * *

In April 1940, after the Nazi invasion of Norway, George Orwell came to see me in a mood of satisfaction that the prospect of imminent disaster often aroused in him. His clothes were baggy and dirty, his face grim, but soon to be wreathed in smiles as the thought of some fresh and terrifying catastrophe entered his mind.

'I've planted my field with potatoes; we shall all be hungry soon,' he remarked in his clipped voice. 'The U-boats are bound to sink most of the merchant ships.'

'Surely not,' I said, with a misplaced optimism not unknown throughout my life, 'new methods of submarine detection have improved enormously.' I offered him a cigatette. 'I'll smoke my own,' he said, producing a dark twist of tobacco from a pouch, and rolling it deftly in a cigarette paper. I watched with interest. From a capacious pocket he extracted a gigantic piece of apparatus.

'What on earth is that?' I asked him. 'A cigarette lighter,' he said. 'There won't be any wood for matches in a few months' time.' Proudly he showed me the mechanism, which he said he had acquired during his service with the P.O.U.M. militia in the Spanish Civil War. It was awe-inspiring. The chief feature was a rope well over an inch in diameter and three feet long from container to tip. Manipulation produced a dull glow of heat at the end. Not without difficulty he managed to bring the dilapidated business-end of his cigarette into contact with the glow and lit it. The gadget was a triumph of misplaced ingenuity.

'How lucky you are,' I said, 'to have such a wonderful lighter.'

'It is rather neat,' he replied, grinning with pleasure and entirely unconscious of the irony of my compliment. 'I reckon that it will last about three-and-a-half years. The war will go on at least as long as that.' A gleam of satisfaction lit up his granite face, as he made this only too modest prophecy. But I never saw him use the thing a second time, the mechanism must have turned out unsatisfactorily.

Three months later I met Orwell again, this time in company with T. R. Fyvel, whose book on Palestine, *No Ease in Zion*, we had published a year or two earlier. The subject for discussion was the transformation of Tory England from the slovenly nation that had come to defeat and almost to disaster at Dunkirk into an up-to-date socialist community which could inspire the world. This gigantic task, impossible as it may seem now, did not appear to us impracticable then. In those days who could have prophesied victory, or even the avoidance of defeat, with the U.S. neutral and the U.S.S.R. surlily hostile? But men like ourselves, too old or too unhealthy to fight, could feed ourselves on little but hope – and dreams of Utopia.* So it was that we felt certain we could ourselves do a great deal to bring about a British renaissance. As I sat listening to the two men talking, the Jew from the Sudetenland who had lived in England since he was twelve and the man from Oxfordshire who had been an imperial policeman in Burma and perhaps despised himself for it, it never occurred to me that our conversation was foolish, that maybe nothing could stop Hitler from becoming master of the world, that (more simply still) the war could be lost.

None of us three – Orwell, Fyvel and myself – was a professional revolutionary, the breed is rare in England. But we thought we knew what a revolution was *not*. It was not a programme, a theory or an ideology. Even when as a publisher I printed yet another hysterical blueprint for a brave but absurd new world, I had grave personal doubts of its practicality. Still less was a revolution a conspiracy, as Lenin had taught. Nor was it the work of a leader, however dynamic, leaders come when there is a movement to lead, and not always then. Revolution, I thought, sprang from a dramatic change of mind and purpose in the majority of the people. The revolutionary urge then spreads like a virus against which no antibiotic is known. It was my hope to stimulate such a change of mind in the only way that was natural to me, by the editing and publishing of books.

The revolutionary idea was socialism, of a sort. Perhaps renaissance

*Fyvel saw active service later in North Africa. Orwell and myself were to meet later in that splendid substitute for active service, the Home Guard. See Chapter 3.

would be a better word – a root-and-branch destruction of the old and decrepit and a planting of new growth. The political struggle, I believed, had not been won, had barely begun. It had merely been postponed 'for the duration'. It was our duty, while supporting the government through thick and thin, to attack what we believed corrupt and class-ridden, denounce what we thought half-hearted, elucidate what must ultimately be done to modernize the social fabric. There were many radicals in those days besides ourselves, some of them trained in that great forcing house of radicalism, the Beaverbrook Press.

Fyvel's idea was for a series of little books, to be known as The Searchlight Books, written by a group of men who had the ability to visualize a new and saner Britain when the war was won. Orwell and Fyvel were to be joint editors, and Orwell was to launch the series with a book by himself on the policy for a Socialist Britain. But Orwell had doubts. For him to write a book in wartime rather than fire a rifle at the enemy was something of a come-down. The Home Guard was already in being, and he was a sergeant in the St John's Wood company. Immersed in the job of being an amateur soldier, he scorned the opportunity of exercising as a professional writer. But Fyvel and I pressed him hard. He listened, grunted and said finally, 'I'll think about it.'

In due course, the two editors lined up a team of writers and publication began. Ten Searchlight Books came out between February 1941 and March 1942, nice little volumes at 2s. each. The ones that sold best were Orwell's *The Lion and the Unicorn* and Cassandra's *The English at War*.* These, and a year later Boomerang's *Bless 'Em All*, published outside the series, had an effect on public opinion which it is hard to exaggerate.

No books could have been more different from each other than these three – Orwell's calm, constructive and full of deep insights into English character; Cassandra's destructive, angry, demagogic, written in simple sentences that a half-wit could understand; Boomerang's good-tempered and devastatingly funny. But one quality these three had in common, radicalism, the feeling that a desperate situation needed desperate remedies. These writers had keen ears; they heard or overheard the conversation in pub and NAAFI, club and canteen, bomb shelter and defence post, in the parlour, the bus and the streets. Somehow their gift of tongues enabled them to express the inmost feelings of a people caught up in a

*Cassandra was the pen-name of the Daily Mirror's famous columnist, W. N. Connor, later knighted, who died not long ago.

war they had not willed but knew they had to fight. They voiced the discontents, frustrations, and hatreds which might well have jeopardized the nation in a time of crisis. By so doing they helped to relax the tensions. 'At least, someone knows what these buggers are doing or will do to us if we aren't careful.' This was a common reaction.

Of these books only *The Lion and the Unicorn* is today in print, and it remains remarkable for at least two reasons. It was the only *positive* work Orwell was destined to write. Its six-point programme for a revolutionary peace comes remarkably close to what the Labour Government actually accomplished during its term of office between 1945 and 1950. The English revolution, Orwell wrote, 'will never lose touch with the tradition of compromise and the belief in a law that is above the state . . . it will show a power of assimilating the past which will shock foreign observers and sometimes make them doubt whether any revolution has happened.' To me, the mild liberal, these words had a sterling ring. They won me to accept Orwell as a political mentor far more honest and likeable than the wild agitators whose books we had been publishing in the years before the war. Compact and original, *The Lion and the Unicorn* was published in February 1941. We printed 7,500 copies which were sold by the end of the year. A second printing of 5,000 copies was necessary. It cannot have been read by less than 50,000 people. Something of its massive commonsense must have penetrated into minds which would have been closed to a less serene appeal. Many doctors, scientists, lawyers, civil servants and business executives generally must have been won over by its arguments to vote socialist when the time came in 1945.

No book presented a greater contrast than Cassandra's *The English at War*. Here was red-hot journalism raised to the highest power, political evangelism, a real-life melodrama. Cassandra got down to brass tacks in the first lines of his Foreword. 'The Generals die in their beds,' he wrote, 'the Politicians catch the last aeroplane away from the Fatherland. The Kings escape over frontiers to raise toy Courts in countries where they are barely tolerated. The Great Merchants disappear from the marketplace to hurl defiance from some foreign bourse. Only the Common People remain. In defeat they pay the price. They foot the blood-soaked bill.' Nine unnecessary capital letters reveal the barely controlled excitement with which this doughty fighter hurled himself into the fray. If words could have killed, the cemeteries would have been filled to overflowing with the bodies of respectable Tories. Cassandra has a fling at the Anglican Church and the Vatican, the Army, the financiers, the industrialists and the businessmen. They all receive their comeuppance in a blaze of rhetoric. 'Let us make sure that, at the end of this struggle, this England, this precious stone set in a silver sea, shall not be lodged again in a vast pawnshop run by peers and bank directors.' In times of crisis Shakespeare provides almost all the best quotations.

Read today by the glowing lights of lamps whose current is provided by the Welfare State's Electricity Board, in a comfortable armchair bought on the never-never, conscious of that six pound a week old age pension to be enjoyed if only we can live long enough, *The English at War* sounds a trifle overblown, the irony too obvious, the manner too chummy. How different it seemed in the chill winter months of early 1941, with the nightly visitation of the bombers, the scarcity of food, the boredom of life, the prospect of a war which might last ten years. Cassandra's book sold like hot cakes, 30,000 copies in fifteen months. I estimate that it was read by more than 250,000 persons. The common people, whom he idolized in it, needed it like a baby needs its mother's milk.

Yet Cassandra had a theme of fundamental importance. Like so many of us who were then on the Left, he was haunted by a nightmare. All this – the war, the unpreparedness, the inequality of sacrifice, the ghastly muddle – had happened before, not much over twenty years ago. This nightmare was present in all our memories. At all costs it must not be allowed to happen again. Let me quote in full the passage in which Cassandra restates this theme with a pen dipped in gall. 'Victory, unprecedented, unparalleled, belonged to us [in 1918]. No nation on earth dared defy us. The seas, the dry land and the air above it were ours. True that ten million men in the pride of their youth had been blotted out as if they had never been born; but we had WON! We had had Blood and Toil and Tears and Sweat, and plenty of it – but we had also gained that which was more precious than life itself – VICTORY! And what a harlot Victory was! – this fairest of all prizes! Disease and Misery were her favours, Starvation, Revolution and Death the fruit of her charms. England's heroes came back not to life as they once knew it, not for the kind of existence they had fought for – but to a new and more rapacious way of living, a society founded on exploitation, a world built by jerry builders and profiteers and run by cynics. The pledges were unhonoured, the ideals discarded. Unemployment swelled into a bloated monstrosity. Veterans with war medals sang in the gutter. Weary, mutilated men who had dragged themselves through purgatory found themselves on the scrapheap. Behind the great gilded cardboard Colossus of Victory, draped with the flags of twenty-three triumphant nations, there was a midden. And in that midden lay the future bedraggled Destiny of Nations.'

Here was the truth, not the whole truth perhaps, but enough in all conscience to make the fears and suspicions of the new generation humanly comprehensible.

There were other Searchlight Books, and good ones too, by Ritchie Calder, Sebastian Haffner, T. C. Worsley, Arturo Barea, Bernard Causton, Stephen Spender, Olav Stapledon and, unexpectedly, Joyce Carey, the only non-fiction work written, I believe, by this brilliant novelist, later revised and reissued.

*   *   *

But it was the army which symbolized for many the power of the old régime, the institution in which class, privilege, obsolescence and stupidity seemed to vie with each other to make defeat inevitable. So it was the army – not the navy which most people admired, not the air force which after the Battle of Britain was worshipped – that became the central point of struggle between Left and Right. The health of the army was examined by Boomerang, a pseudonym for Alan W. Wood, in a pamphlet of only 64 pages bound in paper, called *Bless 'Em All.* This was the biggest bombshell of a book, in terms of sales, that my diminutive firm hurled at the entrenched power of the establishment. Its author was a slim good-looking Australian, known as Lanky, then and later a wit, a philosopher, and a man of the utmost charm who died far too young.

Boomerang started off with a preface in which he emphasized that personally he had been 'very happy in the Army, so this book is not a private grudge. To one like myself from the tie-and-clean-collar class of society, joining the Army is about the only possible means of living with members of all social classes on terms of perfect equality.' A dedication 'without permission' follows to the Rt. Hon. Lord Beaverbrook, P.C. on whose papers he had worked before the war.

After this flying start we come to the first chapter, 'Thank God We've Got A Navy.' The gist of this was Boomerang's observation that 'if any institution is so completely inefficient [as the Army is] that it makes the Englishman the laughing-stock of the world, then the Englishman will merely laugh at it,' instead of turning it inside out. The second chapter, 'You Lucky People', pointed to the serving soldiers' miserable morale, due (he claimed) to the ignoring of war news. The collapse of France in 1940, for instance, was 'likely to be signalled in no way except by a greater drive for better creases in our second-best trousers.' The third chapter, 'Second Childhood', discussed whether army life more closely resembles that of a criminal in prison or a small boy in a kindergarten, and plumps for the latter. 'Your way of life,' he writes, 'has the simplicity of a baby's. Everything is arranged for you. The time you get up; the clothes you wear; the hours you work and play; the time you are sent off to bed at night, tired out by simple bodily fatigue, to sink into the sweet sodden slumber of childhood. . . . You enjoy the simple excitements like riding on lorries, or paddling round a muddy gun-site with great big gum boots on. You revel in schoolboy jokes about sex. You feel your mental age falling lower and lower. Your brain shrinks.'

But I have little doubt that it was the final chapter, 'The Lost Leaders', which drove many of the top people to frenzy. The Army, Boomerang considered, is the last stronghold of the public schoolboy, for short Old Etonian or O.E., who gets most of the commissions in it. The O.E., he continues, 'has a peculiar kind of ritualistic patriotism which makes him ready to sacrifice his life for his country. A great deal of silly socialist nonsense was once written about our O.E. ruling class not really wanting to fight Hitler, because they have "fascist sympathies". Of course they have: they have been brought up that way: Eton is a miniature totalitarian state, complete with führers, gauleiters, mass feeling, mob emotion, uniform clothes, uniform minds, beatings and buggery. But their fascist imperialistic outlook makes them hate Hitler: for Hitler wants the British Empire, and they want it too.

'Again, the O.E. usually has private means; practical experience always shows that the richest regiments are the best regiments. The O.E. has physical courage or, what is equally important, a perfect poise in concealing cowardice. He has self-confidence and a consciousness of his own superiority. He has physical strength and skill at games to win the admiration of his men. All these are big assets.

'I would even defend the standard question asked of candidates for commission: "Do you hunt?" which excites the standard ribaldry of would-be army reformers. . . . Cruel blood sports are obviously ideal training for war, which is the cruellest and bloodiest aport of all. Of course, those who can afford to hunt belong to a restricted social class. You may deplore as much as you like the gulf which yawns between the Quorn and the Bermondsey Bicycling Club. But the gulf is there. Battles have been won by regiments which went into action to the sound of a hunting horn. I have never heard of a charge inspired by the ringing of a bicycle bell.'

The devastating effrontery of *Bless 'Em All* made it an immediate success. The first printing of 5,000 copies was gone almost overnight. Edition after edition followed, until at the end of fifteen months we had sold 37,625 copies, and the sales continued. In fact, I estimate that half-a-million people read the book, perhaps even more. What happened to one copy is shown by a letter dated July 16, 1942 from Salop. Miss Eleanor I. wrote as follows: 'First I read it and I thought it terrific. Then the R.A.S.C. billeted with us read it. "Every word," he said, "is absolutely true, everything he says is perfectly right." Then I took it down to the Canteen and turned it over to the Pioneers, to go round the billets till it falls to bits. At intervals people come up and say "Cor, that book you lent old George – it's all *true*, ain't it – he's got the Army taped all right . . .? True . . . true . . . the word follows your book like a shadow.' From this it's pretty clear that this particular copy of *Bless 'Em All* must have been read by any number of persons from twenty upwards.

As for Lord Beaverbrook, he wrote to Boomerang, on March 18, 1942, two weeks before publication date, as follows. 'Everywhere I hear praise of your book. And now that I have given some study to it, I can well understand the admiration you are winning . . . as the colleague of your newspaper days, I claim a share in the glory of your success.'

This generous letter must have heartened the author, who had understandable doubts about his fate in the event of his pseudonym being penetrated by the military authorities. His friends advised him to deny the authorship if questioned, but he determined bravely to face the music, and the court martial if the need arose. It never did. Wisely the powers-that-be behaved with discretion and shipped the author out of the country to North Africa.

* * *

So, even in wartime, I continued as a publisher to attack the authorities with enthusiasm and a good deal of unfairness. Not even a Churchill in those days could have made up for the crimes committed in the pre-war years by those who should have known better. Twenty-seven and one half new pennies, or 5s. 6d. would have made you the owner of the three books of Orwell, Cassandra and Boomerang, a cheap price even in those days for three closely-wrought sticks of political gelignite fit to fling against the rhinoceros hides of those – and there were still many of them – who clung impenitently to the moribund past.

2

Bombs Over Books

In March 1940 we had moved from our London flat and rented a house near Reading. We moved in just as the German invasion of Norway was beginning. However, I went down myself only at weekends. It was here, glued to the radio, that I listened to the fall of Norway, Denmark, Holland, Belgium and France. It was here that we rejoiced in the great victory of the Battle of Britain.

Foiled by the failure of his fighter planes to make the invasion of Britain possible, Hitler turned to the bombing of cities. On September 7, 1940, the Luftwaffe set out to destroy not only England's past but her future as well. Since the betrayal of Czechoslovakia at Munich just two years before, I had been expecting it. But expecting is not the same thing as believing. H. G. Wells had pointed out the difference to me two years earlier. 'When I was writing *The War in the Air*, 'he had said, 'my mind informed me that one day the aeroplane would become an important transport vehicle and a formidable weapon of war. God bless me, I knew it must happen, but it wasdamned difficult actually to credit such an extraordinary development. It was my biggest problem in writing that novel.'

Now the grim fantasies and fears of Wells' imagination broke loose and began raining nightly down on his venerable head. On September 20, 1940, we published his satirical fable, *All Aboard for Ararat*, and a month later his new novel, *Babes in the Darkling Wood.* It was the third book in one year from England's G.O.M. of letters, a remarkable achievement even for Wells. In November we issued Thomas Mann's novel about another G.O.M. of letters, Goethe, under the title *Lotte in Weimar.*

About 6 o'clock on the evening of Sunday, December 29, nearly 150 German planes attacked the City of London and the East End.

The night was ideal for fire-raising, rainless and clear with a strong wind. An ebb tide meant low water in the Thames, a grave handicap to the firemen who had to fight the flames. Most of the high explosive bombs and incendiaries fell in a rough circle round the Cathedral of St. Paul's, a circle with a diameter of nearly three miles. The defences were unable to cope with the weight of the attack. Over 150 people were killed and over 500 seriously injured. The centre of the British book trade of that day, Paternoster Row and surrounding streets, was wiped out.

The list of firms wholly and partly damaged made up a large proportion of the publishing trade – Blackwood & Nelson, Collins, Ward Lock, Eyre & Spottiswoode, Hodder & Stoughton, Hutchinson, Bagster (the bible house) and many others. The house of Longman, trading in Paternoster Row since 1724, was in ashes, as was their second warehouse in Bermondsey. They lost three million books that night. But perhaps the deadliest blow of all was the destruction of Simpkin Marshall, the largest distributing organization in the book trade. Six million books were lost there. Despite efforts after the war to reinstate it in some at least of its old glory, they never quite succeeded. Ultimately it went bankrupt, owing most publishers a fair amount of money.

From the holocaust of December 29 Secker & Warburg escaped without loss. Our turn was to come a few months later. As for the book trade as a whole, it is a matter of record that no publishing house became a permanent casualty as a result of enemy action, with one exception. The house of Stanford, manufacturers of atlases, reproduced their maps by a lithographic process. The stones so used, split and cracked by the intense heat of the fires, could never be printed from again. For Stanford the blitz was a catastrophe and an irremediable one.

How could publishers stand the financial losses due to the bombing? The answer is simple. The Government before the war had devised a scheme of War Risk Insurance against such hazards, and placed it before the Publishers Association in September 1939. It stipulated a premium of 6% to be paid quarterly. The insurance value of the policy was to be, not the replacement value of the goods destroyed, but the actual value as set out in the balance sheet.

The members of the Council of the P.A. at first looked this gift-horse in the mouth. The premium seemed to them to be high, considering the negligible amount of risk, as it appeared to them then. Since the Council consisted in the main of individuals from large or very large firms, it seemed to them practicable to set aside out of their own profits a substantial sum to insure against any hypothetical loss. This was the view also of Simpkin Marshall! When the Council's decision became known, it was far from popular. Small publishers, myself among them, were alarmed at the prospect of being wiped out by bombardment without adequate compensation. A general meeting of the whole Association was called and widely attended. Simpkin Marshall, luckily for themselves, had changed their minds, though Harold Macmillan, that great individualist, continued to oppose. A publisher's privacy should not, he thought, be invaded by bureaucrats. But, as might have been expected, the individualists were defeated, though by a narrow margin of 39 votes to 38. In the hailstorm of modern war, the majority voted for the communal umbrella. It was just as well. Had it not been for W.R.I., there might not have been many publishing firms solvent by the end of the blitz.

W.R.I. was indispensable, but it created a dilemma for every publisher who considered the matter carefully, whether to value your stock high or low. If you valued it high, you paid a crippling premium in anticipation that the enemy's bombs would fall on your warehouses and destroy your stock. If, on the other hand, you valued it low, the compensation was pitiable and the prudence of years of management could be dissipated in a matter of hours.

* * *

Though we had lost comparatively little in the fire-raid on the City of London our life-blood was draining away month by month, as our stocks of books were destroyed at printers and binders all over the country. We had even had one title over-run and 'captured' in the Channel Island of Guernsey. Some 20% of our stock had already gone, but worse was to follow. As I picked up the morning paper one day in March, I cast my eye over the usual communique from the Air Ministry. It read something like this: 'Enemy bombers crossed the coast in force last night. Bombs were dropped on Plymouth. Some casualties are reported and damage was done to installations.' With such words, scrubbed clean of emotive power, our rulers conveyed to us daily the news of death, wounds and material losses. To those living in unbombed areas and lacking imagination, it might have sounded like a humdrum report in a local newspaper, but to me who knew what bombing meant, the word 'Plymouth' had itself the explosive power of a five-ton bomb. In Plymouth at Brendons was almost all that remained of Secker & Warburg's material assets, here was our last and greatest publishing arsenal.

I got on the phone at once, but the lines were down. Impatiently I waited for news, and next day received a letter from Brendons saying that the damage to their works was considerable, and a full report would be sent in a few days' time. The report never came. Five days later the Luftwaffe struck again. When the dust had settled and the casualties counted, it became clear that Brendons no longer existed. It was never to function in Plymouth again.

At Brendons we lost about 150,000 bound books and half that number of unbound. We lost stereo plates of some of our most important titles. We actually lost manuscripts of new books sent there for composition and manufacture. But above and beyond all this, we lost the whole of our stock of unused paper, beautiful virgin sheets on which we intended to print the masterpieces of the war years and the big sellers out of which I still hoped to make the profits that had so far eluded us. The catastrophe was immense, and even my optimistic temperament was forced to admit it. Barring a miracle, it seemed to me improbable that we could survive.

At Plymouth something like twenty tons of paper, double our ration for one year, had ceased to exist. Its value in pounds sterling would be paid us when the insurance claim had been investigated and settled. If we were lucky, we should be granted a compassionate licence for 7½% of the paper lost, about two new books out of the twenty-five our own paper would have printed. Now we had only our ration to depend on, and this was shrinking fast.

Paper rationing had been imposed from March 31, 1940, at a rate substantially less than publishers, cheerful men as a rule, had expected, 60% instead of the hoped-for 80%. The cut from an unlimited supply to little more than half the pre-war average was severe and ensured a large reduction in the output of books, even though thinner paper was used for printing them. But worse was to follow. The conquest of Norway and Denmark by Germany in March 1940 cut off British paper mills from the main source of their supplies in Finland and Sweden. In April the ration was suddenly reduced to 30% and the Paper Control with headquarters in Reading announced bleakly that it might go to 15%, or in certain eventualities to nothing. However, this panic measure was reversed in June, and with a sigh of relief I learned that the ration had been restored to 60%. Here it remained unchanged for the seven months to February, 1941, in spite of the fall of France and the Low Countries and the heavy losses in paper stocks that the raids of the second half of 1940 must have caused. It was then reduced to 50%. This was the figure, half the average of our pre-war consumption over three years, that we could rely on after the Plymouth blitzes had wiped out the whole of our reserve. It meant that we had some ten tons of paper in a year, enough perhaps to print about 40,000 books and bring in a turnover of, say, £12,000. I was desperate. Without printed books to sell a publisher is not in the race.

One day soon after, as I sat brooding at my desk on these harsh facts of life, I heard a voice outside my door saying goodbye to my secretary. 'Perhaps you'll have some work for us soon. I'll call again next week,' the voice said. It belonged to Mr. Norrington, the London representative of the vast Edinburgh printing house, Morrison & Gibb. I ran across the room and flung open the door. 'Norrington,' I shouted at his back, as he walked down the stairs, 'come here, I want to talk to you.'

At any date till then I would have confessed to a thorough-going disbelief in miracles. When I called Norrington into my room, it was not as a miracle-worker that I welcomed him. Yet surely some intuition dawned on me that sombre morning. Or was it merely the traditional action of the drowning man clutching at a straw? At any rate, I poured out to Norrington the story of the catastrophe which had engulfed me and my firm. I had to tell it to someone who could understand and sympathize, and Norrington was the one who was there. When I had finished, Norrington leant forward. He must by then have been delighted at the prospect of getting a word in edgeways. 'The old man,' he said, referring in the vernacular to the chairman and managing director of Morrison & Gibb, Frederick Haynes, 'foresaw the likelihood of a paper shortage in the event of war and laid in a very large stock of paper indeed.'

'He did?' I said, 'how much?' The words came out fast, like machine-gun bullets.

'I don't know exactly how many tons,' Norrington replied, startled, 'but I should suppose two or three thousand tons at least.'

A ton of paper, I reflected, costs about £36 (in 1972 about £180). Three thousand times £36 works out at . . . why, at around £108,000. My mouth dropped open as I found the answer to this simple sun. Had people really got all that money to put into paper which, after all, might never be required? Apparently they had. Lovingly my mind dwelt on all the paper, ton after ton, ream after ream. Why, if it were stretched flat, page to page, it might stretch to New York, perhaps even to the moon and beyond. Hastily I pulled myself together. This paper was not mine. Mine was in ashes in Plymouth or dowsed in water from the firemen's hoses.

'What does Mr. Haynes intend to use this paper for?' I asked Norrington.

'For publishing projects of his own,' Norrington replied, 'and also to help publishers in a mess, like yourself.' I was silent, as a great calm descended upon me. So we were not perhaps finished yet.

In the coming months and years Haynes did no less than his London representative had suggested he would. Book after book was printed by him for us on his own paper. Nor was his rate for the job excessive. Foresight and generosity are among the most valuable qualities a businessman can possess. They bring him customers and make those customers happy. A happy customer remains . . . a customer. For many years after we were customers of Morrison & Gibb, despite intense competition from rival printers. Foresight and generosity, allied of course to the huge amount of capital involved, paid off handsomely.

* * *

At the end of 1941, depressed by the disasters of the war, I was far from cheerful about the prospects of Secker & Warburg. The fortunes of a small and hitherto unprofitable publishing business was a trivial matter, I knew, weighed against the fall of France, the near-collapse of the U.S.S.R., and the destruction of an American fleet at Pearl Harbour. But this little publishing house was my own creation, a tender plant which I strove day by day to improve and make healthy. In 1940 we had reduced our losses to only £40, in 1941 we were to make a tiny profit (£440). The demand for books was growing, and I was ready to supply them. Ready, but unable. Crippled by an exiguous paper quota which seemed to me unfair, dependent on the magnanimity of a printer who might stop supplying me at any time, my anxieties increased. A small firm must grow. Already I was feeling the symptoms of slow strangulation. Though we might outlast the war, I thought, in peacetime we should be without proper means of defence against the competition of our bigger rivals. The post-war period was to prove that in this respect I was not wrong.

However, in December, 1941, an unexpected development took place, which was to have the effect of increasing substantially the amount of paper available to us. The president of the Publishers

Association, at that time Walter Harrap, one of the shrewdest administrators the trade has ever produced, secured from the Ministry of Supply an allocation of 250 tons of paper, additional to the quota, to ensure the maintenance in print of books, scientific, technical and cultural, considered vital to the war effort. This came to be known as the Moberley Pool, after the name of the distinguished senior civil servant who was to administer it. There were already far too many useful books out of stock. It was a tremendous achievement of Harrap and his fellow officers to have secured so much extra paper for such a worthwhile purpose in the middle of a war which we had not yet begun to start winning. For me and my firm it might well come to mark the difference between survival and collapse.

But to my amazement it became clear all too soon that there were important publishers who regarded the Moberley Pool with extreme suspicion. This group summoned a special general meeting of the Publishers Association to protest against the Pool.

The meeting took place on March 3, 1942, and was attended by every publisher interested in the problem of paper supplies, that is, it was attended by every publisher. The attack on the Pool was launched by Walter Hutchinson, seconded by Daniel Macmillan, and reinforced by W. R. Collins. Tension grew in the Hall as Walter Harrap, president, rose to reply to his accusers. The pool paper, he said, was an extra, there was no question of a new system of allocation of the quota itself. Nor was the principle of censorship involved; every publisher was free, as before, to print whatever books he chose on his own ration of paper. The Council, Harrap said, could not accept the resolution, which was unjustified by the facts.

Surely, I thought in my innocence, Harrap's speech will settle the matter. Never had I made a bigger miscalculation. Douglas Jerrold, of Eyre & Spottiswoode, a man of the extreme right, got up and made a passionate, and, so it seemed to me, irrelevant oration. A new principle had been introduced into paper rationing, he said, and members had not been consulted; discrimination was involved; an inroad was to be made into individual liberty. The late Sir Geoffrey Faber contradicted him. William Longman remarked that, if the opposition motion were carried, the officers and council could hardly do other than resign; they would inevitably be succeeded by inexperienced men. So now at least we knew the issue involved, nothing less than the survival of the P.A. itself. Members sat straighter in their chairs, shocked into a feverish interest in the nightmare proceedings. Gollancz, a man of the extreme left, now took the floor, he was in a somewhat difficult position. He knew that most members would be unwilling to break the continuity of authority vested in the officers and members of Council, and transfer it to the rebels. Yet he believed with blazing sincerity in an individualism that made it almost impossible for him throughout his career to co-operate with any organized business group or association whatever. Gollancz therefore started with a bouquet for the Council who, he said, had not made a false move despite all the difficult and dangerous situations arising from war conditions. But now he believed they had committed a grave error of judgment; it was impossible for any individual or committee to discriminate between the requests for grants. How, he demanded dramatically, was one to decide between a Roman Catholic breviary or a new edition of Karl Marx?

Speaker after speaker got up and continued the debate. But soon it became clear that the rebels, under the spell of Jerrold's and Gollancz's oratory, were more numerous than had been expected. The situation was critical. With shrewd and skilful timing the late Bertram Christian of Nisbet, an ex-president of the Association, rose to move the previous question, which meant postponement of the debate till another day. C. S. Evans of Heinemann seconded. A vote was taken, and the motion was carried by 48 to 28. It had been a near thing. Another half-hour and a majority of the membership might have voted for the ideologues.

Just over three weeks later, a second meeting was held. But by then the bulk of the membership had regained its sanity. When the vote was taken, 61 were for the Council, and only 11 against. It was a notable victory for commonsense, a prodigious defeat for fanaticism. The publishing trade was at last growing up.

In practice, the Pool functioned extraordinarily well. The tonnage of paper grew slowly from 1,000 tons in January, 1942, to 5,850 tons in July, 1948. In all, 9,309 applications for grants were considered and 21,000 tons of paper allocated as a result. The personnel of the advisory committee remained unchanged throughout the entire seven years of the Committee's existence. Each questionnaire accompanying an application – and a complicated form it certainly was, with a mass of detailed information to be supplied, was read by all four members of the committee. Every decision was unanimous. It is impossible to calculate how many thousands of hours were spent in this responsible time-consuming task, which naturally was unpaid. Probably some 500 firms benefited to a greater or lesser extent from the committee's work. But I doubt whether the members of the

Association ever fully realized what a gigantic task was done on our behalf and on behalf of books and their authors by these four men, who stole time from their private lives to assist us. They were the unknown soldiers of the British book trade, unheralded and unsung.

* * *

In September 1941, my wife and I had moved back into London, a top-floor flat at the foot of Primrose Hill, Regents Park. Pamela had long before made her own preparations for the war, simple ones and in her own view adequate. As an offensive weapon she had bought a pound of the best black pepper and kept it in a tin on our window-sill. It was designed for use against enemy parachutists. As a morale-builder she had secured from Ben Huebsch, of the Viking Press in New York, six lipsticks, unobtainable in London, of a peculiar magenta colour known as night cyclamen, which she regarded as indispensable to her appearance. Of these she retained three for use at home and evacuated the rest to three widely separated places in the country, where we might stay in the event of being bombed out. 'I'd rather appear stark naked,' she told me, 'than without the only lipstick that suits me.'

In 1942 and 1943 we made substantial profits; the supplements to our ration which came from the generosity of Morrison & Gibb and the grants from the Government's paper pool at least ensured that. Yet still I was dissatisfied.

Envious of the larger quotas of our legitimate rivals, I decided to lead a campaign for a fairer allocation of paper than that laid down at the beginning of the war by the Paper Control. To do so, I needed allies and soon enough I found them – John Lehmann, then of the Hogarth Press; the late Bertram Christian of the Cresset Press; the manager of Lawrence and Wishart; the owner of the Rationalist Press, and others. A Small Publishers' Group was formed, often referred to in the following months as 'those damned nuisances', and I became its chairman. It was this section of pygmies which I led against the larger publishers, the President and Council of the Association, and looming behind them the almost unapproachable majesty of the Paper Control itself.

Our case was perhaps not quite as strong as I thought it to be in those feverish days of long ago. Small publishers, we claimed, by the willingness to experiment, performed a healthy function which is not adequately performed by the larger firms. This point, not surprisingly, was to be vigorously denied by the larger firms themselves. The

Pamela de Bayou,
the author's wife

25 years

quota system, we went on, was unfair to the small publisher for a number of reasons. First, 'there is a minimum of paper,' he wrote, 'which a publisher needs if he is to maintain a healthy development, by expansion, the finding of new authors, or the replacement of authors who drop out . . .' and we made a comparison with assessments for income tax, where the smaller a man's income is, the lower the percentage of it which he pays away in tax.

But to me it was an argument drawn from the possibility of publishing a best-seller that seemed almost irrefutable. What could a publisher do? Give the best-seller all the paper it needs, and delay and so damage most of the other writers on the list? Or, starve the best-seller, the book most wanted by readers? It could so easily have happened, and in fact it did when we published Orwell's *Animal Farm* in 1945.

There was one last point we made. If the control came to be relaxed by stages, the position of the small publisher would become progressively more desperate. Rival firms, *with whom we had to compete*, would acquire far more tonnage than we could, and so be enabled to crush us with ease by intelligent use of the paper which they had, but which we hadn't got and couldn't obtain by hook or by crook. So, in fact, it happened. Perhaps the outstanding example was the case of Erskine Caldwell, an author we had 'made' before the war and for whom we had published three books, including his masterpiece, *God's Little Acre*. Unable after the war to reprint his books through lack of paper and wholly incapable of accepting for publication even one of the several new books he had written in the meantime, we lost him to a rival firm. So also we lost the chance of publishing the novels of Scott Fitzgerald and Norman Mailer's *The Naked and the Dead*.

Such was our case, and its strength was confirmed at the eleventh hour by information from the U.S. There the rationing scheme had been devised on a graded scale; publishers were classified as small, medium and large; the large ones were cut by 25 %, the medium by 20 % and the small by 15 %. In other words the Americans accepted the principle that the smaller the firm, the larger must be the percentage allocated of its pre-war consumption. There the wind was tempered to the shorn lamb. If only this principle had been accepted in Britain – and it would have cost a trivial amount of tonnage – how much more favourable would have been our competitive position after the war.

Week after week our group met at my office; letters were written to key official personages; a memorandum was prepared; in the end our agitation was so effective that in January, 1944, I was co-opted onto the Council of the Publishers Association, an honour perhaps never before accorded to the representative of so tiny a firm. There I sat round the table, a solitary rebel, with eleven eminent pillars of the trade. Vehemently I argued our case. By the end of the meeting there was probably a majority in favour of doing something substantial on our behalf. But it was not to be. Though I achieved a small moral triumph, the policy of the Control remained unchanged.

Nevertheless, in those long-drawn-out and wearying years, 1941–44, we did publish on such paper as we had some remarkable books. Besides the Searchlight Books mentioned earlier, we issued books by H. G. Wells, Lewis Mumford and Thomas Mann, *To the Finland Station* of Edmund Wilson, followed about a year later by *The Wound and the Bow*. There was Frank Howes' *Full Orchestra*, unwisely rejected by Penguin Books and a tremendous success on our list. The now well-known sociologist and socialist, Richard Titmuss, gave us his *Parents Revolt*, which dealt with the effects likely to result from the halving of Britain's birthrate over the period 1880 to 1940. We had an early book by Henry Miller, *The Colossus of Maroussi*, followed later by his biting study of America, *The Air-Conditioned Nightmare*, one of the finest examples of an apt title I can recall. There were two books by Jacques Barzun of Columbia University, New York, Lord Boothby on *The New Economy*, and Professor Bronowski on William Blake under the title, *The Man Without a Mask*. Two short war novels appeared in 1944, Harry Brown's *A Walk in the Sun*, later to be made into one of the best war films of World War Two, and John Prebble's *Where the Sea Breaks*, recently (1971) reprinted. Prebble's novel still awaits a director of genius to turn this strangely compelling story into a successful film.

* * *

In June 1944, as the enemy tried to repel the Anglo-American invasion of Fortress Europe, the bombardment began again, this time with flying bombs (V1's) and later rockets (V2's). These weapons had, in every sense of the word, an impact on my publishing affairs.

My wife and I in our penthouse had undeniably a room with a view, for it faced due south, and looked across Regent's Park to the southeast, the south and the southwest for a distance of twenty miles right across to the North Downs. From this eyrie in 1944 we observed the bombing of London by the German V weapons. The flying bombs came first and began to sail into London, passing just to the right or left of St. Paul's from where we looked out. Soon we became expert at judging where each one fell. We could trace the direction on a map of London and estimate the distance by counting the number of seconds taken by the noise of the explosion to travel from its point of impact to our ears (1,100 feet a second). It was a grim calculation, and one with a terrible fascination.

One night in August the bombs seemed to be flying into London with alarming frequency, and we kept getting out of bed to have a look. Between four and five in the morning, we were watching when we saw an explosion in direct line with my office. Anxiously we counted the seconds – sixteen, seventeen, eighteen, crash! Just about the time it would take for the sound to travel from Essex Street, Strand to Primrose Hill, Regent's Park. Had my office been destroyed? We could not be sure, but first thing in the morning we heard the news.

My wife and I took a bus to the Strand. There was a cordon at the top of Essex Street. The policeman let us through. The unforgettable musty smell of disaster, familiar to me from a thousand previous 'incidents', was wafted to my nostrils. Before our eyes lay a pile of rubble, where only the evening before I had left, without even a backward glance, an elegant Georgian house of dark grey brick. Through the crazy wreckage of a window-frame hung a red plastic telephone, mine, mutely revealing that business was no longer to be as usual. Everything, it was easy to see, had been destroyed, furniture, typewriters, files, papers, all the paraphernalia of an active firm. The building in which I had worked so enthusiastically for eight years was gone. The delicate network of business operations had surely been shattered. There was one casualty. The caretaker had been killed in the basement by the blast.

No one can fully anticipate a disaster, however much they may insure against it. Nor had I anticipated this one, though I had taken what precautions were open to me by storing every night in the basement the company's books of account and the large volumes in which we kept our royalty agreements with authors, pasted on blank pages. Now, as I surveyed the chaos, I wondered dully whether the firm could survive this hammer blow. Had not our plans and ambitions and hopes been lost in the twisted beams through which a light breeze blew, in the charred fragments of paper on which a hot sun looked down? We had passed through the critical early years of establishing a new publishing house and avoided by a hair's breadth the danger of bankruptcy. In the Blitz we had lost all my painfully accumulated paper reserves in Plymouth. Cursed by an unfair rationing scheme, I was even now struggling to remedy a hazardous paper shortage on behalf of myself and other small firms. Job-like, I cursed God, the enemy, chance and the wind-currents which had borne this ridiculous and irrelevant bomb to my doorstep. And having had my fill of curses, I walked forward wondering what to do next.

On top of the funeral pile stood Senhouse, naked to the waist, filthy with dust, sweating freely. He was engaged in what he was to describe as 'salvage work'. His well-muscled torso bent down, then straightened up, down and up, over and over again. Though I was sad, he was happy – which was not so common. He was carefree, absorbed in a physical task where thinking was a waste of time and his strength could do the job. He saw himself, I'm sure, as a fighter, risking the fall of other bombs, waging his own personal war against the hated Germans, straining every muscle to enable the firm he and I had founded together to rise phoenix-like from the ashes. The picture is printed on my memory. At that moment Senhouse was fulfilled. He was doing something simple and worthwhile, which had nothing to do with the intricacies of business relations, the mysteries of contracts, the necessity of telling harsh truths to authors he knew and liked, all anathema to him.

Suddenly, down the dangerous-looking remains of what had been our staircase, Senhouse stumbled, his arms full of a miscellaneous collection of tattered papers and books. He deposited his load on the pavement, where lay a small pile of objects he had already salvaged, and came up to me. His eyes gleamed with fanatical excitement.

'I've salvaged a lot of useful stuff already,' he said, 'the account books and authors' agreements were safe in the basement and I'll bring them out in a moment.'

'What shall we use for an office?' I asked him, putting a brave front on the tragedy.

'You find an office,' Senhouse said, 'I'm busy here.' And busy he was for the next few days, pulling out of the debris a series of grimy objects of doubtful utility. These were stored fifty yards up the road in the basement of Essex Hall, opposite the establishment of W. H. Allen, a publisher little larger than ourselves, whose owner, Mark Goulden, had kindly lent us a couple of rooms. Here I moved with my staff, all three of them, and settled down to my gloom. A few days later a flying bomb hit Essex Hall, and everything so gallantly salvaged by Senhouse was blown up again. But the account books and contracts were with me in Goulden's rooms, safe at least for the moment.

Slowly over the next week my mood began to change, my fragmented world began to reassemble itself. Almost at once it became known where the personnel of Secker & Warburg was to be found. Letters arrived on my desk as usual. I answered them as usual by dictating to my typist who used a borrowed typewriter. Printers and binders and papermakers called up, sympathized and visited. Some talked to me, others to Senhouse on or near the ruins to which he seemed drawn as if by a powerful magnet. Alan Wood (Boomerang) came to condole and stood with the two directors a few yards from the scene of the disaster, discussing a new book which he was never to write. Almost it was as if nothing had happened.

The fact is that publishing businesses are run, not by letter files or machines or furniture, but by men and women. My staff and I knew what was planned, and if a detail had been forgotten, there was always someone to recall it to us. My most valuable group of letters, kept in a special tray on my desk, had been scattered in tiny pieces to the four winds, but I never missed them. When the answers came in, I knew what had to be done almost without thinking. Though everything had been destroyed, nothing was lost. Were I a business consultant, I should advise my clients to burn all correspondence after a year. Of the total, 99·8% will never be wanted again.*

From the W. H. Allen office, we soon moved to rooms off Kingsway, loaned to us by Jim Pitman (now Sir James Pitman, M.P.) of the famous Pitman publishing house. A month or two later we had found an office of our own, and moved early in January into 7 John Street, Bloomsbury, where we remained till 1961. The weather was icy, the new rooms poorly heated, the stress and anxiety of the last few months had weakened me. Almost immediately I was in a nursing home, critically ill with virus pneumonia. It was mid-April before I emerged.

As I lay in bed or sat during convalescence feebly in an armchair, detached from the swirl of events, I had ample time to survey my life past and present. As if through the wrong end of a telescope, I saw my career public and private, in some proportion. It was not

*The possible loss to historians and biographers is, however, too horrible to contemplate.

much, I thought, in the publishing sphere at least. I was forty-six years old, the head but not the owner of a tiny business with a fair reputation. My salary was poor, my prospects doubtful. One day soon the war would end, and the boom in books which it had created would be over. Would my firm survive the dangerous post-war period? Could it struggle out of the strait-jacket within which paper rationing had confined it before it had grown to an adequate size? Certainly, I had found new authors of distinction, but not surely enough of them. Doubtless I was more competent than I had been ten years before when we had founded Secker & Warburg, yet I wondered whether, even now, I had the financial and business abilities allied to the editorial flair to create a publishing house that was both worthwhile and profitable. Was I perhaps wasting my life to little purpose? In those weeks I came to the edge of despair. Secker & Warburg was too small to matter, too powerless to make a mark, too uncertain to develop a policy.

Yet in the end I drew back from the precipice. Good nursing, good food, my wife's devotion, rest, a holiday by the sea, the good war news, all played their part. The well of energy, drained dry by ten years of almost uninterrupted work, filled slowly up again. Yet I was not the same. I had learned the lesson of mortality.

3
Animal Farm

ONE evening in September 1941, about three weeks after we had settled into our Primrose Hill flat, the front-door bell rang loudly. It was the head porter, a magnificent figure of a man, six foot six inches tall, with a barrel chest, flashing blue eyes and a resonant voice. His name was Richardson. After a little social chit-chat he came to the point with a bang.

'I hope, sir, now that you're back in London, you'll be joining the Home Guard?', he said. Taken by surprise, I considered the suggestion. Naturally I had expected to do my stint as a firewatcher, but to don a uniform and practise the art of war, which I had abandoned over twenty years before, had not occurred to me. I said as much to him, but he brushed aside such trivialities.

'Sergeant Blair tells me you had military experience in the last war,' he continued, 'and he wants you in his own section.' So that was it. Richardson was in the Home Guard with Eric Blair, alias George Orwell, and the two of them were determined to have me in too.

'What is your rank in the Home Guard,' I asked him.

'Company Sergeant-Major, sir,' he replied. 'Regular soldier, Grenadier Guards, first world war, service in India, all over the world. You're the kind of man we need, stiffen up the young 'uns.'

I hesitated. Was the Home Guard still a worthwhile force, I wondered. Perhaps it was. If the German invasion of the U.S.S.R. were successful, as it appeared to be at that time, the Germans might turn west again. There were other reasons for joining. I had no wish to disappoint an important author, nor did I want the head porter of our block of flats to regard me as a man who put his creature comforts before the defence of his country. I put the matter to my wife, who had been listening to the dialogue, only to receive another jolt. 'Of course you should join,' she said, 'it's years since you've taken any proper exercise. Besides, you might look good in uniform.'

So encouraged, I joined the Home Guard four days later and was enrolled in Sergeant Blair's section. Company Sergeant-Major Richardson put me through my paces, and I addressed him on parade as 'Sir'. In our block of flats he addressed me in like manner. It was a good example of the democratic process.

The first sight of the St John's Wood Company on parade in the drill hall in Allitsen Road, a pre-war headquarters of the Territorial Army, impressed me. Here was the enthusiasm to be expected in a volunteer organization, in which a ranker at that time was actually called by his superiors Volunteer-so-and-so, not Private. Boys, young men waiting their call-up, men with a middle-aged spread, veterans of fifty and over, all were mixed up together. As Sergeant Blair fell in as company marker for my first parade, I discerned the zeal which inflamed his tall skinny body. His uniform was crumpled, but it had been cut to fit him by a good tailor. The tricorn cap, bearing the badge of the King's Royal Rifle Corps, of which technically we were a unit, was perched so jauntily on the side of his head that I feared it might fall off. He had bought it himself, since he claimed that forage caps of over size 7 are 'of great rarity. Evidently they [the authorities he so deeply suspected] expect all soldiers to have small heads.' Orwell's expression was Cromwellian in its intensity. Here, I felt, was an Ironside, austere, resolute, implacably determined to destroy his enemies without fear or mercy, if only they came within his reach.

Orwell had joined the Home Guard within a few days of its inception. He had naturally volunteered for the only decent substitute for the armed services which had so unkindly rejected him. For him it was also in some measure a means of expiation for his crime of having been born too late to fight in World War One. Then again, he hoped it might provide him with a second chance of opposing the hated fascists who had wounded and almost killed him in Spain with a bullet close to the windpipe. Besides, he must have felt a deep affection for a force that in the early days had drilled with broomsticks since rifles were lacking, and whose principle armaments had consisted of pikes and bottle grenades. Orwell, except when writing, was an amateur. So for Orwell, in its first year or so, the Home Guard was the ideal fighting force; it was unprofessional; it was volunteer; it was anti-fascist and anti-Nazi; it was certainly not pro-

George Orwell. Charcoal drawing by Pamela de Bayou

de B

Communist; it was rather inefficient (an important point this) and it was animated by a deep affection for the England he loved beyond all else. Orwell, however, had one reservation; the ideological side of his nature could not help suspecting that most of its officers, especially high-ups, were potential fascists. For instance, in September 1940, when his platoon had only one rifle for six men, he complains that they (the unknown high-ups) have stood out against letting the rifles be taken home by individual men . . . 'parked in one place, a bomb may destroy the whole lot.' Yet it was obviously a sensible thing to keep them at H.Q. in times of crisis.

As a man with first hand experience of modern warfare in Spain, Orwell had been given the rank of sergeant, in spite of the forebodings of the authorities who were inclined to regard him as a dangerous red. As a sergeant he commanded a section of some twenty men, to which I was directed. Orwell was delighted to have me in his section, for a number of reasons, mostly rather discreditable. First, he knew me already, a great advantage as he was not one who made new friends easily. Second, he regarded me almost as his social equal, an important consideration since he felt that class barriers were practically insurmountable. Third, I had fought as an officer in World War One, and this gave me a prestige in his eyes which was wholly undeserved. Fourth, despite his normal ranking of women as second-class citizens, babblers certain to reveal military secrets to the enemy, he admired my wife for whose forthright remarks he had a healthy respect. Fifth, he knew me as a liberal who cared as little for the conservatives or the communists as he did. So it was that Sergeant Blair confided in me a good deal and taught me as much as he could remember of the guerilla tactics learned in the Spanish Civil War. But, though I enjoyed performing close-order drill, and was willing to fire a rifle as often and as straight as I could, I was far from eager to be pushed up the ladder of military promotion, as my sergeant hoped. Dubiously I accepted a single stripe after a few months, and later still a second. But the rank of corporal suited me excellently, and at the rank of corporal I stuck mulishly till my disbandment in 1944.

As corporal I became second-in-command of Orwell's section, and stayed with him to the end. The Company Commander, who regarded Orwell and myself as eccentric persons of dubious military value, dumped on us many of the foreign refugees who joined. With strange accents, subtle minds, and a love of indiscipline amounting to genius, these Jews, Polish and Czech, German and French, became in due course a technical section of some excellence. Known in the company as the Foreign Legion, they were unlikely to perform correctly even the simplest movements of close-order drill, but they were quite good at handling the one weapon the Home Guard possessed which had real power and utility, the spigot mortar, in whose mysteries Orwell and I had been trained as soon as it became available.

As instructors in the handling of the spigot mortar, Orwell and I had a number of learners through our hands. The drills usually took place in a garage off the Edgware Road. The spigot mortar was designed to hurl a 50 lb. plastic bomb with very considerable accuracy up to a distance of 400 yards. Thus it was an excellent anti-tank weapon. It was mounted on four legs, each about three feet long with spikes at the ends pointing downwards. These had to be hammered into the ground and took up the considerable recoil when the mortar fired. One night in 1943, when I was not on parade, Orwell took the drill in the garage, which had a concrete floor. Two men, lying flat behind the mortar, were needed to handle it – one to aim, one to fire. Now the mortar had three kinds of bombs each marked in a different colour – a drill bomb, which was wooden and wholly inert, a practice bomb which would leave the mortar at high speed but would not explode on impact, and a live bomb with a war-head able to destroy a real tank, which Orwell and I had each fired to great effect on the ranges at Aldershot. All was ready to fire, but, alas, Orwell had not seen that it was the practice, not the drill, bomb that had been loaded. As the command 'Fire!' was given, the bomb leapt from the muzzle with high velocity, narrowly missing a Home Guard whom it might have decapitated, and bounced heavily off the far wall of the garage. In front all was well, but behind, as the mortar, not being dug in, recoiled, it was another story. Private Smith lost virtually all his front teeth top and bottom, while Private Jones was unconscious for at least 24 hours.

Orwell barely referred to the matter in the days that followed, but he told me some weeks later that he had appeared before a Court of Inquiry. To the best of my knowledge no disciplinary action was taken by the Court, but the cost of a new set of dentures for Private Smith was paid for by the authorities and amounted to over £100, a sum which appeared to Orwell altogether excessive. What significance, if any, this deplorable incident had on my sergeant, I cannot say. He was not soft-hearted and he must have seen far worse casualties on the Aragon front in 1937. In any case, his troubles over his own health and the fact that his store of energy was barely sufficient for the tasks he felt bound to undertake left him little surplus for the minor misfortunes of others.

*　*　*

On his return from Spain in 1937 Orwell was fully and finally convinced that the practice of communism, as he had experienced it in Barcelona, when the anarchists and communists clashed, was intolerable for the democracies of the West. The English people, as he wrote in his preface to the Ukrainian edition of *Animal Farm*, 'had no real understanding of things like concentration camps, mass deportations, arrests without trial, press censorship, etc. Everything they read about a country like the U.S.S.R. is automatically translated into English terms.'* This, Orwell argued, had gravely harmed the socialist movement in England and had distorted English foreign policy. The U.S.S.R. was not in any sense of the word a socialist country and the illusion that it was must be damaging. If a revival of the socialist movement, in which Orwell undoubtedly believed, was to take place, this harmful illusion must be destroyed.

Orwell decided that a simple story was the ideal form for this destruction since 'it could be easily understood by almost any reader.' While living at Wallington, a little country village near London, he saw 'a little boy of about ten driving a huge horse along a narrow path, whipping it whenever it tried to turn aside.' This carthorse was, of course, to become the hero of *Animal Farm*, the magnificent Boxer. This incident was the catalyst which sparked off Orwell's masterpiece – if the finimals could only become consicious of their strength, and unite, they would no longer become our slaves. So similarly with the proletariat, exploited by the rich, as the animals are exploited by their masters.

It took Orwell six years from 1937 to elaborate the story in his imagination. He began to write in November 1943 and finished in February 1944, only three months in which to carry through the most important work of his life. In his essay, *Why I Write*, he remarked, '*Animal Farm* was the first book in which I tried, with full consciousness of what I was doing, to fuse political purpose and artistic purpose into one whole.' This to my mind was the high-water mark of Orwell's career as a writer. Although he described it as 'a little squib, which might amuse you when it comes out' in a letter to

* This and most and other quotation are taken from *The Collected Essays*, 4 vols, Secker & Warburg, 1968.

Gleb Struve of February 17, 1944, Orwell must have known that there was more to it than that. In the same letter Orwell continued 'it is so not O.K. politically that I don't feel certain in advance that anyone will publish it.' On May 1, 1944, Orwell wrote to Philip Rahv in New York, editor of the *Partisan Review*, adviser to Dial Press, a well-known New York publishing house, asking them to have a look at it. 'I am having hell and all to find a publisher for it here though normally I have no difficulty in publishing my stuff and in any case all publishers are clamouring for manuscripts.'

Orwell knew well enough what the trouble was, and puts it in a letter dated August 5, 1944, to J. Middleton Murray. 'I consider that willingness to criticize Russia and Stalin is *the** test of intellectual honesty . . . Russia (is) the only thing the greater part of the British intelligenzia now believe in.' Orwell was right. Rarely can there have been so complete and abject a *trahison des clercs* (in Julian Benda's phrase) as took place between 1936 and 1946. Even Aneurin Bevan, Minister of Health in the Labour Government elected in June 1945, was relieved that *Animal Farm* had not come out before the election. Yet Bevan was no kind of sympathizer with communism.

What then had happened to the manuscript between its completion and the day on which I first received it? The answer to this question is simple and rather frightening. The MS was rejected for publication by three well-known publishers, Gollancz, Faber and Cape. It is worth considering how such an extraordinary blunder could have been committed by three such distinguished persons as Victor Gollancz, T. S. Eliot, poet, critic and a director of Faber & Faber, later to be awarded the O.M., and Jonathan Cape.

There is no doubt that Gollancz turned it down on purely political grounds. Through the middle thirties till 1946–7, he could fairly be described as an ardent fellow-traveller. After that, his enthusiasm for communism had probably decreased. However, the reason given by Gollancz for rejection was the length of the book. He had options under his contract with Orwell for his next two full-length novels, and clearly wanted to preserve them. He claimed (correctly) that *Animal Farm,* slightly under 30,000 words long, was not full-length.†

Michael Howard, author of *Jonathan Cape, Publisher, 1921–71*, a

*Orwell's italics.

†Bernard Crick remarks in his important study of Orwell's recently discovered essay, *The Freedom of the Press* (*Times Lit. Supp.*, September 15, 1972) 'never has a publisher tried harder to keep his hooks into an author whose best books he cordially disliked.'

well-researched history of the firm which Howard's father had created in partnership with Jonathan himself, has dealt clearly with his firm's attitude to *Animal Farm* (pp. 179–80). The many MSS which came into Cape's office at that time were sifted by Veronica Wedgwood and Daniel George. Both read *Animal Farm*. Wedgwood's report is lost, but she has told me that she had found it 'the greatest fun to read, the animals and the farm so marvellously done, it was the literary merits that impressed me. I gave it no particular consideration as a social or political document.' Daniel George, however, aware of the political grounds on which Gollancz had rejected the MS, but undismayed, delivered a favourable report. 'This is a kind of fable, entertaining in itself and satirically enjoyable as a satire on the Soviets. The characters of Marx, Lenin, Trotsky and Stalin can clearly be recognized, and incidents in recent Russian politics are cleverly parodied. There is no doubt that it would find many appreciative readers, though . . . its real purpose is not made clear. Publication of it is a matter of policy. I cannot myself see any serious objection to it.' On these two enthusiastic reports Cape offered Orwell a contract, and 'we all believed the matter to be settled,' Miss Wedgwood wrote to me, 'when Jonathan had the unfortunate idea of asking the advice of a friend in the Ministry of Information, personal and unofficial advice. I think he was genuinely upset when he got a letter disadvising publication on the grounds that it would be very bad for our relations with Russia.' So Cape acted as he conceived that a responsible citizen should act, although greatly perturbed at the reaction he had received from the Ministry. From this it might be argued, and I think it should be argued, that 'responsibility', whether political or social or literary, is not necessarily a desirable quality in a publisher. Irresponsibility or even bad taste may sometimes better serve the public good, and this I bore in mind when in 1966 I published Beverley Nichols' study of Somerset Maugham's marriage, *A Case of Human Bondage*, for which the firm and I were roundly abused in major articles by a large section of the press. However, to advocate irresponsibility and bad taste may be going a bit too far. Orwell in his essay describes the negative reaction of Cape as 'intellectual cowardice', and certainly I'll settle for that. There can be no doubt that courage is as essential to a publisher's make-up as taste, honesty, judgment and skill.

Orwell decided to offer his book next to Faber & Faber, and wrote to T. S. Eliot on June 28, 1944, 'If you read this MS yourself you will see its meaning which is not an acceptable one at this moment, but I could not agree to make any alterations . . . Cape or the M.O.I. (Ministry of Information), I am not certain which, made the imbecile suggestion that some other animals but pigs might be made to represent the Bolsheviks.'

Of the three rejections, that of T. S. Eliot is the most surprising. Here is one of the foremost men of letters in the English-speaking world rejecting the work of a man he knew quite well. One thinks inevitably of Gide's rejection, acting as Gallinard's reader, of Proust's *A La Recherche du Temps Perdu*. That *Animal Farm* like *A La Recherche* was a literary masterpiece makes Eliot's action almost incomprehensible. But it was not turned down on *literary* grounds. In the first paragraph of his letter Eliot writes 'we agree that it is a distinguished piece of writing, that the fable is very skilfully handled, and that the narrative keeps one's interest on its own plane – and that is something very few authors have achieved since *Gulliver*.' High praise indeed, and praise that Orwell must have enjoyed as he read it, for Swift was among his six most admired forerunners. And then – as Orwell's hopes must have been rising that, after all the delays and disappointments, a publisher had at last read his book and estimated it accurately, the terrible doom-laden opening of the second paragraph 'On the other hand . . .'

Having said that he has consulted one other director (in the absence of the chairman, Geoffrey Faber) and that this director is 'in agreement with me on the main points,' he goes on 'we have no conviction (and I am sure none of the other directors would have) that this is the right point of view from which to criticize the political situation at the present time.' How, I wonder, could he have been so sure of the views of those who had not read it? Certainly, so far as Faber was concerned, he was mistaken, unless Faber was naughtily trying to cover up a disastrous blunder of his own, which I doubt. Speaking to me a year or so after *Animal Farm* had been published, he said 'if only I'd been in London that week-end, the decision would have gone the other way.'

Presumably, though it is far from clear, by 'the political situation' Eliot means the situation of the U.S.S.R. as governed by Stalin. With this I could have some sympathy – 'don't be rude to an ally' might be the decent or at least the prudent line to adopt – but this does not appear to be what is in Eliot's mind, for he continues 'I think my own dissatisfaction with this apologue is that the effect is simply one of negation. It ought to excite some sympathy with what the author wants, as well as sympathy with his objections to something. . . . The positive point of view, which I take to be generally Trotskyite, is not convincing.' Here the key word is clearly 'negation'. Farmer Giles rules brutally over his flock, the animals revolt and drive him out, he is replaced by the pigs who soon come to exercise a despotism identical with that of the farmer. This, says Eliot, is negation, for the reader, unable to sympathize with the farmer, can't sympathize with the pigs either. This seems to me an interpretation of Orwell's theme so wrong-headed as to be laughable. It is the essence of Orwell's thought that all rulers, every form of government, must be suspect. Checks and balances are needed. An opposition is essential. For otherwise 'all power corrups, and absolute power corrupts absolutely.' Orwell was aware of this as profoundly as Lord Acton. He had surveyed it from afar in the U.S.S.R., he had felt it in his bones in the streets of Barcelona. He was, after all, temperamentally an anarchist. But he knew that the pure spirit of anarchism can never prevail among fallable human beings. It is this that gives *Animal Farm* its pessimistic and tragic theme, and it is probably this that led Orwell to make it a fairy story, for an actual, functioning anarchist state could exist only in a fairy story.

Finally, Eliot reveals perhaps his most strongly felt objection – 'after all,' he adds, 'your pigs are far more intelligent than the other animals, and therefore the best qualified to run the farm, in fact, there couldn't have been an Animal Farm at all without them: so that what was needed (someone might argue) was not more communism but more public-spirited pigs.' Orwell, of course, never argued that 'more communism' was needed, nor yet (as Eliot suggests earlier) 'a purer communism'. For, to put it plainly, he was not, had never been, and could not possibly have become a communist or communist sympathizer. As for a 'purer' communism, this was what the Trotskyites pinned their faith on, but never Orwell, who despite the view held of him (and of me) at the time was in no sense a Trotskyite.

In this passage Eliot also displays his preference for hierarchies of the intelligent to run the farm (or the state). But, as Orwell well knew, there is no God-given connexion between 'intelligence' and 'public spirit', in fact, a fairly strong case could be made out to the contrary, though there is no room for it to be developed here.

If I have been harsh with so distinguished a writer as Eliot, it is because his letter shows so clearly the ease with which one great writer can misinterpret another. Eliot loved an 'establishment', as we call it nowadays. But, wherever there is an establishment, there is some sort of Animal Farm. It is a fact of life and politics. Orwell knew this. Eliot apparently didn't.

* * *

During the four months while the MS of *Animal Farm* had puzzled and irritated and been rejected by three major publishers, I had been urging Orwell to show it to me, though I was far from clear about its subject or its length. I was his friend, his corporal and the publisher of *Homage to Catalonia* and *The Lion & The Unicorn*, but I was not yet 'Orwell's publisher' to whom everything was offered automatically. Gollancz with his options was Orwell's publisher, though Orwell understood perfectly that he could no longer continue with him and had to find a new one.

On July 18, 1944, Orwell wrote to his agent Leonard Moore, a letter which seems to me of great importance.

> Warburg again says he wants to see it [*Animal Farm*] and would publish it if he can see his way to getting the paper, but that is a big 'if'. If that falls through I am not going to tout it round further publishers, which wastes time and may lead to nothing, but shall publish it myself as a pamphlet at 2/-. I have already half-arranged to do so and have got the necessary financial backing.

This letter suggested that *Animal Farm* had not been offered to me, because Orwell feared I would not have the paper to print it on. This fear was far from being unjustified. However, more important than this, was Orwell's express intention of publishing it himself, if I rejected it.

This indicates a sense of urgency that his 'little squib' must be published rapidly. After all, it had had a six year period of gestation, an intense three months of labour to bring it to birth, and a five month delay, not yet ended, in displaying his brain-child to the world through the good offices of a publisher. Orwell's haste was undoubtedly due to his knowledge that *Animal Farm*, as a satire on the Soviet Union, quite apart from its wider implications, contained a warning of the highest importance to Britain not to worship the false god of Bolshevism or follow his commandments.

There is no doubt that from November 1943 onwards Orwell had entered a period of great activity and vital decisions. He had resigned from the Home Guard and from his job on the Far Eastern Service of the B.B.C. to become literary editor of the left-wing weekly *Tribune*, writing his first *As I Please* column on December 3rd.

Obviously by then he had come to regard Home Guard parades as a waste of time and effort, and the propaganda talks to India as what he was later to call double-talk. In February 1944, *Animal Farm* is finished, in May he writes a text for a picture book on *The English People*, one of a series published by Collins. In June he adopts a baby boy, born on May 14th, and christens him typically, and in the Blair family tradition, Richard Horatio Blair. But before the end of July three major publishers have rejected *Animal Farm*, just when he needed money for the expenses of the baby at a time when his wife had given up her job at the Ministry of Food. In addition to this, his flat in Baker Street had been bombed and he was forced to take a new flat in October in Islington. He was, as his letters prove, short of money.

Writers need money at least as much as any other worker. But there is something which they need even more, enthusiasm for their work. Usually this comes first from their publisher. Throughout my career on innumerable occasions I have noticed how ardently a writer longs for his publisher to read and admire his new book, the fruit of so many months or sometimes years of toil. He will ring his publisher up or write to him or make any excuse to see him to discover what his publisher thinks. Orwell had tried three publishers and had got three negatives. Now he had decided to have one last fling, and show it to me. *Après moi le déluge.* So the letter to Moore gives expression to a feeling of near despair, 'I shall publish it myself as a pamphlet at 2s.' For a professional writer of twelve years standing this is a statement of extraordinary significance, one which perhaps has not yet received the consideration it deserves. Let us suppose that I had in fact rejected *Animal Farm*, and ask what might have happened then. Here no doubt I am on treacherous ground, but I think the risk is worth it.

Of all London publishers Orwell knew me best. I had already published two books for him. With Fyvel he had edited the Searchlight Books for me. The policy of the firm was in line with Orwell's thinking. A rejection by me and my firm would have had a grave impact on his morale. It would have left him with three courses. Put *Animal Farm* in a bottom drawer till the world was ready to appreciate it? Impossible. Its publication was a matter of extreme urgency to him. Try yet again, for the fifth time, to find a sane publisher? Possible, but unlikely in view of the statement in his letter 'I am not going to tout it round further publishers.' Pride was involved here, and a contempt for the intelligence of publishers which was surely not unjustified. There can be little doubt that he would have chosen the third course, and published it himself 'as a pamphlet at 2s.'

Would he have succeeded? It is hard to be sure. Orwell correctly estimated the strong demand for books at that period of the war. Books however are not the same as pamphlets, and *Animal Farm* was planned by him as a 'pamphlet', that is a thin, paper-covered, and fragile object. Would the booksellers have stocked it? Would the public have bought it? And would the reviewers have been sent it for review by their literary editors, when space in the papers was so short? 'After all, it's only a pamphlet,' they might have said.

Then there is the question of printing, paper, and the mechanism of distribution, also the problem of financing it. It costs us £270 to manufacture (say £1,250 at present prices), not a negligible sum. Paul Potts has declared that he had an arrangement with Orwell to publish *Animal Farm* under the imprint of his Whitman Press, which specialized in the production of broadsheets. I do not know whether he had enough paper to print even the 4,000 copies which made up our first edition. Nor can one be sure that the printing would have been completed even as rapidly as ours, and that was low enough.

However, let us suppose that Orwell had succeeded in publishing his 2s. pamphlet as rapidly as we published *Animal Farm*. What then? Would the pamphlet have had the tremendous impact on the world that we achieved with it? In considering this, it is necessary to remember that printing a pamphlet or a book is not he same ast distributing it, let alone selling it. Both have to be transferred from some central office to 'the point of sale', normally a bookshop. No doubt Potts would have done his best to overcome these problems, but could he have succeeded? Could he have got orders from all over the U.K., from Europe, Canada, Australia, New Zealand, South Africa, and elsewhere? It is a hard task for an organized publishing house in peacetime, but in 1944 we were at war, and Whitman Press was hardly organized for such efforts.

So, though publication would in all probability have been effected, the prestige and the success would not have followed. Such is my own opinion. But I have consulted others, a number of publishers, young and old. The large majority are of the opinion that it would not and could not have succeeded as it did, either from the point of view of sales or of prestige. Almost certainly it would not have been sold to a U.S. publishing house, where in fact it had an even greater success than in the U.K. If I am correct, the effect on Orwell might have been, indeed would have been, disastrous. Deep depression, even despair, might have swept over him.

Orwell was most certainly a stoic and a man of iron determination, but he had had much to endure in his life, not merely the early life, but after he had started to become a professional writer. The fifteen years of struggle from 1931 to 1945 to obtain a mediocre or even a pitiful financial return, the constant ill health, when writing was forbidden him as dangerous to his recovery, the knowledge that his expectation of life was shorter by far than the average. In 1943 he was 40. How much longer had he got to get his work done? Perhaps even Orwell's morale might have cracked, had *Animal Farm* failed. And then . . .? *Then there might never have been a novel called 1984.* This book, as I shall show in Chapter 6, was finished only after a tremendous effort, lasting for months, which sapped his vital energies. If *Animal Farm* had not given a tremendous boost to his morale, if it had not earned him money to give him a sense of financial security, it seems to me extremely unlikely that he could have completed it. Half finished it would have been found among his papers after his death, and his executor would have destroyed it in accordance with the testator's strict instructions in his will. In that case the face of English literature in the twentieth century would have changed. Orwell would have died with the work of liberation he had fanatically determined to carry through unfinished.

In July 1944 none of these speculations occurred to me. I was nothing but a small insignificant publisher, hard pressed for paper, with my office wrecked by a V1 bomb. But I had one overwhelming asset, a belief in the value of Orwell's work.

* * *

One day at the end of July 1944, I was lunching at a small pub off the Strand, where the food was at least tolerable at a period when good food was almost unobtainable. The dining-room was on the first floor, but I had finished my lunch and come down the stairs to return to my office not more than five minutes walk away. I was just about to go out into the street when Orwell came hurrying along in his usual shabby war-time clothes. We sat down on a bench in the downstairs bar.

'What's the matter?' I asked him – at that time, with the V1 bombs falling indiscriminately all over London, disaster was always loitering round the next corner – and I was surprised he had come to see me without an appointment.

'I wanted to see you urgently,' he said, slightly breathless, 'I went to the office, but they told me you were here. I've only got a minute to spare.' He looked toward the door, almost as if he wished to get away without more ado.

'Well?' I said.

'I've got a manuscript for you,' he replied, and immediately pulled out of a battered despatch-case a slim typescript in flimsy brown paper covers, which he handed to me. I took it with pleasure, and with some degree of excitement. 'What is it?' I asked.

'Read it yourself,' he said nervously, 'though I don't suppose you'll like it. It's about a lot of animals on a farm who rebel against the farmer, and it's very anti-Russian. Much too anti-Russian for you, I'm afraid.' At this period of the war, the success of the Russian armies advancing into Germany had given many millions a warmth of feeling towards Russia under Marshal Stalin which enabled them to cast a conveniently blind eye on the shortcomings of the communist system.

'What's it called?' I said.

'*Animal Farm*,' he answered. 'I think I can find you some buckshee paper to print it on.' A few moments later he was gone. I walked back to the office with the manuscript in my hand, not yet aware that my firm had received a gift more precious than rubies, and the world a book which it would read for generations.

That evening I read it. I never doubted that it was a masterpiece. Nor did my partner, Senhouse. We told Orwell so immediately.

A few days later, in my London office a great debate took place – was it or was it not politically dangerous to publish this bitter satirical attack on our great ally, the Soviet Union, when its armies were rolling back the German forces, while the U.K. and the U.S.A. had established a mere bridgehead on the French coast only a few weeks before? Senhouse had no doubts – I rather think he felt Stalin might have enjoyed the portrait of himself as the boar dictator. After all, Orwell had christened him with a mighty name, Napoleon. Our young sales manager,* Peter Maxwell, supported him. My experienced London traveller, Charles Roth, was extremely worried. He was a lifelong socialist, and could not really bring himself to believe that Russia was not a socialist state, however flawed. Worst of all, I was under strong pressure from my wife. Whether it was the blood of her Circassian grandmother speaking in her veins, or her belief

*At this time a sales manager's job was *not* to sell books. More books were often ordered than could be supplied; Maxwell's job was to ration the customers.

that Russia had always been a kind of (feudal) tyranny, or the warmth of her feelings for the immense sufferings of the Russian people at the hands of her brutal invaders, or (perhaps strongest of all) her knowledge that it was the Russians who had done most of the fighting since 1941, I'm not sure. But Pamela at that time regarded *Animal Farm* with a complete lack of sympathy. 'If you publish that book,' she said, 'I'll leave you! Don't think I won't!'

Shaken, but not irretrievably so, by her anger – after all, I had survived similar storms before – I went into the meeting. One thought obsessed me – the German armies were in retreat, but their will to resist was not yet broken. Suppose, just suppose, that Stalin made a second deal with Hitler and made peace, or even turned round against the West, the two totalitarian states against the democracies. It seemed almost plausible to me then. In my mind's eye I saw *Animal Farm* published and reviewed. The reviewers would not hesitate to point the moral and indeed adorn the tale. H.E. the Russian Ambassador in London would approach Ernest Bevin, the British Foreign Secretary. It was hardly likely that the Russian leader would welcome being depicted as a pig.

'This foul libel on the Soviet people must be banned immediately,' he would say. Then two smooth gentlemen from the Foreign Office would come round to see me.

'My dear Warburg . . . breach in the alliance . . . situation extremely grave . . . Minister feels sure . . . withdrawal essential . . . perhaps two or three years time . . . as patriotic man surely understand . . .' Then, when it was all over, on a lighter note – 'Off the record, of course . . . reds not our sort of people . . . Stalin awkward customer . . . read little book myself . . . haven't laughed so much since . . . all those pigs round the table . . . wonderful scene . . . reminded me of . . . well, never mind.' And then, as they prepared to leave – 'funny thing . . . damned red like Orwell . . . fought in Spain, didn't he . . . could think it all up . . . well, well, what will these literary gents get up to next?'

Happily I resisted Roth's ideals, my wife's hostility and the fantasies of my own imagination. Slowly I allowed myself to give way before Senhouse's commonsense. All right, I said, we'll publish – and be damned if necessary. Yes, yes, yes! It seemed to me then that I had made a decision of immense importance.

Michael Howard in his book *Jonathan Cape*, already quoted, states that I had no such *crise de conscience* to overcome as Cape had had. But this is not true. The decision to publish was made in the first week of August, 1944, while the war still had nine months to run.

The decision was made, but there were three problems to solve before publication. The first was where to find paper to print it on. Orwell's friends, printers with the 'buckshee' paper, had by now used it up on government work. So the second was to find a printer. The industry had suffered severely from bombing, and little or no new machinery had been bought. The third was how to sign a contract for *Animal Farm* and Orwell's future work, while Gollancz held an option on his 'next two full-length novels.'

The first two problems were solved for us by our good friends in Edinburgh, the printers Morrison & Gibb, though there were to be many delays in production. The problem of the contract was the most difficult of all. In fact, no contract was signed till much later, though Orwell was quite determined by hook or by crook to leave him and come to me,* as Orwell wrote to me on June 13, 1945, saying that he had no intention of keeping his contract with Gollancz, 'in any case you know I will bring you all my books except any which may be written for some special purpose.' That I trusted Orwell's word absolutely goes without saying. His word was indeed his bond. But might not the Gollancz contract bind him against his will?

In a letter to his agent, Leonard Moore, dated July 3, 1945, Orwell writes 'The real trouble is with Gollancz. The contract to bring him my next two novels is still extant. I frankly would prefer not to give or offer him any more books *if we can get out of it*. I have no quarrel with him personally, but it is obviously unsatisfactory to be tied to a publisher who accepts or refuses books partly on political grounds and whose own political views are constantly changing . . . With Warburg these difficulties don't arise. He is less interested in propaganda, and in any case his views are near enough to mine to prevent serious disagreement'.

* * *

In June, 1944, the flying bombs began to fall. In July one partly destroyed our Primrose Hill flat while my wife was in. Fortunately

*It is a matter of fact that the contract for A.F. was not signed by me till October 2, 1945, six weeks after we published it. The delay was due to difficulties with Gollancz over options for his future work. I got the duplicate signed by Orwell back on October 10, and wrote to Moore 'Thank God and all his angels, the new contract for A.F. is in order and in all delight I have signed it.'

she escaped with shock but without bruises or even a single scratch. In August at night our office was completely wrecked, as I have described in Chapter 2. Rapid publishing was not easy in those days. In December Moore reminded me that we had promised Orwell half the advance on *Animal Farm* (£50) before Christmas, and we paid it. Orwell needed this money quite badly. In January I developed pneumonia and was out of action till the end of March, 1945. In February Orwell had gone to liberated France for the *Observer*. In March his wife, Eileen, died. It was not really a pleasant winter for either of us. Yet clearly the war was nearly won, and in May came the end in Europe, V.E. Day.

Meantime the printing of *Animal Farm* was completed. On March 17, 1945, Orwell wrote Senhouse from Paris, wanting to alter one word in Chapter VIII where the windmill is destroyed. 'I wrote "all the animals including Napoleon flung themselves on their faces." I would like to alter it to "all the animals except Napoleon . . ." I just thought the alteration would be fair to J[oseph] S[talin], as he did stay in Moscow during the German advance.' To me this single sentence throws as much light on Orwell's character as any I know.

Concluding the letter he writes 'I hope Fred will have a good long rest [after the pneumonia]. I know how long it takes to get one's strength back.' Indeed, he was to know this all too well.

In June, 1945, came the General Election, and on the morning, around 9.30, I entered the polling booth in McKinnon Street, St. John's Wood, half a mile from our flat, to record my vote, the first in nine long crisis-crowded years. Not for a moment was its destination in doubt. Quietly, almost automatically, I put my X against the name of the socialist candidate on the voting paper and pushed it through the slot into the ballot box. This was the culminating act of the political publishing war in which I had been so passionately involved since the foundation of Secker & Warburg, one of the most satisfying moments of my life. When the announcement came that Labour had triumphed in the Election (though my local candidate had inevitably lost–mine was a sure-fire Tory seat) I could scarcely contain my joy. The political past had died, and reaction had died with it, I believed. The future would be . . . at least, different. I feel sure that Orwell felt the same.

On August 17, 1945, without a signed contract, we published *Animal Farm* at 6s. in an edition of 4,500 copies. Presumably we thought this was adequate to meet the expected demand, though it is conceivable that this was all the paper we could muster. Orwell had had to wait seventeen months from completion before his book was available for readers. The advance was £100, on account of royalties of 12½% to 5,000 copies, 15% to 10,000 copies, 17½% after, reasonable terms for an author of Orwell's eminence. This meant that our advance would be covered by a sale of about two-thirds of the first edition. We were, in fact, out of print in a matter of days, and gave orders for a second impression of 10,000 copies to be ready as soon as possible, but a jam at the printers, almost inevitable in those days, delayed delivery for several months. The total cost of the first printing was £270 plus royalty, a cost per copy of 1s. 2d. plus a royalty of 9d. per copy – in all, 1s. 11d. (0·09½ new pence). To get today's equivalent of these figures it would be necessary to multiply by about 5.

Animal Farm was widely and enthusiastically reviewed, and began to sell very briskly indeed. On August 31, Moore wrote to me '*Animal Farm* is creating a sensation, is it not?' It was something of an understatement. By December very few copies remained in the bookshops. On September 6 Moore wrote Senhouse 'I congratulate you. What a press it is having. You have shown more courage than certain other publishers and you have got the usual reward.' Praise of publisher by agent is not that frequent!

The reviews of *Animal Farm* were many, and on the whole perceptive. Hardly one failed to see its immense originality and distinction. Peter Quennell, J. C. Trewin, T. R. Fyvel, Julian Symons, Graham Greene and Kingsley Martin paid homage to it in signed reviews. Martin, of course, placed a sting in the tail of his review in the *New Statesman*.

'If we read the satire,' he wrote 'as a gibe at the failings of the U.S.S.R. and realize that it is historically false and neglectful of the complex truth about Russia, we shall enjoy it and be grateful for our laugh.' A big 'if' indeed. Greene described it as 'a sad fable and an indication of Mr. Orwell's fine talent that it is really sad – not a mere echo of human failings at one remove.' He went on to suggest it as a suitable subject for Walt Disney. This I had hoped for myself, though it never happened. However, a film was made of it by Halas and Bachelor, the first full-length colour cartoon film ever to be made in the U.K. Trewin remarked wittily: 'Orwell has been both *swift* and sure.' The most violent attack I have been able to discover was broadcast on February 17, 1946, from Lahore. Here, V. G. Kiernan, the reviewer for All-India Radio, spoke as follows: 'As a piece of entertainment the book, though only a hundred pages, is too long, for the joke has only enough humour to support a *Daily Mail* cartoon. . . . Nor is *Animal Farm* remarkable as a piece of propaganda . . . Orwell's "good natured" satire means (if it means anything at all) that in his opinion Stalin and his party are a set of selfish, drunken, bloodthirsty bandits. . . . (While) the Red Army was busy saving civilization, including Mr. Orwell, he, not to be left behind, was making *his* contribution to world progress.' There is a strong whiff here of the Manor Farm sheep, good comrades all, bleating vigorously 'four legs good, two legs bad.'

But I will end with extracts from the long review in the *Book of the Month Club News*. The reviewer was in fact the brother of Frank Morley, who had bought the American rights from me nearly a year before (see next page). Christopher Morley, himself a considerable novelist, wrote in a long review, one of the most perceptive pieces to appear. 'In a narrative so plain that a child will enjoy it, yet with double meanings as cruel and comic as any great cartoon, Orwell presents a parable that may rank as one of the great satires of our anxious time. . . . It is plain enough that the satire is explicitly turned upon Russian communism, yet I wish that the reader might see in it a parable even larger than that. For the impact goes straight to the forehead of any kind of Goliath, any monstrous totalitarianism. It is a smooth stone indeed, sped by a skilful slinger.' 'It has been queer,' he continues, 'to think of this book ticking away like an unexploded bomb deep in the middle of the crowded Main Street of our life. It caused a sensation when it was published in England. One of the most distinguished publishing houses in America shied away from it like a frightened mustang. But when it came, long later, to your committee, we cried with one voice "This is it!" Because it deals in terms simple and unmistakable with the heaviest problem of mankind today, one that no one knows is solvable. . . . Yet man is still a reasoning animal, even if he perishes, he would like to know, in his agony, what it was that doomed him.'

We may say therefore that Orwell's fears for its reception were on the whole unjustified, as were the worries of the foolish publishers, including myself, who feared intervention from a Ministry. Napoleon, the Pig, had conquered the world more permanently than his namesake, the First Consul.

Yet by the end of the year, over four months after publication, twelve or more American publishers, large and small, distinguished and undistinguished, had rejected it, including such top firms as Harper, Knopf, Viking, and Scribner, in some cases apparently on the grounds that it was 'too short for adequate marketing.'* In answer to a letter of mild reproach from Senhouse on October 29th, Moore had replied: 'You may be sure that my American representative is alive to the importance of George Orwell, and you will realize that I am, when I tell you that it was I who saved Orwell's first manuscript *Down and Out in Paris and London* from destruction by the author,† and took it personally to Victor Gollancz. Scribners . . . will not touch *Animal Farm*, and I am sorry to say results have shown that the latter cannot be sold to any of the top-notch publishers in New York. Never mind, we shall get it published satisfactorily there, and the only reason we have not done so up to the present is that America has the jitters regarding Russia pretty badly.'

At Bowes & Bowes, the great Cambridge bookselling house, by December *Animal Farm* was out of stock. Working there over Christmas was a well-known publisher, Frank Morley, who wanted to learn something about the trade of bookselling which might be useful to him as a publisher. At one time a director of Eyre & Spottiswoode, he was at this time a director of the American publishing house of Harcourt Brace. Morley, seeing that his stock of *Animal Farm* had melted away as eager buyers purchased them, borrowed one for himself from a friendly bookseller 'to read over Christmas'. In fact he read it at once and telegraphed me on December 20 setting up a meeting in my office at 3.30 p.m. the next day to discover whether the American rights were still available, which of course they were.

Morley entered my office, then at 7 John Street, off Theobald's Road, W.C.2., punctually on time. We knew each other already, though not well. He told me how he'd happened on *Animal Farm* and what a brilliant little book it was.

'The rights are still free for the United States,' I told him, 'the American publishers seem to me quite mad. Why, we sold out our large first edition in a few days and are reprinting.'

'I'm not surprised, it really is a remarkable little book. Any reason why you shouldn't sell it to me for Harcourt Brace?'

'None at all, except that we don't own the American rights, they're handled by Christie & Moore.'

*A copy of *Animal Farm* was given by Orwell's friend, Frank Horrabin, to David Low, the great cartoonist. Low wrote to Horrabin 'I've had a good time with *Animal Farm*, an excellent bit of satire. As you say, it would illustrate perfectly.' Orwell was quite keen for Low to do illustrations, mainly in the hope that these would assist the sale to an American publisher.

†Nothing is known to me about this (alleged) destruction.

'Never heard of them, what's the address?'

'Their office is a bit outside London. . . .'

'I haven't time for that, must be back in Cambridge tonight. Will you call them for me?'

There was nothing else I could do, reluctant though I was. I did not relish the idea of negotiating *Animal Farm* over the phone with Leonard Moore. He was obstinate and exceedingly deaf, and it was rare for him to remember to stick his hearing aid in position while he talked. Besides, what was the right price? I thought rapidly. It seemed certain to me that we were set to sell at least 20,000 copies, so £750 or even perhaps £1,000 seemed about the right price. Whereupon I asked Morley what offer he was prepared to make. Not more than £250, he said, on a normal royalty basis. That's a poor offer, I told him, it's worth three or four times as much! Offer Mr. Moore £250, said Morley, polite but firm.

There was nothing for me to do except obey. I rang Moore and he came on the phone, of course without his hearing aid. 'I have an American publisher in my office,' I shouted at him, 'who wants to buy U.S. rights in *Animal Farm.*' 'Which American publisher is it?' shouted Moore, 'all the best ones have turned it down.' Naturally Morley could hear every syllable of this dialogue. 'It's Harcourt Brace who are interested,' I told him. Moore heard me all right – I fancy his hearing was much keener when an offer was being made than when a rejection was being conveyed – and in a voice that rang through my room almost as if he were in it, 'Sell it to him,' he shouted, 'sell it to him, none of the others will buy.'

'Very well, I'll do that,' I said, 'but he's offering a very poor advance indeed.'

'How much?'

'Only £250, and it ought to be . . .'

But Moore didn't wait. In a frenzy of eagerness and in the same ringing tones, 'Take it, take it,' he cried, 'we may never get another chance!'

I took it. There was nothing else to be done. In due course a royalty contract was signed with Harcourt Brace and *Animal Farm* was published in the U.S. in August, 1946, twelve months after its British debut. Of the hard-cover edition, the sales to the end of 1971 amount to 150,000 copies. It was a selection of the Book of the Month Club, who sold 460,000 copies between 1946 and 1949. It has sold to date over five million copies as a paperback in the New American library. In all, a total of more than 6 million copies have been disposed of, with the royalties amounting to many tens of thousands of pounds. It continues to sell in the U.S. today at the rate of 350,000 copies a year, mainly in paperback.

The English sales are equally amazing – in hard cover over 70,000 copies, in a Penguin paperback over 2½ million copies, and in an educational edition around 430,000 copies. In all, a total of just over 3 million copies, and still selling in paperback 140,000 copies per year.

There can be very few books indeed to have sold 9 million copies, even over a period of 28 years, and few of those few have been books of the highest quality.

How did it happen that *Animal Farm* made so immediate and so powerful and so lasting an impression on the world, or at least a very large part of it?* There was, after all, little in Orwell's previous work to indicate that he was capable of this supreme effort. There was no one who would have prophesied that Orwell's greatest work was to be, not a novel, not a study however original of social or political life, but . . . a fairy story. Orwell proclaimed it as a fairy story on his title page and he was a man to use words with precision. The writer of rather grey novels, with heroes embodying some aspect of his personal character, had suddenly taken wings and become – a poet, for *Animal Farm* can well be described as a prose poem.

Yet with hindsight it is perhaps possible to trace the steps which led Orwell from the age of 32 through Wigan Pier to Manor Farm. All his life he had been concerned with the problems of society and with politics. He had sharpened the edge of his prose into a lucid and fast-moving style, capable of dealing with complex matters in the simplest possible manner. Since 1936 he had concentrated his effort to attack and if possible destroy the idea of totalitarian rule, so he tells us, and in particular the myth of Soviet communism which, between 1936 and 1946 in Britain (and elsewhere), had deluded millions of working people and fatally infected the minds of left intellectuals who dominated the world of literature and journalism in the second half of the thirties. So he came by the idea of 'a simple story', with political and artistic purpose fused into one whole, describing the development of the Bolshevik Revolution, set in the familiar world of the English countryside, with English animals

*Foreign rights in A.F. were sold in France, Germany, Holland, Sweden, Norway, Denmark, Czechoslovakia, Spain, Italy, Japan, Yugoslavia, Indian vernacular. Illegal editions were printed for Russia, Ukraine and perhaps others. This list is probably not complete.

voicing the sentiments of English characters in a language of Orwellian simplicity. It is, when you come to think about it, a bizarre decision to embody Stalin as a boar and Moscow as Manor Farm, and only slightly less unlikely to represent the English working man as the noble and hard-working Boxer and the sheep as the idiot mob who will always flock (like sheep) to the new leader.

But this merely describes the mechanism. It does not reveal the miracle of the creative process. This must remain a mystery, yet surely it is connected with the fact that Orwell's mind worked on two levels, that of an adult man who fought in a real war and endured endless disappointment and suffering, and that of a child who loved mechanical gadgets and practical jokes, and rejoiced in his own elementary knowledge of botany, natural history and country lore. Early in 1941, on a country walk with Orwell, we reached a railway cutting, and sat down on the slope above it. Soon he got up, ran down to the line and placed a penny on the rail. Before long a train came by, whereupon he retrieved the now flattened penny and showed it to us with a broad grin of delight. Only a writer who had retained the intense and unsubtle perceptions, the huge delights and terrible angers of a child, could have written *Animal Farm*.

When he had finished the writing of it in three short winter months, when the fire of his genius had burnt itself out, Orwell must have known what he had done. He referred to it as 'this little squib', he sent it to a friend with a 'this may amuse you' letter. Mock modesty? I do not think so. It was the silence or the reserve of a writer who *knows*, if not quite surely, that he has made a breakthrough, a unique and important contribution to the world's literature, and dare not say so, dare not breathe a word of it, for fear it may not be recognized by the world. Like a miser who hoards his wealth, the secretive Orwell hid his treasure under a cloak of modesty.

Eleven days before the publication of *Animal Farm*, an American B25 Super-Fortress bombing plane, flying at 30,000 feet, dropped an atomic bomb on Hiroshima. The catastrophic death roll in this harmless Japanese city drove the emperor to sue for peace in a matter of days. The technical breakthrough which made the construction of the bomb practicable had taken five years, about the same period as Orwell had required to conceive, work out and finally write *Animal Farm*. Though the A-bomb was dropped on Japan, it was doubtless considered as a warning to the U.S.S.R. A-bomb and A-farm thus had an identical target, the Soviet Union. Each contained a threat to its existence. That each was launched in the same month of the same year was an ironical coincidence, which has been noted before and is most emphatically worth noting again, for it raises the question of relativity, which is the greater, the pen or the sword, the power of the book or the power of the nuclear armoury.

Orwell, of course, had not foreseen the atomic bomb or its even more horrific successors. But he had foreseen that the world had become one in which such weapons could be produced. Science and technology had made it possible. No wonder then that, as early as 1937, he had proclaimed that 'progress is a swindle', and he might have gone even further and said that it was (or at least might become) a disaster. At the same time he had concluded that the Soviet Union and the myth it was propagating of a Soviet Utopia was the most dangerous threat to liberal values the world had ever seen, and it had to be therefore against the Soviet Union, our ally, that he was forced to aim his book.

With *Animal Farm* Orwell had reached a literary peak that he was never to reach again.* In the quarter-century since it was published, this little book has shown a vitality in terms of sales which to me is conclusive proof that it will remain for generations a classic of English and world literature. One phrase in it at least has entered the language and is being quoted every day in suitable, and sometimes unsuitable, contexts.

ALL ANIMALS ARE EQUAL
BUT SOME ANIMALS ARE MORE EQUAL
THAN OTHERS

It seems incredible that this sentence was never coined before. Orwell had clawed back at least one significant word from the hypocrites and word-mongers and liars, EQUAL, EQUALITY, the word that expresses the most important fact about humanity.

There was nearly five years between the completion of *Animal Farm* and that of *1984*, the last five years of Orwell's life. The quinquennium started well for him, once *Animal Farm* had been accepted, published and attained so rapidly a world reputation. But all too soon the tuberculosis, which had plagued him for so long, began to encroach upon his energy and threaten his life. I shall try in Chapter 7 to follow him along the road to *1984* and death. For Orwell death and *1984* were never very far apart.

* *1984* was, of course, a *political* novel, one of the most profound ever written, and invaluable for its analysis of the use of words to mislead.

4
Embroiled with Kafka

RUMMAGING recently among the office files, I came across a small packet of quarto typing paper, fastened with a paper clip that had turned rusty. The sheet was charred by fire at the edges. In Senhouse's handwriting, in pencil, I read in bold capital letters 'Edwin Muir Correspondence' and just above it in lower case 'all that remains from the bombing'. The words brought back memories. This file, I knew, must be the one containing correspondence about the possibility of translating and publishing a collected edition of Franz Kafka, an enterprise to which Senhouse had been committed for the five war years with the persistence of Kafka's hero, K, attempting to gain entrance to the Castle. It had been salvaged ('all that remains') from the pile of rubble to which a V1 bomb had reduced the office in June 1944. At that time Senhouse must have regarded the Kafka enterprise as doomed. But if he did so, he was wrong. For the enterprise was to accumulate a file fifty times as big as the one in my hand, and was to result in a collected edition of his works within five years of the bombing. Because of the character of the dramatis personae involved, set in motion by the extraordinary instructions of Kafka himself to his friend and literary executor, Max Brod, I have not succeeded in unravelling all the mysteries – to do so would require the services of a first-rate bibliographer, aided by a research student, in collaboration with the razor-sharp intellect of a Sherlock Holmes. My efforts have been rather those of a blundering Dr. Watson, but assuredly I have done my best.

When Kafka died in 1924, he left instructions to Max Brod to burn all his unpublished manuscripts. Kafka believed that to write was 'impossible' – perhaps he meant impermissible. Yet not to write was equally impossible, for him it was an overwhelming need, and he wrote, as he tells us, 'like a man gasping for air to breathe'. This image, however, was not just an image, but an accurate description of what was happening to him – the exhausting effort of putting into words the awesome findings of his imagination had led to the tuberculosis that was to destroy him.* Before his illness, he had published only a collection of short pieces, *Betrachtung* (Observation); a fragment called *Der Heizer* (The Stoker), which later became the first chapter of his novel, *Amerika*; and another story *Das Urteil* (The Sentence). All these by 1916. In 1917 he developed tuberculosis and in 1924 he died, leaving Brod with an intolerable problem, whether to burn the three novels which are now world famous and the many stories, sketches, letters and diaries which reveal the private world of this extraordinary man. What thoughts, we may wonder, passed through Brod's mind?

* * *

Hannah Arendt, author of a long and brilliant book, *The Origins of Totalitarianism* (1951), tells a story for whose authenticity I do not vouch. Brod, the story runs, is strolling down Prague's main shopping street on his way to a coffee-shop a few days after Kafka's death. The editor of Prague's leading literary monthly, let's call him Rudi, meets him.

RUDI – 'You look sad, Max, indeed we are all sad at the shocking news of poor Kafka's death.'

MAX – 'Yes, Rudi, it is terrible that my friend, dear Franz, has left me. He has placed on my shoulders a heavy burden.'

RUDI – 'What burden is that, Max?'

MAX – 'Franz has given me instructions that I am to burn all his unpublished work, all of it.'

RUDI – 'Well, you must burn it then, as Franz wishes.'

MAX – 'It is not so easy, my friend, I have read his work, his novels and stories, all of it. These are masterpieces. How can I burn them?'

RUDI – 'Masterpieces, you say. Then you must not burn them, Max, you must have them published.'

MAX – 'Against dear Franz's wishes, Rudi?'

*This point is well made by George Steiner in the *New Yorker* of July 15, 1972, page 75. The parallel between the death of Kafka and the death of Orwell from the same disease is striking and worth examination by those qualified to write about it. For certain major writers tuberculosis would seem to be an occupational hazard. It is perhaps significant that Thomas Mann's novel, *The Magic Mountain* is placed in a Swiss sanatorium where the inmates are tubercular.

RUDI (thinks hard, then in an emphatic voice) – 'I have it, Max. Publish Franz's work and *burn all your own*.'

Brod, of course, took Rudi's advice and published Kafka's work, but he did not destroy his own which, with the exception of his biography of Kafka, was exceptionally hard to read.

* * *

When Senhouse and I took over the remnants of the original Martin Secker business from the liquidator in 1936, we found ourselves the owners of the British rights in Kafka's novel, *The Castle*, and a collection of short stories, *The Great Wall of China*. There was plenty of stock also, for though Secker had printed only 1,500 copies of each, the first in 1930, the second in 1933, barely a third had been sold, while the rest lay covered with dust unwanted in our basement. It has to be said that neither Senhouse nor I felt able to regard these two books as valuable literary properties for the years to come. How had they arrived on Secker's list?

In 1926 Secker had published an English translation of Lion Feuchtwanger's novel, *Jew Süss*, of which his expectation of sale was so minimal that his first edition consisted of 750 copies imported from the Viking Press, New York. At that time Arnold Bennett was accepted by a vast section of the reading public as an arbiter of taste in the field of literature, and particularly novels. His oracle was promulgated every Thursday evening on the book page of the *Evening Standard*. In 1926 the word went out for *Jew Süss*. The effect was immense, for Secker, rapidly reprinting, sold many thousands of copies.

As a result of this success, he became unwisely convinced that large profits could be made from translating and publishing the best German novels of that era, and bought and issued a considerable number, including further novels of Feuchtwanger. On balance this led to substantial losses, sufficient to have played a big part in driving the business into bankruptcy in 1935. Many if not all these titles were recommended to him by Edwin Muir, then about 50 years old.

Muir was, and remained till his death and beyond, a literary figure of the highest eminence. Poet, critic, novelist and autobiographer, he had a fine knowledge of the German language and had himself translated, with the help of his wife, Willa, a number of the German novels he recommended to Secker. His attention was first drawn to

Kafka's work by an appreciation of it in the late twenties by Thomas Mann, himself already an ornament to the Secker list.

After his experience with *The Castle* and *The Great Wall*, Secker's hopes of producing anything like a comprehensive edition faded. The losses were too serious. He relinquished his options to the agent, Cyrus Brooks of A. M. Heath, who succeeded in selling *The Trial* to Gollancz. This too flopped and Gollancz backed down. Brooks then sold Kafka's third novel, *America*, to Routledge. It was a curious irony that, only a year or two before, I had been compelled to resign my managing directorship of Routledge, partly because I had advocated a policy of issuing novels, which the firm had never done before. *America* too was a flop. Three publishers had tried in vain to put Kafka's main works before the British reading public.

So far the story has been noticeably downbeat, but in 1938 a strange phenomenon became apparent to the watchful eyes of Senhouse and Warburg. *The Castle* had begun to sell, not fast but steadily. In 1939 we were forced to reprint 1,000 copies of it. But this was not the only manifestation of a growing interest. By 1940 we were receiving inquiries from magazines and periodicals in the U.K., and also from the U.S., asking us to authorize a translation of this story or that fable. But, of course, we had no rights in any Kafka material apart from the two works already on our list. Nor did we know who or where was the owner of the rights. Brooks had left the Heath agency for a branch of military service where his knowledge of German could be usefully employed. Audrey Heath remained, but her knowledge of the Kafka situation was slight and her interest in it slighter. Also, she enjoyed poor health and, like so many who dealt with the Kafka affair between 1940 and 1945, was a most dilatory correspondent.

By the end of 1940 Senhouse and I were of the opinion that the time had come for a Kafka renaissance. It was not enough to have reprinted *The Castle* in 1939, especially since three-quarters of the edition had been destroyed by German bombs. It needed another reprint, and Senhouse had discovered that a new 'definitive' German version contained two-and-a-half new chapters (66 pages) which ought to be translated and added to the new English printing. It took him many months, perhaps even a year or two, to find a copy of the definitive *Castle*. But here once again we were up against the basic problem: who owned the copyright of Kafka's work? We had bought *The Castle* from Kurt Wolff, his German publisher, through the Heath agency. But Wolff had been forced to fly from Germany by the Nazis and was in New York, struggling to set up a publishing house in the U.S. Indeed, he was writing to us to inquire about U.S. rights in a new volume of Kafka's short stories, for as he wrote 'I was the first publisher of Kafka, and, as long as he lived, the only one.' But *The Trial* had been published by Verlag Die Schmiede, a firm of which we had never heard. On the other hand we were well aware that Kafka had made Brod his literary executor, which must surely mean that Brod was the ultimate copyright holder. Indeed, Gollancz declared that he had bought the rights in *The Trial* from Brod in Prague in 1935. But Brod had had to flee Prague in 1938 and had gone – where we didn't know. In the end it turned out to be Palestine, with which correspondence was far from easy with Rommel at the gates of Cairo and Alexandria. Edwin Muir, with whom Senhouse carried on an extraordinary voluminous correspondence over the war years, was the accredited translator of Kafka's works into English. He had, he said, written authorization, but naturally he could not lay hands on it – I write 'naturally' because all matters dealing with Kafka I found to be shot through with that peculiarity which illuminates (or obscures) his novels – the conflict between reality and appearance and that between freedom and order. Senhouse, however, in some ways a typical Kafka type, proceeded steadily, in all directions as it were, to a dimly perceived goal. No information of value reached us from America, where there were two Kafka publishers, and still are two today, neither of whom were in possession of useful information. There were other problems, too complex to describe, such as the emergence of rival translators to Muir, one fairly good and two or three bad, who bombarded Senhouse with demands to be allowed to translate this or that Kafka work.

Some time in 1941, quite early in our tortuous struggle, while our books were being destroyed by bombs all over Britain and our paper stock reduced to a pitiable remnant, Senhouse and I came to a decision. It was a simple one, a brave one and a dishonest one – *we would announce that we, Secker & Warburg, controlled all British rights in Kafka's work, published and unpublished, and that when time and paper rationing permitted we hoped to publish a complete, definitive edition of the works of this great modern master.* It was dishonest, because the statement about the rights was untrue. It was, on the other hand, sincere because we fully intended to do precisely what we said we would do.

First, I managed to buy from Gollancz the British rights in *The Trial* and from Routledge in *America*. I also succeeded in securing the

British rights of *The Metamorphosis* (sometimes titled *Transformations*) from the Parton Press. I opened a ledger account for the owner of Kafka rights, whoever he or she might be, into which royalties and payments for periodical publishing were to be entered. We wrote to the *Times Literary Supplement* on the lines of the announcement above. The letter was published. We sat back and waited. Nobody said a word. The technique of 'the big lie' had succeeded again, at least for the moment. Thereafter I suffered infrequent twinges of anxiety, but Senhouse never worried for an instant. He was convinced that he, and only he, was the man to publish Kafka in English. The future owner of the rights would, he thought, willingly and delightedly accept the situation. Things were not to turn out precisely on those lines, but the fact remains that, had we not done what we did, there would never, I believe, have been a well-organized, well-edited, well-translated uniform edition at all.

The problem that baffled us was basic – who was the owner of Kafka's English rights? Until we could discover, communicate and negotiate with him, we were adrift. Sometimes it was possible to believe that Brod was the controller, but he never claimed more than that he was in control *editorially* of Kafka editions. Some believed that proceeds from Kafka's sales went to one of his sisters or his nieces or Mrs. Diamant Lask* in London. There was a missing link. The name of this missing link was conveyed to Senhouse by Muir in March 1943. But he seemed not to have grasped the significance of this, nor did he convey it to me. Indeed he forgot it, for about a year later, when we were informed by Brod in unvarnished words that the copyright owner was in fact Mr. Salman Schocken, he was astonished. Schocken was a German-Jewish business man who had owned a huge department store in Munich. About 1936 Schocken had got out of Germany with much of his wealth, and set up a publishing house in Palestine, and later in New York. Although himself no man of letters, he had an admiration for Kafka as a genius, a Zionist and a saint. In fact, his veneration for him was akin to that of a devout worshipper for his God.

At some date unknown to me, but probably soon after Brod's flight from Prague in 1938, Schocken had made a deal with him and with the beneficiaries under Kafka's will. In return for a life pension Brod was to work on the mass of Kafka MSS, sorting, classifying, editing and preparing them for publication. This Brod did, and, though it is easy to criticize him for the way he did it and the inter-

*Mrs. Dora Diamant Lask, a dear and intimate friend of Kafka.

minable time it took him, one must recognize that the task was one of extreme difficulty. Brod, who is now dead, must be acclaimed as a disciple who performed his duties after his own fashion.

It was not till early 1944 that I became fully conscious of the fact that in the end it was Schocken with whom we would have to negotiate. It was by March or April that Senhouse should have written to him, but I cannot find evidence that he did so. In any case, 1944 was a complex year for both of us, for in June the office was, as I have written, reduced to ashes, and it took some months to find our new home in 7 John Street, off Theobald's Road. Also, as Senhouse wrote on the Kafka file, 'all that remains', there was little enough left.

With hindsight it is possible to see that Senhouse began to go wrong on January 31, 1945, when he lunched with a certain Dr. L. Montano, an Italian publisher to whom he had been introduced in London, about a critical work on Kafka by Herbert Tauber. 'Montano, who works at Bush House,' Senhouse wrote in a memo, 'is a thorough devotee of Kafka and all his works.' This should have warned me of trouble ahead, for 'thorough devotees' of Kafka were capable of generating, and did in fact generate, immense difficulties for us. It was also at last made crystal clear that Schocken was the ace of trumps in the pack, and that his two addresses were one in Tel-Aviv, the other in the Hotel Delmonico, New York. Further troubles were announced in a letter of May 13 from Brod, in which he said 'I am writing in German, as I have to deal with rather complicated matters. Now to grips with the matter . . .' He went on to complain that he had never received our agreement for *The Trial*, although he thought the copy we sent him of our reprint a 'fine production'. He then announced that 'a uniform edition of Kafka's *Collected Works* cannot possibly be published without reference to me, whether directly or through Mr. Heath. It would be better for us to correspond directly, if Mr. Heath continues to handle my affairs as negligently as he has recently done.' He ends by giving his agent one last chance.

It seems extraordinary to me today, first, that Brod had never discovered the sex of Miss Heath during the previous five years, and second, that neither Miss Heath nor Senhouse jointly or severally had succeeded in making it clear to Brod that we were attempting a collected edition. I suspect that Schocken must have written or spoken sharply to Brod about the behaviour of the publishers in London, ourselves, whom he did not know and could not trust.

Brod added 'I have a general agreement with the Schocken Publishing House Ltd. of Tel-Aviv, and in every case our decision must be a joint one.' At last the facts were laid on the line, but why on earth had Brod not done this months or even years before, to Heath and ourselves? How much useless effort and heartache had resulted from this omission, due to folly, vanity or heaven knows what. On May 30 Senhouse woke up, became aware of the dangers, and wrote to Schocken in Tel-Aviv a letter covering 9 typed pages, just over 3,000 words, which dealt exhaustively with the Kafka affair from every conceivable angle and included long passages of wholly irrelevant material. It was the wrong letter to write to anybody, but to Schocken, a business man, it must have appeared as the ravings of a lunatic. It might well be said 'those whom the gods wish to destroy they first make read Kafka'. Sending Miss Heath a copy, Senhouse himself spoke 'of our somewhat prolix and – when taken together, overlapping in content though unified in intensity – letter to Schocken.' Obviously, he had been reading too much German, for it was an inelegant sentence, but the words 'unified in intensity' hits the mark, and was in fact one main source of the trouble.

On July 12 Herr Schocken in person was to arrive at Grosvenor House, Park Lane, London. Senhouse wrote him a note of welcome, asking for an appointment. He got one and kept it and others, but, as will be seen, the results were unfortunate, though of this I was kept in ignorance. The truth began to emerge in a letter from Senhouse to Miss Heath on August 20 just before she was to meet Schocken. 'I think it only fair to give you some understanding of the ground I have gone over with him to date,' he wrote, 'it has been pretty extensive. . . . During the Zionist Conference it has clearly been most difficult to hold Mr. Schocken's attention and I really feel that much time has been wasted . . . to reach the point where we have the future clear-cut before us. You will find Mr. Schocken a charming man, but he is more used to the general Chain Stores contracts and life than to those of publishing. In other words, he understands very little indeed, and the time goes in trying to make things clear. . . .' This was untrue and unfair, a sure sign that Senhouse knew he had blundered.

Now at last the realization dawned on me that things had gone wrong, and that a serious danger existed of our losing Kafka and all the work that Senhouse had devoted to him over the months and years. Indeed, the alarm bell sounded loudly in my ears from another quarter. A friend of Schocken, a refugee from the Bolsheviks, worked at the great bookselling house of Bumpus in London. Miss Dvoretsky was not only an expert on antique books, she had an unrivalled knowledge of German literature, including Kafka. Schocken went to see her and complained bitterly of the disgraceful way he had been treated by Senhouse. He told her that he was determined to find another and more businesslike publisher for Kafka and had approached, among others, Nicolson & Watson, Gollancz, Faber and possibly Heinemann, and was also thinking of Macmillan. Miss Dvoretsky was horrified at the news, for she realized how much Secker & Warburg had done, perhaps more accurately had tried to do, to fit the pieces of the Kafka jigsaw puzzle together. In addition, she knew and admired my wife. Promptly she rang Pamela up, told her how Senhouse had infuriated Schocken and damaged our prospects perhaps fatally. Pamela passed the news on without delay, cursing Senhouse and blaming me, not without reason, for failing to intervene when I should have done. Feeling somewhat guilty, I sprang into action. A very early meeting between Schocken and myself was set up.

Schocken entered my office with a stern demeanour and after a few formal exchanges got down to brass tacks, starting with complaints of his first meeting with Senhouse. 'He was nearly an hour late for the appointment, and, as he knew, I am a very busy man with many things to attend to in London,' he began.* 'He brought with him this Italian publisher, Montano or some such name. I didn't know him or want to know him. They kept trying to persuade me to allow him to do the Italian edition of Kafka. I am not in London for this. There was talk of an Italian printer, Hans Morgenstein or Mardersteig of the Bodoni Press in Verona, who was keen to print Kafka's *Letter to My Father* in German with an Italian text facing it. A luxury edition or some such nonsense. It was a scandal. It was Senhouse I had come to see, to discuss the English edition, nothing else, nothing at all. Kafka's wonderful letter, so typical of his great spirit . . . but it's so personal, so private, I have not even decided whether it shall be published in German. And Senhouse spoke about Mr. Muir, that I must guarantee that *he* shall do all the translations. He is a fine translator, Muir, but he is slow, he never finishes. Miss Heath, she knows nothing of Kafka, nothing at all, why should this woman be allowed to act as agent? Max Brod, he doesn't keep me informed, he

*I have put what followed into direct speech as the simplest and most dramatic way of reconstructing the conversation. Obviously it is only an approximation to what was actually said.

writes long letters, like Senhouse, but they are not businesslike, they do not make things clear to me. I will not go on like this any longer. Kafka is important, he must not be messed about by these muddlers.'

Such briefly was the gist of the harangue, and I listened to it in silence. Poor Herr Schocken had to get this off his chest before anything useful could possibly be accomplished. Besides, I agreed with almost every word he had said. Before the meeting I had read (or re-read) Senhouse's letters, which could not conceivably be described as lucid, still less as decisive.

'Herr Schocken, I am very glad indeed we have met at last,' I said, 'and I have no doubt whatever that we can settle this matter between us. I am a business man, like yourself.' Whether this was true is not for me to say – I have often doubted it. But it was clearly essential that Schocken should believe he was at last dealing with a professional rather than a gaggle of amateurs. I continued, 'I must apologize for my colleague's errors, of which I was unaware till quite recently. I also am an admirer of the work of Franz Kafka, and I am certain that this house, of which I am the executive head, will be able to publish him in the manner his genius deserves.'

Schocken accepted this mixture of half-truths and hopes with a certain degree of scepticism. I then put before him in simple words what had to be done to get the Collected Edition published. There were after all only two real problems – first, Brod's unholy delays in editing and re-editing the major works, especially *The Castle* and *The Trial** – second, the fact that Muir, certainly the best translator available to us at the time, never delivered on the due date or anywhere near it.

So far I was, I thought, doing pretty well. But now Schocken launched an attack on our position from an entirely different angle. 'You have made use of rights that belong to me without my permission,' he remarked, 'and you have made no payments whatever for them.' The answer to this was fairly simple, since we had not yet reprinted any title without a contract, for only *The Trial* had been re-issued up till then, and here we had bought the rights from Gollancz who clearly owned them. As for payment for what we had published and licensed since the beginning of the war, I was ready to pay up immediately and we had money in the bank.

Schocken had one last shot in his locker. 'I have been looking round the bookshops in London, and I have not found a single copy

*This was not, in fact, achieved for several years, in time for us to publish definitive editions of *The Castle* in 1953 and *The Trial* in 1956.

of Kafka in any of them. This is truly disgraceful.' It was, of course, or rather it would have been, had there not been a paper shortage, rationing and a pitiably small allocation to ourselves. Those facts I put before him as simply and as movingly as possible.

I waited. Had I said enough to convince him, but not too much to waste his 'valuable time'? 'Herr Warburg,' he said, accepting me as at least a courtesy member of that business-like Germanic race which had expelled him from Germany and murdered so many of Kafka's family, 'you are persuasive and you are the only one in London to speak to me clearly. When the money you owe me has been accounted for and paid, I will consider accepting your firm as Kafka's permanent English publisher. But I must insist that new agreements between Schocken Verlag and Secker & Warburg be negotiated on reasonable terms.'

'Of course, I shall be happy to agree to that,' I remarked, perhaps a little too quickly, for he wagged his finger reproachfully at me. 'That is not all,' he said, 'I must tell you that, as head of your firm, you have been negligent and careless of your responsibilities. In future, I shall expect you to deal with these matters personally – I do not trust your colleague.'

'That is precisely what my wife has said to me,' I replied.

'In that case, Herr Warburg, your wife is a sensible woman, and you should always pay attention to her advice.'

The meeting concluded amiably. In the months to come, new contracts were signed. The slow but steady development of a Collected Kafka proceeded. It had been a very close-run thing. Senhouse, to whom I gave a heavily censored account of what had been said, was delighted. So was my wife. She claimed that it was she who had saved Kafka for the firm, and I had to admit that there was much truth in what she said.

In fulfilment of our public announcement, after all the endless discussions of the order in which the volumes should appear, we published in 1945 *The Trial*, followed by *The Great Wall of China* in 1946, another reprint of *The Castle* in 1947, and in 1949 *America*. The three great novels were at last simultaneously available. From then on, as other major works of Kafka were translated, we added them to the collected edition. During the years to come, so-called definitive editions with new material were issued. It was, I believe, a publishing triumph, based on Senhouse's knowledge of the works and his persistence, our joint audacity, and, at the end, a confrontation between the formidable Herr Schocken and myself.

Only one question remains to be asked. What quality existed in Kafka's work that prevented its sales between 1930 and 1939, then pushed them almost to the level of big sellers right through the war and beyond? The answer, I think, is simple. It was the feeling of frustration, illogicality and a lurking sense of menace that gripped tens of thousands of men and women, especially in the services, during the war. It was the belief that you were constantly under surveillance by nameless and unknown, but pitiless, authorities, as in *The Trial*, or obstructed by them from pursuing your reasonable objectives as human beings, as in *The Castle*. Nor can it be said that these beliefs have vanished since the war ended. The contradictions in the post-war world have multiplied, though they have no doubt become less immediately oppressive, at least in Britain, which is one reason why the works of Kafka are still read by a substantial number of people. One reason only, for it is W. H. Auden's view, and that of many others, that 'had one to name the artist who comes nearest to bearing the same kind of relation to our age that Dante, Shakespeare and Goethe bore to theirs, Kafka is the first one would think of.'

5

Postwar, 1945-51

THE history of Secker & Warburg between its foundation in 1939 and its entry into the Heinemann Group of Publishers in spring 1952 falls easily into three periods. The first, described in my book, *An Occupation for Gentlemen*, ran from April 1936 to September 3, 1939, the outbreak of World War Two. What were its characteristics? First, the birthpangs, the shake-down of a small group of individuals previously unknown to each other, in particular the working out of some kind of relationship between the two heads. Senhouse, the novice, and I, the trained publisher, two powerful individualists of widely different characters, found understanding of each other a difficult task. I will not say that, like the lion and the unicorn, we battled for the crown, but rather that each of us sought a different crown.

Senhouse, dominated by his previous association with the Bloomsbury Group, hoped for a literary house, small, exquisite and gentlemanly, perhaps like the Hogarth Press without Leonard and Virginia Woolf. His only previous business training had been as a junior executive in a wine import-export firm at Hay's Wharf, where his boss had politely suggested to him, after a rather short career, that his bent was perhaps more towards a literary life. A confirmed bachelor, secretive, clubbable, a man of great charm, prone to sudden fits of anger and melancholia, with a multitude of acquaintances but only a few close friends, he pursued a wayward course, too much so for his own good or that of the firm. But he had great moments and major successes, especially when he followed his own enthusiasms rather than those of his friends, who gave him advice, much of it bad. Unfortunately, you could never be certain whether he was giving you his own opinion or that of the friend with whom he had most recently talked.

The second characteristic of this first period was the series of financial crises which beset us, due of course to the fact that we had started the firm with a wholly insufficient capital.

The third characteristic was the fact that, though as I have said I was a fully trained publisher, all my experience had been in a firm (Routledge & Kegan Paul) which was not only ten times bigger than we were in those early years, but one which published non-fiction books only – no novels – and those mainly of a learned type suitable for the university reader. We on the contrary were concerned with fiction, biography and belles lettres, coupled with a growing list of books on current affairs, social, economic and above all political. The switch tended to baffle me.

We were saved from disaster by one factor of extreme importance, a coherent editorial policy – on the literary side the search for quality rather than sales, on the political a resolute anti-fascism and anti-communism, relevant to the stormy days of the late thirties, which left our bank balance low, but enabled us to enter the war years with half a dozen major authors. An anonymous reviewer of a book on the anti-Nazi Swiss publisher, Oprecht, puts the point well. He writes 'A publisher's self-expression, certainly in the case of a small personal firm, is his production taken as a whole. And it is the consistency and persistence of Oprecht's policy . . . which made him the thorn in the Nazi flesh which he undoubtedly was.'*

The second period, described in Chapters 1 and 2, was the period of the war, easily characterized by paper shortage, the hazard of bombs which destroyed paper stocks, book stocks and our office; and the paucity of authors, involved for the duration in civil or military war-service of one kind or another.

The third period, 1945–51, is the subject of this chapter, and its nature is more complex. It was for us, as for most publishers, a time of renaissance, freed at last from the constrictions of wartime conditions, with members of staff returning from the war and writers settling down to write again. It was to be marked by the entry into the firm of a new personage, David Farrer, who was to become important and remains to this day a key executive. It contains my irruptions into the American goldfields (see Chapter 8) where I began to secure rights in a wide range of American books. It is the period of Orwell's *Animal Farm* and *1984*. It saw the opening of Nazi-occupied Europe and a resumption of cultural ties, which brought to our list such major writers as Alberto Moravia, Simone

*T.L.S. March 10, 1972.

de Beauvoir, André Gide, a little later Robert Musil, author of the classic three-volume novel, *The Man Without Qualities*, and Colette. It saw the debut of a major English writer of the fifties and beyond, Angus Wilson. It contained the Sigma books, an attempt to introduce and explain the extraordinary developments of science in a form comprehensible to English readers untrained in science.

War is a time of waiting, for the soldiers to come home, for more food and better clothing, for safety and most importantly for victory. When V.E. Day came to mark the final defeat of the Third Reich on May 8, closely followed in August by the dropping of two A-bombs and the surrender of Japan, the way ahead seemed clear. We had made a net profit of £14,000 in the years 1942–4, but in 1945 it was down to under £2,000. Time was flying, and I was nearing the crucial landmark of 50 years. Yet progress was difficult. Two of my top executives, John Pattisson, a sort of general manager, and John Lloyd in charge of production, were away on war service. Without them it would be difficult to organize an efficient publishing house and its enlargement, and without growth we were doomed to disaster. Worst of all perhaps, *paper was still rationed.* In 1945 we received only 65 % of our tiny pre-war average. Paper was to remain rationed till early 1948, and this factor was almost disastrous for us. As I have said earlier, it lost us authors we might have had, if only we had been able to guarantee paper to print or reprint their books. We were in the situation of a man attempting to fight a bitterly competitive battle with one arm tied behind his back. The 1945 list contained only 15 titles, of which three were slim volumes of poetry all by Americans. Only Orwell's *Animal Farm* made 1945 into a less depressing year than it might have been otherwise.

At the end of 1945 Pattisson returned from his service in a tank battalion in North Africa and Italy, while Lloyd came back from piloting nightfighters and winning an Air Force Cross over English skies in 1940–1 and Mosquitoes over Normandy in 1944. The 1946 list was hardly bigger than the 1945, and was less distinguished. But now slowly the wheels began to turn. In the summer of 1946 we began to publish the Sigma science books, while in November David Farrer joined the firm as a potential investor with a directorship, as did John Pattisson.

Farrer, educated at Rugby School and Balliol College, Oxford, came from a Yorkshire family, though his branch of it had been settled in Dorset for two or three generations. He was the youngest of three brothers, of whom the eldest was private solicitor to George

VI at the time he joined me. Farrer had been called to the Bar, but practised for only a short time. Next he became an editor for the Amalgamated Press, thence as private tutor to the heir presumptive of the Maharajah of Gwalior. Returning from India to England in poor health, he joined Odhams Press and stayed there through 1938–9, transferring to a censorship job in the wartime Ministry of Information early in 1940. After a few months Lord Beaverbrook was given his name as a likely man to appoint to be his private secretary, working jointly with George Malcolm Thomson. This unlikely pair, as it seemed to me, hit it off admirably, and have remained firm friends to this day.

Till Farrer joined me, he had been drifting, or to put it more politely, experimenting, though his six year term with Beaverbrook, a powerful member of Winston Churchill's war cabinet, must have been one of the most demanding and interesting posts a youngish man could expect to hold.* But once peace had been established and he had inherited some money from his mother, he forsook the world of politics and journalism, a hectic career even without the thunderstorms inherent in coping with the Beaver, for the more placid and slower life of a publisher.

Farrer was something of a gambler. Through the fifties he made many a call to his bookmaker and went often to race meetings. In becoming a publisher, it might be said that he had discovered a more respectable method of gambling, backing unpredictable books and authors, instead of unpredictable horses. It was Senhouse who introduced Farrer to me, suggesting that we needed new capital and new abilities, now that the war was over. After some hesitation I agreed. The hesitation was due to my estimate that Farrer was a dyed-in-the-wool conservative with all the prejudices of his class, while I believed myself to be a socialist or at least a liberal with virtually no prejudices at all. Of course, it turned out that my estimate of Farrer (and of myself) was far from accurate. Farrer, it is true, did have a few prejudices, but he struggled valiantly and usually with success against them.

Years after Farrer had joined the firm, he told me what Senhouse's plan had been for the future of Secker & Warburg. It was simple and unpractical. Farrer was to assist Senhouse on the Secker & Warburg side of the enterprise, while I busied myself with the development of the scientific side under the Sigma imprint. It took the shrewd,

*Farrer has described this period of his life in two lively books, *The Sky's the Limit*, and *G. for God Almighty*.

practical Farrer precisely two weeks to see through the wishful thinking of his friend and supporter.

It was with a gamble that Farrer started his publishing career. In pursuance of his master Beaverbrook's orders, he was in the Curtis Brown office to read the first four chapters and negotiate the serial rights for the *Express* of a full-length book by a 30-year-old Canadian, Major Milton Shulman. Graduated at Toronto in 1934 and qualified as a barrister in 1937, Shulman had contributed stories and articles to American magazines. But then, as the war began, he became an intelligence officer in the Canadian Armoured Corps, and came to Britain. In 1943 he was sent to the War Office to study agents' reports to determine the disposition of enemy forces in France and the Low Countries. In March 1944 he joined the H.Q. staff of the First Canadian Army, took part in the invasion of Normandy, where he continued his intelligence work, for which he was mentioned in dispatches. After the war he was assigned to the task of studying thousands of captured German documents and interviewing many of the senior German commanders, including von Runstedt, Halder, Jodl, von Vietinghoff, Student, Dietrich and others. His material was to be used in the compilation of the official version of Canada's part in World War Two.

The book was to be called *Defeat in the West*, and it was, as the *Evening Standard* said later in its review, 'a panorama, complete and fascinating, of the war as seen from the other (German) side.' Farrer recommended it strongly to Beaverbrook, then rang me up. 'Buy it,' he said, 'though it will cost rather a lot.' I rang Curtis Brown, and read part of the MS, falling for it immediately. Terms were agreed with Curtis Brown, involving an advance payment of £450, equivalent to an advance on about 7,500 copies. This was a lot of money for a book by an unknown Canadian major. *Defeat* was the first book to tell the story of the collapse of the German armies in the West, and the reasons for it. The author came to realize that the Wehrmacht had had victory within its grasp on more than one occasion. How then and why had it failed? To this question the book provided convincing answers. Published at 15s. on April 17, 1947, it sold rapidly and well. All 6,000 copies of the first printing were sold in four months, and a second impression of 3,500 copies was ready in September. 'Of permanent value to historians and of absorbing interest to anyone,' wrote the *Observer*. Since then it has sold many more thousands of copies, and has been set as a textbook in military training courses. *Defeat* was well written, readable and exciting, qualities in a book which Farrer recognized as those most likely to make a book saleable. Such recognition is an indispensable qualification for a publisher. So Farrer's first book had been a major success. It must have given his ego a boost, though it was some time before he found another as good. He had also encouraged me to take gambles myself, and this was important, because I was not a gambler by nature, or so I believed then. Yet the mere fact that I had started Secker & Warburg without enough money should have been enough to convince me that I was wrong.

In the office files recently I discovered two dirty sheets of paper, proudly headed MEMORANDUM on Post War Publishing Policy, dated March 5, 1943. How this survived the bombing of our premises I cannot guess. It reported a discussion between Senhouse and myself with our London traveller, Charles Roth, and another executive. I put forward the idea that we should expand our activities after the war into a series of popular books designed for the non-scientific reader, which would explain some of the prodigious advances made by science and technology since about 1930 – plastics and other substitute materials; radio, television and radar; aircraft; and medicine with its wonder drugs. Little did I know then that only seventeen months later the biggest scientific advance of all would be demonstrated in all its fearful majesty on the cities of Hiroshima and Nagasaki. Senhouse dissented. Like many literary men in those days he had a strong distaste for, and a lurking dread of, science. He suggested instead a series on 'the psychology of the varied allied nations' and 'books in various foreign languages', though he never made clear to me what he meant by this. These remarks and others I found unhelpful. In the end I went ahead with the science series, which I christened Sigma Introductions. Just over three years later the first four titles were published.

The editor of the series was Kurt Mendelssohn, M.A., Ph.D., F.Inst.S., an expert in the field of low-temperature physics, a fellow of Merton College, Oxford, now an F.R.S. He got together a good team. The first volume of the series was David S. Evans' *Frontiers of Astronomy*, 'easily the best book of its kind for the past 20 years' wrote *Science Progress*. There followed Dr. I. Berenblum's *Science versus Cancer*, J. G. Daunt's *Electrons in Action*, Dr. E. S. Duthie's *Molecules Against Microbes*, explaining the chemical attack on bacteria, including penicillin. Other volumes appeared in 1947–8–9, in all some 25 books, including larger ones outside the series. Notable, I think, was Mendelssohn's own contribution, *What Is Atomic Energy?*, probably the first study of the atom bomb in any language apart from H. D. Smyth's *Atomic Energy for Military Purposes* – published by the Princeton University Press. To me one of the most appealing volumes was Gordon Ostlere's *Anaesthetics and the Patient*, which explained the recent improvement in the technique of anaesthesia due to the use of the deadly South American poison, curare with which the Indians tipped their arrows. In tiny quantities curare had the effect of relaxing the muscles. Indeed, this gave it its deadly quality, for when the muscles of the heart relax and fail to pump the blood through the body, the body dies. But, when administered in small amounts, the muscles relax, which reduces enormously the amount of anaesthetic required for an operation, especially through the stomach.*

The price of the Sigma series was 7s. 6d. (37½p) each. They ran to 160 pages or over. All the volumes were illustrated, some by the brilliant artist, Victor Reinganum. The series sold well, though I have been unable to secure sales figures. Yet the profit was too small to leave an adequate margin. Many times I argued with my colleagues that they would stand an increase to 8s. 6d. (42½p) or even 10s. 6d. (52½p). I was convinced that this would not seriously reduce the sales. But always in the end I lost the battle, if not the argument. So finally this series and the larger books that went with it were discontinued, and we lost the chance of becoming popular science publishers on a substantial scale. Yet even today I doubt whether enough writers are conveying to the public the news of developments in science and technology, at least with the accuracy and simplicity demanded. A good scientist is not necessarily a good writer. I wish a new university course could be created for men and women anxious to devote their abilities to this immensely difficult task.

* * *

On January 29, 1944, Senhouse despatched a copy of *Sainte Colline*, the novel of Gabriel Chevallier which followed *Clochemerle*, to his friend, Norman Douglas, in chilly war-time London, S.W.7, not in the Italy he loved. Senhouse asked him 'whether you make anything

*Some years later Ostlere published a novel which had a gigantic sale. It was written under a pseydonym, Richard Gordon, and was titled *A Doctor in the House*! Feverishly I looked up my contract with Ostlere. Alas, I had an option only on his next work *in the field of science*.

of it, whether you think it is possible to translate it, and if so whether you could possibly undertake it.' Now *Clochemerle* had been our very first big success, published only a few months after we had taken the firm over from the liquidator. Yet, despite the difficulties of a novice firm, we had sold nearly 8,000 copies in the first sixteen months, a major factor in averting an early bankruptcy. Senhouse continued calmly 'I may say we had ideas before the war of making it the second publication after the success of *Clochemerle*, but I took against the book on a second reading, and so did Edwin Muir, whose wife at one time thought she would try her hand at translation. So here we are back again, with a contract for the book, to wait for your opinion as to what you think the English will think of it.'

It seems odd to me now that we had not signed a contract for *Sainte Colline* long before the war had begun. After all, a publisher must be crazy to reject (or not to accept) a clearly saleable follow-up to a major success. Yet this must have been what Senhouse had done, as he admits in his letter. Under the influence of a highbrow critic, Muir, he had taken against the book, even though Godefroi, the translator of *Clochemerle*, was delighted with it and had, in fact, translated a specimen chapter in 1938. However, under pressure from me early in 1941–2 the matter came up again, but now Godefroi was unable to translate through pressure of work. Muir's wife, Willa, agreed to do it, though it would appear that she never even started it and in 1942 returned to us Godefroi's specimen chapter which Senhouse had naughtily sent her 'as a guide'. Soon after this we signed a contract for *Sainte Colline* with his agent and the consent of the Trading with the Enemy Department of the Board of Trade, since France was occupied by the Germans. But no suitable translator was available till late 1944, when Godefroi was ready to go ahead. Yet even then Senhouse continued his secret war to sabotage *Sainte Colline*, sending it to Douglas with a fairly obvious hint that it was perhaps not worth publishing or that, if it was, it was too difficult to translate.

On March 4 Douglas sent Senhouse his report, and I reprint here this hitherto unknown piece of Douglasiana.

> I should like to see an English translation of *Sainte Colline*; it would do our people good to read it – open their eyes. Catholics might be annoyed at some passages and Puritans at others – so much the better.
>
> It interests me because I know something about French boys and their professors and parents and lives at school. Here is sound reasoning, sound characterization and sound observation, though the author does not even

hint at a significant feature in the life of College boarders. This would have rounded off the description and hurt nobody.

The picture is held in a relatively narrow frame. The author has done his best in the way of drollery in the opening chapter, but it is less *intriguant* than that of *Clochemerle*, which has more fun and a broader human basis, so far as I can remember. I question whether an English version would be profitable from a business point of view. No; I don't see the requisite public for it. Critics like Raymond Mortimer would be sure to review it well as an authentic and instructive and entertaining document – which it is – and if the sales depend on people like him I would be inclined to go ahead.

I fear they don't
Prognosis: unfavourable.

However, in his covering letter he remarked 'I am secretly hoping that you will print it all the same. Most entertaining.' This report from Douglas more than cancelled out the allegedly unfavourable one from Muir. The secret sabotage of *Sainte Colline*, if indeed it existed, ceased. However, the 1942 contract had become out of date by then. There had been a change in Chevallier's London agent, and a change in his French publisher, due no doubt to the war. France, and Chevallier in Lyon, had been liberated. Now we had the problem of explaining to a sceptical French publisher that we were unable to adopt his plan for defrauding the British Income Tax authorities for his sake. Then there was an alarm that another English publisher, Methuen, had a prior option. Legal opinions were taken, and somehow we won the argument. Finally the paper shortage that was strangling us caused yet more delays.

But all these labour pains proved to be worthwhile. We published on April 27, 1946, and sold out the first edition of 5,000 copies on publication, the second impression of 2,300 copies went in two months, another 2,500 copies sold rapidly. Though never as great a success as *Clochemerle* and its sequels, it has sold ever since and still remains in print. From then on there was no hesitation in taking his future books. *Clochemerle-Babylon*, sales over 30,000, published in 1955, showed the village in an age of transition from the pastoral simplicities of the twenties into the era of jazz and motor cars, the cinema and the telephone, with the old Torbayon Inn become a three-star restaurant, thus giving the voluptuous Mme. Torbayon an opportunity to display her magnificent bosom to a wider and more discriminating group of admirers. *Clochemerle-les-Bains*, sales over 15,000, appeared in 1964. It examined the devious methods by which a simple well of spring water gets turned into a full-scale spa to the substantial benefit of a select few of Clochemerle's leading lights.

I think the Clochemerle trilogy will endure. Chevallier writes with much of the spirit of Maupassant, though a much more cheerful Maupassant. Most of his novels are conceived in a vein of wit, irony and irreverence, with a knock-about element. Here is the atmosphere of the Mediterranean, the pagan joy in buxom women, rich food and good wine, physical well-being, all the things which are becoming so desperately scarce in the world of the seventies. Will the next generation, will even the present one, believe that the France of Chevallier's novels, or something like it, ever really existed? Chevallier, with all his cynicism, belonged to an age of innocence, destroyed for ever by the war, the German occupation of France, and the double-edged advances of science and technology.

A work of major importance was published by Knopf in the U.S. early in 1947. This was the first volume (1889–1913) of *The Journals of André Gide*, to be followed by three others. It was no accident that we acquired the rights, since it was we who had published his last previous book, *Return from the U.S.S.R.* in 1938 to the fury of the communists, for *Return* was Gide's brief but shattering account, after a trip to Russia, of his disillusionment at the sight of the socialist utopia of his dreams. A month after the *Journals* appearance Gide was awarded the 1947 Nobel Prize for Literature,* and we decided to go ahead with translations of a number of his hitherto untranslated works. There was no doubt that in 1947 and for some fifteen years beyond Gide was a dominant force in European literature. Our enthusiasm roused the house of Cassell to activity, and between us we made available to English readers some fifteen of his most important novels, philosophical *contes*, plays, and works of sociological exposition. Gide, of course, was a homosexual, admired by many of the known and unknown homosexuals of the day. His writings on the subject may well have contributed to their self-assurance, and so paved the way to that change of opinion which culminated in the liberalizing Act, passed into law by the Labour Government in

*This was 'our' second Nobel prize, following the award to Thomas Mann in 1929. 'We' were to gain a third when the Japanese novelist Kawabata, was awarded it in 1970 (see Chapter 15), and a fourth when Heinrich Böll, whom we had just taken on to the list, was given it for 1972. My author, Dennis Gabor, was to receive the Nobel Prize for Physics in 1971, some months before we published his second book for us, *The Mature Society*, in 1972.

1967. Oddly enough Gide's works are no longer in demand, but a time will surely come when some at least of them will be wanted by English readers.

Many other interesting books were published by us between 1946 and 1950 – Rayner Heppenstall's *The Double Image*, a study of four French Catholic writers, where beneath the devout surface is revealed a tendency towards heresy and the private myth; Ruth Benedict's *The Chrysanthemum and the Sword*, an analysis of a society, Japan, based on premises fundamentally opposed to those of the West; Eric Partridge's two dictionaries, *Forces' Slang*, 1939–45 (examples *bat your flap* for 'shut up!' and *skirt patrol* for 'a walk with the intention of finding feminine company'), and *Name into Word*, proper names of persons, places and things which have passed as words into the English language (*sukey*, 'a tea kettle, clearly a diminutive of Susan'); Jon Kimche's *Seven Fallen Pillars*, a sustained indictment of British policy towards Arab and Jew in the Middle East since 1919; Hester Chapman's *Great Villiers*, a biography of the second Duke of Buckingham, 1628–87, reputed the richest and handsomest man of his day. Even this handful gives some idea of the wide range of subjects we were prepared to cover.

There were also, of course, some excellent novels, including Penelope Dimont's *Johanna*. Why do I mention this unknown writer? Because Dimont turned into Mortimer, and Penelope Mortimer's name is now very well known indeed. She declared recently that *Johanna* sank like a stone on publication, though in fact it actually sold 1,600 copies out of 2,250 printed, not a quite negligible sale for a first novel at that time. She also states that people now tell her it's the best thing she ever wrote, a tribute, no doubt, to my critical insight in picking it. When she had completed her second novel, which 'I took ages to write', she showed it to me, and if I am to believe her, I advised her to go away and read the history of the Peloponnesian Wars. 'I was utterly crushed and couldn't write anything for years,' she wrote. For this I must apologize, though I have no recollection of my extraordinary remark. But why should this advice, odd as it may seem, have upset her so deeply, and did she in fact follow it? If so, it clearly did her some good, for now 'I reckon to complete a book in around four months . . . I use no notes, no story outline. I go straight at it, starting at 9.00 a.m. and continuing till I'm exhausted.' Lucky Penelope!

The climax of our fiction publishing, however, came in the first half of 1949. I cannot believe that my firm, or indeed any other firm, will ever again publish four books, three novels and a book of short stories, of such importance within fifteen weeks. If ever I had to justify my career in publishing, it could well rest on the period March 24 to July 7, 1949.

On March 24 the first book of a brilliant new English writer – *The Wrong Set* by Angus Wilson (see Chapter 18).

On April 28 the novel which many critics think his greatest – *Dr. Faustus*: the life of the German composer Adrian Leverkuhn as told by a Friend, by Thomas Mann (see Chapter 16).

On June 8 the final work of the greatest English writer of the decade – *1984* by George Orwell (see Chapter 7).

On July 7 the first full-length novel of the major Italian writer – *The Woman of Rome* by Alberto Moravia.

As I write these resounding names on foolscap paper lined in pale blue ink, I feel a sense of pride, of exhilaration, even of awe. Had this really happened to me? Since indeed it had, I have become almost convinced that I was a greater publisher then than I thought myself, perhaps a greater publisher then than later. Yet at the time, it seemed different. How had it appeared to me then? The short stories of *The Wrong Set* appeared to me exceptionally fine, but unlikely to sell many copies since short stories 'don't sell'. *Dr. Faustus* was obviously an important Mann novel, but so complex and difficult that its future was hard to estimate. *The Woman of Rome*, since it was the story of a Roman prostitute, had obvious sales possibilities, but Moravia then was a little known writer in England, and the book was hardly obscene, despite its story. Only in the case of *1984* did I believe that we had both an English masterpiece and a major seller. It was only a year or two ago that I came to realize what A Golden Year 1949 was for us.

But there is always a price to pay for success, and in less than eighteen months from the end of 1949 we were suffering from a substantial lack of capital to meet the growing costs of our operations and our overheads. In 1948 and 1949, for instance, we issued 36 titles, double the total for 1946. Furthermore, the post-war inflation had begun and was gathering strength. In Chapter 9 I shall discuss the drastic move by which we tackled this problem.

6

An English Classic Reborn

IT must be a rare, perhaps even a unique, event in the 20th century for an English editor and an English publisher to discover or uncover an undoubted English classic which has languished in a good deal of obscurity since its author's death in 1697 – to uncover, enlarge, edit, publicize and establish once and for all that it is a book for the many. The classic I refer to is Aubrey's *Brief Lives*, described by Arthur Bryant as 'one of the most enchanting books ever written.' Yet this is what we and a brilliant young man were fortunate enough to achieve in 1949.

In the libraries of the Royal Society in Burlington House, and of the Corporation of the City of London at Guildhall, and in the manuscript room of the British Museum, but most of all in the Bodleian Library at Oxford, there lay for many years, virtually unread, many hundred sheets of MSS, written in a beautiful but difficult seventeenth century handwriting. Heavily corrected, with gaps, with curious tricks of shorthand, wickedly unorganized, they set a fiendishly hard task to one who would decipher, read and digest them. These MSS were the works of John Aubrey, born in the hamlet of Easton Pierse in Wiltshire in 1626 'about Sun-riseing, being very weake and like to dye that he was Christened before morning prayer.' However, he was to enjoy a long life for those days, dying in 1697, while still vigorous. It must surely be said that Aubrey did indeed enjoy his life, for he was possessed throughout it by an undying and overwhelming and indiscriminate curiosity about peoples' lives, characters, accomplishments and possessions. The Aubrey family had come up in the world during the last two generations, and Aubrey went up to Oxford at the age of fifteen. At twenty Aubrey became a student of the Middle Temple, though he was never called to the Bar. But, speaking broadly, the long years of his life were spent in the unending compilation of books that were never completed.

Aubrey has been described by Isaac D'Israeli as 'the little Boswell' of his day, but in general as an antiquary, as indeed he was, for it hurt him to see all around the destruction by neglect of the relics of the past. 'In my grandFather's dayes,' he wrote, 'the Manuscripts flew about like Butter-flies. All Musicke bookes, Account-bookes, Copie books, etc were covered with old Manuscripts, as we cover them now with blew paper, or Marbled paper . . . gloves were wrapt up no doubt (at Malmesbury) in many good pieces of Antiquity. Before the late Warres a World of rare Manuscripts perished here about. . . . About 1647, I went to see Parson Stump out of curiosity to see his Manuscripts, whereof I had seen some in my Child-hood; but by that time they were lost and disperst; his sonns were gunners and souldiers, and scoured their gunnes with them.' But these losses were due to neglect and ignorance. What was to come was far worse. For the Puritans, like so many revolutionaries before and after them, had a zeal to destroy whatever they did not like, and of this there was plenty. By the time they had fought and won the civil war and executed the king in 1649, there was no power to curb their zeal. Stained glass windows were anathema to them – 'at Croydon in Surrey in the Rebellion, one Bleese was hired for half a Crown per day, to break the painted Glass-Windows, which were formerly fine.' By his middle twenties Aubrey saw valuable records of the past being burned and smashed, and this must have increased his already powerful urge to save what could be saved from the holocaust. This was the treasure he poured into his books or his notebooks.*

There can be no doubt that the greatest of all his works was the one which came to be known as *Brief Lives*, which he compiled between 1669 and his death. But it took a long time to be fully born and revealed to the world, and this was not surprising. Consider his method of work.

'Having decided to write a life, Aubrey selected a page in one of his notebooks and jotted down as quickly as possible everything that he could remember about the character concerned; his friends, his appearance, his actions, his books and his sayings. Any facts or dates that did not occur to him on the spur of the moment were left blank, and as Aubrey was so extremely sociable that he was usually suffering

*I have made copious use in this chapter of Aubrey's *Brief Lives*, edited with an Introduction by Oliver Lawson-Dick, Secker & Warburg, 1949.

from a hangover when he came to put pen to paper, the number of these omissions was often very large. . . .

'He then read over what he had just written and put in any stories that he thought were even vaguely relevant, wrote alternatives to words and phrases, inserted queries, numbered words, sentences and paragraphs for transposition, disarranged everything. Any facts that occurred to him later were jotted down quite at random, in the margin if there was still room, otherwise on another page or in the middle of another life, often in a different volume, sometimes even in a letter to a friend. And there the text was left, for he rarely made a fair copy of anything that he had written because, as he confessed, he "wanted patience to go through Knotty Studies".'* Even the optimistic author despaired at last of ever reducing his life's work to a manageable shape.

This sprawling book was to be printed for the first time in 1797, exactly a hundred years after its author's death, by James Caulfield of William Street, Adelphi. Its title was '*The Oxford Cabinet*, consisting of engravings from original pictures in the Ashmolean Museum and other public and private collections; with biographical anecdotes by John Aubrey, F.R.S. and other celebrated writers.' But Caulfield ran into trouble and was refused access to the manuscripts in the Ashmolean Museum through the malign influence of Edmund Malone who claimed to have an exclusive right to use of the material. Although Caulfield challenged Malone's intervention in a pamphlet, printing on the title-page the words 'I will a round unvarnished tale deliver,' he failed in his purpose. *The Oxford Cabinet* contained only 48 pages; the bulk of Aubrey's jewels still lay hidden in the Bodleian Library.

Twenty years later in 1813 things took a turn for the better. Two clergymen printed a substantial volume which remained for 85 years the only edition available of *Brief Lives*. Incomplete, inaccurate and heavily expurgated, it was a godsend to scholars who had access for the first time to Aubrey's lives of Shakespeare (500 words), Milton (1,800 words), Hobbes (over 5,000 words), Harvey (over 2,000 words) and others. The Victorian writers stole from him and reviled his work as mere gossip, yet modern research has shown that often enough it was Aubrey, not his critics, who were in the right of it.

It was not till 1898, two whole centuries after Aubrey's death, that Andrew Clark edited and published an edition of *Brief Lives* at the Clarendon Press, Oxford. The object of this work was to place the

**Brief Lives*, page xxi.

entire contents of the four main manuscripts beyond the risk of perishing, and is invaluable for scholars, but not for the plain reader. It was not till 1931 that a selection of the *Lives* was published by John Collier, with a sympathetic account of Aubrey's character. It bore the rather catchpenny title *The Scandal and Credulities of John Aubrey*, the first attempt to introduce Aubrey to the general reader. Only after World War Two was *Brief Lives* at last printed at length in a form which made it possible for the ordinary reader not merely to appreciate the book but to realize that it was, in fact, a classic of English literature, fit to be ranked with such as Boswell's *Life of Johnson*, Pepys's *Diary* or Evelyn's, or Burton's *Anatomy of Melancholy*, etc.

It was a young man, Oliver Lawson-Dick, who accomplished this triumph of scholarship between the ages of 25 and 28.

Born in 1920, L-D was educated at Westminster School. Here he first became familiar with *Brief Lives*. In the History VI form of the school at that time a great schoolmaster, now the Oxford professor, John Bowle, historian of the British Empire, used it as a source for the study of the seventeenth century, and here L-D was introduced to the old gossipmonger. Here he was encouraged as part of his work to write a pastiche of a Brief Life, using another boy in the class as a model, as Angus Wilson had done some ten years before.* No doubt L-D had read at school the passage of Aubrey where he admits his absolute inability to finish a work begun with such enthusiasm, and accumulating sentence by sentence and page by page over 30 years. 'Considering therefore that if I should not finish and publish what I had begun,' he had written, 'My Papers might either perish, or be sold in an Auction, and some body else (as is not uncommon) put his name to my Paines: and not knowing anyone that would undertake this Design whilst I live, I have tumultuarily stitcht up what I have many yeares since collected: I hope, hereafter it may be an incitement to some Ingeniose and publick-spirited young Man, to polish and compleat, what I have delivered rough hewen: For I have not leisure

*John Bowle recalls in a letter to me Angus Wilson as a better pasticheur of Aubrey than L-D. He describes Angus at that time as 'intensely observant – gazing at people with those grey-blue eyes – very alert. And witty. He had a great sense of fun and loved to raise a laugh. But I thought he would be a literary critic, a man of letters. I thought he would be a writer, not an academic man. But I did not really foresee his creative power, did not realize it was formidable.' Still and all, Bowle may be said to have helped two distinguished writers in their earliest years and who can say how many more of whom I have no knowledge. A great schoolmaster has a value no less than the great historian he has now become.

to heighten my Stile.' Such was the urgent appeal to posterity by the old man.

As we have seen, Aubrey had had a long time indeed to wait, nearly 300 years, before an 'ingeniose' young man heard and obeyed him. In 1941, Lawson-Dick, after being accepted for a commission in the Welsh Guards and failing his medical, had become in September 1941 one of a four-man team of the Government's Fuel Rationing Enquiry with Lord Beveridge, Sir Stephen Tallents and Lord Pakenham. Later he had been granted a civilian commission in B.O.A.C., plotting with three other pilots the trade routes to the major European centres as they were liberated from Nazi rule. His was the first unarmed aircraft to land at Warsaw, while the field was still being swept for mines. His too was the first into Berlin. It was after his demobilization and after taking a history degree at Christ Church, Oxford that he settled down to work on the *Brief Lives.*

He worked in his mother's modest house at the foot of Box Hill near Dorking, commandeering the dining-room and its large table. He existed on the pitiably small allowance his mother, a widow, was able to allow him. Here accumulated the thousands of pieces of the Lives, as he managed to decipher them from the manuscripts. Sorted into small heaps according to subject, they were the basis of the definitive text which was ultimately to emerge. One day a blackbird flew in through the open window and scattered the work of months all over the floor. For three days L-D despaired, almost ready to abandon the near impossible task of sorting. But in the end his determination triumphed, work was resumed and a newly minted English classic was brought to birth.

By what methods did he proceed? First, he had to learn how to read Aubrey's seventeenth-century handwriting and the shorthand tricks which he employed. As he had told me, this took him many weeks. Then, having read through the manuscripts until he knew them thoroughly, he made a selection of 134 out of the 426 Lives which Aubrey had begun. Why did he discard so many? Some were too short, one of only two words 'Mathematical Boyes'; some were valueless, for instance of John Holywood Aubrey writes only 'Dr. Fell is positive that his name was Holybushe.' Parts of lives selected were omitted. For instance, The Life of James Harrington is a sizeable one of over 1,200 words, but the first sentence is omitted, as it reads: 'James Harrington, Esq; the son of . . . Harrington of . . . in the Countie of . . . by . . . daughter of Sir . . . Samuel was borne at

. . . (Sir . . . Samuel's house in Nottinghamshire) anno. . . .' Such sentences convey nothing to the reader, except that Aubrey did not know how to fill out the missing details. L-D also made a choice between alternative words in Aubrey's MSS and differing versions of some favourite story, in one case as many as seven appear in the MSS. Aubrey's mistakes have not been corrected, except where he twice misquotes from famous poems. In fact, the editorial operation can be compared to the fitting together of a giant jigsaw puzzle, where the pieces have been thoroughly shuffled and deposited in large and small heaps in a number of English libraries. It would seem to me that the editing of the *Brief Lives* must have been among the most complicated tasks ever to be undertaken by an English editor. Yet this task was, in fact, performed by a young man who, after taking a degree and after five years war service, came untried and untrained to a work which had baffled all his predecessors. It was a kind of miracle, as if old Aubrey, sitting in that part of heaven reserved for major English writers, had made manifest to his devoted disciple how he wished him to finish the job he had left half done.

But it was not only a pure, reliable and unbowdlerized text that L-D provided the reader, he also wrote as an introduction a 50,000 word study of Aubrey's life and times, which Edmund Wilson, writing in the *New Yorker*, described as 'A masterpiece of its kind – for, using wherever possible the words of Aubrey himself, put together from the scattered writings, he has succeeded in producing an intimate portrait of his subject embedded in the density of current events.' No better brief account of L-D's edition can be given than another passage in Edmund Wilson's review. 'Aubrey's accounts of his contemporaries and of the men of the preceding period . . . take you quite out of the Hall of Monuments of the established reputation and the accepted classic, and into a world where all these celebrities are still alive and kicking or have not long ceased to be so. The whole ferment of the Elizabethan Age and the vigour of the century that followed are still exciting and fresh in this book. I have never read anything else that made me feel in quite the same way what it must have been like to live then, to find oneself part of an England that was venturesome, unsettled, and eager, that was opening new horizons. John Aubrey, not one of its giants, brings its heroes down to human scale. He becomes, with Mr. Lawson-Dick's edition, an unmistakable and a manageable classic.'

After some hesitation, due to the announcement of another edition of Aubrey's *Brief Lives* edited by Anthony Powell* – an extraordinary coincidence more common in publishing than might be imagined – we accepted L-D for publication. Our hopes of its success were greatly increased by the wild enthusiasm of Eric Bligh, a friend of Senhouse, an experienced antique bookseller and a formidable bibliographer.† Bligh thought that our promotion of the book was inadequate, but he admitted that it was difficult to convey to the public briefly how remarkable it was. 'The full text of the chief Lives in its integrity *for the first time*,' he wrote Senhouse, 'I think Aubrey is wonderful, but the public *must be told, and why*.'

Both Senhouse and I were aware that we were about to publish, not only one of the best short biographies of an English writer, but an edition of *Brief Lives* which might give it for the first time its legitimate place as a classic of English literature. We therefore decided to make a handsome volume of it. Height 10 inches, width 6½ inches, bulk 1½ inches, printed in a large Garamond type on laid paper, with a buckram binding, it looks even today a handsome volume. In the poverty-stricken days of 1949 it stood as almost an *édition de luxe*. It ran to 114 pages of introduction, including the Life and Times of Aubrey, and 408 pages of text, including a Bibliography, a Glossary of Persons and an Index. It cost some £1,000 for a first edition of 2,000 copies, excluding royalty, and was underprices at 30s., equivalent at today's prices of £7.50. It received a superb press. Bernard Shaw in a private letter to the author referred to 'my amazement at the sheer industry its compilation and transcription must have cost you. The old liar must bless you from his grave.' Ogden Nash called it 'one of the most enchanting books ever written,' while G. M. Trevelyan wrote 'what an incorrigible, lovable old gossip he is.' W. H. Auden declared in the *New Yorker* 'Aubrey is the first "modern" English prose writer . . . his feeling for the significant scrap is so unerring that he can tell us more about a person in a sentence than most writers in a page.'

But of the many who praised it then and later, none hit the nail on the head so precisely as the late Robert Pitman in the *Sunday Express*: 'I report the success story of a strange literary partnership. A partnership which in just ten years has set up a new name besides favourites like Pepys on the bookshelves: which from a mass of

*An excellent edition, good of its kind, but neither so full nor so authoritative as Lawson-Dick's and without the biography of Aubrey.

†Under the title *Tooting Corner* we had published Bligh's own autobiography three years before.

scrawled and blotted manuscripts at Oxford's Bodleian Library has carved a lusty, virile, impudent book. For a year and a half – supporting himself – unsponsored by Government or college – Lawson-Dick worked privately at the papers. Three hundred years after Aubrey began his work, the first complete edition of Aubrey came off the presses. The result was extraordinary. The publishers hoped to please the scholars. They did not know that the public would demand the book too. Through Aubrey's eyes thousands of readers saw the people of the 17th century Britain for the first time.'

It is not often vouchsafed to a publisher to give to a wide English public a 'new' classic, and to establish it as such, a book which has now been read by many thousands and will be read by many tens of thousands more in the years to come. From the beginning its sales were impressive, and have continued steadily ever since. Today, over 12,000 copies of this expensive book, priced between £4 and £5, have been sold. Besides these, Penguin, who issued it in their Peregrine Books in 1962, sold 13,000 copies, and re-issued it again in 1972.

Soon after the publication of *Brief Lives* I wrote to L-D. 'We should have a talk early in the New Year (1950) about the possibility of your editing another brilliant if obscure book of English letters.' A naive suggestion perhaps, though at one time consideration was given to Aubrey's interesting work *On Education*. But it was not to be. Although my wife and I remained his friends through the years, I never published another book for him.

L-D travelled widely in the years to come, set up a distinguished public relations firm with the chef and restaurateur, Robert Carrier, and wrote a number of useful books, but none which began to compete in importance with *Brief Lives*. In the modern world a scholar is hard put to it to make much of a living, and L-D's demands on life were great. He made money, and spent it, and died young and tragically on May 1, 1964 at the age of 43 years. He might have been happier if he had stayed at Oxford. In him England lost a great scholar and an unusual man, handsome, witty and a trifle sardonic. I deeply regret his passing.

Aubrey was buried in the church of St Mary Magdalen in Oxford. He had hoped that someone would put up a memorial there to him. After L-D's death his mother put up such a memorial as Aubrey and his editor had hoped for. It was in the Chapel, the oldest part of the church and originally separate from it.

JOHN AUBREY
1625–1697
Lies buried in this Church
Biographer and Antiquary
An Original Member of the
ROYAL SOCIETY
This stone was erected at the wish of
OLIVER LAWSON-DICK, 1920–1964

A friend of Oliver's was the film star of the twenties, Lillian Gish. When she heard of the memorial, she sent a gift of money to the church for its beatification in his memory. So Oliver's name is mentioned in prayers on his birthday, May 21, as a benefactor of the church. This church is in the gift of Christ Church, Oxford, where Oliver was a scholar (and I an exhibitioner). It was at Christ Church that Oliver became his individual and essential self (and it must be said that Christ Church was not without influence on me). Thus Aubrey, L-D, and Warburg, writer, editor and publisher of *Brief Lives*, owe more than most to that magnificent foundation of Cardinal Wolsey. If it be said by those who review and those who read this book, that 'it is nothing but the work of a gossip, and many of its anecdotes are untrue,' as they said for 300 years of Aubrey's *Brief Lives*, I shall know how to answer them, even from beyond the grave.

7
1984

WITH the publication and success of *Animal Farm* in August, 1945, Orwell's need for money had become less acute. The royalties on *Animal Farm* to the end of 1945 must have amounted to about £600, worth at least £2,500 at the 1972 level. To put it another way, I should suppose it would have taken him a year's hard slogging to earn as much by journalism and other occasional writing. He must also have received a number of advances from the numerous foreign publishers who had bought the right to translate. Of course, when *Animal Farm* was published in New York in August 1946 and became a selection of the Book of the Month Club, Orwell became really well-off for the first time in his life. This period can be seen as a high-water mark in his career, when his morale and his hopes were at their peak, and lasted at least a year or eighteen months.

It was probably in September 1945 that he took me out to lunch. He told me how delighted he was to stand me a lunch in return for the many I had stood him since I had known him. We went to a restaurant in Percy Street, off Tottenham Court Road. It was a hot and steamy day. Orwell took off his jacket and hung it over the back of his chair. Almost at once up came the manager to tell him that this conduct could not be allowed in his restaurant. Orwell's reaction was immediate and rather to my surprise fiery. He called the manager a 'bloody fascist' (not, it will be noted, a bloody commie – he expected a different type of interference from them), stood up, put on his jacket, and walked out, leaving me to tag along behind. At a restaurant about fifty yards away, we went in and sat down, but to the best of my recollection Orwell did not remove his jacket again.

It was probably on that occasion that Orwell told me how he had longed for years for a success. 'Every writer wants a big seller,' he said, 'it's not so much the money he cares about. A man writes to be read. The more copies of a book are sold, the more he's read. Unless a book sells, a writer feels himself to have failed.' When *Animal Farm* began to sell, to really sell, Orwell for the first time must have felt himself to be at last a successful writer. Since he had wished for nothing so much as this since his teens, it is easy to imagine how great at that moment was his euphoria.

On February 14, 1946 we published Orwell's *Critical Essays*, in the U.S. titled *Dickens, Dali and Others*. Once again, as with *Animal Farm*, the contract was not signed till after publication – one day only however. All the essays were reprints. This type of book was not easy to sell in those days any more than it is in these, but *Critical Essays* sold. The first printing of 3,000 copies sold out in a few weeks following what Senhouse described as 'a blaze of reviews', and the second printing of 5,600 copies went within a year. Orwell's name was now a name of power, everything he wrote was a matter of interest to the literary world and beyond. It was clear to me his publisher that we must take over his books from the Gollancz list and reissue them. I waited eagerly for news that he had embarked on a new novel.

I find an office memo of mine dated June 25, 1945 [not 1946] which reads in part 'George Orwell has written the first twelve pages of his novel, but of course disclaims knowledge of when it will be finished.' Could he really have started *1984* as early as this? I don't know. But certainly in April 1946 Orwell gave up his journalistic work for six months and on 23 May went to Barnhill, on the island of Jura, where he was to live for two-and-a-half years, mainly in the summer, while he spent the rest of his time in London.

But London had its problems for him. Eking out the tiny coal ration of those days with 'blocks of wet peat of which I happen to have a few' didn't keep him warm in London – in the country, Orwell said, 'you can go out and scrounge firewood.' To Dorothy Plowman he complained, 'I am constantly smothered under journalism – at present I am doing 14 articles a week,' and to Arthur Koestler 'I have become more and more like a sucked orange.'

By June 22, 1946 Orwell had freed himself. Writing me from Jura he said 'I have done no writing for nearly two months . . . I've been very busy getting this house running, beginning to break in the garden, etc. My sister is here and works for me. . . . This is a nice house with 5 bedrooms and bathroom and I am getting it properly furnished by degrees. . . . The only great difficulty is transport – we are 7 miles from anywhere and 25 from a shop. . . .' Here was Orwell's Utopia, a smallholding in a wet and bleak landscape, miles from anywhere, with a climate utterly unsuitable for a man with a grave weakness of the lungs. Here was Orwell's main workshop, where *1984*, that most metropolitan of novels, was thought out, drafted, re-written, and typed by Orwell himself. Here was a place to be happy in, quiet, soothing to his jaded nerves, away from the complexities of social and business relationships, which irritated and baffled him. In this tiny world, with the sombre hills rising behind the house and the sea lapping the shore a few yards in front, he could and did create the horrific world of *1984*. Here was the place in which the lonely monk, the doomed pilgrim, overstraining what strength remained to him, ensured his death. Orwell's island Utopia was as fatal for him as Winston Smith's anti-Utopia in London 1984 was for Winston. But somehow I cannot bring myself to believe he need have died so soon.

And yet . . . Writing in *Tribune* on December 6, 1946, Orwell considered the case of H. G. Wells. 'A novelist does not, any more than a boxer or a ballet dancer, last for ever. He has an initial impulse which is good for three or four books, perhaps even for a dozen, but which must exhaust itself sooner or later. Obviously one cannot lay down any rigid rule, but in many cases the creative impulse seems to last for about 15 years: in a prose writer these 15 years would probably be between the ages of 30 and 45, or thereabouts.' Did Orwell consciously or unconsciously apply this 'rule' to himself? What were Orwell's 'three or four books'? Surely a selection of the great essays, *Homage to Catalonia* (1937–8), *Animal Farm* (1943–4) and *1984* (1946–48). There was a sense in which Orwell's work was complete when *1984* was written. Soon after reading it for the first time, I asked myself 'Where can he go from here? How can he revive the spirit of man so utterly and odiously destroyed in Room 101 by O'Brien, the grand inquisitor?' Here was Orwell's ritual or fictional suicide, the death of 'the last man in Europe',* to be followed in a little over a year by the real death of the living man.

A strange comparison exists between Orwell's thinking and that of a man of a different race who lived 10,000 miles away, the great Japanese writer, Yukio Mishima. He too believed that the creative span of a writer's life is limited to about 25 years. Mishima wrote his first book at the age of 20. He committed suicide both ritual and real at the age of 45 (see Chapter 13).

*A suggested title (by Orwell) for *1984*.

So perished two of the greatest writers of our age, both of whom must surely have won the Nobel Prize if only they had cared enough to prolong their lives into what they believed would inevitably be the mediocrity of their later years. It is not for me, their publisher, to criticize them. They gave their lives for literature, as a few have done before and a few will do after them. In the Soviet Union the present-day martyrs to literature must also be counted. To all of them, as a man who has devoted his whole life to literature as midwife or publisher, I pay the only tribute to them which is open to me. I remember them.

* * *

On July 1, 1946, after hearing from our author, Humphrey Slater, that Orwell had actually started on a new novel and that it was likely to be a long one, I wrote to Orwell to remind him that we had no contract for it yet, and on July 8 Orwell sent me an invitation to visit him in September. 'You'll have to walk the last 8 miles . . . so can you make do with rucksack luggage and a couple of haversacks? But it isn't a really formidable walk. . . .' To me however it seemed formidable, and that no doubt was the reason I never went. On August 23 Orwell expressed sorrow that I couldn't come, but stated 'I have stored up a considerable reserve of health and energy. I have literally started another book, but haven't got far with it. . . .' Orwell returned to London for a visit in October and on November 28 I sent him a copy of Norah Montgomerie's *Scottish Nursery Rhymes.* At this time Orwell was contemplating a book, perhaps only a short one, on nursery rhymes. In *Tribune* on December 21 he had a piece on Nonsense Poetry, starting off with *See-Saw, Margery Daw* in two different versions, and continuing with Edward Lear and Lewis Carroll.

On January 25, 1947 he wrote to Rayner Heppenstall, who had produced Orwell's own script of *Animal Farm* on radio and was probably asking him for something else. 'I can't promise anything more at present, I am too busy [on *1984*]. I've still got ideas about fairy stories. I wish they would dig up and re-broadcast my adaptation of *The Emperor's New Clothes. . . .'* Senhouse and I sent Orwell a number of books on these subjects, but nothing was to come of it. The concentration on *1984* left him no spare time or energy. The discs of *The Emperor's New Clothes* have not reappeared, so far as I know, which is a great pity. Long before I knew of them, I had regarded Orwell as akin to the child in that story, for was he not perpetually pointing out, to a sceptical world, emperors such as Stalin who had no clothes and imperial edicts of all kinds whose virtues were invisible to all sane men?

Back on Jura on April 11, 1947, though 'in most wretched health since January', Orwell wrote to me on May 31, telling me that he'd made a fairly good start on the book and 'written nearly a third of the rough draft . . . I keep pegging away, and I hope that when I leave here in October I shall either have finished the rough draft or at any rate broken its back. Of course, the rough draft is always a ghastly mess . . . but all the same it is the main part of the job.' Orwell hoped to finish the final draft fairly early in 1948, barring illnesses. To me it is amazing that he was less than a year late, despite his illness, in completing the most demanding novel he was to write.

What was my own state of mind about the book *before* I received this letter? I had known, of course, that Orwell was a major writer ever since I had read *Animal Farm* three years before. Since its publication over eighteen months before, I had known that he was now *recognized* as a major writer in the widest possible circles. But in November 1947 Senhouse had told me of disquieting news from mutual friends of Orwell's recklessness of his health and indeed of his life. From that moment, both as his publisher and as his friend, I was intermittently racked with anxiety about his health and the possible failure to complete his new novel. Now on receipt of this letter I knew something about what the novel was going to be. 'I don't like talking about books before they are written, but I will tell you now that this is a novel about the future – that is, it is in a sense a fantasy, but in the form of a naturalistic novel – of course, as a book of anticipations it would be comparatively simple to write.' This description left a blurred impression on my mind and slightly depressed me – novels about Utopias or anti-Utopias were not my favourite reading, nor the public's. So far as I could recall only Aldous Huxley's *Brave New World* had ever had much of a sale. If Orwell had only said to me, this is a novel about London under a totalitarian dictatorship, I should have had a much clearer picture of what was to come and perhaps a less severe shock when I first read *1984*.

In this same letter Orwell went on to tell me about 'a long autobiographical sketch – *Such, Such Were the Joys* – which I originally undertook as a sort of pendant to Cyril Connolly's *Enemies of Promise*, he having asked me to write a reminiscence of the preparatory school we were at together.' Orwell thought it too long to print in a periodical and too libellous to publish without risk of a successful prosecution. In fact, the principal person libelled lived for many years beyond 1947, and the long piece did not appear, except in the U.S. where the libel laws are less stringent, until it was included in volume IV of *The Collected Essays, Journalism and Letters of George Orwell*, 1968.

'Maybe sooner or later I might do a book of collected sketches,' wrote Orwell in the same letter. This most definitely set up hopes of an eventual autobiographical volume. What an extraordinary work it might have been – *Such, Such* followed by *Paradise at Eton*, and finally by *Burmese Trumpetings*. But for all those, including my colleague Senhouse, who went to Eton, what a lucky escape! For the present rulers of Burma? It's hard to guess whether they would truly have admired it.

But there was never to be an autobiographical volume, although there were diaries, London Letters to the *Partisan Review* and the long series of *As I Please* pieces in the *Tribune*. All these contain a modicum of autobiographical material, as do the essays. But somehow I doubt whether Orwell would ever have wished to write one. He was as secretive about his private life as any man I ever knew.

* * *

Before Orwell left for Jura in April 1947, he had wrestled personally (not through his agent) with Victor Gollancz. He had asked Gollancz on March 14 to release him from the terms of a contract signed in 1937 for his novel, *Keep the Aspidistra Flying*, a contract by which Orwell was bound to give him the first refusal of two other full-length novels, and this even though the contract was ten years old, and even though I had published his last (*not* full-length) novel, *Animal Farm*. I doubt whether many such contracts are in force nowadays. The literary agents would crucify any publisher who tried to enforce such an agreement.

Orwell's letter is not without interest. He wrote to Gollancz 'I know that I am asking for a very great favour. . . . Since (1937) you have published three books of mine but you have also refused two others on political grounds . . . the crucial case was *Animal Farm*. At the time when this book was finished, it was very hard indeed to get this book published, and I determined then that *if possible* I would take all my future output to the publisher who would produce it, because I knew that anyone who would risk this book would risk anything.' These final words of Orwell are strong words, and words that, when I read them over 20 years later, give me an intense feeling of satisfaction. *Would risk anything.* What a wonderful thing to have said about you, even if in my view there is a slight degree of exaggeration.

Gollancz, obviously reeling under the impact of Orwell's démarche, begged him to think again, and Orwell did. On March 25 he returned to the attack. 'I am afraid of further differences arising, as in the past. You know what the difficulty is, Russia. For quite 15 years I have regarded that régime with plain horror . . . I don't think my feelings are likely to change so long as the Communist Party remains in power. I know that your position in recent years has been not very far from mine, but I don't know what it would be if, for instance, there is another seeming rapprochement between Russia and the West. I know Warburg and his opinions well enough to know that he is very unlikely ever to refuse anything of mine on political grounds. As you say, no publisher can sign blind an undertaking to print anything a writer produces, but I think Warburg is less likely to jib than most.' At this Gollancz threw in the sponge, and Orwell thanked him for his 'very generous action'. Had Gollancz not done so, I would have fought, at least if Orwell had allowed me. But, in fact, from the day I signed a contract for *Homage to Catalonia* on September 1, 1937 until the moment of victory ten years later, I had never doubted that I was Orwell's publisher and that Orwell was my author. It was an alliance to be terminated only by death. Free now from the 1937 contract, Orwell signed a contract with me for his next three books. It was dated July 14, 1947, Bastille Day. Orwell had escaped from his prison.

Now that Orwell was free of any publishing commitment, I pursued the negotiations started in January with his agent for a reprint of *Coming Up for Air*, which we sent to the printers on June 6, 1947. It was to be followed by *Burmese Days* and *Down and Out in Paris and London*. Orwell regarded *The Clergyman's Daughter* as a poor novel which he had published only because he needed the money so badly, nor did he seem keen on *Keep the Aspidistra Flying*. He was a poor guardian of his own work, for later I had to steal a copy of one of these novels from the Holborn Public Library in order to reprint it – replaced by six copies of the new edition when it was ready.

In a letter to me dated February 4, 1948, from Hairmyres Hospital, East Kilbride, near Glasgow, Orwell blamed 'the beastly cold of last winter' 1946–7 for the serious worsening of his health. It was a post-war winter when a tired Britain suffered greatly from coal shortages, frozen railways, electricity cuts, as well as a poor diet – meat for instance was still on ration. 'I didn't feel well all last year except during that hot period in the summer. Before taking to my bed I had finished the rough draft of my novel all save the last few hundred words and if I had been well I might have finished it [the final draft] by about May. It is just a ghastly mess as it stands, but the idea is so good that I could not possibly abandon it. If anything should happen to me, I've instructed Richard Rees, my literary executor, to destroy the MS without showing it to anybody, but it's unlikely that anything like that would happen.' A specialist had diagnosed tuberculosis of the left lung, and five days before Christmas 1947 Orwell had entered the sanatorium.

A friend and admirer of Orwell's was David Astor, editor of *The Observer*, to which Orwell had made many contributions in previous years. Astor had arranged to have a supply of streptomycin flown over from the U.S. in a determined effort to halt somehow the disease which gripped him. At that time it was a rare drug, not available in Britain. Orwell started on it early in February for a two-month course. On February 22 I visited him in Ward 3 at Hairmyres.

Orwell was sitting bolt upright in bed when I went into his room, wearing a shirt. He greeted me with a smile that was both welcoming and wintry. He told me he thought the antibiotic might be doing him a bit of good, but the actual injections, which seemed to him to be all too frequent, were exceedingly painful. He showed me his arm which was marked by the scars of numerous needles. But he seemed cheerful, and naturally we discussed all manner of matters connected with the publishing and promotion of his books. From this talk, which must have lasted about two hours, I remember particularly one remark he made which has always seemed to me to throw light, not only on the character of his literary output, but also on the way he sorted out his views on the social and political problems of the world.

At that time my wife and I had living with us a young man, Michael K., about 25 years old, a refugee from Hitlerite Austria, whom Orwell had met many times and liked. They had a common interest, not in politics, but in fishing and the use of mechanical gadgets and engines, which Orwell adored. Orwell inquired about Michael, how was he, what was he doing. 'He's gone into an advertising agency,' I said, 'much to his sorrow, for, as you know,

George, his deepest wish was to become a farmer and make two blades of grass grow where only one grew before.' Orwell looked puzzled. 'That's an odd thing, Fred,' he remarked, 'Michael's Jewish, isn't he?' 'Half-Jewish,' I told him. 'Extraordinary,' said Orwell, 'it seems strange to me that Michael should want to be on the land. After all, Jews are nearly always interested in money.' About eight months later, Orwell was to review Jean-Paul Sartre's *Portrait of the Antisemite*, which I had just published. The book seemed to annoy him, for he wrote me on October 22, 'I have just had Sartre's book on anti-semitism to review. I think Sartre is a bag of wind, and I am going to give him a good boot.' This he certainly did, writing among other things 'The facts would not square with M. Sartre's atomised vision of society. There is, he comes near to saying, no such thing as a human being, there are only different categories of men, such as "the" worker and "the" bourgeois, all classifiable in much the same way as insects. Another of these insect-like creatures is "the" Jew . . . it is true that there are two kinds of Jew, the "Authentic Jew" who wants to remain Jewish and the "Inauthentic Jew" who would like to be assimilated; but a Jew, of whichever variety, is not just another human being.' And yet Orwell was surprised at Michael's love of the land!

Orwell was a very sick man at the time he wrote this review, desperately struggling to finish *1984* before it was too late. Nor would I have quoted it against him, but for one reason. Orwell, I believe, did himself have a somewhat 'atomised vision of society', he did tend to agree with the view expressed by Plato in *The Republic* that all objects which are red are red because they partake of 'redness' and that the 'idea' of redness is an important concept, as are all other abstract nouns, e.g. beauty, freedom, evil, elasticity, etc. It would be interesting if some literary critic were to examine Orwell's work from this point of view. It might perhaps throw light on why Orwell's most successful literary work was *Animal Farm*, where the various animals stand for types rather than individuals, while in *1984* the hero, the heroine and the grand inquisitor are somewhat colourless, and the proles are simply . . . the proles.

* * *

There is no doubt that the streptomycin did a great deal for Orwell. By the end of May he could get up for a few hours a day, sit in the sun when it was warm and hoped to get out in two or three months. He hoped that on leaving he would require no further treatment, and could go back to Jura 'instead of hanging about in Glasgow or Edinburgh.' At the end of June he was 'playing a lot of croquet which seems quite a tough game when you've been on your back for 6 months,' as he wrote to George Woodcock on May 24. Jura was where Orwell wanted to be, his Mecca, where the loner could be alone, where he could wrestle with the creation of *1984* and with the Angel of Death. Two weeks later he was back in Jura, but in September his health began to enter on what was to be the final collapse.

It has been said by some that Orwell was careless of his life, reckless as in the narrow escape from the whirlpool off Jura, when his adopted son, Richard, was in the boat with him. In other words, that he might have killed himself by gross negligence. I do not believe this for a moment. Orwell was a stoic. What he considered tolerable would have been felt to be quite intolerable by many. There are constant references in his letters to a lack of warmth. Did he get proper food? I doubt it. Journeys from Jura to London and back must have produced for him, as for far fitter people, the weariness of the long-distance traveller. Did he stay indoors when the wind and the mist and the rain made it dangerous for him to go out? I doubt it. But this falls far short of an unconscious, let alone a conscious, urge to suicide. What it does show is a failure on Orwell's part to recognize in time the need for precautions, his dislike of having to behave like an invalid, something akin in fact to the feelings of passengers in a car who refuse to strap on their safety belts or those who visit tropical paradises without first getting themselves innoculated. It is said that on one of his monthly trips to Glasgow for a check-up, he failed to reserve a room for the night when a conference was meeting and all the hotels were booked full, in consequence of which Orwell trudged from one place to another seeking shelter for the night. No doubt he would have been carrying a fairly heavy bag with him. It was directly after this trip that he had his first breakdown. Indeed, in a letter to Julian Symons of October 29, 1948, he writes 'Ironically it started with my going back to the hospital to be re-examined, and being upset by the journey.' What Orwell needed, and didn't get till it was too late, was a competent nurse to keep him in order, or better still a wife who would not take 'no' for an answer.

But on September 6, when he wrote me, there was an element of optimism in the letter. 'I am about half way through the revision of my novel and unless I get ill again . . . I should have it done in time to let you have it early in December. My health seems to be getting much better . . . I am going up to Glasgow to be X-rayed again, and perhaps after that they will let me get up a bit more . . . but I can't walk far or do anything requiring the smallest physical strength.' It may well have been this trip to Glasgow which is the one referred to in the previous paragraph.

But soon after this Orwell must have been faced with a terrible decision. During September it is clear that he was getting worse, and this deterioration must surely have been due, either to the Jura climate or to hard work on *1984*, or most probably both. Yet what could he do? He had returned from the sanatorium and the streptomycin treatment about six weeks before. Yet already the ominous symptoms were returning. Two courses of action lay open to him – to stop writing *1984* and hope (against hope?) for a measure of improvement, or to finish the book within three months, as he knew he could, and damn the consequences. He chose the second alternative. He gambled once again with his life, as he had done in the Spanish Civil War twelve years before, and perhaps in the whirlpool a year before, and perhaps on other occasions of which we know nothing. But this time Orwell was to lose. Yet, if Orwell had *not* gambled, it seems to me improbable that *1984* would ever have appeared in print.

On October 22 Orwell was over half way through the revision of the second half of *1984*. He wrote me on that day 'I shall finish the book, D.V., early in November, and I am rather flinching from the job of typing it, because it is a very awkward thing to do in bed, where I still have to spend half the time . . . the book is fearfully long, well over 100,000 words, possibly 125,000. I can't send it away because it is an unbelievably bad MS and no one could make head or tail of it without explanation. On the other hand a skilled typist under my eye could do it easily enough. If you can think of anybody who would be willing to come, I will send money for the journey and full instructions. I think we could make her quite comfortable.'

Senhouse received a similar request a few days later. Both of us tried our best to find a typist to type what I hoped would be one of the great books of our time. But we did not succeed. The thought of that long journey, the eight mile walk at the end of it, the lonely homestead by the sea, the stony paths, the two sea crossings to be endured from the mainland to Jura, proved too unattractive to every girl we interviewed. I had to cable my failure to Orwell, who finished the revision early in November, and then typed the MS himself. On December 4 he posted it to me. This failure on my part still haunts me. It was perhaps the last straw. On January 6, seriously ill, Orwell went to the Cotswold Sanatorium, Cranham, Gloucestershire.

In the same letter of October 22, Orwell wrote 'I am not pleased with the book, but I am not absolutely dissatisfied. I first thought of it in 1943. I think it is a good idea, but the execution would have been better if I had not written it under the influence of T.B. I haven't definitely fixed on a title but I am hesitating between *Nineteen Eighty-Four* and *The Last Man in Europe*.' The final decision on title was Orwell's, but it had my strong approval. The typescript must have reached me about December 9. I read it at once.

* * *

When a publisher reads the MS of an author's book for the first time, he will know what his opinion of it is. He may think that it is a fine book or even a masterpiece, only to change his opinion later as a result of discussion with his colleagues or a hostile press. And of course vice versa, a low opinion changed by the enthusiasm of others. In the case of *1984*, my original view of the novel is available, since on December 13, at most four days after receipt of MS, I dictated a report for my colleagues to my secretary. I reprint this below in full, precisely as it was. I was certainly the first man in Europe (indeed in the world) to read the novel *The Last Man in Europe*, now known as *1984*. What I expected from it is hard to say, that I read it with a deep excitement is certain. I knew then what it had cost Orwell to write, though of course I could not know the full price he would have to pay.

F. J. W'S REPORT ON 1984

This is amongst the most terrifying books I have ever read. The savagery of Swift has passed to a successor who looks upon life and finds it becoming ever more intolerable. Orwell must acknowledge a debt to Jack London's *Iron Heel*, but in verisimilitude and horror he surpasses this not inconsiderable author. Orwell has no hope, or at least he allows his reader no tiny flickering candlelight of hope. Here is a study in pessimism unrelieved, except perhaps by the thought that, if a man can conceive *1984*, he can also will to avoid it. It is a fact that, so far as I can see, there is only one weak link in Orwell's construction; *he nowhere indicates the way in which man, English man, becomes bereft of his humanity.*

1984 is *Animal Farm* writ large and in purely anthropomorphic terms. One hopes (against hope?) that its successor will supply the other side of the picture. For what is *1984* but a picture of man unmanned, of humanity without a heart, of a people without tolerance or civilization, of a government whose *sole* object is the maintenance of its absolute totalitarian power by every contrivance of cruelty. Here is the Soviet Union to the nth degree, a Stalin who never dies, a secret police with every device of modern technology.

Part One sets the scene. It puts Orwell's hero, Winston Smith, on the stage. It gives a detailed and terrifying picture of the community in which he lives. It introduces the handful of characters who serve the plot, including Julia with whom Winston falls in love. Here we are given the telescreen, installed in every living-room, through which the secret police *perpetually* supervise the words, gestures, expressions and thoughts of all members of the Party; newspeak, the language devised by the Party to prevent thought; the big brother (B.B.) whose face a metre wide is to be seen everywhere on placards, etc.; doublethink, the formula for 100% political hypocrisy; the copiously flowing synthetic gin, which alone lubricates the misery of the inhabitants; the Ministry of Truth, with its three slogans – War is Peace, Freedom is Slavery, Ignorance is Strength – and its methods of obliterating past events in the interests of the Party.

The political system which prevails is Ingsoc = English Socialism. This I take to be a deliberate and sadistic attack on socialism and socialist parties generally. It seems to indicate a final breach between Orwell and Socialism, not the socialism of equality and human brotherhood which clearly Orwell no longer expects from socialist parties, but the socialism of marxism and the managerial revolution. *1984* is among other things an attack on Burnham's managerialism; and it is worth a cool million votes to the conservative party;* it is imaginable that it might have a preface by Winston Churchill after whom its hero is named. *1984 should be published as soon as possible, in June 1949.*

Part Two contains the plot, a very simple one. Winston falls in love with a black-haired girl, Julia. This in itself is to be considered heretical and illegal. See Part 1, sec. 6 for a discussion of sex and love, but in any case 'the sexual act, successfully performed, was rebellion. Desire was thoughtcrime. . . .' A description of their lovemaking follows, and these few passages alone contain a lyrical sensuous quality utterly lacking elsewhere in the book. These passages have the effect of intensifying the horrors which follow.

*This judgment has nothing to do with my political sympathies at that time. By then I was almost certainly a floating voter.

Julia and Winston, already rebels, start to plot; contact O'Brien, a fellow rebel as they think; are given 'the book' of Emmanuel Goldstein, the Trotsky of this community; and Winston reads it. It is a typical Orwellism that Julia falls asleep while Winston reads part of the book to her. (Women aren't intelligent, in Orwell's world.)

Goldstein's book as we may call it (though it turns out later to have been written by the secret police) is called 'The Principles of Oligarchical Collectivism' and we are given many pages of quotations from it. It outlines in a logical and coherent form the world situation as Orwell expects it to develop in the next generation. (Or does it?) It would take a long essay to discuss the implications of the astounding political philosophy embodied in this imagined work, which attempts to show that the class system, which was inevitable until circa 1930, is now in process of being fastened *irrevocably* on the whole world at the very moment when an approach to equality and liberty is for the first time possible. The book is quoted in Part 2, sec. 9, which can almost be read as an independent work.

Before passing to Part 3, I wish to call attention to the use made by Orwell of the old nursery rhyme, Oranges and Lemons, said the bells of St Clements. This rhyme plays a largish part in the plot and is worth study. It ends, it will be remembered, with the words 'And here comes the chopper to chop off your head.' This use of a simple rhyme to achieve in due course an effect of extreme horror is a brilliant and typical Orwellism which places him as a craftsman in the front rank of terror novelists.

1984 by the way might well be described as a horror novel, and would make a horror film which, if licensed, might secure all countries threatened by communism for 1000 years to come.

Part Three contains the torture, breakdown, and re-education of Winston Smith, following immediately upon his arrest in bed with Julia by the secret police. In form it reminds one of Arthur Koestler's *Darkness at Noon*, but is to my mind more brutal, completely English, and overwhelming in its picture of a thorough extermination of all human feeling in a human being. In this part Orwell gives full rein to his sadism and its attendant masochism, rising (or falling) to the limits of expression in the scene where Winston, threatened by hungry rats which will eat into his face, implores his torturer to throw Julia to the rats in his place. This final betrayal of all that is noble in man leaves Winston broken and ready for re-education as a willing adherent of Ingsoc, the necessary prelude in this society to being shot for his 'thoughtcrime', for in Ingsoc there are no martyrs but only broken men wishing to die for the good of their country.

'We shall meet in the place where there's no darkness.' This phrase, which recurs through the book, turns out to be in the end the brilliantly lit passage and torture chambers of the Ministry of Love. Light, for Orwell, symbolizes (I think) a horrible logical clarity which leads to death and destruction. Darkness, as in the womb and perhaps beside a woman in the night, stands for the vital processes of sex and physical strength, the virtues of the proles, that 80 % of the population of Ingsoc who do the work and do not think, the 'Boxers' of *Animal Farm*, the pawns, the raw material without which the Party could not function.

In Part III Orwell is concerned to obliterate hope; there will be no rebellion, there cannot be any liberation. Man cannot stand against Pain, and the Party commands Pain. It is almost intolerable to read Part III which, more even than the rest of the book, smells of death, decay, dirt, diabolism and despair. Here Orwell goes down to the depths in a way which reminds me of Dostoievsky. O'Brien is his Grand Inquisitor, and he leaves Winston, and the reader, without hope. I cannot but think that this book could have been written only by a man who himself, however temporarily, had lost hope, and for physical reasons which are sufficiently apparent.

These comments, lengthy as they are, give little idea of the giant movement of thought which Orwell has set in motion in *1984*. It is a great book, but I pray I may be spared from reading another like it for years to come.

* * *

There is little in this report which I would today alter, except perhaps my belief that, in describing the 1984 régime as Ingsoc, Orwell was making 'a deliberate and sadistic attack on socialism and socialist parties generally,' including even the mild socialism of the U.K. This was definitely not Orwell's intention, as he was to make clear soon enough.

To the best of my knowledge, the typescript revealed no signs of the agony of its typist, Orwell himself. We prepared the book for press with extreme urgency. There was the question of Orwell's health – he must be alive to read and correct the proofs. He must be alive too to enjoy what I expected to be one of the biggest and most enthusiastic receptions a book could have. It has been my experience that the successful publication of a book can and usually does act as a tonic, an elixir, a magic potion, strong enough to improve or even restore its writer's health. I have at least two particular cases in mind. Then there was my enthusiasm and that of my colleagues. Lastly there was the extreme importance of the book itself, both literary and political. This, in fact, was a book on which there must be no delay.

We promised Orwell publication in June. Writing to a friend, he said, June in publishers' language means July. But in fact we did publish in June, on the 6th.

On December 21, 1948, Orwell wrote me 'I am really very unwell indeed and am arranging to go into a sanatorium early in January . . . I'm glad you liked the book. It isn't a book I would gamble on for a big sale, but I suppose one could be sure of 10,000 anyway* . . . I have a stunning idea for a very short novel which has been in my head for years, but I can't start anything till I am free from high temperatures, etc.'

On January 6, 1949, seriously ill with tuberculosis, Orwell went into the Cotswold Sanatorium, Cranham, Gloucestershire. A few days later I telegraphed him there 'Heard you arrived stop Hope you stood journey not too badly stop Should like come see you Friday let me know if possible by return whether this all right stop You must underlined get better this time however long it takes and whatever it costs.' On January 14 I received a long letter from L. Simmonds, a bookseller of 16 Fleet Street, Strand, London, E.C.4., a friend and warm admirer of Orwell. After giving me some (unasked) advice, for which he apologized ('you may well feel that I should attend to my own affairs') about the pricing of Orwell's novels, the bulk of paper to be used for printing them, the desirability of an illustrated edition of one of them by David Low, the great cartoonist, etc., he prophesied that, if *1984* was as good as I had told him it was, 'it would fly into top figures for sales'. Simmonds had also told me that he, and one or two of his friends, would raise £500, a largish sum in those days especially for booksellers, to send him to Switzerland, remarking that 'he is far too precious to lose'.

In answer to my telegram, Orwell telegraphed 'Look forward to seeing you Friday Do bring Pamela Car will meet you.' On Friday my wife and I went down to see him. We had various matters to discuss with him. First, I was keen to tell him of the high hopes we had for the sale of *1984*, which might produce a boost to his morale, helpful to a man in so perilous a situation. Second, I wanted to tell

*We printed in fact a first edition of 26,000 copies, see below.

him of Simmonds' generous offer. I had already written him on January 19 'your future is important to more people than yourself... you are a much loved writer and your public wants you to get well and wants you to do everything that you can to this end.' Third, there were a number of minor points to discuss in connexion with the publishing details of *1984*.

But, more important still, Pamela and I felt it was essential that Orwell should be under the personal care of an absolutely first-class specialist in tuberculosis, since clearly it was now a matter of to be or not to be. We had in mind Dr. Andrew Morland, whom we had known for many years. He was a doctor of the highest reputation, with a long experience of tuberculosis cases, who had himself suffered from it in his younger days. In addition, he had been in charge of D. H. Lawrence during the last years of his life, which, we thought, should give him a keen understanding of the mind of a creative writer with all his hopes and fears, and of course a sensitivity sharper than the normal.

A car met us and took us to the sanatorium, where we were conducted to a small grey-brown wooden hutment or chalet built, with others, on a large flattish piece of ground. It was bitterly cold, the air he was breathing must have been nearly as chilly as the ice cold air in the sanatoria of the magic mountains in Switzerland.

It was obvious to me that Pamela had formed a low opinion of the place, and she lost no time in asking a few questions.

'Don't you feel cold in here?' she said.

'It's a bit cold sometimes,' said Orwell, 'but they're going to let me have an electric blanket.'

'Well, why haven't they given it you yet?'

'I expect it'll be here tomorrow or perhaps the day after.'

'Why not today? If they've got one, they could bring it at once, George. Ask them for it. But what I want to know is what the doctor thinks about your condition.'

Orwell looked at her, but he didn't answer. Pamela looked at him sternly.

'Don't tell me he hasn't told you what he thinks,' she said.

Orwell stammered a little. 'As a matter of fact, I haven't seen him yet . . .' Pamela seemed about to explode, when Orwell went hurriedly on '. . . but a woman doctor comes and visits me every morning.'

Pamela's face cleared a little. 'Well, what does she think?' she asked sharply.

This time Orwell began to look worried. 'She's an Austrian,' he said, 'but I think she's thoroughly competent and kind, and asks me how I feel and all that.'

'Is that all? Doesn't she listen to your chest with that . . . that thing?'

'A stethoscope,' I put in, at last finding a use for my tongue in this frightening dialogue.

'No,' said Orwell. 'I'm afraid she doesn't. I expect they're understaffed here, you know, she probably hasn't got time.'

'But you've been here for ages,' Pamela said, 'nearly a month.'

'About two weeks,' Orwell said.

'It's monstrous, absolutely shocking,' Pamela remarked angrily. Pamela had been married before to a painter, who had died of T.B. after a year. She knew far more than I did of the symptoms and treatment of this disease.

'George, you must ask to see the doctor in charge today or at latest tomorrow.'

'I expect he'll come and see me fairly soon,' Orwell replied, 'the place is really very comfortable, they look after me quite well. I expect the doctors know what they are doing.'

The reply was so typical of him – he couldn't bear to make a fuss – and so heartrending that I could hardly believe my ears, but at least it made it easy for Pamela to beg him to see a London specialist. She came out with it immediately. 'George, I want you to see Dr. Morland. We'll get him to come down here and give you a thorough examination, and I hope he'll be able to take you into his hospital, University College Hospital. You'll feel much better in London than in this . . . this field. And of course all your friends can come and see you whenever you want. Will you let me ask Morland to come down?' The argument went on, but the best that Pamela could achieve was that Orwell would think it over.

'Promise me one thing, George,' Pamela said finally, 'the instant you feel you'd like to see Morland, let us know, Fred or me. I *know* he'll come if we ask him, and I know he'll get you into U.C.H.' Orwell promised, but it was not till May 6 that Orwell sent off his S.O.S.

On the train journey back to London, Pamela looked at me sadly 'I don't think he'll live for more than a year,' she said.

During the next four months till May, Orwell was sometimes a little better, more often rather worse. A number of decisions were made. Orwell wanted *1984* spelt out – he refused to let the American publisher call it *The Last Man in Europe* – he criticized the first blurb we sent him – he refused to allow the Americans to drop the appendix on Newspeak from the book – he also refused to let the Book of the Month Club cut the text, by shortening drastically the passage quoted from Dr. Goldstein's imaginary treatise – he tried once again but again unsuccessfully to persuade us to reissue some of George Gissing's novels, especially *New Grub Street* which he greatly admired. His mind was intensely active, but clearly the physical odds against him were growing.

I wrote to him from time to time, giving him details of the progress to publication of *1984*. On March 8, for instance, I wrote him 'publication date is now virtually fixed for June 14, and the book will definitely be a June choice of the *Evening Standard*. George Malcolm Thomson [then literary editor of the *Standard*] is more than enthusiastic about it . . . there was a big fight in the selection committee of the Book Society whether it should be their choice. As I understand it the protagonists were – pro-*1984* V. S. Pritchett, anti-*1984* Compton Mackenzie. The Noes had it after about an hour and a half, mainly I believe on the grounds that the book has ideological implications and that the Book Society members prefer to read books which will in no way remind them of present-day realities.' This reaction is not unknown today, and never fails to infuriate me. My letter to Orwell continued 'I do feel that Mackenzie's religious instructor – he is a Catholic – should be notified, surely good Catholics should be in favour of such books as yours.' I went on to tell him of bookseller enthusiasm and good advance orders, that we had fixed the first printing at 25,000 copies, '. . . and have already thought it prudent to buy paper, now unrationed, for a first reprint of 10,000 copies. It seems to me we are going to be successful in pushing your masterpiece into best sellerdom.'

On March 31, Orwell wrote Sir Richard Rees, saying that he had redrafted his will. On April 8 he wrote him to say that the Book of the Month Club had agreed to select *1984*, although he had refused to cut a word out of it, as they requested. 'So that shows that virtue is its own reward, or honesty is the best policy, I forget which.' Orwell had not felt so strongly about editorial interference with his earlier books, but since he wrote *The Road to Wigan Pier* he had been a sea-green incorruptible. Orwell must have known that this selection would have been worth at this time a minimum of £40,000. Would every author have taken the risk, especially at a time of critical illness, when he feared he might be an invalid for the rest of his life?

On April 14 he wrote to his American editor, Robert Giroux, 'I am now on the way to recovery and shall be out of here before the summer is over. I have my next novel mapped out . . .' Yet, *the very next day*, he wrote to T. R. Fyvel 'I've been horribly ill the last few weeks. I had a bit of a relapse, then they decided to have another go with streptomycin . . . this time only one dose had ghastly results . . .' And two weeks later, April 22, he wrote me 'I am somewhat better, and have been sitting out a little in a deck chair when the weather is fine.' What did he really believe?

On May 13 I wrote Orwell '. . . I had better report progress . . . but first I do hope your health is not too shocking. I heard from Sonia Brownell yesterday that she is coming down to see you over the weekend, and I hope to hear from her . . . that you are improving. . . . Unless [we] are living in a world of illusion, *1984* is going to be a smash hit . . . advance sales have already reached a total of 11,000 copies . . . all sorts of little indications tend to show that this is the book people are waiting for. . . . By advancing our publication date by a week we have stolen a three weeks run on the second volume of Winston Churchill [*The Second World War*: Their Finest Hour] who comes out on June 27. His book will of course have an enormous sale . . . and we think it is a matter of some importance to get your book well and truly launched as far ahead of his as possible. I have just sent a copy of *1984* to him . . .'.

But on May 16, three days later, a terrible change for the worse had occurred. Orwell wrote 'I am in most ghastly health, and have been for some weeks . . . too feverish to go over to the X-ray room and stand up against the screen . . . I am afraid it will show that both lungs have deteriorated badly.' At last it seems that Orwell had realized his mortal danger; up till then he had appeared not to allow himself to fear the worst. This was the stoic element in his character, combined with the fatal trait of not wanting to be thought a nuisance.

The letter continued 'I asked the doctor recently whether she thought I would survive and she wouldn't go further than saying she didn't know.' Was it this sentence that shocked Orwell into a realization of the brutal facts. It seems likely. The letter went on 'If the "prognosis" after this photo is bad, I shall get a second opinion. Can you give me the name of that specialist you mentioned? . . . *They can't do anything*,* as I'm not a case for operation.'

I replied immediately, on May 18. 'Dr. Morland's address is No. X

*My italics.

Harley Street . . . one of the leading chest specialists in England. You will like him if you see him. If you would wish me to get in touch with him myself, I will be happy to do so . . . I am sure there must be things that can be done, and that Morland will know what they are.' On May 20 Orwell replied 'I've spoken to the doctor here. She says she has no objection to a second opinion (she says she knows Dr. Morland). Could you be kind enough to get in touch with him on my behalf and fix up a suitable date with Dr. Kirkman here for him to come and see me. If you know him well, could you impress on him that I *don't* want to be cheered up but given an expert opinion on whether I am likely to stay alive, and, if so, how long.' He also wrote a postcard to Pamela, thanking her for putting Morland's name before him so forcefully.

On May 25 both Morland and Orwell wrote me. Morland wrote 'I have just returned from seeing this man at the Cotswold Sanatorium. I found that he has rather severe disease of the left lung and a relatively slight amount on the right. He has made some progress in the right direction since January but his improvement has been slow and undulating.

'I discussed his outlook with him as fully and frankly as possible but in a case like this prognosis is hazardous.

'Provided he rests properly he should continue to improve but it may well be that after a number of months he will stagnate or even relapse. One point I am quite clear about is that if he ceases to try to get well and settles down to write another book he is almost certain to relapse quickly.

'With further rest I do not anticipate a cure but he might well reach a stage at which he could do several hours writing a day combined with physical rest. He would then reach the stage which we call the 'good chronic', i.e. able to potter about and do a few hours sedentary work.

'His resistance must be fairly good as he stabilized well last year and *should not have broken down had he not foolishly over-exercised.*'*

On May 30 I thanked him for his report, which, I said, 'is a good deal more encouraging than I had dared to hope. . . . It is clear that at worst Orwell has a fighting chance.' I went on to discuss with him future policy about 'the best way to handle this difficult patient,' and also to ask whether it would not 'be possible or desirable, once he has somewhat recovered from the present collapse, to come to a sanatorium nearer London.'

*My italics.

Orwell's letter, too, was as satisfactory as could be expected. He found Morland 'very nice and quite encouraging'. What worried Orwell was that Morland had told him 'it is necessary to stay still and do no work for what may be a long time, possibly as much as a year or two years. I don't think I could stick it for two years, but could manage one if absolutely necessary.' Another matter that disturbed him was that 'I shall have nothing ready for next year.' He went on to hope that I would come and see him early in June.

On May 30 I wrote Orwell a long letter which I am quoting almost in full, since it gives a clear picture of Orwell and *1984* and his publisher at that time.

'My dear George,

'I was delighted to have your letter of Friday, and to know that you found Morland pleasant and not too discouraging. As a matter of fact the report he has given me about you is far more encouraging than I had dared to hope. Morland is perfectly clear on one point, which is that "if he ceases to try and get well and settles down to write another book he is almost certain to relapse quickly." This from your point of view is probably the devil.

'On the other hand, however, very definite hopes are held out to you that at a certain stage not too far away you can be allowed safely to work on writing for several hours a day, provided that the work is combined with a very large amount of physical rest. So the target is worth aiming at, and it is even suggested that beyond that is a still more satisfactory target, that you will be able eventually to potter about and do a few hours sedentary work.

'It must therefore be crystal clear to you the limits within which your life is set, and since as you have told me and as I know myself from direct observation, you are as keen or keener than any man to stay alive, I am hopeful. But this disease is one which apparently you cannot cheat, and you cannot trust your feelings of being well or being better, but only the sharp scientific test of how much infection is actually present in the lungs. So however much better you feel next month or in August or in October, for God's sake don't start working until you are given the all-clear.

'I do not mean this letter to appear to you as a lecture, but as I said to you before there are so many people who want you to stay alive that it is your duty to do just that; Richard, of course, first and foremost, but also your readers, whose numbers will shortly run I hope to hundreds of thousands, and your friends who would miss you terribly, and not least your humble servant and publisher, F. J. Warburg.

'I am planning to come down and see you on Sunday, June 12th, four days after publication of *Nineteen Eighty-Four*, by which time some of the reviews should have appeared, and we may have some slight idea as to sales possibilities, though of course it is really too soon after publication to form a proper opinion. But I am convinced that you will earn in England, and I have no doubt in America too, far more money than from *Animal Farm*, certainly enough even after tax deductions, to last you for say three years or more, even allowing for the heavy expenses of treatment in a sanatorium. This does not mean that we should not be glad to publish a second volume of your reprinted essays, say in the autumn of 1950, in the hopes that before the end of 1950 you will have recovered and had time to write your next novel.'

There is no doubt that advance interest in *1984* for weeks before publication was intense. So too was the interest in Winston Churchill's *Their Finest Hour*, his history of Britain in 1940–41 when 'we stood alone'. Orwell had given his hero the christian name of Winston, a clear indication that in Orwell's mind the defence of British freedom had rested during the war on Churchill. Yet Orwell's Winston had come to a dishonourable and disgusting defeat. Whether Churchill read the copy of *1984*, which I had sent him before publication, I do not know. But, if he did, he might well have disliked it and dismissed it with some such remark as 'morbid rubbish, the fellow's a bloody defeatist'. Yet Churchill, had he said this, would have been wrong. Orwell was no defeatist. Pessimist though he was in normal circumstances, and doubly pessimistic and exhausted as he was when he typed the last few pages, Orwell wrote *1984* not as a prophecy but as warning. What he was saying, with all the demonic power and intellectual analysis of which he was capable, was 'this, or something like this, has happened in Russia, *don't let it happen here*.' In addition, he gave future freedom fighters a vocabulary of sentences newly minted by him, which would serve to elucidate the language of tyranny and expose its hypocrisy.

On June 8 we published *1984* in an edition of 25,575 copies. By the end of October we had sold 22,700 copies. By March 1950 a second printing of 5,570 copies was ready, in April a third printing of 5,200 copies, in November a fourth printing of 5,000 was ready. These lasted till April 1951, when a fifth printing of 7,570 copies became available. These five printings totalled 49,917 copies. In the next 15 years to 1966, a further 21,400 copies were sold. Between 1966 and 1971 the sales averaged about 2,000 copies a year, bringing the total number sold to 81,250 copies of the hard-cover edition alone.

The paperback edition was published by Penguin and has sold 804,300 copies by 1972, and is now selling at the rate of 150,000 copies a year. Together with 10,000 to 15,000 copies sold in special editions, the sale must now have reached one million copies, give or take a few thousand, an extraordinary figure for a novel that is not designed to please nor all that easy to understand.

In the U.S. the sales were equally magnificent. In hard cover, around 170,000 copies, rather more than double the British sale. As a selection of the Book of the Month Club, it sold 190,000 copies between June 1949 and March 1952. As a paperback in the New American Library it sold 1,210,000 copies between 1950 and 1957, 2,052,000 copies between 1958 and 1965, and from then till 1969 another 5,571,000. It was also published in Reader's Digest Condensed Books, where the distribution in the 18 months of its life there ran to 596,000 copies. From these figures it would appear that *1984*, like *Animal Farm*, is selling better each year.

The reviews of 1984 were far more enthusiastic than those of *Animal Farm* and much longer, due in part to the fact that recovery from the war was substantial, paper rationing had ceased, and postal communications over the world had become easy. But there was more to it than that – Orwell had been recognized (at last) as a major writer of world significance. Then again *1984* was a full-length novel, if a strange one, while *Animal Farm* was a fairy tale and short, about one quarter the length of its successor. At the time I had a strong impression that throughout Europe, so recently freed from the Nazi tyranny, *1984* was thought of as a political *act* rather than a novel, a dire warning not to allow their liberty ever again to be endangered. In the U.S. too its political importance was deeply appreciated, and Americans regarded Orwell as a right-wing prophet who loathed socialism, the left and the welfare state. About this there was to be trouble later, since Orwell's hatred of privilege, poverty, unemployment, hereditary titles and the like was strong and undeviating. In Britain, on the other hand, *1984* was dealt with by critics much more as a literary work than a political tract for the times. If I am right, this presupposes that in Britain the fear of despotism or totalitarianism was extremely slight, compared to the apprehension across the waters to east and west.

1984 was chosen as book-of-the-month by the *Evening Standard* and reviewed by George Malcolm Thomson. He came out with his view of it right at the start. 'In some respects, the most important book published since the war. It will arouse a storm of controversy. Many people are going to hate its message. But they will hate the book only because as a novel its impact has such power, violence and lucidity.' Controversy there certainly was – Frank O'Connor wrote 'it doesn't so much smell as stink to high heaven . . . not a good book.' – Edward Shanks found it too strong for his taste and asked 'must we assume that the love of power is an absolute passion, as the love of goodness, or God, is not?' Peter Quennell was tepid – J. B. Priestley was depressed by it, and thought that, now that Queen Anne's dead, 'it's a new Rabelais, not another Swift, we need.' Others were hostile to it, largely, I think, because they understood it as prophecy not warning, and as we islanders all know 'Britons never, never, never shall be slaves.'

But on balance it was greeted with paeons of praise. Bertrand Russell wrote 'it depicts with very great power the horrors of a well-established totalitarian régime of whatever type. It is important that the western world should be aware of these dangers,' and later he described it as 'the book that has interested me most [in 1949].' E. M. Forster said the same, while admitting 'it is too terrible a novel to be read straight through.' Rebecca West considered it as the book of the year, describing it as 'a remarkable book because it succeeded in depicting not only a set of circumstances, but how characters would have reacted to them . . . a superb effort of the imagination.'

Religious papers for the most part praised it. *The Tablet* referred to the need for the grace of God to help man escape the dangers of the lust for power, while the *Catholic Herald* wrote 'most important of all is the analysis of the underlying motive which keeps the wheels going in this triumphant totalitarian world . . . the lust of power. Here Orwell . . . comes full circle in history to the fall of the Angels and the fall of man.' The socialist papers were mostly full of praise, never expecting for a moment that Ingsoc could possibly be confused with English Socialism, and indeed how right they are! V. S. Pritchett, who fought so gallantly but in vain to make *1984* a choice of the British Book Society, described it as a book that 'goes through the reader like an east wind, cracking the skin, opening the sores,' and to my joy quoted the first two paragraphs with their magnificent opening sentence, 'It was a bright, cold day in April, and the clocks were striking thirteen.' It is difficult to imagine a sentence more chilling than this to open a horrific novel. *Striking thirteen.*

A particularly interesting review came from Professor Geoffrey Durrant, writing in the *Sunday Times* of South Africa. He describes the plot and the social system and remarks that 'there is nothing especially original in this, though it is all most logically and clearly presented. Orwell shows his real brilliance in his discussion of the methods used to control the minds of the people. He has realized more fully than any other writer in this field the central importance of language and the degree to which corruption of language may help a tyrannical government.' He considers *Newspeak*, 'where there are no longer such words as "freedom", "self", "criticism" and so on – they are all included in the one word *Thoughtcrime.* Is this fantastic? The reader has only to look round him to see that a similar process is already going on . . . in South Africa. . . . And are we not well on the way to using the word "communism" as a synonym for "thoughtcrime" . . .' In contrast to Professor Durrant, the *Cape Times* review includes the following passage – 'It is equally frightening to realize that many of the conditions he describes already exist in mild forms under the Socialist régime in Britain.' For the words 'in mild form' all of us here in Britain should perhaps be grateful. I am sure that it is Orwell's creative work in the field of language and its misuse that has helped to give *1984* a perennial life, which no mere sci-fic thriller could possibly match.

Perhaps I have given too much space to a consideration of *1984*'s reviews, yet a much fuller study would reveal a great deal of interest about the characters and the morale and the ideas of the critics and the countries of which they are citizens. This is true particularly of the U.S. The book was as great a success there as in the U.K. It was also, like *Animal Farm*, a selection of the Book of the Month Club. It received enthusiastic reviews from such notable thinkers as Arthur Schlesinger, Jr., Alfred Kazin, Paul de Kruif and others. An unusual discussion of it was made in one of Alistair Cooke's famous *Letters from America* on B.B.C. radio. It was printed under the title 'Joys of Unlimited Individualism'. Cooke says that its great popularity 'is due to the fact that it attracts something in American thinking that is phoney, and alarms something . . . that is genuine.' The phoney attraction is 'that they look on it exclusively as an attack on the British Labour Government or on communism, or on both as fatal and inevitable partners.' The genuine alarm, Cooke goes on, is due to the assumption that the more government you have, no matter of what sort, your own personal character and tastes will be all the more threatened.' It is true, Cooke says, that Americans are conservatives, and some of their views would shock socialist ministers, but it is also true that 'what the American deep inside him wants to conserve, to keep, is his right to be an anarchist.' This is a shrewd insight, as applied to *1984*, for there is no doubt in my mind that the socialist reformer in Orwell's unconscious was tied like a Siamese twin to a conservative anarchist. This emerges most clearly from a reading of *Animal Farm*, but is also present in *1984* in full measure.

* * *

On June 15 I went to see Orwell at the Cranham sanatorium. A note I made at the time states that 'he is undoubtedly better than at his low point of some weeks ago when he saw Morland. The high temperature of that date, the feeling of exhaustion and disintegration appear due to pleurisy rather than the tubercular infection. George's present condition is shocking, but he is hopeful.' Orwell also told me, to my great relief, that he would move nearer London when he started feeling better, but this decision appeared to be due mainly to a wish to be nearer his London friends rather than any dislike of Cranham or any wish to put himself directly under Morland's care.

I detailed to him the large sums of money he was likely to earn from *1984*, amounting to between £10,000 and £15,000, of course a gross underestimate as it turned out. By now he had an accountant, and had turned himself into a limited company.

Orwell was concerned about some of the American reviews of *1984*, one of which described it as 'timely as a label on a poison bottle.' They suggested that it was something he expected to happen in the Western world during the next forty years. I took down a statement from him at his bedside, and reproduce here the brief notes I made at the time. 'I don't think 1984 is what will happen – but I do think, allowing for book being parody, that something like it could happen. World is growing in this direction at this moment – danger lies, not only in structure imposed on socialism by necessity to prepare for atomic war, etc. but also in acceptance of totalitarian outlook by intellectuals of all colours – moral is, don't *let it* happen. It depends on us – *why* Orwell assumes that if socialism came into being, there would be several superstates (à la Burnham) in opposition to each other, and pretend to be much more in opposition than they are. In that case, mortal enemy of Anglo-America would be Eurasia, and you don't take the name of your opponent. So call yourself *Ingsoc* and not *Communist* – after Labour party breaks down dealing with hard problems, if it does, tougher types will take over, drawn from ranks of present left, but not sharing its liberal aspirations – Attlee, Cripps, Bevan, O.K. – older men fairly safe, but young tough fiends abound.'

These are Orwell's *ipsissima verba*, as I summarized them in pencil on Cranham notepaper. On my return to London I dolled them up and sent them to the American newspapers, where, if Alistair Cooke is right – and he almost always is – they didn't do two pennorth of good.

We also discussed how best to follow up *1984*, since clearly Orwell must not work on a new book for twelve months minimum. Orwell had come round to the idea of a book of essays more miscellaneous than the earlier volume, *Critical Essays*, but he wanted two new essays to add to the 40,000 word collection already available. One of these was the piece on *George Gissing* which he had done for *Politics and Letters*. However at that time the piece had been lost, while the company was going into liquidation. The second was to be the *Joseph Conrad*, on which he had been working for some months. The new novel he had in mind was to be a novella of 30,000 words or so, with a Burmese background, a novel of character rather than ideas, so he said.

* * *

Such hopes as I had of Orwell's partial recovery were shattered by his letter to me of August 22, 1949. 'I have Morland coming to see me again this evening,' he wrote, 'on and off I've been feeling absolutely ghastly. It comes and goes, but I have periodic bouts of high temperatures.' Soon Morland informed us of the situation, and my wife begged him to take Orwell into his own University College Hospital without delay. Morland was undoubtedly a fine doctor, and apart from that it was bound to be warmer and less draughty in London than at Cranham. Morland promised to do his best – few people refuse Pamela anything she really wants. By September 3 Orwell was brought back to London by ambulance and installed in U.C.H.

In the same letter Orwell wrote 'As I warned you I might do, I intend getting married again (to Sonia) when I am once again in the land of the living, if ever I am. I suppose everyone will be horrified, but apart from other considerations I really think I should stay alive longer if I were married.' The news, as Orwell says, was no surprise to me. Earlier, Sonia had asked me for advice about the marriage, and I had pointed out some of the pros and cons. With me the feeling was strong that Orwell had a better chance of recovery with a woman he loved to help him. On October 3 they were married.

I saw Orwell a few times in U.C.H., but nothing significant took place. Clearly he was desperately ill. Early in the morning of January 21, 1950, Morland rang up and told us that Orwell was dead. The passionate pilgrim had come to the end of the road. One of the great masters of English prose was no more.

As I write this, it is by chance almost 21 years to the day since Orwell's death. My sadness at his passing has come of age, but it is still, and I think it will always be, a day of deep regret. For the young, he must be a writer of the past whom they are expected to study in their Eng. Lit. courses. The communist virus, against which he manufactured such powerful antibiotics, has become less virulent, at least in Britain. Communism itself has aged and become duller and less attractive. Yet Orwell's books will always be an indictment of those who are bent on the destruction of liberty, and their name is legion. Freedom of speech, of the press, freedom to publish books, to perform plays, to film, to paint pictures, to make sculpture, to compose and print music, all these are still in danger in most places in the world, including Britain and the U.S. In the years of revolutionary change, which must surely come during the next few decades, there will be as great a need as ever for the Orwellian courage and lucidity, and for the books of Orwell himself.

In this book I have tried to pay some of my own debt to Orwell by describing as accurately as I could the conditions under which he wrote his major books and how he faced them. As his publisher from 1937 onwards I perhaps know more about this than anyone else. To a future biographer, and there will inevitably be one,* I hope that at least some of what I have written may be of use.

*It is now announced that Bernard Crick has been offered and has accepted the important task of writing the authorized biography with access to all the papers. He has, it seems to me, a massive commonsense and a balanced outlook indispensable for the task. He should do it well. The book, I am pleased to say, will be published by Orwell's publisher, the house of Secker & Warburg.

8

The American Goldfields

Now I must go back a year or two in time to early 1947. That was when the nightmares began, the same one repeated. I'm in New York on a publishing trip, I've been there three or four weeks, but I've done nothing yet to carry out my task. Desperately, with only a day or two left, I pick up the 'phone, but I can't get through to a publisher or an agent or an author. In my dream I hurry, dashing about here and there. All in vain. The failure is absolute . . . I wake up in a state of anxiety, shouting.

It wasn't difficult to analyse this dream. Clearly I had a deep unconscious urge to return to New York, which I had not visited since 1934–5, just before I was expelled from the firm that had trained me. The 1934 trip had yielded me one author of importance, Lewis Mumford, who had come to me, when I set up my own firm, with a now famous book, *The Culture of Cities*.* Maybe I could find other remarkable authors in the American goldfields.

My wife encouraged me, even though it meant she would be left alone for six weeks, for she knew there would not be enough money to send both of us. I put the matter to my colleagues, estimating the costs at £500. Senhouse was opposed and Pattisson was lukewarm, but Farrer gave me enthusiastic backing. He'd been to New York with Beaverbrook and could visualize the possibilities. He knew also that we were too small to pay a director a decent salary or even to survive for long without growth and rapid growth at that. In September, 1947, after careful planning, I embarked for the goldfields, one of the earliest of the post-war prospectors.

New York in 1947 was a different city from what it has now become. It is not just that the cloud-capped towers on the southern

*Information about Lewis Mumford can be found in *An Occupation for Gentlemen*, pp. 137–9.

point of Manhattan Island are now more closely packed together. The atmosphere is transformed. In 1947 it was a confident city, rejoicing in a war they had won to become the undisputed masters of the world. The atom bomb was at their disposal, and they believed that they alone had the know-how to make it. Most of the world owed them money and would be grateful for Marshall Aid to keep the wolf from the door. The Soviet Union had far to go before they could recover from the hideous devastation of the German armies. There was as yet no Red China, no smog, not much mugging. The world was a good place then for the Americans, and New York was the greatest city in the world. They had no wars of importance to fight, Korea and the horrors of Vietnam lay far ahead. Even the age-old negro problem was, they believed, capable of a solution by means of a gradual evolution on liberal lines.

The S.S. *Mauretania* on which I sailed was a crack liner. On it a first class passenger was wrapped in luxury, overfed in a restaurant on food utterly unobtainable then in London, and cared for by a steward trained in the Jeevesian tradition. But, once installed in your hotel, the effort began. Hercules himself would surely have rated a publishing trip to New York among his twelve famous labours. Ideally, you needed the stamina of a long-distance runner, the diplomatic finesse of an ambasador, the capacity for drink of a Falstaff, some at least of the wisdom of Solomon, and of course an A to Z knowledge of the theory and practice of publishing which few publishers ever acquire. Certainly I had none of these qualities in full measure, but I was determined to have a go.

What did I hope for on that first trip? First, to buy one or two books to pay the expenses of the trip and leave a profit. Second, to spy out the land, collect information, and meet a number of American publishers I did not yet know. Third, to establish in the minds of American publishers and agents that my tiny firm, with its small and somewhat amateur staff, existing on a paper ration too ridiculous to mention, was in fact a powerful or potentially powerful house with an adequate present and a glorious future. Undoubtedly, the third objective was the most difficult to achieve, yet in it too I succeeded, because the Americans simply could not believe that the British publisher of Wells, Orwell, Mumford, Mann, Edmund Wilson and Kafka, could possibly be short of paper. Probably this was the first major confidence trick of my publishing life, though it was not the last. It was not even consciously intended or planned, for I'm a stupidly truthful man on the whole. But my American friends wanted to be deceived, wanted to think me a success, wanted to believe the firm was more important than in fact it was. All I had to do was to allow them to think what they wanted. I told no lies. It simply wasn't necessary.

The first appointment I had on this crucial first trip was with Ben Huebsch of the Viking Press, whom I'd known in London for many years. Huebsch had originally published under his own name, issuing some of the most advanced literary works of the early years of the century. He was, for instance, the first publisher of Joyce's *Ulysses* in the U.S. He belonged undoubtedly to the horse-and-buggy era of American publishing, a sort of one-man firm, writing his letters longhand, his own editor, production manager, and advertising executive, who actually went out into New York himself to sell copies of his new publications to the booksellers. Fortunately for him and for Viking, he allowed himself to merge with them in the early twenties, a loved and respected editor till retirement in his eighties, when it was said of him 'Huebsch is taking it easy now – he's stopped going to the office on Sundays.' Some years ago he died.

I entered his office, which was small, dingy, and spectacularly unimpressive, with some hope of success. Huebsch, of all New York publishers, seemed to me the most likely to offer me something worthwhile. Time passed, without my daring to put all to the test and ask bluntly what he had to offer me. Nervously I glanced at my watch, and Huebsch, noticing the gesture, picked up a book from a near-side table and handed it to me. My spirits rose.

The volume was clad in a royal-blue dust-jacket, on which in large white upper and lower case letters appeared the title *The Middle of the Journey*. Below this was a lozenge-shaped inset in yellow, depicting a quiet country road, some trees and a few houses. Below this were the words 'a novel by Lionel Trilling'. I looked at it blankly. The author's name meant little to me. 'A first novel,' Huebsch remarked, unemphatically, 'which I haven't read myself, but they tell me it's good. We're publishing it in three weeks' time.' A few minutes later I left him, with the book in my bag. I was far from excited. If Huebsch hadn't bothered to read it himself, how (I assumed) could it possibly be worth publishing? When I returned to my hotel that evening, I took *The Middle of the Journey* out of my bag and set it on a table. There it remained, unread, for nearly two weeks, overlaid by books, manuscripts, galley proofs, catalogues and miscellaneous litter. One morning I began to clear up the clutter in my room, and found *The Middle of the Journey*. Trilling's novel can't be worse, I thought, than the rubbish I've been offered so far. Brushing aside my melancholia, I sat down to read. All that morning I read, with greedy fascination, and again that evening. By 2 a.m. I had come to the final sentence: 'the creel would not fit on the rack with the bags, nor would the bowl, so he kept these on the seat beside him.' Not perhaps in themselves stirring words, but for me (when I came to them) the fitting conclusion of a masterpiece. 'At last,' I said to myself, 'a real book.'

The next day I still thought it magnificent. But slowly there came crowding into my mind those second thoughts so familiar to publishers – it can't possibly be as good as you think it is. Sternly I put the case against myself as a wishful-thinker. 'Do you really imagine that this, the first book to be given you by the first American publisher you have visited on your first visit to New York for your own firm could be worthwhile, let alone a masterpiece? As a publisher of twenty-five years standing, you can't be such a fool. Come off your high horse and admit that you're set on finding at least one book before you leave, and have promoted this one to a position it does not deserve. Remember that this book must have been read by at least half-a-dozen English publishers before you got round to it. They didn't think it worth buying, did they? Why should you?'

But I overcame my doubts and went to see Huebsch to make a deal. 'Trilling's novel is a masterpiece, Ben,' I said, 'of course I want to buy it.' Huebsch looked at me with some amusement. 'A clever technique of bargaining, Fred,' he replied, 'you think I'll sell it to you cheap just because you tell me it's a masterpiece.' Perhaps he was right. At any rate, I bought British rights from Viking for an advance of $500 on account of a 12½% royalty.

* * *

What were the qualities in this novel that had so excited me? I tried to discover them when I wrote the blurb, perhaps the most difficult blurb I ever had to compose. 'Under the hot sun of a New England summer,' I wrote, 'Laskell . . . is recuperating from a severe illness . . . shaken in body and uncertain in mind. The time is the latter part of the 1930's, before the conflict of faiths had blazed into war and the cold clash of ideas which envenoms civilization to-day. . . . Laskell, in his middle thirties, is set among old friends from the city and new acquaintances of the village. We meet Nancy and Arthur Croom, ardent young radicals whose belief in human progress is unbounded.

There is Kermit Simpson, wealthy and ineffective, who longs for all to be as comfortable as he is. There is Emily Caldwell, strong in her femininity, the wife of . . . the local handyman, drunken, lecherous, and knowing. And their young daughter Susan, whose end is tragic. Above all there is Gifford Maxim, brilliant dialectician and secret agent of the Communist Party, whose break with the party provides the starting point for the drama which follows.

'. . . From the beginning it is clear what is at stake, nothing less than the soul (or the sanity) of Laskell himself. But it is by no means clear whence come the threats, who are his antagonists and who his enemies, until the author has led us deep into the labyrinths of the human psyche.

'For this is a novel of detection, in which the reader must discover for himself which of the author's characters are guilty, and why they are guilty, and above all what it is they are guilty of. And the search is more exciting for those who can grasp its full implications . . . because on its success rests the hope of safety for those now living in a threatened civilization. . . .'

The Middle of a Journey was published on October 14, 1948, a year or more before Whittaker Chambers, an ex-communist, accused Alger Hiss of turning over confidential State Department documents to the Soviet Union. Two trials followed. In the end Hiss was convicted of perjury, though many doubted, and still doubt, his guilt. A feature of the trials was the possibility or otherwise of secret papers being concealed in a pumpkin. Obviously there were parallels between fiction and fact.

Recently I wrote Trilling to inquire whether he had any personal acquaintance with the two antagonists, and his reply of May 22, 1972 is full of interest, particularly as illuminating the way in which novelists make use of the material in their own lives. 'I did not mean to write a novel at all, only a long short story. . . . But it seemed to need something else, and in response to that need Gifford Maxim, which is to say Whittaker Chambers, presented himself, together with such political explicitness as he brought, which had to be considerable, for he was the most political man I knew. It was he who gave the novel such largeness of reference as it has and made it as long as it is.

'I had had some acquaintance with Chambers at college. . . . He was at an early age a very commanding person, and a first-rate poet. . . . In the very early thirties he was a figure of some importance in the Communist Party, to which for a time Diana and I were drawn.

In 1930 or 1931, he "went underground". Among those who knew him, it was thought that he was doing espionage work for army installations. If so, he was the most manifest spy that ever slunk around a corner; he seemed to make a point of looking clandestine and sinister and he solicited his bourgeois friends to act as mail drops. He tried to recruit Diana, but she refused. His connections . . . were with the Russian apparatus, rather than with the American party. . . . Around 1934 or 1935, he became disaffected . . . and "broke". In his attempts to "establish an identity", which the novel makes much of, he turned to his old friends, who believed . . . that he was in mortal danger.

'The novel's representation of Chambers is . . . pretty literal. Naturally, when the Hiss case broke . . . the novel was thought to bear upon it. I had no acquaintance with Alger and Priscilla Hiss . . . but Arthur and Nancy Croom, whom I drew from a couple I did know, seemed to be sufficiently like the Hisses in temperament and political disposition to make it appear that I knew all about the Chambers-Hiss relationship. . . .'

It is over 25 years since Trilling wrote *The Middle of the Journey*, but he has not yet written a successor, though he still hopes to do so. He has had instead a brilliant academic career in literature at the University of Columbia, New York. We have published most of his work since then, as Viking Press has in the U.S., starting with the influential *The Liberal Imagination* in 1951. It is, of course, a sad blow to a publisher when a brilliant first novel has no successor, but it is not uncommon. A main theme of Trilling's has been the conflict between the moral and the sensual, the ego and the id, and this figures prominently in *The Middle of the Journey*, where the sane, civilized and sceptical Laskell is swept into a sexual episode with a married woman, Emily Caldwell. But Laskell is not swayed by political emotions into a blind anti-communism by the ravings of Gifford Maxim nor into the sneaking fellow-travelling of the Crooms, who might have been modelled, but were not, on the Hisses. Laskell is a man in equilibrium, who considers the agonizing problems of his life from one point of view and then from its opposite, making his decision on each problem separately, and only when the time for a decision can no longer be delayed. It is Trilling's concept of equilibrium which I found important when I first read his novel. I find it important still today. It is this which, in my opinion, makes *The Middle of the Journey* a major post-war novel by an American.

* * *

It was a major American critic, already our author, who recommended to me John Horne Burns' first novel, *The Gallery*, published by Harper six months earlier. Why such an extraordinary work had not been bought already by a British publisher seemed to me incomprehensible. Such an omission could hardly be possible today. *The Gallery* is the Galleria Umberto in Naples, an arcade of shops, bars and less reputable places where Italian lives had got mixed up with those of American (and British) soldiers. Here came every conceivable type of person, in search of drink, conversation, women, the black market, or merely passing through. The book consists of a series of stories and episodes recreating the passions and crudities boiling up in this wartime cauldron, based on the writer's own experiences as he moved from Casablanca to Fedhala to Algiers and finally to Naples for the last half of the book. We published it on September 7, 1948, and it received an enthusiastic reception. The *Times Literary Supplement* wrote 'he recreated some facets of the life moving through the Galleria . . . bar-keepers, G.I.'s, tarts, queers, W.A.C.'s . . . examined with a compassion and an understanding that amuse, excite and move with a dexterous versatility . . . a book of the highest promise.' The *Evening Standard* wrote 'almost every page quivers with the sense of unbearable outrage . . . a raw remarkable novel.' Such reviews set the literary world ablaze, sales soared, the first edition (2,870 copies) and the second edition (2,850 copies) were gone in a flash. Then, due to the lack of paper, the book went out of stock at the moment of maximum demand. It was a tragedy. Nevertheless, we went on to sell around 11,000 copies within five years.

No doubt, this 'sense of unbearable outrage' led to the change Horne Burns referred to in his statement, 'when I went to Italy in 1944, I experienced an annihilation of myself – and a re-birth.' Its nature is indicated in *The Gallery*'s first portrait, 'The Trenchfoot of Michael Patrick'. On page 16 he writes 'What was there here in the sweetness of this reality that he'd missed out on in America? He'd opened a door into a world that had nothing to do with merchandising and selling, with the trapped four-four beat of boogie-woogie, with naked girls shaking their navels through cigar smoke on a runway, with nervous old ladies totting up their insurance, with the fact that he wouldn't live to be twenty-eight, with the smell of a world like a slaughterhouse, with groping and misunderstanding and cruelty. He felt himself inundated with the loveliness that men seek in a woman's arms, that old nuns sense on their deathbeds. He saw for the first time in his life that the things which keep the world going are not to be bought or sold, that every flower grows out of decay, that for all the mud and grief there are precious things which make it worth while for us to leave our mothers' wombs. . . .'

On October 30, 1949, we published his second novel, *Lucifer With A Book*. This was the story of a young man and a young woman, both veterans of the war, idealists with a passion for teaching, arriving at a swank 'private' school. Here their fight against the prejudices, snobberies, materialism, vice, and growing militarization which infect the Abercrombie Academy (coeducational) is the dominant theme. Once again the two veterans of the system struggle in vain and are crushed. It was Horne Burns 'rebirth' which enabled him to protest, first against the curruption of society in the U.S., then against the American school system. It was his passionate hatred of American society in almost all its aspects that disturbed and ultimately destroyed the admiration for him among his own countrymen, and especially the critics. This clairvoyant foresaw too much for his own good, and reported on what he saw with an outspoken or even an outrageous abandon that was unbearable.

Lucifer had a less than enthusiastic press in the U.S. In the U.K. C. P. Snow in the *Sunday Times* wrote 'His first book was bubbling with gusto. So is *Lucifer*.' The *New Statesman* described it as 'brilliantly funny and acutely, even poetically, perceptive'. But the sales were a disappointment after *The Gallery*, the subject was rather too far away to interest British readers.

To help publicize *Lucifer* Horne Burns came to London and we gave him a party. He arrived early, as we had asked him, but long before the guests were due he was begging to be allowed to leave. A strange and overpowering shyness possessed him, but he stayed to the end because he was a man of his word and scrupulously polite. It was probably in 1951 in Boston that I saw him next, when he asked me to breakfast. With him was a young man and a flat-chested girl he introduced to me as his fiancée. This was a surprise, as I had assumed until then that he was exclusively homosexual.

His third and last book, *A Cry of Children*, was published on October 10, 1952. It was a novel which dealt with a limited number of characters in its analysis of a love affair which lasted not very long, but went very deep, a tale of sacred and profane love. Murray, concert pianist and composer, Catholic by upbringing, studious, ambitious and a bit of a prig, meets Isobel, a girl with a sordid past, lovely, greedy, sensual and shrewd, with the shrewdness of those who have had always to fend for themselves. They live together in a small apartment built in the shadow of a church, against a background of industrial squalor. Symbolically, the church and the factory are juxtaposed, the life of the spirit against the crude urgencies of life under the military–industrial complex. In this cramped space the couple fight the primeval campaign of sex and affection, wealth and poverty, oppositions that can make or destroy one or both of the antagonists.

The reviews of *The Cry of Children* appears to be lost or at least mislaid, but Farrer, who was Horne Burns' editor, remembers that it 'must hold the record for being the most savagely and *unfairly* criticized novel of the century.' The statement may be regarded as exaggerated, and the sales were far from negligible (5,000 copies), yet it does make clear that there was a powerful irritant in Horne Burns' works which turned the critics against him. Light is thrown on such matters in a substantial piece by Brigid Brophy in the *Sunday Times Magazine* of 1963, the only sustained critique of Horne Burns so far to appear and one to which I am greatly indebted. Miss Brophy records as her 'very serious opinion' that he 'was by far the most talented, and the most *attractively* talented, American novelist to emerge since the war.' She concludes her pioneering essay with the words 'May he be not one whose name was writ in water.'

This prayer is one which I echo. To ensure, so far as I can, its fulfilment, I have recorded in what follows some of the more important exchanges that took place between the writer and his English publisher, hoping that they may be of use to some future biographer. For there is as yet no critical study or biography of this strange, secretive, handsome, vigorous, shy, sensual, puritanical, jesting character, an accomplished pianist with a fine tenor voice, and this is a major scandal in the sphere of American letters which should be put right while those who knew him still live to remember. It was no mean critic who so strongly recommended *The Gallery* to me during my 1947 trip. It was Edmund Wilson himself.

* * *

The first letter from Horne Burns to me that survives is dated October 31, 1951. It is written from Villa La Bicocca, Carbignane, Firenze, Italy. There he lived till his death in the autumn of 1953. The correspondence, which is intermittent, deals mainly with *The Cry of Children* and with a completed novel, never published, originally titled *Maiden Voyage*, but later changed to *The Stranger's Guise*. The first letter is gay and lively, and is written by hand, as many of the later letters are. 'It's most appropriate that I should write you for the feast of All Hallows,' he begins, 'a frightful phrase for me, a Roman Catholic. Shortly I'm sending Miss Helen Strauss [his agent] my third novel, *A Cry of Children*, which has cost me so much blood these last two years. She seems a bit unhappy that I choose to stay in Tuscany indefinitely – I've taken a house here, and I'm very happy. As the last of the romantics, I find everything in Tuscany – good cooking, a kitten, a collie, and the love that I need. Everybody in this tiny village is Communist, and they treat me marvellously. I haven't much desire to return to the United States, which may be a sign of supreme weakness in my character. At any rate I live sumptuously on $45 a week. I hope you'll like *A Cry of Children*. It seems to have a depth and a sweetness I never dreamed myself capable of.'

This letter was completely unexpected by me, coming (I would suppose) after a long interval of silence. Of course it delighted me since, as I wrote him on November 7, 1951, 'I cannot offhand think of any novel coming to us in the next twelve months that I am more anxious to read.' This was not publisher's gush, but sincere, for then as now I regarded his work, flawed though it was sometimes with sentimentality, as that of a major novelist.

The same letter continued 'I should not dream of criticizing your stay in Tuscany, especially as you find everything there that you need. But you are a novelist, and if living there means no novels, I am against it, not only because we would not have the pleasure and (I hope) the profit of publishing them, but also because you would be frustrated and feel, sooner or later, that you had wasted your life. . . . That you do not wish to return to the U.S. is neither here nor there; for some things the U.S. of A. is just dandy and for other things it must be pure hell. I do think you should go back from time to time and sniff the air of modern capitalism, if only because you are living in a Communist community.'

It was three months before the typescript was sent to his agent, who 'responded with an airmail letter of such superlatives that I feel moved to mail you the carbon copy this very evening,' he wrote. Within 48 hours, on February 21, 1952, I read it and wrote him that it was 'a moving and powerful and at times extremely funny novel . . . the Catholic influence is very strong and this I like. Superlatives are justified.' By the end of March terms had been agreed with the agents and on April 24 I wrote Horne Burns 'How much I enjoyed reading it. . . . It is more like the usual conception of a novel than your two previous books and shows you treating character in a straightforward way rather than with the irony or satire of *Lucifer.* . . .' On April 28 Horne Burns answered 'I received a tantalizing letter from you, hinting of two enclosures 1) your own blurb 2) a reproduction of the jacket, but neither was enclosed; so I concluded that your secretary was dreaming of bank holidays and Brighton.' He went on to thank me for a copy of Dino Buzzati's novel, *The Tartar Steppe*, which he had recommended to me for translation a year or two back in Milan where he had met the author. 'I gushed at him,' Horne Burns wrote, 'for an Italian he has a strange closed character and, since I'm not a great talker, communication between us was virtually impossible. He loves skiing and La Scala – the second a passion I share.' Later in the letter he goes on 'Maybe I'm becoming too Latin in my tastes – fatal for an American novelist. My love affair with this country goes on and on. Why is it only here I feel a sense of life as it is and might be, even though I recognize all the defects of Italians and their government? E. M. Forster felt it 50 years ago. (He was here the other day, but I didn't go and pay court.)'

Reading his letters then, full of humour, exuberance, and interest in all around him, I had no forewarning that he was little more than a year away from disaster. He did, however, have many problems, because owing to a series of muddles on the part of his American agent or publisher, the cheques he was expecting had not arrived. 'If I don't get a check by the end of the week,' he wrote, 'I'm thinking of selling my 35-year-old body to rich American doxies who pass through here.' But before the end of May he told me he had at last received 'a generous disbursement of advance'. He had also read some Katherine Mansfield short stories in Italian, and remarks 'Jesus, she makes me look pretty cheap. I don't think I'll ever write again, though I've promised Helen [Strauss] the Fourth Novel for Christmas.' To this I replied, 'I would never have thought that her short stories would have made you feel so cheap as a writer. I think you need a tonic.'

A tonic perhaps was what Horne Burns needed. With *The Gallery* he had shot up into the literary firmament like a rocket. *Lucifer* had shown a slow-down in the dizzy ascent. Now clearly he was worried about the reception of *Cry*, he refers to 'pre-publication jim-jams', and had already seen 'a depressing and superficial review of it from the U.S. I suspect that Harper was rather less than enthusiastic about it.' There is nothing an author senses more swiftly than a lukewarm attitude of his publishers. Fortunately I had written him on August 26 a strong letter of support 'I read it in proof with even greater admiration . . . this really is a powerful novel, likely to appeal equally to men and women . . . I am very optimistic about its sales possibilities, etc.' In a final paragraph I concluded 'I realize more clearly than ever before how strong a hold the Catholic doctrine has upon you, and how fundamental is your detestation for industrial civilization. This makes it perfectly clear why you find in Italy a home which home itself does not provide. All the same, you should go back for a refresher course, even if only to stock up your hatred of towns like B [Boston].' Yet it must be remembered that, in spite of his anxieties, he had almost completed his fourth novel before his third had appeared. Horne Burns seemed to be borne along on the full flood of creativity.

On November 14 I wrote him what I hoped might be a cry of reassurance. 'Don't take this too tragically,' I told him, referring to the hostile press for *Cry*, and he replied 'Thanks for your letter, which reads like a rich uncle trying to console his nephew being flunked in third year Latin. I'm not taking it at all tragically, I'm finishing my fourth novel, *Maiden Voyage*, which I hope will silence the critics for a spell, until I give birth to the fifth. I begin work at four o'clock every afternoon. Around about three I begin to get nervous (when I write I experience agonies that only the damned could conceive) even though I've thought it all out in advance, and strange changes happen when I sit down before this damnable Italian "writing machine". So I play with my shepherd dog or my white kitten, but that doesn't really help at all, and at four I go to the slaughter.' What writer has not experienced these tortures! However, in spite of all, Horne Burns believed he had 'never written a novel with such love and calm. Walking through these huge cold rooms, I often weep stertorously, and think I'm already mad, or that a writer is too romantic or too neurotic, and ought to be suppressed.' Yet he is firm in the belief that his book has 'an equilibrium I never before possessed.'

On February 23, 1953, Horne Burns informed me that he had finished. The novel had changed its title, without warning to me. It was now called *The Stranger's Guise*. 'The chosen few – what a phrase! – who have read it' he wrote 'say that it has something I never had before. But that's what comes of living in Italy and writing about Her . . . it's no rewrite of *The Gallery*. When I start copying myself, I'll raise pigeons and train dogs.'

Yet it was not (I think) till April or May that he sent 'a piddling one-third of the novel' to me, and goes on 'I've worked so hard on the fuckin thing that I no longer trust the judgments of my Italian friends, who are too kind. . . . The white cat has had three kittens, two of which have been destroyed; the dog, Lucky, is in a dubious state. This is the House of Sex,' to which I replied by return 'I wait for the arrival of the second third. . . . You say yours is the House of Sex, but you give the impression that it is a Slaughter House.' The remark was intended as a joke, and was certainly in poor taste. Yet within little more than three months this lovable man was dead. What had happened?

There were rumours – too much drink, too much sexual indulgence, sunstroke, pneumonia, the loss of a loved one. Yet a man so full of life as Johnny rarely dies of a broken heart. Was he in fact in despair about his work, for *The Stranger's Guise* was criticized severely and rejected by Harper? But we did not reject it, though we criticized it, but the criticism was constructive.

On June 26 Horne Burns wrote me 'I almost believe the long agony of this winter hasn't been in vain.' His agent wanted a carbon copy of the MS to sell to magazines. 'Naturally I'll mail her one, for I love money – or at least the good things it buys.' There is no thought of death here. 'Would you like a puppy by air freight? Lucky presented me with fifteen in nine hours of labor. This is the house of fertility.' On June 14 Farrer wrote Horne Burns a three-page letter of criticism. It was warm, polite, frank, detailed and everywhere constructive. 'It contains the best things you have ever written . . . it also contains the worst. I get the impression that in parts of it neither your mind nor your emotions were really engaged. . . . But once you have tackled it, you will have produced a book that is immensely worthwhile.'

To this criticism on July 17 Horne Burns thanked Farrer 'and the house for taking the trouble you have. Perhaps I'm getting older, for I find the report 98% just in its findings. . . . I know now precisely what must be done. . . . I can't afford another scalping. . . . No, your remarks were not harsh. I prefer to be brought up short by my editors than by the critics and the public.' This was the last letter from Horne Burns that we received. Within weeks he was dead. Rupture of a blood vessel in the brain had killed him. He was buried in his beloved Florence, though later the body was exhumed and reburied in the family plot in Brookline, Mass.

What happened to this novel after the death? Was it destroyed or does it still somewhere exist in typescript, wholly or partly corrected? If it has been destroyed, I would regard it as something of a calamity. For in my opinion the novel even unrevised had so much that was good in it that it could and should have been published posthumously. I'm sure that Farrer would agree with me. Horne Burns was a major writer, despite the American critics who treated him so scurvily. I want to read again John Horne Burns's novel, *The Stranger's Guise*. It marked a further stage in his development, a transformation.*

Many trips to the U.S. followed the one of 1947, and few of them yielded a harvest of less than six titles. But in 1966 I made my twelfth and last. I was almost twenty years older, and I had found them exhausting. Besides this, there was the transformation in the atmosphere, not only the air pollution or the growing violence in Harlem and elsewhere, but in the social and political climate Conversation with American friends could become embarrassing, though the hospitality, consideration and politeness remained unimpaired. There was the problem of the blacks, which was the problem of the whites. There was the everlasting Cold War, which in the days of Senator McCarthy affected the morale of many of my authors. Above all by 1966 was the growing menace of the war in Vietnam. Yet there were few, even as late as 1966, who doubted the possibility of victory or believed that the expenses of the war could damage the social or political or financial health of the U.S. A shrewd and knowledgeable friend, a lecturer at the Massachusetts Institute of Technology, said to me when I questioned him – 'America is a very wealthy country, and there can be no doubt that she can afford a big war in Vietnam *and* a constant improvement in our social well-being.' But he was wrong.

Perhaps my reluctance to return – it was never a final decision – sprang from a conversation at a dinner party in Boston given in honour of my wife and myself. After the meal, feeling relaxed and somewhat mischievous, as may happen when you are meeting people ten times wealthier than yourself, I said to a number of men, all Americans, sitting by me 'it's funny when you look round the world at the five major powers – there's the Soviet Union, terrified of an attack from China in the east and from the Nato powers in the west – there's my own country going slowly and imperturbably into bankruptcy – and there's your own great country with a negro

*This typescript does exist, and I am hoping to be permitted to read it soon.

problem you can't solve and a war in Vietnam you can't win.' This remark was tactless enough, but I made matters worse with my concluding sentence 'only France and China are sitting pretty.' Since at that time General de Gaulle was probably the most unpopular foreign statesman in America, and China was regarded as a sinister and aggressive power liable to join with the U.S.S.R., overrun 'civilization' and destroy the American way of life, this was adding insult to injury. My listeners remained fairly calm, but the son of a famous American ambassador to South Vietnam, Henry Cabot Lodge, decided that I could not be allowed to get away with such offensive rubbish. With chilly politeness he lectured me at length about the rightness of the Vietnam War, ending up with the words which have haunted me ever since – 'I think you will agree with me, Mr. Warburg, that America does not need a military victory in South Vietnam, but she must be seen to have prevailed.' Was not that sentence what Americans call 'gobbledegook'? That depends on the meaning of the words 'military' and 'prevailed'. In any case, Mr. Lodge's remarks depressed me unutterably.

9
A Deal with Heinemann

IN the spring of 1951 I had gone on my third American trip. I bought James Agee's short novel, *The Morning Watch*, on the advice of James Stern, who knew him well. Foolishly it was the only one of his handful of books I ever published. I bought Eric Hoffer's book of aphorisms, *The True Believer*. Hoffer was a longshoreman of San Francisco, whose book dealt with the awful dangers of fanaticism. In the U.S. it did well, in part because a photograph of President Eisenhower was published in the press carrying it under his arm with the title showing. Eisenhower was known to have admired it, but in the U.K. it fell flat and its sales are too trivial to record, yet it is a book I am pleased to have published. But, in commercial significance, there was only one book in it, James Michener's *Return to Paradise*.*

It was just as well that I came back to London with this hidden but unrecognized treasure in my possession to help us through the difficult years ahead, for I was met on the platform of Waterloo Station with dread tidings. Secker & Warburg was running out of money. This was not due so much to trading losses, although the wartime boom in sales was over, as to the post-war inflation. Despite the substantial capital Farrer had introduced to the firm, and £1,500 put up by Pattisson, the rising costs of paper, printing, binding and the rest ate up the money available, and ate it up all the faster since the number of titles published each year was increasing steadily. We had plugged the capital gap by borrowing a high percentage of our book debts,† but the news I now received was that this borrowing

*Discussed in Chapter 10.

†Booksellers pay publishers for books with an average credit of two months in the U.K. and six months overseas. It can be assumed that roughly one third of a publisher's annual turnover is permanently locked up in debts owed by booksellers, a sum of approximately £15,000 or more at this stage in our career.

device had to be phased out over a period of months. Inevitably we were bound to run out of cash before long. Since none of the four directors were able to risk more of their own money – it is doubtful in fact whether any of them had any more to risk – we had to look elsewhere. But where?

In those days as now new publishing houses were normally financed by the optimistic men who fancied their chances. Often enough they were outcasts or voluntary exiles from established firms, as I was, who can no longer tolerate what they regard as the old-fashioned, penny-pinching, ultra-conservative behaviour of their elderly bosses. But when a young firm comes unstuck and has no wish to take in new untrained partners who will inevitably want to rule the roost, if only to protect their money, the field is narrow, normally a printing house or a binder (to secure printing or binding contracts in what was a highly competitive world) or a papermaker (to sell his paper) or a larger publisher with capital to spare who wishes to be associated with, or control, or conceivably suppress, a potentially dangerous rival. My own view was that we had less than two months to solve our problem. Senhouse was more optimistic or pretended to be. Indeed, with the ominous figures right in front of his nose, he denied that there was any serious crisis at all. Further, he contrived to give the impression that, if by some unlucky chance a crisis should arise, he knew places where he could collect many thousands of pounds when we really needed it, though whether from friends in the City, from one of the notables of his home county of Cumberland, or from relations never quite became clear. Senhouse played the rôle of Micawber expecting something to turn up with such conviction that we were almost deceived by him.

The best concrete suggestion came from Farrer, who remarked 'Frere told me when I joined the firm that if ever I had a publishing problem, I should consult him first.' No one in the book trade for more than a week could have failed to know who A. S. Frere was. Short, dark-haired, sun-tanned in appearance, with a fine aquiline nose, he seemed to radiate determination and power. I had met him a few times at publishing affairs, but scarcely knew him personally. But as head of the great publishing house of William Heinemann, he was a sort of emperor of the trade, with a business ten or twenty times as big as mine, and a list of authors of the utmost distinction, among them Graham Greene, J. B. Priestley, D. H. Lawrence and Somerset Maugham.

But this sensible suggestion was vigorously opposed by Senhouse, who clearly had a dislike or at least a distrust of Frere. Instead, we began to search in other quarters without making any real progress. Soon it became apparent that Heinemann was not only the most desirable but probably the only port in the storm. Ignoring Senhouse's opposition, I asked Farrer to see Frere urgently. Senhouse, unable to stay in London to face the music, sad, angry, and desperate, went on holiday. He did not return till after the crisis was over. Perhaps there was nothing else he could do. Since his colleagues were pursuing a course that he regarded as fatal, he wanted to have no part in it. Yet from a French seaside resort he sent us a stream of postcards, letters and cables. 'There isn't a night that I don't think of you and your worries,' he wrote, 'but once at a distance I cannot do more than concentrate my moral assistance as a force which is positive. . . . Of course, I would not have gone, had I foreseen a breakdown. . . .' But he did not return. If only he had not assured us so strongly before he left that he could at a few days notice find enough cash to solve our crisis, at least temporarily. When we put his assurance to the test, we discovered to our horror that it was worthless.

'Talk to Frere,' I said to Farrer, 'and do it soon.' So Farrer talked to Frere, probably at the Garrick Club, that centre of cabals and conspiracies, of which they were both members, and received a dusty answer. The shock of Frere's rejection and the realization that Senhouse's promises were nothing but hot air, led Farrer to the verge of collapse.

Inexorably our situation worsened. Every week I sat at my desk with a list of creditors and the amounts due to them. The extent of our bank balance was obviously known to me. It was normally rather less than half what was required to keep the creditors happy. Like a juggler with a dozen balls to keep in the air at once, I strove valiantly, but one day soon I knew there must be a failure. If one ball fell to the ground, if one creditor sued, the other eleven – much as they might have liked or admired us – would promptly have issued their writs.

Soon my anxiety became unbearable, and a new thought occurred to me. Had Farrer, I wondered, put our case to Frere with sufficient power, outlined our latent possibilities, emphasized the prestige of the imprint. Perhaps he had, perhaps not. After all he'd been with me only four years, his total publishing experience. It was I who had founded and fathered the firm. Perhaps I had the knowledge and could find the eloquence to convince the sceptical Frere that we were worth backing. I rang up Dwye Evans.

Evans, a senior director and editor of Heinemann, was in his forties, the son of C. S. (Charlie) Evans, who had been the head of Heinemann before Frere, and had died in 1944. He had been a brilliant picker of new talent in the thirties. With his son I was on good terms. When I told him of our plight and asked him whether he would introduce me to Frere, he agreed immediately, and a day was fixed. It was probably in June 1951 that this, in publishing history, momentous meeting took place, momentous because our deal with Heinemann set a pattern which was followed, for better or worse, many times in the years ahead.

Evans took me to the first floor of the Heinemann offices in Great Russell Street, where Frere had his inner sanctum, and led me in. I was, naturally, nervous, as I realized all too clearly that, if I failed with Frere, there might be a sudden, sickening and messy end to all my hopes. I shook hands with Frere and sat down in the low armchair at the side of his desk. From it I looked up at Frere, seated in majesty. I felt like a supplicant before the great king as I waited for him to speak.

But Frere did not speak, he looked at me coolly. It is suppliants who must speak, state their case, and beg for mercy. I had not prepared a first sentence, indeed I had not prepared my case in detail, trusting to my knowledge of the facts to make my points spontaneously. I opened my mouth, and the words came out loud and clear, 'I come to see you, Frere, in two capacities – first, as the man who presides over an insolvent firm, second as the head of the most distinguished young publishing house in London.' Frere smiled, not broadly but slightly and sardonically. He was himself an outspoken man, too outspoken for his own good, he often said. Probably he appreciated my opening words, for I had certainly laid the gist of my case before him in one medium-length sentence.

This first sentence I remember accurately, even though I spoke it over twenty years ago. But what followed I do not remember, except that Frere agreed in principle to assist us with money, technical help and advice. But first I had to appear, for cross-examination as it were, before the whole Heinemann Board, for which purpose I had to travel down to Kingswood, Surrey on the following Wednesday.

Accompanied by Farrer, down I went to Kingswood, and came to the great double block of mellow red brick, neo-Georgian offices, designed and built for Heinemann by Gerald Wellesley, later the Duke of Wellington, in 1927. They stood like some Whig landowner's residence or even a palace for a small nation's royalty, with magnificent rosebeds and a fine herbaceous border. Playing fields and woodlands surrounded this publishing fortress, which would have impressed even an important visiting publisher. On me the effect was tremendous.

Farrer and I entered the Kingswood boardroom, about forty feet long and fifteen feet wide, with windows all along its length. At an enormous long table sat the Heinemann Board, with Frere at its head. On Frere's left sat H. L. Hall, the finance director who was Frere's closest confidant. I was seated on Frere's right. Including Farrer, who sat more or less opposite me, there were present Dwye Evans, Louisa Callender (an editorial chief), B. F. Oliver (in charge of the Windmill Press, which printed for and belonged to Heinemann) and one or two others. I felt like a heretic on trial before a court of the Inquisition, and the analogy is not too far-fetched, for – though I did not fully realize it on that day – I did hold views on publishing which those present at the meeting might have regarded as heretical, had I voiced them clearly.

For nearly two hours questions were hurled at me from all sides. Most of them came, not unnaturally, from Hall, the finance man. He had no wish for a recapitalized Secker & Warburg to go bankrupt on him after a dismal year or two. But actually the questions were somewhat superficial. Question: Why don't you publish novels which sell better and make you a real profit? Answer: We would if we could. But since we're not able to pay big advances, like Heinemann, and haven't a powerful selling organization, like Heinemann, we have to take the best of what we can get. But some questions went deeper. Question: Why are your overheads so high? Answer: We can't get them down; none of the directors are paid enough to live on; our only hope is to increase the turnover without a corresponding increase in the overheads. This was the best answer I could discover at short notice, but the question was not really answered and remained deadly. Soon I began to get ruffled and a trifle angry, but apparently I did not show it, for Farrer wrote to Senhouse the next day 'the atmosphere grew more friendly and cordial as the meeting proceeded. ... Heinemann made no effort to get better terms than we offered.... Above all I have been impressed by the palpable goodwill shown to us by all the Heinemann directors. Fred has certainly made a hit with Frere.' In my own view it was with Hall (always addressed as H.) that I made my hit that day. Before the meeting, after Frere had told him what his plan for us was, H. must have been worried. He had, as a financial animal, the greatest mistrust of small publishers who issued books they fancied and hoped for the best, with disastrous results. Apparently he did not believe that I belonged in this category. Months later, when he came to our office with his confidential secretary-assistant Mrs. Edna Mercer, to examine the account books, they came into my room after doing the job and announced in a tone of such astonishment that I can hear it in my mind's ear to this day, 'really, you've kept the books quite well. I've looked at dozens of small publishers' accounts in my time, but never a nice set of books like yours.' Between H. and myself a high degree of mutual confidence prevailed right up to his retirement in the early sixties.

It would be tedious to explore in detail the terms of the Heinemann deal. Briefly, in return for their investment, they received a preference dividend, as did David Holt, our young sales manager, who also put up money, and thereafter the profits (if any) were to be divided in a proportion which my colleagues and I with our legal advisers regarded not merely as fair but as generous to us. Of course, the Heinemann directors (Frere and Hall) had a majority of votes on the board, and could do (almost) anything they liked with us, but – and this surely is the root of the matter – they trusted me as executive head of the firm to do my best, while listening carefully to financial and other advice when offered, while I trusted them not to abuse their position of power. It was central to the agreement that we should have complete editorial freedom to select the books we wished to publish without consulting Heinemann, provided (at first) that the advance did not exceed £300. It was typical of the negotiations that no mention of this was incorporated in any binding form. Both sides remained satisfied through the years. But, as I realize now, it might so easily have turned out differently.

The essence of the arrangement between Heinemann and ourselves was the division of duties. Heinemann took over the responsibility for finance, not only by the purchase of shares, but by the guarantee of an overdraft which grew through the years to £100,000 and over. They took over accountancy and the collection of debts. They took over distribution to booksellers and other customers, one of the most complex and expensive overheads in publishing. Finally, they took over the travelling of our books throughout the U.K. and Ireland, except in London where our own able and likeable rep, C. R. Roth, continued to charm the booksellers. Also, they sold for us overseas, where a vital 40% or more of a publisher's turnover is located.* They took over in fact what makes a publishing house a *business*. In this respect, one publisher does not differ from another in kind, but only in efficiency.

What was left for Secker & Warburg to do? Everything that was individualist or personal, all those matters which caused me to give my first volume the title *An Occupation For Gentlemen*. They included the finding and selection of books to publish (a problem of taste and judgment); the establishment and maintenance of friendship or trust with the authors (a problem in the psychology of human relations); the construction of a list with a coherent and therefore recognizable flavour, which will attract new and suitable writers to publish with you rather than with another firm (a problem involving literary, social, political or other flairs); the finding of types of production, distinguished and suitable for the type of list in question (a problem of aesthetics); the planning of methods of promotion appropriate for the list. Such abilities cannot normally be found among business men, though there are naturally exceptions, because the business man is concerned with problems of a different character, his aim is profit and growth. The publisher's aim is quality, and growth is a secondary consideration. The problem of group publishing is the harmonization of profit and quality, and this is not an easy task.

Heinemann's experiment in group publishing with Secker & Warburg worked, and worked well, though it was not to work with another, most distinguished, publisher who joined the group a few years after we did. Why did it work so well? I think because Frere and I understood, not so much each other, as the true nature of the situation in which we were mutually involved. On April 23, 1952 I wrote Frere, telling him he and H. had just been elected to the Secker & Warburg board, adding 'there is no doubt in my mind that we will be immeasurably strengthened by the presence on it of two of the acutest minds and strongest personalities in the publishing world.' The next day Frere replied 'something more than conventional thanks for your letter. Publishing has a mystique of its own, and the lean and bleak economic facts have little to do with the worth and integrity of an imprint. We may, or may not, be able to improve "the banker's eye view" of it, but we are happy to be associated with your imprint and, in maintaining it, you may be assured of nothing but sympathetic co-operation from us.' This is the letter of a publisher before all else. It is also the letter of a man who proposes to run his

*Later, we travelled our own list throughout the U.K. and Eire.

group, not as an empire but as head or prime minister of the most powerful publishing house in a commonwealth of publishers. Frere was as good as his word. I had nothing but minor clashes with him for many years, and when the big clash came it was not over an internal but an external group affair.

It was, of course, the relationship between Frere and myself which led to our growth and success. Yet this relationship was not based on a close friendship or a clear understanding of each others' personalities – no two men could have been more different. It was based on agreement about the way in which a publishing group should function, and on the fact that I knew my job as a publisher, as a Secker & Warburg type publisher, well enough to do it at the least adequately.

The reason perhaps why two such unlike personalities as Frere and myself could and did see eye-to-eye is that we were both born before the twentieth century had begun. Our ideas were formed in a world utterly different from today's. Frere had described publishing in his letter to me as having a 'mystique', I might well have described it as an 'adventure'. Such words would not be used today by the masters of publishing houses, where efficiency is the password to the citadel of profits. Such words would be regarded as coming from amateurs, dilettante, or elderly has-beens, and there is a sense in which this is perfectly true.

The publishers of my vintage, born between 1890 and 1914, came into a world of traditional values, where professionalism was almost a dirty word and efficiency the trademark of a scoundrel. At a public school to 'swot' was far worse a crime than to bully. Coolness and panache were in fashion. Concern, if felt for the grave problems of the day, should be hidden. Progress was certain, or almost certain. In 1914 we went to war, praying that it would not be over before we 'got a crack at the Hun'. We fought for honour or to right a wrong, not for any sordid reason. Many never returned, many of those who did were crippled either physically or psychologically. Among those who returned without a crippling handicap was Harold Macmillan, a prime minister and a publisher, perhaps as typical an example as any of the finest products of that Edwardian generation who lived and flourished superbly into the next and the next but one.

The next generation, the masters of publishing today, had a different experience. They were too young to experience the first world war, they had to endure it. With food rationed, father away or perhaps killed, mother worried or over-worked, they had a miserable beginning. Followed the 1929 crash on Wall Street and the great depression, which made jobs hard to find and putpaid to any hopes for a revival of the splendours of the past. Hitler came to power in 1933, and three years later the outbreak of the civil war in Spain. Panache was no longer enough, honour was an outdated word, even hope was a feeling that had to be deliberately hoped for.

Inevitably they reacted to their dismal heritage, cursed their fathers who had brought these plagues upon them, and made their adjustment. They went to the second world war, not for glory, but to win it, and if possible to win it without losing their lives. They were practical men, believing in efficiency. They had an overwhelming need of success – success rather than achievement – and because they so desperately needed success, they tended to be ruthless. I do not believe that such men could have conceived the Heinemann group type of organization, and if they had done so, I do not believe they would have made it work, for to them a publishing house must be not only distinguished but successful, that is, profitable. Once it is profitable, the large-scale centralized organization must by its own logic demand greater profits. So a new scale of operations is prescribed almost inevitably, and must be carried out, and then we are nearing the point when a publishing house is no longer a mystique, an adventure or a quality system, but an organization for the production of profitable commodities on an ever greater scale. Soon their sons, the teenagers and twenty-year-olds of today, already in revolt against their elders' ideas, are likely once more to change the face of publishing in ways which cannot now be foreseen. Already it is clear, however, that many of them, including some of the most brilliant executives, are leaving firms where they had previously been happy. Some because the growth in size of the firm and its exclusive concentration on profits has disgusted them. Some because they fear, rightly or wrongly, the American ownership or part-ownership of British firms. This has grown substantially in the last decade. They believe, as I do, that book publishing is a direct reflection of the British character and way of life, and should not therefore be in foreign hands. Some simply because they want to 'run their own show', as I did when I left Routledge & Kegan Paul who had trained and promoted me. A slide has started, but it is still too soon to guess whether it will grow into an avalanche.

The Heinemann deal was well received in American booktrade circles, a matter of great importance to us as we bought many titles from them direct. A letter to me from a senior director of Random House, Donald Klopfer, ran in part as follows 'I do think it's a happy affiliation, because I know you will get a square shake from Frere, and the whole Heinemann outfit seem like fine people to do business with. I am sure you will retain your identity.' This letter is significant, for Klopfer was the man mainly responsible for the Random House group of publishers, which today includes Knopf, Pantheon and others. He and Frere were close personal friends. Both belonged approximately in the same age group. It would not be surprising to know that they had built and created their groups after consultation with each other. These two groups, Heinemann in the U.K. and Random House in the U.S., seem to me the only two publishing groups with vitality, with a loose but durable system of control, the only two who have not sacrificed quality for the sake of growth and profit. In groups, as in individual firms, it is the character of the key executives which is decisive.

The other great source of books was the literary agents of London. Most of them accepted that we had gained in financial strength and in the power to sell without losing the vital freedom to publish what we wanted to publish. Only the biggest literary agent of all, Curtis Brown, was sceptical. I went to see Juliet O'Hea, one of their young middle-level executives. She was distraught. 'In a year or two,' she said, 'you'll be turned into just another department of that huge production machine. The originality and boldness of your publishing will disappear. It's inevitable.' 'It's not in the least inevitable,' I replied, 'we are quite strong enough to maintain our integrity, and we shall do so. Wait and see. There'll be no changes except for the better.' Publishing history and the pages of this book show which of us turned out to be right.

Senhouse in due course returned from his holiday, and inquired why there was no clause in our agreement with Heinemann which allowed us to get out of the group when we became solvent again. Farrer explained this fact of business life to him in extremely plain words. Senhouse, I think, never wholly recovered from the realization that the firm was no longer 'his' firm. Though he stayed on to retire some fifteen years later, his heart was no longer in it. So in only four years Farrer had become my second-in-command. It was inevitable, and it was not a moment too soon. We had to prove to Heinemann on the one hand that we were competent, and on the other that we would not be pushed around.

In January I went down to Kingswood to brief the six Heinemann reps who were to carry our titles through the U.K. I sat in Frere's normal seat at the head of the long boardroom table, and began the briefing. After a few minutes Frere entered through a door behind me. Instantly the atmosphere became electric. Frere had the ability, when he wished, to produce an atmosphere akin to the calm before a powerful thunderstorm or a raging hurricane. He walked slowly down the table and sat down. 'Go on,' he said to me. With my heart beating fast, wondering why he had intruded, I continued with my briefing. Slowly the tension decreased. After quarter of an hour, Frere got up and walked slowly out of the room. 'That was perfectly adequate,' he remarked as he passed my chair. The incident was trivial, but it was important. It has stuck in my memory all these years. It had made me understand one aspect at least of Frere's complex character – he was a shy man rarely at ease in the abrasive conflicts of business affairs. Not till he returned home at night and shut his door behind him, could he relax in the peace and security of a happy marriage.

10

Making Good, 1951-5

THE year 1949 I have called 'The Golden Year', though I did not recognize its character at the time. The year 1951 might well be called 'The Year of Decision', for the deal with William Heinemann, agreed in that year and finalized in the following spring, had set us on a new course. For better or worse nothing could ever be the same again. Before the deal power had rested in a quadrumvirate, Senhouse, Farrer, Pattisson and myself, and this could create a difficult position. Where the Senhouse policy differed from the Warburg policy, a deadlock could arise, for on the whole Farrer tended to side with me, ready to take risks in attempting new tasks, while Pattisson was normally to be found in the Senhouse corner. Now however the final arbiter on policies was Heinemann. Since Frere backed me, especially if Farrer was with me, clashes were scarce and I followed my star without hindrance.

The years 1951–5 were a testing time for Secker & Warburg, we had to make good, to turn the losses into profit without lowering the quality of our publications. Within two or three years of the association we had achieved this aim, and thereafter the rein on which Heinemann rode us was so slight as to be almost imperceptible.

* * *

In the spring of 1951, before the Heinemann deal, I made my third trip to New York, and made serious contact for the second time with Helen Strauss, head of the literary agent department of the huge William Morris organization on Madison Avenue. Miss Strauss was at that time rising to the top among agents, a serious rival to Bernice Baumgarten, of the Brandt and Brandt agency. These two remarkable and likeable women, as different from each other as chalk from cheese, might well be considered the most successful dealers in authors' rights in New York at that time.

Miss Strauss greeted me warmly, and in the course of our conversation offered me the British rights in James Michener's new book, a sort of sequel to his *Tales of the South Pacific*,* published in the U.K. by William Collins. Why this book, *Return to Paradise*, was not accepted by Collins I never discovered. Possibly they were never offered it.† But to me it seemed a big nugget to pick up in the American goldfields. Clearly Miss Strauss thought so too, for she put a high price on it. It was already the Choice of the Book of the Month Club. Flushed with enthusiasm at my strike, I would have accepted on the spot, had I not been uneasily aware of the state of our finances in London. Instead, I cabled my office.

Instantly, a violent controversy broke out. Farrer approved of my accepting the offer, Senhouse and Pattisson did not. An official cable informed me that my maximum price should be £250. But to Farrer this appeared a blunder. Behind his colleagues' backs he cabled me 'my personal view Michener is pay up to sterling 500 if necessary.' In the end I paid £350, worth nearly £2,000 today, so becoming the publisher of a writer who was to become one of the greatest money spinners among the novelists of the last 25 years. The success of *Return to Paradise*, published October 11, 1951, was undoubted, it earned its advance in its first year, while its sales in Australia and New Zealand were in excess of 2,000 copies.

Michener was a foundling, who never knew who his parents were. Brought up in a poorhouse, 'I missed a whole cycle of childhood, but I've never used it as a device for self-pity.' Farmed out to a woman who called every evening for the children she cared for and took home for the night, he listened to her reading him Emerson's essays and the work of other nineteenth century novelists. Almost inevitably he became a Quaker, a tough-minded liberal, who has fought fiercely but sensibly on some dangerous battlefields, such as the persecution in the McCarthy years of the Hollywood Eight. While working on his book about the killing of four students at Kent State University, he was bugged, but not bewildered, by the F.B.I.‡

*Later it became *South Pacific*, one of the most successful musicals ever made.

†The paradises of which Michener wrote were an atoll, Polynesia, Fiji, Espirito Santo, New Zealand, Australia and New Guinea. He adopted a somewhat unusual technique, a documentary essay on each one with a short fiction to follow, developing the essay's theme.

‡I am indebted to Alex Hamilton for the details of Michener's early life, *The Guardian*, London, 23.2.72.

Michener was a late developer, both in writing books and in courting girls. The years before his fortieth were years of preparation, but they were used to good effect. His energies were controlled, like the torrents of a great river by a dam. Once released they burst forth from 1946 onwards in a steady succession of books, small and great. His three major novels, *Hawai* (1960), *The Source* (1965), and *The Drifters* (1971), must contain some half-a-million words each, equivalent to 18 novels of average length. Michener is one of the great masters of narrative, who found a huge reading public eager for his books, not only in the U.S., but in South-East Asia. But in the U.K. he has had a very thin time. The top reviewers gave him short 5-line reviews, saying approximately 'another novel by Mr. Michener has just appeared. Readers will know what to expect.' The suggestion was that readers could expect a long or very long novel of indifferent quality. But frequently he was ignored entirely. At last, however, Maurice Wiggin has made amends in the *Observer*, October 15, 1972. 'Michener gets on better with the reading public than with reviewers,' he writes, 'possibly because he writes very good stories in a style straightforward without a trace of showing-off but undistinguished. . . . Yes, but he does produce a really absorbing story rich in incident, in character, fully and deeply imagined and meticulously worked out. . . . It is writers like James Michener and Daphne du Maurier who keep the novel going as a viable public entertainment as distinct from a private joke.' Justice at last to the most underestimated writer of this generation.

With *The Source* we broke through for the first time to major sales in the U.K. *The Source* was a chronicle of the land of Palestine from prehistoric times to date, the theme the unending conflict between the religious man and the pagan, a story which belongs to the Western rather than the Eastern world. Hence its gigantic success in the U.K.

* * *

There have been times, especially when she wondered why she had, when my wife has claimed that she married me in order to persuade me to publish an English translation of Colette. Her novels, she told me, had been an enjoyable part of her reading in early childhood, an education which no English child would be likely to experience. Until the war was over and paper off ration (in 1948), no progress was possible, but then Pamela started her campaign, and assisted by Spencer Curtis Brown, a powerful agent who had no financial interest whatever in the project but simply admired Colette as an exciting writer, she succeeded. A number of Colette's novels had been published before the war by Gollancz, but the translations had been mediocre, their reception unenthusiastic, and all the titles were now out of print. The way ahead seemed clear. In this particular project Senhouse was with me hand in glove, as he had been with the translations of André Gide a year or two earlier.

We went to work with enthusiasm, only to discover that the road ahead was not clear, but full of obstacles. Colette, like many other writers, had had little understanding of the publishing process and not overmuch ability in the handling of money. She had scattered the fruits of her talent round the publishing houses of Paris, and to make a deal for a collected edition of her major works was a task demanding time, tact and tenacity. Fortunately for us, and still more fortunately for Colette, she had in the person of her third husband a patient negotiator who knew what had to be done.

Maurice Goudeket was an able business man, and he set speedily about the work. Even so, it took him several months before he was in a position to sign a contract with us for publication on stated terms of many of Colette's most important books. Of the 19 titles we announced in our first prospectus, only the two volumes of *Chéri* and the four volumes of the *Claudine* series had been previously published. Raymond Mortimer, a fervent admirer of Colette, had advised us throughout on the editorial side of the enterprise, and we had all agreed to start with *Chéri* and *The Last of Chéri*, the favourite novels of Colette herself. *Chéri*, published on July 27, 1951, sold better than any of her other books, and with her enchanting short novel *Gigi* (1944) has been the prime factor in making her known to and loved by the English public. This is hardly surprising, since *Chéri* is the classic and compassionate study of a love-affair between a young man and a woman about twenty years older, with an inevitably unhappy ending, while *Gigi* has an almost fairytale quality – the young daughter of a *grande cocotte* who marries, while still a virgin, the wealthy business man who discovers he not only desires but loves her.

Twenty-one of Colette's books appeared under our imprint, including a volume of short stories. There was also a book called *Earthly Paradise*, a sort of autobiography containing extracts from her extensive writings. The enterprise was a considerable, if not a runaway, success. Certainly it lifted Colette in England to a place among the major European writers of the century. Certainly too it added much lustre to the Secker and Warburg imprint, and it is one of the ventures in which I felt and feel enormous pleasure and pride.

The great problem in publishing Colette is that of translation. As Mortimer wrote in his Preface to *Chéri* 'her vocabulary is enormous, and savoury with archaic and regional words. From her imagination images rush profusely like bees from a hive. . . . She can foreshorten the French language as boldly as Mallarmé; she has trained it to obey her caprices like a pony in a circus. All of which is a perpetual feast to the reader, a chronic headache to the translator.' I believe that most of the translations we produced are, though not perfect, as good as can be expected in an imperfect world. Certainly we took infinite pains to find the best translators available.

Armed with our contract, with our coherent plan of volumes to be published, with our translations, with Goudeket's approval, and not least with our own immense enthusiasm, we attempted to interest an American publisher. But it was far from easy. Blanche Knopf said 'no' after long consideration, Helen and Kurt Wolff of Pantheon found it too expensive for the resources at their disposal, but at last it found a home with Farrar, Straus, then a youthful quality house, directed with almost superhuman energy by the youthful Roger Straus. The American contract, like the British, took many weeks to organize, but at last it was ready for Colette's signature. Around September 1951 I took it across to Paris to present to her.

At that time Colette was 78 years old, Grande Officier of the Légion d'Honneur, the highest rank in the order ever awarded to a woman, and member of l'Académie Goncourt, the most respected figure of the Paris literary world. Sidonie Gabrielle Claudine Colette had come a long way since her birth in 1873 in Burgundy, the daughter of a Parisian mother and a father who was a French army officer. Before she was twenty-one in 1893 she had married a writer known as Willy, who had urged or even bullied her into writing a series of novels, which he signed in his own name, and later jointly with her – Colette Willy. Of these the four *Claudine* books are well-known, from *Claudine At School* to *Claudine Married.* Into them Willy insisted she insert as much sexy material as possible. Despite this interference the *Claudine* novels, autobiographical as they are, remain delightful to read, while Claudine herself must rank with Gigi and with Chéri as three of the outstanding characters in Colette's world. *Chéri* was written in 1920 while she was married to her second husband, Henri de Jouvenel, a distinguished political figure and diplomat – Colette had left Willy in 1906. By Jouvenel she had her only child, a daughter. But in 1951 she was with Goudeket, to whom she had been married in 1935, a man years younger than herself, living in an apartment overlooking the geometrical gardens of the Palais Royal, still writing, but stricken since 1943 with a most painful arthritis of the hip. This was the woman I was to meet, and I looked forward to it eagerly, if with some trepidation.

Goudeket and I met by appointment at Véfours. This now famous restaurant only three doors away from the Colette house had become a meeting place for their friends. The new owner, Raymond Oliver, a friend of Colette, had taken it over and launched it with a brochure by Colette, a drawing by Christian Bérard and an article by Jean Cocteau. A number of the tables were named after great French writers. We sat naturally in the one labelled Colette. Lunch was on a massive scale and lasted two hours, Goudeket was treated by the maître d'hotel with the deference due to a queen's consort. But at last it was over, and we walked the few yards to 9 rue Beaujolais. The great moment had arrived.

Goudeket led me into Colette's room, and there she was, half sitting, half lying on the bed she called 'the divan raft on which I have been floating now for years,' propped up by an infinity of cushions. I approached the bed and bent over her outstretched hand. 'Il me fait grand plaisir, Madame Colette.' I handed her an enormous bunch of tiny pink roses packed together, which I had bought from a street flowerseller. Colette seemed pleased, she stared at them, then buried her nose in them, a long straight nose under the dark brown eyes and the bulging forehead partly covered by thick wavy blonde hair – Colette thought her forehead too masculine for a woman to show. The conversation began. Out of her mouth came the French sentences in a rich Burgundian accent, which I found difficult to comprehend. 'All the morning I've been here by the window,' she said, 'listening to the cries of the children playing in the garden, so sweet, so lively . . . the birds too fly past my window, many birds, blackbirds, thrushes, sparrows, swallows.' I listened. Was it sincere, was it an act, was it simply a way of starting a conversation? Probably it was all three, certainly it was charming.

I looked round the room. Walls and ceiling were red, the furniture seemed massive, the room seemed to me to have a heavy quality, rather like a prison holding secure the tiny figure of that great woman who, tied though she was to the bed, had a lightness and a vivacity that nothing, not even her years, could keep in check. There on the mantlepiece, a few feet in front of her bed, were the coloured crystals, the paperweights enclosing some mysterious object within them – fortune-telling amuses me, she had said, it's like my paperweights – the huge Brazilian moths, a brilliant blue, set pinned and lifeless against their supports.

Goudeket had left the room. 'How is your arthritis, Mme. Colette?' I inquired. 'Ah, mais je souffre beaucoup, beaucoup . . . but I do not tell *him*, he does not know, it would make him too sad. . . .' She put her hand to her hip, to point out to the stranger from London precisely the location of the terrible disease that gripped her.

It was the only question I asked her, and perhaps this was fortunate. I had come to give her a valuable document to sign, not to take from her the answers to questions she had been asked a thousand times. Colette herself has expressed her views of those who came to question her. 'For a time that is happily under my control,' she had written a year or two before my visit to her, 'I lie here their prisoner. I assume an air of finding their presence natural, but I am the one who has been summoned to appear. . . . They think I possess a store of general ideas. It is not for me to enlighten them, to explain that I am living off that fund of frivolity provided for the aid of those who live a very long time. . . .' Thank God, I did not ask her the questions she so disliked – that premature wrinkle? – that raised scar? – that profound weariness? – your literary plans, madame?

There was more besides, but not much more, and the words have vanished into thin air like the cries of the children in the garden. Perhaps I was alone with her only ten minutes, only five. Perhaps she said nothing but the few sentences I have recorded. Yet the sound of her voice, the sight of that ravaged face with the lines of passion and pain which still allowed the delight of living to shine through, remain with me.

Soon Goudeket returned with the American contract I had brought with me. He put the large four-page document in her lap. 'What is this, Maurice?' she asked vaguely. 'You know what it is, my dear, the contract for the American edition of your books,' Goudeket told her. 'It has been beautiful all morning,' Colette remarked, 'such a lovely morning, the birds. . . .' Goudeket cut her short, 'Here's your pen, you sign at the bottom of page three.' Colette signed. 'Pauline will witness it,' said Goudeket, and called her in. I stared entranced at the figure of this famous person, who had entered Colette's service at the age of fourteen and stayed for forty years. Very dark, with yellowish protruding eyes, which had a rather wild expression in them, she calmly took the document and signed her name on it. Soon after I went away. It had been a powerful experience which I have tried, in vain, to pin down. But, like the blue Brazilian moths, I'm afraid that in trying to pin it down I have killed it.

Three years later, in 1954, Colette died at the age of 81. She was the first woman in France to be given a state funeral. Goudeket has recalled her own words as an epitaph 'And when you lie down across the dizzying wavy path, if you have not already shed your curly locks one by one, nor one by one your teeth, if your limbs have not worn out one by one, if the dust of the world has not, before your last hour, sealed your eyes from the marvellous light, if you have right to the end kept in your hand the friendly hand which guides you, lie down smiling, sleep happily, and sleep privileged. . . .'

* * *

It was about 1951 or 1952 that Tosco Fyvel asked me to become a member of the Society for Cultural Freedom (S.C.F.). 'Never heard of it,' I said, 'what's it do?' 'It's aim,' he replied rather solemnly, 'is to promote Western culture and defend it against the communist culture of the East.' That sounded fine to me, after all I'd been fighting the Communist myths with some vigour since 1936. But I must admit I was surprised to hear that our culture was in peril, and that a society actually existed to protect it.

Questioning elicited a number of facts hitherto unknown to me. It appeared that a conference of the Soviet Union and its satellites had recently been held in Wroclaw, Poland (previously Breslau, Germany) at which the nature of communist culture had been defined and steps taken to broadcast its values, not only to the deluded citizens of the West, but to the Orient and particularly India. In Paris a new organization, the Congress for Cultural Freedom, had been formed with substantial funds at its disposal to combat this allegedly horrific threat. The English S.C.F. was an offshoot of the French C.C.F., and financed by it. It had a tiny office in London, a permanent secretary, typing facilities and a small library. 'How do you join it?' I inquired.

F. 'I simply put your name down on the list; there's about 180 members.'
W. 'What's the subscription fee?'
F. 'Nothing at all.'
W. 'What's the idea? Don't members actually *do* anything?'
F. 'Just general support of the causes for which the Society stands.'

It seemed to me odd, but there were a number of well-known names on the list. 'Put me down, if you think I can be of some use,' I told him.

Weeks passed, then Fyvel rang me. 'There's to be a ballot for a new S.C.F. committee,' he told me, 'We want you to stand.' I stood – where was the harm? When the votes were counted, I found myself elected, and when the committee met, Malcolm Muggeridge was made chairman and I was appointed treasurer. The committee included Stephen Spender, Harman Grisewood, T. R. Fyvel, Michael Oakeshott and several others. As treasurer I received £400 a quarter from the Paris H.Q., this was my budget. Apparently I was launched on a mini-career of a new kind.

At an early stage I learned that the committee was thoroughly dissatisfied with the way our funds had been used in the past. But to find new ways proved tricky. The rival culture we were supposed to be fighting was invisible, while our own Western culture was valued in conflicting ways by the members. Sterile discussions dragged on for months, and Muggeridge, an impatient man, pressed for our dissolution. 'There's altogether too much cultural freedom already,' he is reported as saying, 'any man who hasn't got a platform to sound off from must be a fool.' But it is rare for committees to dissolve themselves, especially when real money is automatically coming in, and at last a plan for action was agreed – we would send John Clews, our new paid secretary, ex-student of Birmingham University and a practised speaker, to student gatherings in the U.K. and Europe to keep their organizations safe for democracy (Western model). Out he went to fight the good fight against the communist champions of democracy (Eastern version). Once a month he reported. Doubtless Clews did an excellent job, but soon the committee became bored to tears, all of them were far beyond student age. They needed desperately something more showy.

Slowly a new idea was born in the mind of Spender or Muggeridge or another; we would have a cultural magazine, as the French already had (*Preuves*) and the Germans (*Der Monat*). Fyvel made a reconnaissance in Paris. Weeks passed. Magazines cost a deal of money to produce, and usually lose it in six months or less. The £1,600 a year budget which I nursed was chicken-feed. Where would some real money come from? Apparently there was a British source, a millionaire, it was said, known to Muggeridge, ready to make a substantial contribution. I never heard his name. But the bulk of the money would be generated in Paris by the Congress.

Soon it became known that the Congress money was American in origin. I was informed that the money would come from American Foundations or the American State Department, channelled to Paris through the American Federation of Labour. Even at the time this seemed to me a ridiculous and unlikely story, which I neither believed nor disbelieved. But the matter seemed to me then and seems to me now unimportant. Britain needed a first-rate cultural magazine, literary, artistic and social, to fill the gap left by the lamentable death of Cyril Connolly's brilliant *Horizon*. This was my personal objective right from the start, and to hell with propaganda. The best recommendation of Western culture was, simply enough, Western culture.

Nevertheless, this money, which I now assume to have been in part at least C.I.A. money, caused a rumpus among the intelligentsia at the time, and again a few years ago. But in the early fifties the C.I.A. was not by any means the hated organization it is today. Then the Russians appeared hostile, even dangerous, while the Bay of Pigs and the brutalities of the Vietnam involvement lay in the future.

One day in May 1952 I was deputed to accompany Muggeridge and Fyvel to Paris to discuss with the Congress the new magazine and its problems. We set off by night ferry. Their H.Q. was located on the avenue Montaigne, opposite the luxurious salon of a great French coutourier. In a huge room on the first floor we found ourselves facing three men, always referred to by Muggeridge as the Comedians, though why I never discerned. Bureaucrats? Yes. Cold war warriors? Certainly. But they were able and talented people doing their best in a nebulous cause. Without them there would have been no *Encounter*. On the left was François Bondy, editor of *Preuves*, which printed serious and often stodgy articles, social, political, and economic, designed to show that West was best and no doubt about it. No doubt, this is an unfair description of a useful magazine, but then *Preuves* was, I feared, likely to be the suggested model for ours. On the right sat Mike Josselson, the financial and administrative brains of the Congress, a New Yorker who had come up from the bottom, and worked for the Allied Psychological Warfare Branch during the War. His dislike of communism was deep and genuine. In the middle sat Nicholas Nabokov, emperor in this palace, a distinguished composer and musicologist, cousin of V. (Lolita) Nabokov, exiles both from their native land. With raven black hair greying, piercing eyes, aquiline nose and a high complexion, he made a deep impression on me. Discussion began, everything seemed about right, an American editor would be appointed, Spender would be the English editor working in Paris. 'In Paris?' I inquired, roused from my complacency. 'In Paris, of course,' said Nabokov, 'we have all the files here with the material on the U.S.S.R., Stephen will commute between Paris and London, the magazine will be printed in France.' At last everything became clear to me – the new magazine was to be a carbon copy of *Preuves* but in English, again the cold-war warriors publicizing communist theories by attacking them, giving them an audience they did not deserve and would not otherwise obtain.

'No,' I said firmly, 'certainly not, this is a recipe for disaster. Do you think any intellectual, west or east, will pay the slightest attention to an English magazine printed in Paris? It must be printed in London, and it must appeal to English readers if it is to have any worthwhile circulation. And it must not be specialized.' An argument began, my colleagues backed me, deadlock. 'We must consult higher authority,' said Nabokov. The next day we returned to London.

Muggeridge was in a foul temper, but a week or two later Paris conceded the victory. Secker & Warburg would distribute, but not manufacture, *Encounter*. The American editor was to be Irving Kristol. Spender rang me, and came to call. He sat down, looking flustered, and informed me that he was deeply worried about becoming editor of *Encounter*. 'Why should you be worried?' I asked him, 'You're obviously the right man for the job, and what a marvellous job to have, a first-rate English cultural monthly.' Spender continued to look pained. 'John Lehmann won't like it,' he said, 'he thinks he's a much better editor than I am, and that he ought to edit *Encounter*.' 'But he isn't the one who's been asked,' I replied mildly, 'it's you we want and you should be able to do it splendidly.' Spender had made his confession. I had absolved him. He went away, purged of the guilt feelings which so often invaded him.

The first *Encounter* was that of October, 1953. Ten thousand copies were printed and the issue was sold out. Over the years it has gone from strength to strength. Its circulation has probably quadrupled. Its present editors (1972) are Melvin Lasky of the U.S. and D. J. Enright of Britain. The marriage of England and America has been peaceful, with only a few stormy interludes. Long may it prosper! As assistant midwife at the birth, I look upon it with pride.

With the appearance of *Encounter* the shadowy existence of the Society for Cultural Freedom might have been thought to have ended, but to my surprise it still had one task to perform, and a not insignificant one at that. Under the management of Malcolm Muggeridge a remarkable character reached Britain in the fifties, a defector from behind the Iron Curtain, Tibor Szamuely. He brought with him his wife, a daughter and a son, and his library. Apart from these the family had nothing but the clothes they had worn on the journey. Without delay Muggeridge rang me and instructed me to provide the refugee with £250 from the fund of some £2,000 still remaining at my disposal as Treasurer of the Society. After a few questions I obeyed my Chairman's order and sent the money. 'They've got to buy some clothes,' Muggeridge informed me, 'and some food, of course.' Some weeks later a request for another £250 was made and complied with. But by then I was becoming inquisitive and restless. There seemed to be nothing constructive about the draining away of our fund. 'I want to see Szamuely,' I told Muggeridge. Soon he arrived at my office alone.

Szamuely was a Hungarian Jew born in Moscow in 1925. On both his father's and his mother's side he was born into the communist aristocracy, in particular his uncle had been the agent of the red dictator, Bela Kun, who had carried out the merciless execution of many thousands of the bourgeoisie after World War I. A close friend of the family was Rakosi, the man closest of all non-Russian communist leaders to Stalin during the years of the great purges. But Szamuely had a 'flaw' in his character which alienated him from his family and a distinguished career in Budapest and Moscow – he ceased to believe in communism or even marxism, and developed political views far to the right of those held by even the more extreme members of the Tory party.

The rot had started when he was twelve in 1937, following the 'disappearance' (that is, the murder) of his father in a Stalin purge. By 1941 he had completed his secondary education and worked in a factory during the war, but in 1944 he had volunteered for the army, but had soon been invalided out and studied for two years in the History Department of Tomsk University. After a year in Hungary on the Soviet Control Commission, he returned to Moscow in 1947, working as a journalist, and finally graduated with honours at Moscow University in 1950. It was no doubt in this year that he read an English copy of Orwell's *Nineteen Eighty-Four*. This must have inflamed his already strong anti-Soviet feelings. One day he was heard to make a nasty crack about Stalin, as a result of which he landed in the Lubljanka Prison and later in a prison camp in

Southern Russia. His sentence was eight years, which he would never have survived had it not been for Rakosi, who made a personal appeal to Stalin to release him. The request was granted, the only case known of Stalin granting the plea of a non-Russian communist for clemency. In his thirties Szamuely became a lecturer in politics and history in Budapest University, which was where Muggeridge first met him and plotted his defection, promising him his help when he arrived in England. In due course, Szamuely wangled himself into Ghana to lecture, and after two or three years took off by plane for freedom.

When Szamuely arrived in my office in 1964, he presented a striking appearance, very short for a man and broad, with a wide face, dark brown hair, strong features, with a keen look in his eyes behind the spectacles. He addressed me in faultless English without a trace of a foreign accent. His mastery of slang and the vernacular was at least as good as mine. I am still uncertain how this was possible for him. It is true that he spent nearly two years at the age of eight at the Bertrand Russell Beaconhill School while his father was over here as the G.P.U. watchdog with a Russian trade delegation. Dora Russell, who was then running the school, remembers him well, and reports that he took part in a children's play as an agitator! It has always seemed a delicious irony that his father, this high G.P.U. official, had chosen for little Tibor a school famous for what many thought to be an over-permissive atmosphere.

Szamuely and I got on well from the very beginning, though I had to overcome a certain horror at his extreme right-wing views. Soon enough I discovered that he had written books, and here it seemed to me was a field in which a constructive future for him could be arranged without further recourse to the dwindling funds of the Society. After discussion it was agreed that we should commission from him a history of the Soviet Union. He produced a list of chapters for what would have been a magnificent work. In his own words it was to be 'a concise one-volume history, covering the whole existence of the Soviet Union, showing both the fundamental continuity of its policy and the profound transformation of country and people . . . setting out the facts without bias or favour . . .' etc. We gave him an advance, from the firm's not the Society's resources, and were to give him many more advances over the years. With absolute confidence in the importance of the book, I sold it to the U.S., France, Germany and Italy. They were agog – a trained historian who knew Russia from the inside could and would, they thought, reveal more than ever before and more truthfully.

For a year or two at least I lived in Cloud Cuckoo land. But one day the truth began to dawn on me. Before Book I, chapter 1 in his table of contents, was typed the words 'Introduction: the Decline of Tsarist Russia', obviously a 5,000 word piece on the antecedents of the Bolshevik Revolt. Obviously but mistakenly, for this section began to grow. I complained to Szamuely, who replied that it was a difficult section for which he had had to read many books, later he thought it might have to run to as much as 20,000 words, later still that he feared it would have to be a book of its own, about 80,000 words, to be published separately in anticipation of the major work to follow. There was nothing to be done, except to stop paying him further advances, which amounted by then to some £3,000. Fortunately for Szamuely he had now fully established himself in British society. He had many friends, appeared on television, wrote for the *Spectator* and the *Sunday Telegraph*. He had also been appointed lecturer in Russian History at Reading University.

Looking back on these events, and with infinite sadness at his sudden death in 1972, I realize what went wrong. It was not that Szamuely could not have written the *History of Bolshevism* and written it brilliantly. But never could it possibly have been contained in one volume. For Szamuely was an expansive character and a talker, one of the greatest talkers I have ever met – and these include Isaiah Berlin, Maurice Bowra, Angus Wilson, Alistair Cooke and others. Larger than life himself, he enlarged all he touched. Sentences became paragraphs, paragraphs sections, sections chapters, chapters books, and never could he have lived long enough to write down his thoughts, his knowledge and his experiences. Even so he would have achieved more, had he only been able to control his most unruly member, his tongue. But a fine talker loves to talk. Szamuely made of a five-minute conversation a long half-hour. Szamuely, it must sadly be said, talked his life or at least his work away. But how delightful an experience it was to listen to him, especially his tirades about some political blunders in the U.S.S.R. or in Britain.

That 'brief' Introduction to the never written *History* became a work of 180,000 words, called *The Russian Tradition*, an analysis of those strands in Russian history which led 'inevitably' to the Bolshevik Revolution. It will, I hope, be published in 1973. Of all the books he was never to write, I regret most his autobiography. What a marvellous book that could have been. Perhaps with the help of his widow, Nina, one of his many friends who are writers could construct a biography? For this unique character deserves a biography in English, for two reasons – first, because he has had one of the most improbable and dangerous of lives, second because his love and admiration for England was unbounded, though not uncritical. When he was naturalized in 1969, with myself as one of the four referees, he is reported by Kingsley Amis to have said 'You know, this makes everything all right. Even dying, I'll be able to tell myself that at least it's in England.'

On February 6, 1952 I finished dictating to my secretary a long report on Gore Vidal's sixth novel, *The Judgment of Paris*. I was enthusiastic about it, and proposed making an immediate offer. The offer was never made. Instead, a big bust-up took place inside the firm which led to my being forced to reject it. This was perhaps the most foolish, if not the greatest, editorial defeat I ever endured. Vidal had been previously published by John Lehmann, his novel *The City and the Pillar*, one of the earliest homosexual novels. It had been successful (8,000 copies sold) and was well known. Vidal, however, had fallen out with Lehmann and elected to offer his new book to me as a quality fiction house likely to appreciate his work, which I most certainly did and do.

In this battle I was supported by our young sales manager, David Holt, and by our experienced London traveller, Charles Roth, who wrote 'I would not be surprised if it sold 10,000 or 15,000 copies . . . the author's fertile imagination carries one along . . . publication would be certain to cause a stir, possibly even a rumpus, but I think its literary merit would protect it from being attacked as mere pornography.' 'Rumpus' it certainly created inside the firm. Against me were Senhouse, Farrer and Pattisson, united in an unholy trinity, supported from the outside by the formidable George Malcolm Thomson, then literary editor of the *Evening Standard*, who wrote in his report to us 'It fails because it is not written with sufficient wit, delicacy and erudition . . . it would not surprise me at all if the Director of Public Prosecutions took a dim view . . . one day he will.' One day he did, as Chapter 12 relates, but *Judgment of Paris* was not the recipient of his attentions. It was no doubt the possible threat of prosecution that forced me to raise the detested white flag, for, though I did not regard it as likely, it was at least conceivable. To bring my colleagues and our good name into the precincts of the Old Bailey was a burden I did not care to take upon myself alone.

Judgment tells the story of a wealthy young American making the grand tour in Europe and North Africa, searching not for the beauty of landscape or art, but for the beauty of love. In Rome he finds the worldly and ambitious Regina (Hera), in Cairo the coldly intellectual Sophia (Athene), in Paris the womanly Anna (Aphrodite). Between these three our hero, a latterday Paris, must make his judgment and bestow on the winner the golden apple. These sharply contrasting *affaires* were frankly described. In its day twenty odd years ago the episodes might have appeared shocking to many besides my colleagues, explicit both hetero- and homo-sexually. But this book was a high-powered artificial comedy, not at all realistic, and it was played, not for nervous titters but for open laughter.

As for the opposition, Senhouse couldn't abide it and twice threatened to resign if the book were accepted. But this was no surprise to me since he regarded all American novelists as virtually third-rate, regretting that Henry James, whom he deemed godlike, was no longer alive. Pattisson 'couldn't feel any enthusiasm... judged from a serious critical standpoint it fails miserably.' Farrer, on whom my hopes rested, let me down for once – 'a devitalized book which I found extremely boring . . . much of it in very questionable taste.'

Sadly I wrote a long personal letter to Vidal, explaining in some detail how much I admired the book and why I was not going to publish it. This chore, which I have only rarely been forced to undertake, is perhaps the most difficult to perform successfully in publishing. But on this occasion all went well. Vidal wrote me a delightful letter from which I quote – 'My work has always enjoyed the fiercest enmity of American book reviewers and booksellers, though the last always come around when I produce a best-seller. Worse than hostility, however, are the solemn admirers who scratch about for "moral values" and "affirmation", ignoring the fact that one has tried to be funny. You are exactly right when you say I have written an "artificial comedy". English reviewers believe, almost correctly, that Americans never write it, consequently they are suspicious of any American who attempts to work outside the naturalistic tradition. I always felt that, much as Lehmann professed to admire my unique genius, he was secretly of the opinion that I was a homosexual Jack London who could be relied upon for innumerable tense and squalid dramas dealing with the vagaries of the old, all composed in basic Americanese.'

What was the book's fate in the U.K.? From my standpoint a reassuring one. I tipped off Heinemann who asked the agent, Curtis Brown, to offer it to them. Heinemann took and published it, and sold nearly 6,500 in a year or two. A steady stream of books by Vidal, novels and general works, have appeared since then, not on my list but on that of Heinemann. At least it was better than seeing him on the list of a deadly rival. As for the reviews I have only the *Observer*'s, where it was reviewed top of the column with novels by H. W. Meyerstein, Jocelyn Brooke, and Laurens van der Post, a most distinguished trio. 'Certainly the most ambitious novel of the week,' wrote David Paul, and added 'he has all the materials, if not the talents, of a modern Petronius.' Not precisely fulsome praise, but more than enough to keep the booksellers happy.

Foiled in my purpose to publish, I read my colleagues a tremendous lecture on their shortcomings and editorial blunders which, as I put it, 'must not be indefinitely repeated'. But this was merely a smoke-screen to cover the fact of my retreat. Certainly they had made a serious blunder by profitability standards, but I had allowed it. Certainly they had been careless and irresponsible for believing that their personal hang-ups were based on critical judgment. But it was I, the executive head of the firm, who should have told them to go to hell. Since I had the power, I should have wielded it. In the years to come I often did so . . . and sometimes, alas, it was I who blundered!

* * *

On June 13, 1955, I published an anonymous book called *A Woman in Berlin*. It described what it was like to be in Berlin during the first few weeks of the Russian occupation, a story of rape, loot, hunger and devastation. It was not a great book, but it was a very good one, and I believed that, even ten years after the war was over, it would interest the British public, indeed I believed emphatically that it could be and would be a best-seller.

It was probably my friend, James Stern, a distinguished writer himself,* who suggested it to me. He was at that time living in the U.S. and had translated it for Harcourt Brace. The bona fides of

*His short stories had already been published by Secker & Warburg, and a large selection of them are in print under the title, *The Stories of James Stern*, Secker & Warburg, 1968.

the book was vouched for by the distinguished archaeologist, C. W. Ceram, author of the best-selling *Gods, Graves and Scholars*. In his introduction he wrote – 'the author of this extraordinary document was in her early thirties when she began her diary on April 20, 1945. In Rousseau's introduction to his *Confessions* we find the words "I am commencing an undertaking, hitherto without precedent, and one which will never find an imitator." No sentence could be better suited to introduce this work.' That's as may be, but certainly it must always rank high as a minute-to-minute account of the sack of a great capital city.

Although the book had not apparently sold well in the U.S. (under 2,000 copies, I believe), I soon discovered that three other publishers were bidding for it in England. Promptly I offered the largest amount (£300) which at that time was authorized without consulting our Heinemann colleagues. It was not enough. I raised my bid, still not enough. At £700 I secured it, and was promptly faced with the necessity of informing our finance director, Hall, at Kingswood.

He and I had always been on excellent terms. I visited him once a month for a long talk followed by lunch, and wrote him innumerable letters on every conceivable financial aspect of the business from pricing to promotion, from overheads to overstocks. To these letters he replied at considerable length. Our friendship or partnership surprised all around us, for I had been cast at the time of the Heinemann deal in the rôle of reckless and profligate spender (which I was not) and he in the rôle of unimaginative and tight-fisted dictator of policy even to his own firm (which he was not). I learned a great deal from H. Leslie Hall, which was of use to me then when we were struggling and has been of use to me ever since.

When I rang him and told him what I had done, he was furious, or pretended to be, but it was too late for him to intervene. 'D'you think the bloody book will earn all that advance, Fred?' he inquired, in a voice that expressed hope rather than rage. 'Of course it will,' I replied, as confidently as I could manage. Hall ended the exchange on what I should describe as an amiable note – 'God help you if it doesn't sell, I'll flay you alive for this.'

And what happened? The two Sunday papers, *Times* and *Observer*, reviewed it on the day before publication. They were hardly enthusiastic and my heart sank, though not far, since I was aware that the advance sales were nearly 15,000 copies, far more than was necessary to cover the advance. But other influential papers took a different view. The *Daily Telegraph* wrote 'This is far beyond importance or ordinary interest. It is the actual report of life in Berlin from April to June 1945 . . . it is a book which requires to be written and which needs to be read.' And read it was. At 18s. (90p) it was not a cheap book for those days, yet it sold in the first year over 27,000 copies and went on selling for many years after. Hall was delighted, and remarked ambiguously that 'he wasn't surprised'. Later it was published as a paperback by Panther Books on their first list. Clearly my hunch, based on no kind of reasoning but simply on the effect the reading of the book had made on me, had paid off, the prestige (and the profits) were big. Publishing is an art not a science, and hunches (including mine) are not always wrong.

11

Whose Bridge Over the River Kwai?

DURING the fifties I went regularly to Paris on buying trips, usually once a year. We already published some fine French writers, but we hoped for others. It was the Paris trip of autumn 1952 that led to our publication of Pierre Boulle's famous novel, *Le Pont de la Rivière Kwai.*

Most of our Paris business was channelled through the Agence Denyse Clairouin, run by Mlle Marie Schebeko, who spoke and wrote excellent English, and Madame Doussia Ergaz, a widow, who had excellent connections in the literary world and was herself a talented novelist. Broadly speaking Schebeko controlled the business, Ergaz the literary side. I was fond of both of them, and they undoubtedly favoured Senhouse and myself because of the adventurousness and distinction of the list, and my wife because of their belief that she dressed as well as or better than the best-dressed French women.

As usual in November, the awards of the annual literary prizes had been announced shortly before I arrived. Contrary to common belief, France is not a great book-buying nation, as Germany is, and new novels in particular sell poorly and for the most part are unprofitable. What the French publisher needs and aims at is one of the prizes, and above all the Goncourt. A Goncourt prize-winner rarely sells less than 100,000 copies, and quite a few as many as half a million. I remember discussing with René Julliard, head of the important Julliard publishing house, the extraordinary number of novels on his list. 'We have twenty-seven first novels this year,' he told me, 'we can't afford to lose any chance of winning the Goncourt.' The system in England, is (I'm happy to say) utterly different, though four years ago The Booker Prize, a substantial one of £5,000, was offered for the first time by the well-known industrial firm of Booker McConnell, sugar producers, shipowners and producers of an excellent rum. The winners, however, have so far achieved sales of less even than a moderate Goncourt sale.*

In 1952 the goodwill of Agence Clairouin led them to offer me four of the prize-winning novels of that year, including the Goncourt and the Renaudot. All four of them I rejected. French prize-winning novels are no sure-fire success in the U.K.† But I had been reading in the Paris papers some excellent reviews of Boulle's *Kwai*, which had just appeared. I asked Ergaz why she had not offered me this novel. 'It is not good enough for you,' she replied, 'it is not worthy of the distinction of your house. It is more for Cassell or Hodder.' So do the virtuous reap the bitter fruits of their virtue. 'I would very much like to read it,' I said, 'at least the hero is a British colonel.' *Kwai* was fetched from a distant shelf and reluctantly given to me, I read it and bought it for an advance of £100 on a/c of the normal royalties for a translated book. I felt sure that English readers would find a soft spot in their hearts for a crazy old warhorse like Colonel Nicholson.

The plot of this novel was simple enough. The time is the last two years (1944–5) of World War 2, the place Indochina and Burma, the subject a bridge to be built across a river of vital strategic importance to the Japanese army fighting a tough rearguard action against the advancing British. The Japanese intend to use British prisoners in the neighbouring P.O.W. camp to construct the bridge, which will be made of local timber to a Japanese design. It is here the trouble starts, for the British colonel will not permit his men to work properly at their task except on his own terms and to the design of his own bridge builder. After a violent confrontation the Japanese commander gives way and the bridge is built. Unknown to the British colonel, however, it is secretly mined at night by British saboteurs from rear H.Q., ready to be blown up when the first train, full of V.I.P.'s and generals, is crossing it on this gala occasion. At the crucial moment, when all is set and ready for the successful execution of this daring act of sabotage, the British colonel, unaware till then of what is in the wind, pathologically proud of the British bridge and its British design and the British workmanship involved, meets his death in an idiotic and successful attempt to *prevent* the bridge's destruction. A

*Another important prize in England, worth £1,000, is awarded annually by the great bookselling house of W. H. Smith and Sons.

†For an exception, see page 294, *Le Dernier des Justes.*

brief report to H.Q. by the one surviving saboteur makes a final ironic comment on the affair – 'Two men lost. Some damage done but bridge intact thanks to British Colonel's heroism.'

Once the agreement was signed, we looked for a translator. We had recently commissioned a book, *The Stronghold,* from Xan Fielding about his wartime expeiences in Crete. The work was nearly finished, and the writer was running out of money. He hoped to get some French translation from us. Fielding claimed to be (and was) bilingual in French and English, and we sent him *Kwai* to read with a view to his translating it. On February 2, 1953 he wrote me – 'I enjoyed *Kwai.* Boulle must have been in the same Far East false-nose-and-whisker racket as myself – Force 136 which he calls Force 316. I remember there were a number of Frenchmen . . . operating with the F.F.I., who became "unemployed" with the liberation of France. The thing's authentic all right . . . I know the technical jargon which Boulle uses on almost every page, sabotage and para-military terms . . . I was also connected with some of the wretches who worked on that railway he describes and with their guards. . . .' Can there ever have been a more extraordinary coincidence? We gave Fielding the translation and he did it promptly and with great skill. *The Bridge Over the River Kwai* was published on March 29, 1954, in a printing of 4,000 copies, sold briskly, and reprinted. Boulle was compared by some reviewers to Kipling. *The Times* thought he wrote 'with great intelligence – his tone is often slightly satirical in a manner recalling George Orwell.'

Meantime, as soon as we had the translation and later the proofs, we tried to interest an American publisher in the book. So did Clairouin. But it was a tough job. To my knowledge it was rejected by at least five major New York houses – Simon & Schuster, Harper (twice) who called it 'a very bad book', Knopf (Blanche Knopf in person), Farrar, Straus (because of doubts as to its suitability for the American market and also because of 'its all-male cast'), and Viking Press (by the magnificent Ben Huebsch himself, reading it in London). How did five such eminent firms, each fully capable of assessing the literary merit, saleability and narrative power of *Kwai,* fall down so disgracefully on this project? Are British publishers as insensitive and foolish as our American colleagues? It was finally accepted by a less known firm, the Vanguard Press, who issued it with great skill and most successfully. Vanguard and we ourselves still have *Kwai* in print, and have each published a dozen or more of Boulle's books since then.

There must be many who have seen the magnificent film which was made from Boulle's novel. Sam Spiegel was the producer, David Lean the director, and the star part of Colonel Nicholson was played by Alec Guiness, though I believe it was first offered to Noël Coward. Another actor who had read the book and longed to play the part was Charles Laughton. 'Lean was tempted, and so was I,' wrote Boulle, 'but finally we thought him a little too old and quite a lot too fat to play the part of a starving prisoner. But he went so far as solemnly to promise to lose 40 lbs, if he was given it.'

The film rights were competed for by at least three different companies, including Ealing Studios (Sir Michael Balcon), and the negotiations, which we conducted on behalf of the French publisher, became so tortuous that in retrospect it is hard to disentangle them. But the final result is clear enough, we sold it for three million francs, then about £3,000, to karl Foreman, a U.S. citizen, and Zoltan Korda, both of London Films, but not actually to London Films itself. On our side negotiations were conducted by Senhouse, who cannot be described as a tough negotiator, assisted by Pattisson. In retrospect, it seems to me that we got about half of what we should have got for the rights. Senhouse however seemed unperturbed. He had enjoyed what he described as 'a grand telephonic auction', and the price obtained was less important than the fact that a film would be made. Julliard too was satisfied; he had got the price he'd fixed before the bargaining began. Farrer and I, however, felt lugubrious, for in May we learned that the advance would be paid with 'commission en sus', a phrase I had never previously heard. What it meant soon became clear enough – neither Clairouin nor ourselves would receive any part of the purchase price. After selling the rights for one of the most successful films ever made, we came out with a negative profit, comprising the cost of letters, cables, phone-calls, lunches to film executives and a hundred or two hours of our working time. But in this matter of price it was Farrer and myself who were proved wrong, Senhouse and Pattisson who were proved right. When the film was shown and broke all records, the sales of *Kwai* in paperback and hardback soared and it has never stopped selling since. Collins' Fontana Paperbacks were the publishers in 1956, and have sold to date some 675,000 copies, paying royalties to the author and ourselves of well over £20,000! But the film, brilliant though it was, had cheated. In it, that remarkable bridge of fiction *was* blown up (in spite of Boulle's frantic pleas to the director over a period of two years), British strategic plans were fulfilled, but the author's irony was brought to nothing.

And that, I would have thought, was the end of the story, but Pierre Boulle has informed me otherwise. A bridge over the River Kwai was destroyed, not however by British saboteurs, but on April 3, 1945, by an American bombing squadron with a Colonel Henderson in the lead plane. Was this Boulle's bridge? Certainly not. Boulle's bridge existed only in his vigorous and realistic imagination. How did all this come about?

In Paris at the beginning of the fifties Boulle was a young writer 'living in the lowest sort of hotel, practically starving. . . . I well remember how I was thrilled to the marrow when I was told that an intelligent British publisher had taken an interest in *Kwai*.'* He was equally delighted to discover that his novel had been bought for films and would bring him something under two million francs (£2,000) out of the three million francs paid, though to this day 'people believe it brought me thousands of millions'. This talented young man had already written an excellent thriller, *William Conrad*, where a Nazi agent is placed in Britain to be 'a sleeper', ready to perform some horrific act of sabotage when the right moment came, but is unable to do so because he feels himself utterly English when the moment arrives, a theme (as I realize now for the first time) clearly parallel to that of *Kwai*.

'A fortnight before Christmas 1951 – I well remember the date – I had an idea for *Kwai*, I really knew it was going to change my life. I did not regret, I have never regretted that the film rights were sold for a relatively modest sum.' Boulle set to work and finished the first draft, now he had to find names for Colonel X, Colonel Y, and the River A. He opened an atlas and 'looked carefully at the maps of Burma and Thailand, either country being fit for the historical background of my story. That is how I discovered the river Kwai, running where I needed it. The name sounded good and I hesitated no longer.'

Now the plot of the novel demands that the scene had some unusual features – 'a large flat plain on one side of the river (enabling the saboteurs to see and hear the arrival of the train from a long way off) and on the other bank hills covered with thick jungle conveniently disposed for the saboteurs to conceal themselves and have a fine view over the British prisoners' camp – also a flat space between these hills and the river, providing for a large curve of the railway after it crossed the bridge, etc.' Boulle is of the opinion that, although

*Quotations from Pierre Boulle's letter to me of 24 September, 1972.

there is no physical impossibility about such a terrain, it is a little unlikely that any such existed. Certainly it did not exist on the banks of the Kwai, for when the producer and the director visited the river, they returned horrified and abused the author vigorously for placing his story in such an impossible spot. In fact, they chose a location in Ceylon and there that fictional bridge was constructed. But it was not the Ceylon bridge which was bombed by American planes in 1957 when the film was shot – that would certainly have led to a tremendous international crisis – it was a bridge over the river Kwai, though not of course Boulle's.

One day in 1958, a Colonel Henderson, of the United States Air Force, went to the movies, and sat happily through a showing of the *Kwai* film then having its first season in New York. 'When I saw the movie for the first time,' he relates 'I felt I'd been there before.* The more I thought about it, the stronger the feeling grew. . . .' During World War Two, he had served as a B-24 Bombardier in the C.B.I. theatre, and flying in the lead plane had bombed a bridge over the Kwai river, which he now suspected was Boulle's. Today, a Master Navigator, recalled to service during the Korean War, he holds an important post in the Strategic Air Service at Barkdale A.F.B., La. But his feeling of *déja vu*, the belief that it was he, and not the fictional English Colonel Nicholson, who had destroyed the bridge must have waxed and waned, for it was to be ten years before he put his belief to the test.

In 1968 Henderson was back in Thailand during the build-up of U.S.A.F. forces, and there was no time to solve the puzzle. 'After I returned in 1968 to the United States from service in South Vietnam I wrote the U.S. Air Attaché in Bangkok,' he relates, 'who confirmed that Boulle's bridge had been near the town of Kanchanaburi, that there were two bridges, and that the steel one still stood.' Colonel Henderson was given the name of a Mr. Boonpong Sirivejapahdh, who had managed a canteen in the P.O.W. camp there, and later had become a successful business man in Bangkok. Boonpong, it was said, had secretly helped many prisoners to survive.

Boonpong's information fascinated the colonel, who two years later volunteered for a second tour of duty in S.E. Asia, arriving in the Central Highlands of South Vietnam during August 1970. Five months later he obtained six days of R. and R. (rest and recreation) in Bangkok and met Boonpong there, who told him where the bridge of his dreams was situated near Kanchanaburi. He went to inspect it

*Information about Colonel Henderson and his raid is drawn from his own account in *Air Force Magazine*, February, 1972.

and returned convinced that here indeed was the site of the bridge he had destroyed. There was, he thought, too much evidence on the site to allow the colonel to come to any other conclusion. 'I know now,' he writes, 'that it was shattered by the 436th Bomb Squadron of the 7th Bomb Group.' The date was April 3, 1945. Henderson was in the lead plane, but only one of his bombs was released in the first attack and secured 'a direct hit on the ten-foot-wide bridge, which looked like the thin edge of a knife-blade even at this low altitude.' Soon the planes came under heavy attack, but escaped over the Bay of Bengal in the direction of Rangoon. Henderson's plane crash-landed on a beach where the plane was destroyed with minor injuries to Henderson and the tailgunner.

The evidence which convinced Henderson was a brochure issued by the Thai Tourist Bureau stating that Kanchanaburi is the site of Pierre Boulle's bridge, mentioning that a wooden bridge had once stood a hundred metres down stream from the still standing steel bridge. They add that the wooden bridge was dismantled after the steel one was completed. Here the Bureau appear to have adopted the ending to the novel as written by the author (where the bridge is left intact) rather than the ending of the film where it is blown up.

How could the Tourist Bureau come to believe that the bridge at Kanchanaburi was the bridge of Pierre Boulle's novel? The answer must be that *they did not*. Shrewdly, once the bridge had become famous all over the world as the popularity of Boulle's novel and film spread, the Bureau selected a site not too far from Bangkok, in a convenient bend of the river to attract tourists, and inscribed on a large wooden board 'HERE STOOD THE BRIDGE OVER THE RIVER KWAI'. Who can blame them? Profits from tourism are important to small countries and are not despised even by large ones. Isn't there a house in Baker Street, Number 221B, shown to visitors as the residence of Sherlock Holmes?

The destruction of a real bridge, strongly defended by A.A. guns and fighter planes, would seem to be an easier task than the obliteration of a phantom bridge. Once again fiction is shown to be stronger than fact. Boulle's imaginary bridge has been incorporated into the real world. It would be the devil of a job now to remove it. One final thought. I am waiting eagerly for an English colonel of the right age to manifest himself, claiming to be the pathological character in the novel named Colonel Nicholson. That will be the day, and what a glorious libel action might ensue.

12

A Slight Case of Obscenity

IN 1951–2, when my firm tottered on the edge of bankruptcy, I had taken the gamble of a deal with Heinemann. This policy had been one of make-or-break, but there had been no alternative to it. Three years later another deadly hazard faced the firm, prosecution on a criminal charge at the Old Bailey, the charge of 'publishing an obscene libel, to wit a book'. In today's permissive society, when 'dirty' books, pictures, plays and films abound and are discussed seriously in the media, it is hard to imagine the situation as it was in the early fifties. Let me attempt to recreate the atmosphere.

The English are on the whole a tolerant people, where even the politicians, as Orwell pointed out, rarely if ever murder in order to gain power, as they have done in so many other advanced countries.* Yet beneath this quiet exterior lies concealed a Puritan streak, shared with the great democracy across the Atlantic, which drives both countries to enact laws and regulations which appear odd and even unnecessary to foreign eyes. Though the English have done nothing to compare with the colossal American blunder of Prohibition in the 1920's, we do go berserk at times and start prosecuting those who are discovered to be infringing the alleged moral code. One particularly revolting example of such madness occurred as late as 1963. It led to the forced retirement of John Profumo, an excellent minister of war in Harold Macmillan's conservative government, and still worse to the suicide of Stephen Ward, an osteopath and artist, son of a Church of England Canon, and friend to many an 'establishment' figure.†

*The problem of Ulster is a very special case. Its problems and perplexities lie far outside my terms of reference.

†See, for instance, *Scandal 1963*: a Study of the Profumo Affair, by Clive Irving and others.

Since 1868 when Chief Justice Cockburn had laid down the legal test of obscenity in a manner that must definitely be described as unhelpful, there has been every kind of incident – Dr. Bowdler thought the Bible was obscene – in 1877 Annie Besant and Charles Bradlaugh were successfully prosecuted for publishing a book on birth control – in 1888 a London publisher, Henry Vizetelly, went to prison for three months for publishing a translation of Zola's *La Terre* – in 1895 Havelock Ellis had a terrible time with his book, *Sexual Inversion*, and his publisher betrayed him by pleading guilty at the last moment.

In this century the crusade continued. In the twenties the bonfires burnt briskly for a time. Radclyffe Hall's mild lesbian novel, *The Well of Loneliness*, was suppressed in 1928. The poems and paintings of D. H. Lawrence were viciously attacked. James Douglas, a star journalist on the *Sunday Express*, thundered loudly against the depravity of this or that book, presumably to the satisfaction of his readers. In 1932 the poems of the extraordinary Count de Montalk were prosecuted. Asked by the judge what punishment he thought he deserved, he replied, 'My Lord, I think I deserve to be sentenced to six months in Buckingham Palace.' But instead he got six months in Wormwood Scrubs prison, and on appeal the sentence was confirmed. Of course, these bonfires seem petty compared to those the Nazis stoked with such infinite gusto after 1933.

During the war there was a lull, perhaps because modern war is itself the ultimate obscenity or more probably because there was not enough paper to print pornography. After the war most writers and publishers assumed that the authorities regarded John Bull, toughened by bombing and hardship of all kinds, as adult enough to be permitted to choose his own reading without supervision. But in 1954, unheralded, a powerful attack was launched on writers and publishers. If there were reasons for this, they are unknown to me, for the number of doubtful books – doubtful in the eyes of the authorities – seemed to be no larger, if no smaller, than normal.

The crime of publishing an obscene book was then known as a misdemeanour. Though less serious than a felony, which includes such acts as murder, rape and blackmail, it could land you in prison for an unspecified term as well as saddle you with a substantial fine. In 1954 this type of prosecution was brought under the common law, not by statute as is normally the case in American obscenity trials, which is why my American friends, sympathetic though they were, tended to underestimate the perils that surrounded me. Even some

English friends were ignorant enough to inquire why I had not taken the precaution of insuring against the risk, a question so wrong-headed as to make me angry.

But, apart from the legal penalties, there are other disadvantages for the defendant in an obscenity trial. You are accused of being a pornographer, or rather a purveyor of his productions. The pornographer at least writes the stuff, even though it may be, in every sense of the word, a low level of creativity. But the publisher himself is concerned merely to make money out of someone else's 'filth'.* Socially, it's really rather disgraceful, or was in those distant days of the fifties. There was no guarantee then that all your friends would rally round and commiserate with you if you were found guilty. Indeed, if you happened to be a member of a good club, you might well discover a polite request for your resignation in the morning's mail. Again a conviction on a criminal charge is no laughing matter in the U.K. or anywhere else, it remains on your record for ever. And why should it not? The pornographer aims to make profits out of the sexual weaknesses of his fellows. Like any trafficker in dangerous drugs, like any white slave-trader, he should be suitably punished when he's caught and convicted. So many people thought in the fifties, so many people still think today. As for myself I had not pondered these matters deeply in 1953, and for the simplest of reasons: I did not intend to publish pornographic books. But the crime of which I was to be accused can be committed unknowingly, and it is this possibility which sets it apart from all, or at least most, of the crimes in the criminal calendar.

The first act of the drama took place in the Isle of Man. A young policeman from there had passed out of (I think) Hendon Police College, top of his class, defeating the less talented students from England, Scotland, Wales and Northern Ireland by a fair margin. Returning to his island home, this keen officer found the absence of prosecutable crime well-nigh intolerable. Eager to dissipate his boredom, he visited the local bookshops and there discovered two novels, one *The Philanderer* by Stanley Kauffmann, published by my firm, the other, *Julia*, published by Werner Laurie, which he judged an affront to decency. A local action followed, the books were condemned, the bookseller who had sold them was fined £1 on each book. This happened in the silly season of the summer of 1953 and attracted a few meagre paragraphs in the great London dailies. This

*I suppose today 'pornographer' has come to mean a purveyor as well as a writer of pornography.

absurd incident must have alerted a zealous Home Secretary to the existence, hitherto unsuspected, of pornography in the lists of reputable publishers.*

A charge made against a publisher of publishing an obscene book can be tried without a jury in England and Wales, and in London by stipendiary magistrates, a body of men unlikely on the whole to give a book, or a burglar, the benefit of the doubt. If a publisher doesn't like the look of his local magistrate, he can demand trial at London Sessions or the Central Criminal Court, the Old Bailey, where the costs are higher, the penalties of conviction graver and the publicity more widespread. Here a judge and a jury of twelve will see what they can do for him.

Though my publishing record was unsullied in matters of this kind, I had a smattering of information before my troubles came upon me, and should have known well enough how to conduct myself. Yet when Sergeant K and Detective-Constable B knocked at my door and found me at my desk, I lost my temper.

There is no excuse to be offered on the grounds that I was taken by surprise. The two gentlemen from Scotland Yard had considerately advised me of their coming. Nor were they impolite. They sat on the far side of the desk, quietly smoking, and inquired whether I had published *The Philanderer* a novel by Stanley Kauffmann, an American, issued in New York a few months before under the title of *The Tightrope*. 'Why do you want to know?', I inquired nastily, and they replied that they had 'reason to suppose' that the book was obscene.

This well-known phrase is really a masterpiece of obfuscation. They didn't say they had read it themselves, and found it filthy. They didn't even state unequivocally that they had read it at all. There was more the suggestion that friends of theirs, some study group perhaps surveying the contemporary American novel, had come unexpectedly upon *The Philanderer* and mentioned casually to them over a drink that it did not conform to the strictest canons of decency. This opinion they were passing on to me for what it was worth, confident that I would know how to deal with a potentially

*It is argued by C. H. Rolph in *The Trial of Lady Chatterley*, published by Penguin, that the Director of Public Prosecutions was alerted to the five hard-cover books prosecuted in 1954 by their mention in the Reiter case, which had taken place some months earlier where they were mentioned in court as being more obscene and therefore more worthy of prosecution than the cheap paperbacks Reiter had published.

embarrassing situation which irked them and their friends no less than it did me and my associates.

For a moment I was almost persuaded that this was a storm in a teacup, and I toyed with the idea of slipping them £5 each, with a promise to withdraw the book from circulation. The urge to appeasement passed, fortunately no doubt, and was succeeded by a lively irritation. 'I don't think it's obscene,' I said indignantly, 'and I wouldn't have published it if I had. If you attack it, my firm and I will defend it with all the force at our command.'

So there it was on the table, a challenge to the Director of Public Prosecutions, the man without whose say-so no worthwhile criminal proceedings can get started in England. His representatives, Constable B and Detective K looked hurt, rather like a family doctor and a specialist who have just advised a patient to give up smoking, only to be informed that the patient will not only continue smoking but has decided to increase his drinking as well. They stiffened, and asked a lot more questions, most of which I thought irrelevant. But there was one question, the answer to which interested them very much indeed – 'Do you, Mr. Warburg, take full responsibility for acceptance of *The Philanderer* by your firm?' Later on, this question turned out to be crucial.

The weeks went by. I sailed to New York on business and returned. Winter gave way to spring, and in due time a writ was served on us and on Werner Laurie. Of course, we consulted our legal advisers. Mr. Thurston Hogarth, then a partner in the firm of Oswald Hickson and Collier, now with another firm of solicitors, experienced in all problems connected with the publication of books, read *The Philanderer*. He thought it was a book that most definitely should not be suppressed, indeed it seemed to him on the whole a rather moral book. Yet he knew it would shock the susceptibilities of many readers, and, as he put it, 'past precedents for this kind of prosecution did not enable me to paint a very happy picture to Fred Warburg.' Speaking of the jury he added that 'it is not seemingly in human nature to think that you yourself can be corrupted, but easy to think that other people have not your moral fibre . . . to predict a jury's reaction is something akin to fortune-telling.' However he thought he could offer us 'some glimmerings of hope', but he was certain that to plead before a metropolitan magistrate was a recipe for disaster. It was the Old Bailey or nothing, and for this we needed the best counsel available. He recommended Rodger Winn, later P.C., C.B., O.B.E., and later a Lord Justice of Appeal.

Soon we had a consultation with Winn in his chambers. Hogarth was delighted to note that Winn agreed we had some reasonable chance of success at the hands of a judge and jury. We discussed defence policy with him and the evidence to be called. But at that time no evidence was permitted as to the obscenity or otherwise of the book from any person however distinguished. Winn was greatly worried about a passage in the middle of the book describing a sordid scene in the hero's childhood. Curiously this passage was not one of the many later read out by prosecuting counsel in his speeches to the jury. After this consultation I estimated the odds against us as 6 to 4, and had no doubt whatever that a full-scale battle at the Old Bailey was infinitely preferable to fading into guilt before a magistrate. So the decision was taken after calm deliberation. Nevertheless, it was risky.

What was the novel about, which was to be the cause of so much excitement, the pivot of a case now firmly established in English legal history under the title of Regina versus Fredric Warburg? The book opens with the hero, Russell Conrad, in the bedroom, indeed actually in the bed of Suzanne, a beautiful blonde model. Their affair has been ardent, but it is clearly coming to an end, and Russell is annoyed because Suzanne has ended their liaison before he's ready to end it himself. Russell has a lovely wife whom he adores, and who adores him. He's an intelligent man and an idealist, reasonably well off, with a splendid career in a public relations job opening before him. His trouble is that he can no more stay away from the girls than a drunkard can keep off the bottle. In describing Russell's jobs and love affairs, the novel gives a down-to-earth picture of the manners and morals of New York society as it then was. It shows the hero as racked by conscience at his own infidelities and terrified of being found out by his wife with a divorce to follow. Kauffmann gives a good clinical analysis of the childhood origins of Russell's compulsion to get into bed with any good-looking woman who gives him the eye, and, ranging himself firmly on the side of the angels, disapproves of his hero's behaviour as beastly, unsatisfying, and likely to bring him disaster in his career. We leave Russell at the end, starting on a new and extremely important job, but already entangled in another liaison, which the reader can guess will put paid to his job, his marriage and all his other bright hopes.

If this description of *The Philanderer* makes it sound like a moral tract, the fault is mine. The author's insight into the art of seduction, and his ability to make his female characters behave as they so often do in real life, is admirable. Any intelligent reader will find much in this book to delight him, as Russell slides enjoyably to destruction. Such was the novel which caused all the hullabaloo in 1954, and was to provide agreeable matter for discussion in the summer throughout literary society, and in clubland, and in wider circles yet.

Having consulted the legal oracles, my colleagues and I drove down to Kingswood to get our decisions approved by our Heinemann directors. Frere's advice was clear – take your medicine from the magistrate, it's less dangerous, cheaper and not so widely publicized. 'Nor will there be an acquittal,' I replied, 'we would have to plead before the magistrates at Clerkenwell, who have just accepted a plea of guilty for the Werner Laurie novel.' Frere remained sceptical, and Hall agreed with him on financial grounds, Legal expenses in the High Court might ruin our profits. But determinedly we stuck to our guns, and Frere abandoned his attempt to knock some 'sensible behaviour' into our high-principled skulls. 'If you insist on acting like bloody fools,' he remarked, 'get on with it. But don't say I didn't warn you.' So, on this crucial matter, Frere acted in the spirit of our agreement. Freedom to select our books and publish what we wanted was extended to mean, even if what we wanted was or might be pornographic. I have often wondered since then whether Frere would have given us the same advice, had he known that he too was to be tried on an obscenity charge only a few months after me.

The first publisher to go on trial had been Werner Laurie, whose imprint no longer survives. They had pleaded guilty and been fined £30 or thereabouts. Press interest was half-hearted, since a plea of guilty with apologies cannot arouse much enthusiasm. We came next. There was a summons against my firm and another against the printers who had printed it for us. Accordingly on May 26 my colleagues and I drove to Clerkenwell Police Court, London, N.1, and stood waiting in the large dreary hall. When Winn arrived, he greeted me briefly and disappeared into some secret chamber of the building where unimportant non-legal persons, such as defendants, were not allowed to penetrate. Emerging a few minutes later, he beckoned me over, and in the firm but kindly tones of a medical specialist informing a patient that his disease demands an instant operation, told me that a summons was about to be served on me personally. Would this make any difference to the policy we had decided to adopt?

What did I feel at this crisis? Just as anybody else would have done – scared! Not visibly so, perhaps, for the bruise to my morale had not yet had time to swell. Confusedly I considered what my wife would say if she were present. I contemplated asking my colleagues' advice. Then I realized that this was a decision that was all mine, no one else was going to shoulder it for me. 'Well,' I asked Winn in a final effort to avoid a decision, 'what do you suggest?'

'In view of the fact that you have let it be widely known in advance that you intend to demand trial before a judge and jury, I think it would be rather pusillanimous if you should change your plans now that you are personally involved.' This sentence, long and involved as it may appear to those who read it, penetrated slowly into my bemused mind and exploded there with deadly effect. 'Pusillanimous: adjective, small-minded, hence cowardly.' Rather cowardly, but by the same token somewhat prudent, quite a lot safer, much less worrying, and a good deal cheaper. A fine of £50 instead of maybe £500. A prison sentence of. . . . But my mind rebelled at the consideration of prison sentences of whatever length.

As I stood there with Winn, gazing distractedly at the unbeautiful ceiling, I almost decided to choose the coward's path. The case could begin and conclude that very morning. No waiting, no worrying, no more time for preparation, no opportunity for regrets. The words 'I'll take what's coming now' hovered on my lips. What I said was 'We'd better go to the Old Bailey as planned, hadn't we?'

There was not much of interest after that. The big moment came when an officer of the Court made his way to where I stood bashfully at the back with my colleagues and presented me with a sheet of paper headed 'Summons'. At this I stared in a dazed manner until the officer indicated that I was no longer an entirely free agent, but was to accompany him to another part of the courtroom where I had to face the magistrate. Formal evidence was given. The magistrate sat fingering a copy of the book, into which he had inserted numerous slips of paper to mark passages he regarded as doubtful. He seemed astonished that we had not pleaded guilty. Like most lawyers he approved of precedents, but we were ignoring them in a most distasteful way. Before long we were all headed straight for the high jump at the Central Criminal Court.

Why had the D.P.P.* decided to summon me personally? It must have been a change of plan on his part, for it was only two days before the case was to be heard by the magistrate that the police called at my office (in my absence) and subpoena-ed from my harrassed secretary the letters that showed me to be personally responsible for

*D.P.P. does not refer to a single individual, but to the office generally.

accepting the book for publication. The reason must have been that the D.P.P. had become aware, since we had made no secret of it, that we intended to ask for a judge and jury and that we meant to make a fight of it, unlike Werner Laurie who had grovelled. Possibly he hoped to scare me, the managing-director and villain-in-chief, into accepting a magistrate's verdict. But he may have argued differently, believing that the publicity of an Old Bailey trial, if followed by a verdict of guilty, would scare off a number of other publishers who had published or might be about to publish obscene books. Certainly the three publishers who followed me at intervals into the Old Bailey were given no choice – the magistrates refused to consider their cases. One last point. To prosecute an abstract entity such as a limited (or incorporated) company is a somewhat impersonal performance. Such an entity cannot sit in the dock between warders, cannot plead in a hypothetical voice through abstract lips. It is invisible. But, with a live defendant, you can deprive him of his business suit, dress him in prison garb, lock him up for six months, expose him to the indignity of being pushed around by warders. To achieve all this, the D.P.P. needed a flesh-and-blood publisher, a person, a body. In fact, he needed me.

Now came a month of waiting, a period made harder for me by the vituperative criticism of the law on obscenity from my wife, and by the consideration shown me by my colleagues, an attitude unusual for colleagues in the normal course of business. Friends, thinking to amuse, promised to visit me in prison and bring me a 'nice book' to read. Even the first time I heard this miserable joke, I regarded it as in bad taste. One thought did buoy me up, the belief that *The Philanderer* was not an obscene book, whatever the jury might find, and in this my wife was a comfort to me, for she insisted that *The Philanderer* was so boring that no jury would be able to finish reading it. Her attitude, however, reflected harshly on my abilities as a publisher. Nor was it borne out by the fact that the novel had had a brisk sale on publication. It merely confirmed my view that women are more familiar with the facts of sex than men, and therefore less scandalized by them. From this premise I deduced that female jurors would be more likely to champion my cause than men, especially since they might be expected to have a soft spot in their hearts for philanderers. All this surprised the lawyers, whose views on women seemed to me hopelessly old-fashioned.

In due course the anguish of suspense was behind me, and the day fixed for the hearing arrived. The news had got out that a hitherto reputable publisher was to be tried on a criminal charge, and an enormous crowd jostled each other at the side door of the Old Bailey to ensure themselves seats in the courtroom. By 'enormous' I do not mean such numbers as are required to fill Wembley Stadium or Carnegie Hall. I have in mind a modest hundred or so persons, a trivial number where a notorious murder case is scheduled, but undoubtedly impressive where a case about a book and its publisher is the only entertainment offered to the public. Only a handful got seats, for in an English court the number of individuals actually present so that 'justice may be manifestly seen to have been done' is not excessive.

My wife naturally had a new hat for the occasion. She looked both lovely and anxious, something that women of personality can usually manage with ease. I could not help wondering whether she still believed *The Philanderer* to be as boring a book as she claimed. I could not help wondering also whether there wouldn't be a temporary period of forced separation for us when the trial was over. I wore a smart but sober double-breasted suit, rejecting a buttonhole as too flippant, but selecting a lively tie to indicate that I regarded the proceedings without apprehension.

* * *

Old Bailey is a name of sinister significance in the annals of England. A street in the City of London, Bailey is said to be a corruption of Balehill, an eminence close by St. Paul's on which stood the house of the bailiff. Thus it was a suitable place for a gallows where men could see from a distance that the full penalty of the law had been visited on the unfortunate criminal. For more than a thousand years the place had been associated with a dock and a gibbet. A place of evil omen indeed, and most insanitary in the old days, for Stow reports in his *Survey of London* that 'there was a large cistern with divers cocks which received the waste water of the prison of Ludgate for the use of the neighbouring inhabitants.' Newgate Gaol was close at hand till Dickens' day to receive those committed to it from Old Bailey. But Newgate Gaol is no more, and in 1906 a new stone-faced courthouse replaced the old and takes up nearly all the space originally occupied by the prison.*

This hideous building had a frontage of some 150 feet, on which columns, windows and allegorical figures of the female sex struggle for predominance, topped by a dome, and the dome topped by the

*The Old Bailey has now been enormously enlarged.

figure of Justice with sword in one hand, scales in the other. In the main hall in letters impossible to ignore, you may read 'Defend the Children of the Poor and Punish the Wrongdoer'. Proceeding inside you mount a broad flight of marble stairs to the long gallery on the first floor, from which the four courtrooms open out. Some twenty feet from the floor, the frieze of the walls carries such inspiring inscriptions as 'London Shall Have All Its Ancient Rights', surmounted by a vigorous painting of the bombardment of the Old Bailey by the Luftwaffe, and 'Moses Gave Unto the People the Laws of God', crowned by an obese Moses in a bath-towel descending from Mt Sinai with the tablets.

The No. 2 Court of the Old Bailey is a large chamber, some 60 feet wide, 100 feet long, and 40 feet high. It is panelled in dark wood to some 12 feet from the floor, and the rest of the walls are painted cream. The chairs and benches are padded with green leather, picked out in gold with the arms of the City of London, Domine Dirige Nos. Its capacity must be around 120 persons, and a visitors' gallery high up off the floor, and entered by a separate stairway, will seat a score or two more. As I walked into it, with my wife's arm in mine and my colleagues close behind me, I identified without difficulty the great chair with the royal arms on which the judge was to preside, and facing it across the well of the court that ill-omened rectangle known in England as the dock, within which an accused person sits during his trial and stands to receive his sentence – or his discharge, not too common an event here.

The dock, an institution blessedly unfamiliar to Americans, is Flemish in origin, *dok*, meaning a birdcage or rabbit hutch. It was first used in the seventeenth century, and popularized, if the word is appropriate, by Dickens in *Oliver Twist*, since when it has been used many million times by all classes of society. In 1610 part of a room at the Old Bailey where criminals were housed was surrounded by a spiked fence, and this was known as the *bail-dock*. One James Goodman, unwilling to entrust his fate to a judge and jury, leapt over the spikes and escaped into the narrow streets of the London of his day, an athletic feat which it was not in me to rival. Recently there has been a growing agitation for the abolition of the dock on the grounds that it prejudices a prisoner's defence, since the prisoner in it must appear to be guilty. Why otherwise is he in a dock at all? In my view, a prisoner should sit with his legal advisers as in American courts. Any society dedicated to the abolition of docks can have my subscription for the asking.

The case before mine was ending. Mr. Justice Stable was presiding. A weedy fellow in his thirties stood accused of knocking an old woman over the head and stealing a few pounds out of the till. Soon after my own case had opened, this thug was brought into court to hear the jury's verdict of 'guilty' and to receive a sentence of seven years, with some blistering remarks from the judge on the brutal nature of his crime.

In a few minutes the awful moment came when it was my turn next. My cheeks felt hot and my legs wobbled, but I defeated the urge to flight in time to accompany an officer of the Court in the direction of the dock. This action of mine is known technically as 'surrendering to bail', which had been granted on 'recognizances of my own finding' at the Clerkenwell Court. The amount had been £25, a trivial sum it seemed to me in the light of the gravity of my alleged offence, and clearly the authorities thought so too, for it was increased to £100 for the publishers who came after me.

So it came about that on Tuesday, June 29th around 11.30 a.m. in No. 2 Court before Mr. Justice Stable, I was firmly separated from an anxious wife, from colleagues exuding moral support at every pore, from the whole comfortable world which had not had criminal charges levelled at it, and led by the warder into the dock. I had arrived at my finest hour, or if you look at it the other way round my most infamous, with the whole complicated apparatus of the Crown in readiness to ensure that I didn't get out of Court without an indelible stain on my character.

With the case not yet begun and the twelve chairs in the jury box empty, I felt conspicuous and went down the stairs at the back of the dock which led to the cells. Halfway down a warder stopped me and ran his hands over my body. It was the first time I had been frisked, and I was far from pleased. A simple dialogue followed.

'What have you got on you?' the warder asked.

'The usual things, cigarettes, a few pound notes, my keys.'

'What are you in for?'

'A book.'

'A book? What in hell d'you mean, a book?'

'A book,' I said, 'this one, *The Philanderer*, this is a case about a book.'

The warder looked disgusted. He must have considered it a sheer waste of the court's time to deal with dirty books. The Old Bailey deserved better than that.

It would be hard to give an adequate account of the judiciary of

England in a single paragraph, and I shall not attempt it. George Orwell wrote in *The Lion and the Unicorn* that 'the hanging judge, that evil old man in scarlet robe and horsehair wig, whom nothing short of dynamite will ever teach what century he is living in, but who will interpret the law according to the books and will in no circumstances take a money bribe, is one of the symbolic figures of England.' That's putting it harshly, but there's not much doubt that the English judge in full wig, towering above the mere mortals in his court, is a figure to strike terror in the heart of even a hardened criminal. For me it was of almost no importance that he wouldn't take a bribe. What mattered was to have a judge who was aware of the century he was living in and of the truism that the indecencies of yesteryear become the commonplaces of today.

There is a word to be said, too, about juries at the Old Bailey. I cast an anxious eye over mine before the trial began, and indeed at frequent intervals while the case was in progress. A nicer lot of individuals I have rarely seen together in one place. My difficulty lay in deciding whether they were confirmed readers, resolute not to allow themselves to be deprived of intellectual sustenance, or even, when I looked at one or two of them in the back row, whether they had been taught to read, and had remembered what they had been taught. A jury at the Old Bailey is not a blue-ribbon jury, but a group of men and women as liable to look first at the racing page, the gossip column or the fashion news as to turn their mind to the more serious aspects of world affairs.

A few minutes later the trial began, or, as the lawyers say, was called on. I ran back up the stairs and re-entered the dock, sitting down in the hard Windsor chair provided, with a warder on either side of me. The jury filed into the jury box. There was a pause, we all stood up and Mr. Justice Stable made a dignified entrance. We all bowed, and he sat down in his great chair. The stage was now set for the First Act. Scene One was packed with action.

'How do you plead, guilty or not guilty?' the Clerk of the Court demanded, as I faced him across the courtroom. A good friend of mine was married to the daughter of a distinguished American lawyer, Morris Ernst, who had in his day defended many a doubtful book against a charge of 'having a tendency'. This friend had lunched with me a few weeks before, and passed on a pearl of wisdom from his father-in-law which came to me now in the hour of need. There are two essentials for a successful defence on an obscenity charge this great man had laid down: the first a good lawyer, the second a strong conviction of your own innocence. Now I felt was the occasion to display the latter. In a voice that rang through the courtroom I shouted my plea, 'Not guilty.'

Soon after this, to the consternation of the Crown, the judge ordered me out of the dock. 'Many distinguished men have sat in the dock at the Old Bailey before Mr. Warburg,' he said, 'but I do not consider it – and I am sure, members of the jury, you will agree with me – a suitable place for the defendant in this trial. He may sit with his legal advisers.' The jurors beamed with delight at being consulted by so eminent a personage almost before the case had begun. They would do nothing, their bewildered smiles indicated, to harass the judge in his conduct of the case. In some bewilderment myself I stood up. I did not exactly run out of the dock, but in a jiffy I found myself seated between Hogarth and my co-director, Farrer, in the well of the Court. I now had a much poorer view of the proceedings, since the dock is strategically placed to overlook nearly every quarter of the room, but I felt incomparably more at ease.

The trial began, and Mr. Mervyn Griffith-Jones,* prosecuting, opened for the Crown by telling the jury that the two defendant companies, the publishing house and the printers, were firms of good standing against whom nothing was known, and that the defendant was a man of the highest integrity with an unblemished record. Then why in heaven's name, I thought, put me to all the anxiety and expense of defending myself? Why not exhibit a copy or two of *The Philanderer* for trial in the dock and let it go at that. These early sentences were about the only ones in counsel's speech with which I was able to find myself in any kind of agreement. Soon, I must confess, I took a cordial dislike to him, as he expressed his views in a most forceful manner about the depraving influence of Kauffmann's novel. I looked up at the judge to see how he was taking it. But he sat aloft, unruffled. The nine men and three women, on whom my fate ultimately depended, were putting up a good show of being interested, but I wondered how long this would last.

At the end of his speech, prosecuting counsel produced a sheaf of typed pages which he proposed to hand to the jurors. These pages contained the list of passages the Crown claimed were obscene. Mr. Winn rose from his seat to object, and the judge upheld him. He turned towards the jury and said, 'Would you mind reading it *from cover to cover*. Read it as a book. Do you follow? Not picking out bits

*Now a High Court judge.

that you think have, shall we say, a sort of immoral tendency, but read it as a book. Do not discuss it with your friends and relations because they may not appreciate the legal tests that you ultimately have to apply.'

This decision of the judge was something of a triumph for the defence. Sentences and paragraphs may seem decent enough when they are read in their proper places in a book. But when they are read out, one after another, the impression can easily be created that the book is nothing more than 'a filthy concoction'. But now the jurors had to read it all straight through, there was to be no short cut for them, they would have to discover for themselves what the Crown called 'the objectionable passages' by reading a full-length 80,000 word novel.

My feeling of sympathy for the jurors in having this homework thrust upon them was not excessive, for in an obscenity trial at that time there was precious little for them to do but listen to two speeches and a summing-up. No long hours were spent hearing 'expert' evidence, for such evidence was not allowable. The uninstructed might imagine that the author himself would be allowed to tell the jury why he wrote the book the way he did, that the publisher would have a chance of explaining how he came to publish it. Nothing of the kind. Malcolm Muggeridge was in court at our request, a knowledgeable reviewer capable of dissecting the book for the benefit of the jury. So was Graham Greene, one of the best novelists of the day. As friends of mine, they might have been able to add a word or two about my own unblemished character. Instead, they sat amiable but gagged, ghost witnesses till the close of proceedings. After only an hour or two in court on June 29, the jurors were presented with a copy each of *The Philanderer* and sent home to read it. The Court rose, and we all went away till Friday morning, a three-day interval in which I tried to keep calm and resume my duties as a publisher.

The second and final day of the trial came, and an even bigger crowd clamoured for admission, for the news had got out that for the first time in a generation a publisher was giving the Crown a run for its money. Indeed, the betting in the clubs at this stage must have firmed up to evens. An impartial summing-up was expected. Of course, no one knew how the jury would find, whatever the summing-up, for no jury had had a lively modern novel to read in years.

No record appears to exist of the final speeches for the defence and the prosecution. But my view of them remains naïvely clear.

Winn had put forward a masterly and subtle defence of *The Philanderer* and its publisher, taking in on the way the necessity for freedom of publication, the value of literature to society, the difficulties of the defence in an obscenity trial, and much else besides. Griffith-Jones on the other hand had used every trick of the mob orator to bring about my downfall, banging on the table, sneering, quoting the most succulent passages he could find. He had given what seemed to me a ham performance like a third-rate villain in an old-fashioned melodrama. But, of course, on this matter I speak with no impartiality at all. All the same, when Griffith-Jones lifted up the skirts of his gown and sat down, I felt it was not a moment too soon. He had made even me feel guilty. In what moment of thoughtlessness had I ever considered making a contract to publish this vile product of an author's diseased brain? Why had my colleagues permitted me to go ahead with it? How had the printers consented to manufacture it? Did I not deserve what I was likely to receive – crushing remarks from the judge, a heavy fine, a term of imprisonment? Wrapped in gloom, I waited for the judge's summing-up.

This speech, now famous throughout legal and literary circles wherever English is understood, seemed to me to pack more commonsense on a difficult theme into a short space than could possibly be expected. It was delivered extempore, with the help of a few notes. The jury enjoyed it – the judge was treating them as grown-ups, even as keen and intelligent readers. For myself I enjoyed it then and I enjoy it now. Often when I have half an hour to spare I read it through.*

* * *

The judge disclosed to the jury quite early on that sex is essential to procreation and hence to the continued existence of the human race. He said that this was not his fault, nor that of members of the jury, nor (by implication) that of the author or publisher of *The Philanderer.* The mistake, if it were one, he said, could be attributed to the great Creator of life, and the jury should overlook it. Indeed, he went so far as to suggest that it was nothing to worry about, and should be accepted without dismay by all decent law-abiding people. Here he

*The full text of the speech is printed as an appendix to the novel with which it is concerned. It also appeared in the year of the trial as an elegant 16-page pamphlet, signed by the man who spoke it, Wintringham N. Stable himself, printed by the American publisher, Alfred and Blanche Knopf, to give away to friends at Christmas.

was of course in direct conflict with the Crown, which had tended to maintain that passion was 'sheer filth'.

From this solid beginning he went on to make some sound remarks about the function of literature in general, and of the novel in particular. He considered that the contemporary novelist held up a mirror to the society of his own day, precisely as the great Victorians had held it up to the society of the nineteenth century. 'This is an American novel purporting to depict the lives of people living today in New York, and to portray the speech, the turn of phrase and the current attitude towards this particular aspect of life there. If we are going to read novels about how things go in New York, it would not be of much assistance, *would it*, if, contrary to the fact, we were led to suppose that in New York no unmarried woman or teenager has disabused her mind of the idea that babies are brought by storks or are sometimes found in cabbage patches or under gooseberry bushes?' The 'would it?' came out of his mouth like the crack of a pistol shot.

By this time the prosecutor must have felt that the sooner the Court adjourned for lunch the better. But the judge had another rod in pickle for him before then. He had already asked implacably 'are we to take our literary standards as being the level of something that is suitable for the decently brought up young female aged fourteen? Or do we go even further back than that, and be reduced to the sort of books one reads as a child in the nursery? The answer to that is *of course not*.' Again the crack of a pistol shot. 'A mass of literature is wholly unsuitable for reading by adolescents,' he continued, 'but that does not mean that a publisher may not make it available for the general public.' Next he dealt with the Crown's contention that books like *The Philanderer* would poison the minds of teenagers. 'You have heard a great deal about the putting of ideas into young heads,' he said, 'really, members of the jury, is it books that put ideas into young heads, or is it Nature?' Stable clearly understood the perils of the passage through adolescence, travelling, as he put it 'through an unknown country without a map, a compass, and sometimes even a guide. It is the natural change from childhood to maturity that puts ideas into young heads.'

The court then adjourned for lunch. I was beginning to feel more cheerful. At least some jurors would realize, I thought, that *The Philanderer* was a serious novel, not a piece of nastiness. When we resumed, his lordship took up this very point. 'You may agree,' he said, 'that it is a good book, or a bad book, or a moderate book. It is at least a book, the creation of a human mind and it depicts people created by the author in the environment in which portions of their lives were spent. You may agree, or you may not, that it is not mere pornographic literature, the filthy bawdy muck that is just filth for filth's sake.' This was precisely what I felt.

Soon after this Mr. Justice Stable stopped. He had spoken for about one hour and a half. It was not a moment too long for me. To listen on an otherwise disagreeable afternoon to the wisdom of Nestor, the charm of Cicero and the forcefulness of Demosthenes is a boon rarely vouchsafed to twentieth-century man. Despite my urgent wish to clap, I restrained myself. The judge looked at the jury, as much as to say 'I've done my part pretty well, now it's your turn,' and the jury left the box. I stood up, stretched my legs and walked over to sit by my wife while the jury considered its verdict. I was not without hope. Unfortunately my wife, who had borne earlier anxiety with the stoicism of a Spartan mother awaiting the return of her son from battle, now lost her nerve. As the minutes passed, her alarm became plainer still. She appeared to think that, in view of the summing-up and on account of the sterling character of her husband, the jurors should not be wasting time in aimless chit-chat between themselves. They should have given their verdict of *not guilty* without bothering to leave the box.

After 50 minutes back came the jurors. It was nearly 4 o'clock. The courtroom buzzed with the confused sounds made by a number of people waiting for something dramatic to happen. Mr. Justice Stable looked at the jury. The foreman rose and faced him. My throat was dry. 'How do you find, members of the jury, guilty or not guilty?' demanded the Clerk of the Court. NOT GUILTY. It was a unanimous verdict. There was no cheering, but everyone in court seemed pleased. The jurors looked happy, as well they might, since they had had a short and rather entertaining trial of a kind which had never been heard at the Old Bailey before.

The case was headlined that evening and the next day in an immense variety of London and provincial newspapers. *The Times* in a leading article paternally headed 'A Wise Approach', observed that 'Mr. Justice Stable has helped us to preserve a balanced judgment, when confronted by the unfamiliar and the unpleasant in literature, by discouraging a witch-hunt against publishers which would be as capricious in its justice as witch-hunts traditionally are.' This appeared to be the general view. Many people believed that it heralded a new deal for literature and that the three cases pending would be dropped. Letters of congratulation arrived on my desk in a steady trickle from Brazil, New York, Denmark, India, France, and from the great state of Texas. One of them quoted Edmund Gosse's remark – 'Let us say we would rather see English literature free than decent.' I wondered whether this was not going a bit too far. Certainly the D.P.P. thought so, for soon the new batch of summonses was delivered, against three more publishers, with others held in reserve. The Public Prosecutor might have lost a battle, but he was still determined to win the war.

* * *

The trial was over. I walked out of the Central Criminal Court with my wife and my colleagues a free man, not only physically at large but cleared from the stain of a criminal conviction. It was one of the greatest moments of my life. We had defended a vital principle, freedom of publication, with complete success. In terms of money it had cost us little,* in terms of extreme anxiety it had been expensive. What had we actually achieved? The answer was slow in coming, but in the end there can be little doubt that The Philanderer Case had released the wind of change, a stiff breeze which helped to blow us for better or worse into the age of permissiveness.

But it did not look like that during the months ahead. About three months after our acquittal, a new trial began before the Recorder of London, one of the regular Old Bailey judges. The accused were the large publishing house of Hutchinson & Co., who published this book and its predecessor, and their then managing director, Mrs. Katherine Webb, together with the unfortunate printer, who is always dragged into such cases because the law demands it, in my opinion wrongly. The book was a novel by Vivian Connell, called *September in Quinze*, a rather sordid story of a character clearly based on Farouk, ex-king of Egypt, and his exotic life on the French riviera. The Recorder interpreted the law in a very different manner to Stable. 'It is fortunate,' he remarked early in his summing-up, 'that the recent campaign against pornographic literature has resulted in at least one decision which is of great use to the courts now.' But he was referring not to the Philanderer trial but to the Reiter case, where a publisher of cheap paperbacks had issued a number of nasty little books which no 'responsible' publisher would

*I recall our costs as being some £600, say £2,000 in terms of 1972–3 money. Today I reckon the costs would be at least four times as much, and more than that if many witnesses are called.

even have considered. The legal definition of obscenity, he said, 'is designed to protect the weak rather than the strong-minded. A book which would not influence the mind of an archbishop might well affect the mind of . . . a callow youth, a girl just budding into womanhood.' There could hardly have been a more direct contradiction of Stable's interpretation. He accepted (in theory) Stable's argument that a jury must consider the book as a whole, but added 'when you come across one of these lurid passages, it is quite impossible to ignore its influence,' which makes nonsense of what went before. Referring directly to Stable, he went on 'passages have been read to you from his summing-up . . . but remember he was dealing with one book and you are dealing with another . . . a different book altogether.' The jury found the defendants guilty, which was scarcely surprising. Delivering sentence, the Recorder fined each of them £500, a swingeing penalty. Addressing the unfortunate Mrs. Webb, who was seated in the dock, he said, 'you are lucky to have received only a fine, I have had to consider carefully whether I should not send you to prison for six months.' Mrs. Webb, who had claimed in evidence not to have read the book before publication, collapsed with a nervous breakdown.

By now I think I have established that the atmosphere of 1953 in the book world was much tenser, and the perils much greater than 20 years later. Gloom descended on the world of literature. The blue pencils were resharpened. Legal experts received increasing numbers of doubtful typescripts from publishers for reports of their corrupting qualities. But now, as before, no one could divine what was obscene and what was not. The informed, who followed the development of the campaign from ringside seats, as it were, waited for the fourth trial, where A. S. Frere and William Heinemann Ltd. were charged with publishing Walter Baxter's novel *The Image and the Search*, issued by Putnam in New York. Baxter was in the dock with Frere.

We knew instinctively that this trial would be decisive. If the Crown lost, it would have to throw up the sponge; if it won, we might expect further rounds in the grim contest. No one foresaw the extraordinary course that this trial would take and the long drawn-out agony of suspense that awaited Frere, Heinemann's chairman, and Baxter.

Four days after the summing-up in the Hutchinson trial, I wrote to D. Kilham Roberts, a barrister and full-time secretary of the Society of Authors. 'This letter contains a plea,' I wrote, 'for urgent action in defence of freedom of publication. . . . So far as the Recorder is concerned, no book shall be published likely to bring a blush to the cheeks of schoolgirls.* . . . I see no particular reason why *every* general publisher could not be successfully prosecuted whenever the authorities choose to take action, I do not think I exaggerate the situation.' Nor do I now. I sent copies of this letter to J. B. Priestley, Graham Greene, prominent members of the Society's committee, and a strong letter to the President of the Publishers Association. The first necessity, I wrote, is to press for an alteration in the law. Priestley was in 'substantial' and Greene in 'complete' agreement with my views. The second necessity was to allow 'expert' evidence. Slowly the movement gathered momentum. On October 27 I wrote to R. Code Holland, chairman of the libel and obscene libel group of the Publishers Association, asking him to collaborate with the Authors Society and appoint a joint committee to prepare 'a suitable draft (Bill) for consideration by the Home Secretary. . . . I want to give up agitating in this manner and to feel it is in reliable hands . . . or must I go on making myself a nuisance?'

On October 18 Heinemann and Frere were tried before Mr. Justice Devlin. *The Image and the Search* was quite a difficult book to defend. It contained numerous passages of an explicitly sexual character. Throughout it called a spade a spade. Its theme was of a woman who had lost a dearly loved husband in the war and embarked on a series of erotic encounters to find herself again. Redemption through sex. A Jesuit priest was present to give evidence for the publishers, but as usual the evidence was inadmissible. I was in court, and heard the speech for the prosecution. By shutting my eyes I was readily able to imagine myself sitting once more through my own case. Speeches for the prosecution throughout the series followed a set pattern – 'Members of the jury, I call your attention to page 17 or 117 or 217, read from there.' Often I felt that the jury was bored by the constant repetition, and would have cried out if they had dared, 'I say, old man, we've read the book, you know.' The defence, on the other hand, took trouble in all the cases to analyse the book as a whole.

Mr. Justice Devlin's summing-up was strictly neutral. He declared that he did not wish to be a thirteenth opinion on the jury, and left it to them. The jury was out for four hours, and then returned to announce a disagreement. The judge sent them out again, and after an hour they came back in two minds once more. They were dis-

*It was believed at the time that the Recorder was determined to hear *all* the obscenity cases. For him, a sincere and ardent evangelical, it was to be a crusade. But higher authority seems to have intervened.

missed and a re-trial was ordered, to the surprise of many. The case was fought hard all over again a month later before Mr. Justice Lynskey. Again the jury disagreed. The Crown at last gave up. Frere and Baxter were discharged, having endured for six months an ordeal to which sensitive men should not be subjected without allowing them to say one single word in their own defence.

On the same day the fifth trial was held. The book charged was one which should never have been attacked. After ten minutes the jury returned a verdict of Not Guilty. The case attracted almost no publicity. The campaign ended 'not with a bang but a whimper'. All emotion had been drained away in the interminable battle over the bodies of Frere and Baxter.

Meantime, writers had at last taken steps to protect themselves and their publishers from an out-of-date law. The Authors Society had set up a strong committee, under the chairmanship of Sir Alan (A. P.) Herbert, with C. R. Hewitt (C. H. Rolph) as secretary. Members included Roy Jenkins, Lord Lambton, Rupert Hart-Davis and R. Code Holland (appointed by the Publishers Association), and a number of authors, including V. S. Pritchett, Dilys Powell, Guy Chapman and H. E. Bates. After five years of struggle and negotiation, the Obscene Publications Act, 1959 emerged after passing, almost miraculously it seemed to me, through both the Commons and the Lords. The Act was something of a bargain between the bill drafted by the Committee of Authors and the needs of the office of the D.P.P. While accepting most of the demands made by the committee. which were concerned with the needs of 'reputable' authors and 'responsible' publishers, the D.P.P. got in return much stronger weapons against the more blatant and clearly worthless forms of pornographic material. The two most important concessions were – in future, a book must be read as a whole, evidence of experts was admissible whether publication was 'for the public good' or 'in the interests of science, literature, art or learning, or of other objects of general concern.'

This great and liberating Act was challenged in 1960 by the D.P.P. in a trial which started on October 20 in Court Two of the Old Bailey. The book challenged was D. H. Lawrence's famous novel, *Lady Chatterley's Lover*. The trial was on a stupendous scale and lasted six long action-packed days.* My old enemy, Mr. Mervyn Griffith-Jones, senior Treasury Counsel at the Old Bailey, appeared

*The transcript has been edited by C. H. Rolph, with a brief introduction, under the title *The Trial of Lady Chatterley*, Penguin Books, 1961.

for the Prosecution, as he had done in the five cases in 1954. For the defence three famous lawyers had been engaged, Gerald Gardiner, Jeremy Hutchinson and Richard du Cann. There was no 'prisoner at the Bar' – the defendants Sir Allen Lane and Hans Schmoller of Penguin Books, sat with their solicitors, as I had done at my trial after Stable had lifted me out of the dock. Nevertheless, there is one vital difference between the Chatterley trial and the trials of the year 1954. The 1954 trials were dangerous to *defendants*. *Chatterley* was a test case, only the *book* was in danger.

Even under the less stringent Obscenity Act, 1959, it was difficult to believe, if you were the Public Prosecutor or his advisers, that so 'notorious' a book as *Lady Chatterley's Lover* could be let loose on the innocent and corruptible British public. They wanted desperately to stop it, but they did *not* want to send Lane or Schmoller to prison if they got a conviction. To put it mildly, the news that Sir Allen Lane, founder and head of Penguin Books, was in prison, and for publishing a work of one of the greatest writers of the twentieth century, might have led, if not to a general strike, at least to a crisis of unforeseeable proportions. Lane graciously played along with them. Although he had printed a first edition of 100,000 copies and advertised the book extensively, he did not actually distribute copies to the shops. The book was on sale only in a technical or Pickwickian sense. Although the duel was of enormous importance, it was not deadly, the buttons were not off the foils, the winner (like an Olympic contender) could expect, not the wounding or death of his opponent, but a gold medal.

This was the end of the crusade. There have been plenty of obscenity cases since the Penguin trial, and they have taken place under new rules. Rolph was to say in a broadcast of March 20, 1973, 'it can certainly be said that this sensational case, and the acquittal which ended it, were the direct consequences of Warburg's decision to challenge the D.P.P. to a stand-up fight.' With that verdict I would be inhuman not to agree. But with my name must be linked another, that of Mr. Justice Stable. Without him, we would in all probability have gone down to defeat. Who, I wonder, was responsible for appointing Stable to conduct the Philanderer case? Had we been tried before the Recorder, the odds against our acquittal would have been, say, 20 to 1 against. Stable may or may not have been a great lawyer – I am not qualified to judge – he was something better, he was a man, not a pedant but a humanist. Filled with a gusto for life, keenly interested in the society around him, he had emancipated himself effortlessly from the frigid attitudes of the past.

For him the Law and its interpretation could not be learned from the textbooks by the study of precedents, for he knew that ultimately a law must be acceptable to that part of society which is involved with that particular law. For the very first time in this field a breath of fresh air had blown through the oppressive atmosphere of Old Bailey, and in the field of literature things can never be the same again. To Stable I own a deep debt of gratitude, which I have tried to pay in part in this chapter. But there are innumerable others who owe him a debt, though many are not aware of it. Writing in the *Evening News* on November 19, 1954 H. E. Bates wrote as follows:

'The profession of authorship is important, not only because it gives you something to read, but because it gives employment to a vast number of people. Without authors there would be no printers, binders, booksellers, agents, plays, films, theatrical managers, editors, advertisers, newspapers, magazines. Half your radio programmes would be cut and half your television. . . . To suppress literature therefore is to suppress them all. . . . To institute prosecutions against responsible publishers and authors for alleged obscenity . . . is a step towards suppression.' There can be few on either side of the Atlantic or anywhere else who will not agree with him.

Now, nearly twenty years later, I have set down my impressions of that prolonged tussle for my own satisfaction and to prove yet once again that 'the price of liberty is eternal vigilance.' But it is, of course, a mite more than that, for someone sometime must take action, must take a risk. 'Isn't it awful?' creates nothing but melancholy, 'I must do something about that!' raises the blood pressure and can sometimes produce a miracle. And yet the consequences of what was achieved in the fifties have not been entirely satisfactory.

In an obscenity trial two great principles are in conflict – freedom of publication on the one hand and the social health of a nation (the public good) on the other. The second principle is at least as important as the first. Art is frequently pornographic, not only literature, but painting and sculpture. There's nothing to be done about it, except to see that such art is not destroyed. But there's little to be said for hard-core pornography, which can reasonably be described as 'sheer filth', to use the phrase that popped out of the mouths of judges and prosecuting counsel with such monotonous regularity in 1954. The trouble then was that it was being applied to books that did not deserve it. Yet how do we know whether the phrase 'sheer filth' is or is not applicable to a book? Assuming for a moment that 'filth' should be stopped, I see no better way than trial by judge and jury. The power to convict should never be vested in one man, be he magistrate, judge or censor. Nor should it ever be vested in a committee of allegedly well-intentioned persons. If they could ever agree with each other, which seems doubtful, the opinion would carry no weight whatever. Think of the lobbying which would take place by interested parties to get 'their' man elected. Think how pompous and self-righteous each of them would become, if he had the power to approve or condemn any particular work. The merits of a jury are obvious – they are chosen at random, they are anonymous, they include or should include high and low, rich and poor, men and women. There is only one qualification they should possess, the ability to read, speak and understand English.*

An obscenity trial cannot measure 'a tendency to deprave and corrupt those into whose hands a book may fall,' for, as E. M. Forster has pointed out, there is no available definition of depravity or corruption. It has been said that a more eminent judge than Cockburn was on the bench the very day that Cockburn gave the world his most inappropriate definition of obscenity in the Hicklin case. This was Mr. Justice Blackburn who remarked casually, 'an act of this sort is in fact a public nuisance.' Could we not, even at this late date, settle for that? What an obscenity trial does measure is public taste, and public taste fluctuates from generation to generation, and indeed more rapidly than that. Nor does it always become more liberal. It can go up or down. Since it is taste which is being measured, it seems harsh to try a defendant in a criminal court. Could he not be tried in a civil one, and fined in the event of conviction? There will no doubt be objections, for some of the more extreme puritans among us may hope for prison sentences under the law rather than a fine. But fines can be big as well as small, and to make the punishment fit the crime should surely be practicable. In the U.S., to the best of my knowledge, most obscenity trials are under civil law. I have little doubt that battles will be fought from time to time in the struggle between the artist and the censor. For this war is one which will never be won so long as people are seriously interested in the art of literature, and that, I hope, will be for a very long time.

*C. H. Rolph has put forward powerful arguments against juries in obscenity cases. John Calder suggests the use of lay assessors, to sit on the bench to assist the judge. I would welcome this, but only if the assessors were chosen at random and not allowed to act too frequently. The assessors should be able to outvote the judge, if it comes to a disagreement.

13
The Japanese Connexion

As a publisher I have been forced by the requirements of my trade to read all or part of innumerable books, running no doubt into thousands. Some have occupied less than five minutes of my time, others an hour or two, yet others as much as two or three days. A small percentage of these books I have published, because I thought them, at the time, worthwhile. Yet many of this small percentage were not books which I would have read either for pleasure or instruction or illumination, had I not been or become their publisher and so accepted the responsibility of doing whatever a publisher can do for an author on his list. It is one of the deepest pleasures of my retirement to be able now to read or re-read some of the books which speak powerfully to me.

But the ordinary man or woman is no better off than me. He has a job to do which will occupy the greater part of his waking life, while she, if she has no job, has the arduous chores of housekeeping and the demands of motherhood. Faced with the spectacle of the crowded shelves of libraries and the colourful displays in the bookshops, even a keen reader may despair, and by the age of thirty will have abandoned all hope of reading any but a small proportion of the world's masterpieces or even the books he would like to read.

Why then should I have become so excited on my American trip of spring 1954 at the possibility of publishing novels from the Japanese? Surely no worthwhile Japanese literature existed? Certainly none had hitherto been translated. It was difficult enough to sell even the best French, German, Italian or Scandinavian novels. Did the Orientals write books? Who had ever heard of a contemporary Indian or Chinese literature? And yet, when Harold

Strauss, a senior editor of Knopf, began to talk to me, I listened with rapt attention.

In 1943 Strauss, an air force lieutenant concerned with excruciatingly dull publicity duties, put in an application to transfer to military government, expecting to be sent to Europe, since he had a fair knowledge of several European languages. He was accepted and sent to train at Charlottesville, Virginia. However, the mysterious powers-that-be switched him, just before his course was complete, to Northwestern University, Chicago, to learn Japanese. Strauss regarded the transfer as a waste of his time, but he could hardly have been more wrong. After six months he was shipped to Monterey, California to await the great MacArthur's pleasure. Soon he was summoned and settled into a job in Japan 'scanning' books and magazines to see which of them were worthy enough to receive a ration of paper, which was naturally in short supply.

The job excited him, for he came to realize for the first time that contemporary Japanese literature had remarkable qualities. 'As you may suppose,' he wrote me on December 21, 1972, 'I was not content to be semi-literate. From 1945 till 1953 I worked like the devil, using Japanese primers, to become literate. I was in Japan only for one year after the end of the war, though I've been back eleven times since, but my work threw me into contact with generous advisers such as Osaragi and Kawabata.' He also came to know the great Japanese specialists, Donald Keene, Howard Hibbett, Ivan Morris and others.

Here, in fact, was the right man in the right place at the right time. It can't have been long before an idea dawned in his publisher's mind – to translate and publish some of the finest modern Japanese novels. It is strange to realize that the discovery of Japanese literature and the availability of translators from the Japanese was due to the entry of Japan into World War Two and the subsequent occupation of Japan. Without that, recognition of its importance might have been delayed for years.

On his return to New York Strauss discussed the project with Alfred Knopf who encouraged him from the beginning and authorized him to go ahead. Contracts had to be signed, translators found, there was much to do. It was not till early 1954 that he confided his plans to me. When he'd finished, I told him I felt sure we'd back him up to the limit in this highly speculative venture. I had remembered my wife's pleasure and my own in reading Murasaki's *Tale of Genji*, translated by Arthur Waley, whose six volumes rested on my library shelves at home. Within three years we had published four modern Japanese novels.*

From the beginning this affair intoxicated me, it was a journey into the unknown, a voyage of discovery into a strange country which had suddenly erupted in 1941 into the Western world, a nation of terrifying power whose bombers had destroyed a huge American fleet in Pearl Harbor. To have the privilege of introducing a new and major modern literature into Britain was as satisfying as the re-establishment of Aubrey's *Brief Lives* as a classic six years earlier. The value of Japanese literature is clearly set out in a long article in the *Times Literary Supplement* of August 20, 1971 by Ivan Morris, himself a fine translator of some of the books we have published. 'What I would stress above all,' he writes, 'is the combination of distinctive "Japaneseness" with emotional accessibility. The idea that Japanese culture "all comes from China" [or that] "it has all become completely Westernized" is still accepted by people who should know better. In fact, Japanese culture is probably a great deal less derivative than England's; and, in spite of a hundred years of relentless Western influence, Japan in 1971 remains in many ways remarkably Japanese. Though certain types of writing were deliberately . . . based on foreign models, the great majority of the works are uniquely Japanese, and they include some of the most impressive writing in world literature.'

The first Japanese novel we issued was Jiro Osaragi's *Homecoming* on August 15, 1955, a study of a man banished from Japan and from wife and child to Singapore, returning after the war to revisit his battle-scarred homeland. Its sales were indifferent. Next on February 13, 1956, came *Some Prefer Nettles* by Junichiro Tanizaki, often referred to as the grand old man (or Mann) of Japanese letters. This was a short and subtle story of a modern bourgeois sick of his empty domestic life with his wife. Both take lovers, and the breach becomes too wide. Divorce follows, undertaken with a polite sophistication to marvel at. On February 11, 1957, came Yukio Mishima's *The Sound of Waves*, a kind of Daphnis and Chloë story in a Japanese setting, and on March 25 Shohei Ooka's *Fires on the Plain*, translated by

*'For distinguished service in introducing Japanese literature to America and to Europe', Strauss was awarded the Kikuchi Kan Prize, one of only three foreigners ever to receive it. Kikuchi Kan was a wealthy man with a cosmopolitan outlook far ahead of his time, a moderate writer but a great editor. He left the money for prizes on his death. They are awarded by *Bungei Shunju*, a leading literary magazine.

Ivan Morris. On July 1, 1957, came Yasunari Kawabata's *Snow Country*, a study of the possibility of love in an earthly paradise, a geisha in a hot-spring resort in the mountains with a wealthy dilettante free of all worldly cares. Kawabata was to win the Nobel Prize for Literature in 1968 and, in 1972, to commit suicide, quietly and untheatrically, his work done, in the fullness of his seventy years. The fate of Mishima, who was perhaps the greatest of them all, will be discussed later.

Four of these five writers had been published by Knopf: the exception was Ooka. How well had Strauss chosen! Tanizaki, Mishima and Kawabata must rank with the finest writers in the world today. All three are now dead. Only one, Tanizaki, died a natural death. Further books by these authors followed, and books by other writers too. Today over thirty Japanese novels have appeared under my firm's imprint, and quite a number of books about Japanese culture generally.

No doubt I had heard about Ooka's *Fires on the Plain* from its translator, Ivan Morris. It was over ten years later that I was alerted to the significance of Masuji Ibuse's *Black Rain* by C. P. Snow (Lord Snow) who, reviewing in the *Financial Times* one of fifty copies available in England, wrote 'a novel that turns Hiroshima into a major work of art, utterly unsentimental, unsparing but not at all sensational.' As a result we bought British rights and published it with all the energy that its quality demanded. No two books could offer a greater contrast.

For me *Fires* has seemed *the* book of World War Two, as Erich Remarque's *All Quiet on the Western Front* was *the* book of World War One. Each is an account and an indictment of the obscenity of war. *Fires* is the only outstanding book by Ooka, stemming directly, as the translator points out, from the overwhelming emotions he himself experienced in the Philippines. The central character, Private Tamura, suffering from tuberculosis, is thrown out of his defeated and disorganized unit to wander in the jungle with nothing but a few potatoes to eat. 'Tamura's persistent effort to avoid total degradation, to retain a grip, however tenuous, on human dignity,' as Ivan Morris writes, is the mainspring of the novel. Slowly Tamura descends to 'callousness, murder and cannibalism. But the ultimate abomination he resists: he can kill his fellow creatures, even eat their bodies, but he will not murder in order to eat.'

Ibuse's novel, *Black Rain*, is the work of an entirely different kind of writer, who has written novels and stories of quality about themes other than the war. Wise, sophisticated, kindly, with his emotions under an apparently effortless control, he describes the fall of the atomic bomb on Hiroshima and its effect on the life of that city and its population, on a number of clearly drawn characters, and on the central figure of the elderly Shigematsu whose interest in life is breeding carp. the *Times Literary Supplement*, reviewing it on March 26, 1971, writes, 'Shigematsu comes across as a scrupulous, tidy-minded man, observant and full of alert curiosity, a sort of Pepys without the pranks: indeed, his account of the bomb and Pepys's of the Fire of London can usefully be put side by side. Without any moralizing, Ibuse communicates the will to survive, the determination to establish routine, the way in which discipline, self-discipline, bureaucracy and sheer human endurance alternately recede and show themselves in a time of vast disaster and distress.' We may have need in the decades ahead of the sanity and coolness of such a writer as Ibuse.

None of the Japanese novels have been runaway successes to date, though some have sold well to satisfy a publisher. I would estimate that we have made a modest profit overall on the series, especially since a number of titles have been sold to paperback houses, and as time goes on and new volumes are published further profits are probable. Since the press has been on the whole favourable and very often enthusiastic, the reason for a somewhat disappointing result must lie elsewhere. I believe it is due partly to the very different philosophy of life prevalent in Japan and partly to the actual structure of the novels themselves. They seem to lack drama and they tend to finish not with a climax but with a slow dying fall. Fundamental attitudes differ also. The Japanese attitude to death differs fundamentally from ours in the West, and is strongly present in the pages of most of the books. Similarly strange to us is the Japanese attitude to sex and love. Love is certainly regarded by Japanese writers as dangerous and completely undesirable. Men should at all costs avoid loving women, though the love of a woman for a man does not bring her as much danger, especially if the man does not respond to it. It is sad to think that the mind of the English reading public is too narrow or too inward-looking to appreciate the delights of a strange but powerful foreign literature. In the U.S. Knopf had an easier task in selling Japanese books on a worthwhile scale, for the obvious reason that America is more mixed up with Japan than Britain, at least till now. Yet the Japanese on the other hand most certainly read and enjoy and even understand a wide range of English literature.

A visit to Japan has never been possible for me, a source of deep regret since it has deprived me of friendship with my Japanese authors. Yet one I did meet twice the most fertile and probably the most interesting of them all. Yukio Mishima came twice to London. He came into my office with his wife walking two steps behind him. After shaking hands they sat down beside my desk, Mrs. Mishima in a chair two feet behind her husband's. Mishima and I talked for an hour or more, his wife said not one word. She seemed perfectly content to remain peacefully in the background.

Yukio Mishima, married man with two children, writer of countless novels, stories and plays, a certain Nobel prize-winner had he lived, most popular of authors in Japan, wealthy, sophisticated, physically fit, committed suicide at the age of 45 on November 25, 1970. With four friends, all officers of the nationalistic Shield Society founded by Mishima, he broke into the headquarters of the Eastern Defence Force in Tokyo, made prisoner General Mashita, the chief of staff (actually a friend of Mishima's), barricaded himself in his office, then walked on to the balcony and harangued for nearly ten minutes some 1,000 soldiers in the courtyard below. He accused the Japanese people of being 'drunk with prosperity' and of having forgotten their patriotic spirit. A Samurai himself, he urged them to remember the Samurai code and to defend the traditions of Japan while serving their emperor to the death. He spoke of Japan's disgrace in losing the war in the Pacific and demanded that the slate should be wiped clean and the corrupt politicians thrown from office. The audience seemed unsympathetic. Returning into the room, Mishima unsheathed his sword, knelt on the floor and plunged it into his belly, drawing it from left to right in a seven-inch cut. One of his companions, as planned, attempted to sever his head from his body and succeeded only at the fourth blow. This primitive and to a Westerner barbarous act was and is in Japan a deeply traditional and revered form of suicide, known as seppuku, and is perfectly legal. Throughout Japanese history the leaders defeated in a great cause have committed seppuku, and been admired by later generations far more than the victors. Perhaps this may be compared with the British celebration of their great disasters, such as the retreat from Mons and the forced evacuation from Dunkirk.

In what great cause had Mishima been defeated? Surely not a national one? Mishima and his 100 men of the Shield Society cannot rationally have expected to overthrow the government and change the policies of the nation. In a letter to his friend, D. J. Enright, a poet and novelist who lectured on English literature for some years in Tokyo University, he wrote a few days before his death 'I have believed that knowing without acting is not sufficiently knowing . . . I wrote everything in my last novel . . . finished on the very day of my action in order to realize my BUNBURYUDO (fusion of literary and military arts) . . .'* For me, however, the act of seppuku cannot be considered as part of the military art, nor was it in any case 'fused' with the literary art by the fact that his last novel was completed on the same day as his death. To me there was muddle in Mishima's mind, or, if Mishima's mind was clear, then the so-called military art was brought in to veil from public gaze the fact that his suicide was for entirely personal reasons.

Of these there were many, and the idea of suicide had been present in Mishima's mind for twenty years. For Harold Strauss, his American editor who knew him well, 'one element of the suicide is Mishima's narcissism . . . Mishima was a weakling who was rejected by the Japanese army a couple of months before the end of the war when they were scraping the barrel. Mishima was also quite short. He told me several times that the rejection left a deep scar on his psyche and that is the reason why he turned to body-building and the traditional sport of kendo (duelling with wooden staves). . . . He was in superb physical condition at the age of 45 when he died. But to maintain this rigorous schedule of training must have taken its toll as he grew older. He also said to me . . . that he did not want to live to be 50 and become fat and flabby. His pride in his body was as great as his pride in his literary talent. . . .'†

Gore Vidal writes rather savagely about him‡ in his review of Mishima's *Sun and Steel*, a brief and curious philosophical autobiography, in which his future suicide is clearly foreshadowed. Vidal quotes a passage from page 25, 'specifically I cherished a romantic impulse toward death, yet at the same time I required a strictly classical body as its vehicle; a peculiar sense of destiny made me believe that the reason why my romantic impulse toward death remained unfulfilled in reality was the immensely simple fact that I lacked the necessary physical qualifications.' On this Vidal comments with brutal commonsense 'this is grandstanding of a sort far beyond the capacity of our local product.'

In a considered essay on Mishima in the *Times Literary Supplement*

**London Magazine*, April, 1971.
†Letter to me from Harold Strauss, April 1, 1972.
‡*New York Review of Books*, June 17, 1971.

of August 20, 1971, Donald Keene, a friend of Mishima and a translator of his books, wrote 'no event since 1945, the defeat at the end of a long and bitter war, has shaken the Japanese literary world as much as Mishima's spectacular suicide.' Within weeks all copies of his books were sold out in the shops and his publishers had to reprint with extreme haste to satisfy the demand. Other Japanese authors analysed his motives from every angle. In the press and on television distant friends and even mere acquaintances cashed in with anecdotes and tearful regrets that they had not done more to avert this disaster. The reactions to the death of George Orwell were not dissimilar, though on a minor scale. Orwell after all did not commit suicide, and few besides myself were aware of the close connexion between his labours on *1984* and his death. Yet there is a resemblance. Orwell may be said to have come upon death in order to complete *1984*, while Mishima came upon the sharp point of his sword only after he had completed his longest and finest work, *The Sea of Fertility*.

A comparison between Mishima and Orwell in some detail might well prove fruitful. Each had an intense love of his own country and a deep awareness of his country's traditions; each felt a strong sense of duty for the thing that must be done; each experienced an ardent (and thwarted) wish to fight and if necessary die for his country; each hated what Orwell named the smelly little orthodoxies; each was deeply concerned about politics and showed it both in action and in writing; each tended to regard women as subsidiary beings to men; and each felt a loathing for the disastrous impact of technology on human living, in Orwell's pithy phrase 'progress is a swindle'; each was well versed in the classical literature of his own country.

In many ways, of course, these two great writers were quite unlike, partly perhaps because Orwell did not find his bent as a writer till he was thirty, while Mishima found his at twenty or even earlier. Partly also because with Mishima success and wealth came early, while with Orwell it was only in the last five years of his life, years mainly of sickness, that success came at all and wealth did not follow success till he was on his deathbed. In the early pages of my chapter on *1984*, I have compared Orwell's views with Mishima's on the brevity of a writer's creative period. Orwell died at the age of 47,

Mishima at the age of 45. Can it be that Orwell believed unconsciously that on the completion of *1984*, his task was done? Certainly for Mishima the completion of his great tetralogy, *The Sea of Fertility*, the first part of which was published this year under the title *Spring Snow*, marked the end. He could not and would not have done it before, any more than Orwell could have left *1984* unfinished. In fact, in the weeks before his death Mishima wrote several letters expressing a consuming concern that his American publisher would not honour his contract to publish the four volumes of *The Sea of Fertility*, a concern that was wholly misplaced. Knopf and Secker & Warburg are bringing out these novels as rapidly as the difficult task of translation permits.

Now the three great novelists, linked by friendship, each firmly rooted in the Japanese literary tradition, are gone. Tanizaki, Kawabata and Mishima are dead. It would appear that we shall not look upon their like again. The newer writers, Abé, Endo, Oë, Yasuoka and others, it is said, have cut the umbilical cord which bound them to the past. It is sad to think that this is true, for it was in great part the Japaneseness of these writers that made them great, and ironically made them less than popular with the English-reading public. When Kawabata won his Nobel prize in 1968, as Donald Keene relates in the article already quoted, 'he stated with characteristic modesty that Mishima, a genius whose like was seen only once in 300 years, deserved the honour more than himself.' Certainly, Keene adds, Mishima wanted this international certificate of high distinction. In August, 1970 Mishima told Keene that 'he had written enough for one lifetime and had put into *The Sea of Fertility* everything he had learned as a writer. "When I finish the book I'll have nothing left to do but to die," he said with a laugh, and I laughed too, unable to take him seriously.'

14
Nothing Succeeds Like Success

THE triumph of Secker & Warburg at the Old Bailey in 1954, after which our name and reputation became known to tens of thousands of new readers all over the world, gave my morale and that of my colleagues a tremendous boost. We felt that we were becoming or even had become an important house which was certain to succeed. It also turned me into a writer, a talent of which no signs had previously been viable.

To be a writer, it might be said, demands an overcoming of a certain kind of inhibition. Horne Burns' rebirth, as he had called it, had been in part the result of the destruction of his New England puritanism by the sensuality of Naples. And was my puritanism destroyed at the Old Bailey? In a way, it was. I have treated the affair unseriously in Chapter 12, yet the trial was a serious matter. As Dr. Johnson has written 'Depend upon it, Sir, when a man knows he is to be hanged in a fortnight, it concentrates his mind wonderfully.' Hanging, of course, was not in question, but my reputation could be at stake. There was another worry as well. Faced with a criminal charge, a man with a clean record tends to believe that somehow he must be guilty, for if not why has he been charged? This was how I had felt for a time, if only for a short time. I had known *The Philanderer* was a strong book for those days, I had known that prosecution was a possibility, and yet I had gone ahead. I had been of such stuff as criminals are made of, and this sent a shock wave through me, from which fortunately I had recovered before my trial. But the close-fitting bourgeois plating round my character had been pierced in a new place, and like a snail whose shell has been damaged I was not quite the same man after as before.

The damage was not, of course, something that I could accept. I blamed it on those who, so it seemed to me, had been responsible for inflicting it, the Director of Public Prosecutions and his servants, the foolish law on obscenity which had brought me into the dock, and finally the dock itself. It was not that I was wrong to do so, indeed I am certain that I was right. But, before I had been charged, I had not bothered to attack these enemies of literary freedom. Now I was about to do so, and to some effect. Now I had a cause of some importance. Now, though I didn't realize it yet, I had something to write about.

It was Kingsley Martin, editor of the *New Statesman*, who asked me to dine at the Whitefriars, a Fleet Street club where once a month the members and their guests assembled to listen to a talk on some subject of topical interest and discuss it. Present was to be an important person from the D.P.P's office. The subject – Obscenity and the Law. During the debate I got up and, staring fixedly at the D.P.P's man, announced in the course of a short speech and in ringing tones 'of course, Mr. So-and-so is an honourable man, so are they all, all honourable men.' The audience rather liked it, and so did Martin, for he asked me to write him a short piece for the *New Statesman*, which I did. It appeared, somewhat transmuted, in his diary column the following week.

Not much to be proud of really, yet I suppose that many publishers have a mild inferiority complex. They deal in writing, yet they cannot write. Some months later my wife pointed out to me a long piece in the *New Yorker* about some of the richer Jewish families of New York. Reading it I discovered that little or no mention had been made of the English branch of my own family. Encouraged by the trifling success of my appearance, courtesy of Kingsley Martin, in the *Statesman*, I decided to write a letter of complaint to the *New Yorker* about their omission. A week or two later I posted a sizeable letter to the editor, written in a style which I imagined appropriate to their columns. To my astonishment, the letter was published, and a substantial cheque paid. A letter from William Shawn, the editor, suggested that they would like to see more of my work. Of course, there was none. What to do? Racking my brains, I decided that there was one subject of which I had some first-hand experience, the feelings of a man accused of a crime he had not intended to commit. It was a long piece and it took me many weeks of research to complete. Much of it is reproduced in Chapter 12. It appeared in 1957 under the same title, *A Slight Case of Obscenity*, in the splendid section of the *New Yorker* titled 'Onwards and Upwards with the Arts'. From then on, there was no holding back. In three years I had crossed the divide which separates a publisher from a writer. The first volume of this autobiography followed two years later. How lucky I was to find a sympathetic editor prepared to give many columns of a distinguished weekly magazine to an unknown.

* * *

The risk of committing an offence under the law of obscenity has certainly played quite an important part in my publishing career, not because I had a specially dirty mind or any particular love of the genre, but because a quality house, such as we aimed to be, often publishing 'avant garde' literature, has to run certain risks in this field. Many firms however, did not, either through fear of the consequences or because their sensibilities were disturbed by a sexual theme.

The break-through from too much purity to too much licence came in the fifties, as I have already related, but it did not come in time for Jo Ackerley to remain with the distinguished house which had published his books till then.

It is only fair to admit that the problem that his publishers, Chatto & Windus had to face was a hard one, in fact there were two problems and two books. The first was called *We Think The World of You*, and should probably be described as autobiography with fictional elements. It tells the story of the middle-aged Mr. A. and his love for Johnny, a young, rather spineless ne'er-do-well and fatalist, serving a six months sentence for theft. Johnny has a young and beautiful pedigree Alsatian bitch, and wants A. to look after her for him while he's in prison. A. refuses – he has only a cramped apartment in the London suburb of Wimbledon – but visits Johnny's family – mother, father and fiancée – in the East End for news of Johnny who never bothers to write him. There he falls in love with the exquisite bitch and ultimately buys her from them and takes her home. The second book, *My Dog Tulip*, recounts the loving relationship between A. and the Alsatian, combined with a detailed account of her food and excretory functions, her sex life and mating, and the obstetrical element of her giving birth.

Chatto had little hesitation in rejecting *We Think* on the advice of Leonard Woolf who described it as 'criminally libellous' and spoiled by 'sexual naiveté'. Towards the end of 1955 it came to me and I read it. On December 21 I wrote to Ackerley 'it raises difficult problems, not only for us, but for you. As to its merits I have no doubt whatever . . . the picture of a working-class family is superbly done.' My main objection to the book was fundamental. In the narrative as it then was, A. takes Johnny to bed in a homosexual episode. Since it seemed highly unlikely that the account was not autobiographical, this scene alone was a criminal libel on Johnny and, equally important, it was a self-incrimination of Ackerley. I told him so. 'The day after you publish it,' I said, 'the police will be round to arrest you for practising homosexuality.' Had Ackerley realized this before I told him? I rather doubt it, for he looked slightly stunned and took the MS away. Later he was to offer it to Girodias of the Olympia Press in Paris, who returned it with the remark 'not nearly dirty enough and far too English.' It was to be five years before I saw it again.

Meantime Chatto had been fretting over the MS of *My Dog Tulip*, 'your non-libellous dog essays', as I called it. They came at last to a half-hearted decision to publish with substantial cuts and an advance of £100. Understandably discouraged, Ackerley refused. 'The drastic cuts you wanted seemed to destroy the "beastliness" which I wished to restore to the life of beasts,' he wrote them. Besides this he thought the advance was inadequate. He had a bank overdraft of £100 and wanted another £100 for a holiday. Such are not infrequently the problems of authorship, even for a writer so brilliant, so well-known and with such powerful support in the literary world as Ackerley.

On May 2 Ackerley wrote telling me he would drop the MS into my office in a week or two. 'It seemed to me,' he wrote, 'that [Chatto's] strictures completely destroyed my picture. I make no claims for that, except that it is a true portrait of a dog, the only true portrait, I think, ever written.' I thanked Ackerley for his letter, 'delighted to know that you will let Tulip off the leash into my office . . . we will certainly give her kennel room while we put our best minds at work on the subject of the book she has written. . . . The book sounds utterly fascinating.' And so it did to my wife and myself who had kept an Alsatian (male) for many years.

The MS arrived, and I wrote to Ackerley on May 20 'I have read it . . . I must admit to flinching at one or two passages, especially where Tulip drags her would-be lover across the floor in the most indelicate manner possible. But I am basically in sympathy with your whole conception . . . it charmed me, it made me roar with laughter, [I thought] you had given a most bitchlike representation of this beautiful animal . . . this is the most original book about a dog

I have ever read, the most unexpected, and quite certainly the best written.'

A few days later I made him an offer – £200 advance (essential) on 10% to 5,000, then rising, only a few sentences to be cut, and those on grounds of libel, not obscenity. However, I also warned him that 'nothing said above enables me to guarantee that English printers, craven as they are, will consent to print. . . . However, we will exercise persuasion!' Ackerley accepted, but at the end of August he was still tinkering with the MS and asking me whether this should be included or that changed. However, on September 14 I acknowledged the MS ready for the printer, and also told him we were sending it to our legal advisers . . . 'don't take this too seriously, but it is a precaution perhaps worth taking in view of the unique character of your book. The young man who acted for us in the Philanderer case is available.'

To Thurston Hogarth it went, with my letter asking whether it would 'have a tendency to deprave or corrupt those dogs into whose paws it might fall and whose minds might be open to such immoral influences,' slightly adapting the well-worn (and rather soiled) definition of obscenity. 'What are you worrying about?', Hogarth replied promptly, 'dogs can't read, hence no section of the public is open to corruption.' This was the briefest and most enjoyable of the many opinions I've had from him on this subject.

Meantime we tried to sell the American rights. A dozen U.S. publishers urgently demanded to read it. One found it chuckle-provoking, another a disappointment, another not a good-selling possibility, another a regretful decline. Only one man wrote a letter of rejection at some length and worthy of respect, Bucklin Moon, a novelist of considerable distinction, then working for the Bobbs-Merrill Co. 'An original and exciting job,' he wrote, 'I liked the book myself tremendously . . . the result, I'm afraid, would be a good press but limited sales.'

Moon was right. We published it on July 16, 1956, at 10s. 6d. (52p). We got a huge press for it, mostly enthusiastic, only a few nasty. Out of the 4,000 copies we printed, we sold only 2,000 in the first year, and few after that. This little book, on which the author had lavished so much care, was a flop. Years later it was issued by another firm, and is generally accepted today as a minor classic.

As for *We Think The World of You* the story was even more disappointing for me. Ackerley re-submitted it to us about 1959. The homosexual incident where A. goes to bed with Johnny had been excised. The book seemed as good to me the second time round as the first. The atmosphere in publishing had changed too with the passing of the more permissive Obscenity Act, 1959. Yet Senhouse and Farrer, disturbed at Ackerley's openly admitted homosexuality, stood firm against me. They pointed out that *Tulip* had not sold well. In vain I argued, and in the end I yielded. About four years later, the book was published by the Bodley Head. It won the £1,000 W. H. Smith Prize for that year. When the cheque was handed to the beaming author, he made the briefest speech of thanks I ever heard, approximately as follows – 'Thank you for the £1,000 – I shall take myself off to Japan with it – couldn't afford to go there otherwise – I've always wanted to return.' The distinguished personage who handed the prize to Ackerley was Lord Longford, whose recent illiberal report on Obscenity was a nine-day wonder. A strange book for Longford to support? Yes, indeed, if Longford had read every page of the prize-winning book. But, as he told my wife, he hadn't.

* * *

On September 17, 1956, we published a first novel by Jack Reynolds, *A Woman of Bangkok*, a detailed and sympathetic study of a young man's enslavement to the fleshly charms of Bangkok's most famous courtesan, White Fox. It had a big success, and I waited eagerly for the second novel to be submitted. But it didn't come when promised. Again and again I wrote the author, still living in S.E. Asia, for news of progress. His reply, though deeply discouraging, has always remained in my memory. 'Recently I was crossing the river here in a punt,' he wrote, 'I had the novel, almost complete, in my despatch case. In mid-stream I stumbled and lost my balance, the case fell into the water, and a crocodile swallowed it.' True or false? Who knows? But in any case the most ingenious excuse I have ever received for non-delivery of a manuscript.

* * *

From time to time I have written about a book which I had unwisely rejected, either through my own stupidity or weakness, or through that of my colleagues, and sometimes both. *A Woman About Town*, not its actual title, came into quite a different category. The agent who sent it me recommended it to my personal attention as a lively and unusual autobiography with a considerable sales potential. Although I normally disregard agents' enthusiasms since they naturally tend to overpraise the products they are offering, in this case the character of the book was enticing, since it purported to be – and indeed was – a narrative of the writer's love affairs with a number of men who might or might not be drawn from life. When I started to read it, the expectation of possible libel had not dawned on me, though surely it should have done, until nearly halfway through the narrative when the heroine took a new lover. At this point my attention was riveted on her story. Surely there was something familiar about this new man, almost as if I knew him personally and rather well. Feverishly I read on through another 30 pages of typescript to the end of the affair. There was no longer any doubt. This was a clinically exact, unkind and richly amusing portrait of Sir John P., a wealthy city man, entrepreneur and industrialist, then in his early sixties, married and with one son.* He was not an intimate friend, but my wife and I knew him well enough and had been to parties at his large house whose walls were adorned by a number of valuable paintings – impressionists and a selection of moderns.

The author had described in her book her first meeting with him, his pursuit of her charms until at last she had agreed to live with him. It was clear that, while the affair lasted, Sir John had been between marriages. There was in all this nothing particularly immoral or even unusual. What gave the narrative such penetration was the author's insight into Sir John's character. She had brought out his boastfulness, his meanness, his glee at victories over business rivals. But above all it was his hypocrisy of which she had given so compelling a picture. Sir John's feeling for her had been sexual, nakedly sexual, yet he needed always to hide this from himself. He talked a great deal of his earnest desire to improve her cultural background, her appreciation of music and painting. He sent her to courses, brought teachers to the house. It seemed to him magnificent, mais ce n'est pas la guerre. That had been fought in bed, and when that was over the liaison had ended.

For some days I pondered how to deal with this situation, then I phoned Sir John and asked him to call on me as soon as possible. Suspicious and annoyed at being summoned by a man whose income was clearly but a fifth of his own, envious of my friendship with talented writers whom he did not know, and almost certainly convinced that I wanted to borrow money off him, he came the next

* Sir John P. is not his real name. I have slightly disguised him, though he cannot be libelled, since he died some years ago.

day at 11.30, dressed for tennis, with a racket in his hand. 'I can only spare you a few minutes, Fred, I'm going to have my weekly lesson with the pro at Queen's Club,' he announced on arrival. I told him about the book and the passage dealing, so it seemed to me, with himself – Would he like to read it? Certainly he would. I sat him down in a comfortable chair for a 15 minute study of the author's vitriolic pen-portrait. He finished and looked up at me. 'It's me,' he said, with a massive simplicity which I admired. 'You wouldn't want it published, would you?' I asked him. He shuddered. 'No, certainly not! You won't publish it, will you?' 'Of course not, J.P.' A few minutes later he left in a thoughtful frame of mind. The matter was never referred to again between us.

I returned the MS to the agent, telling her of the libel which made publication, not perhaps impossible but most certainly risky. So far as I know the book, despite the skill of its character drawing, its undoubted merits, was never published. If I had dared to publish it, I might have called it *The Woman of London*, *La Londiniana*, a sort of pendant to Moravia's famous novel *La Romana*. But it was not, of course, as great a book as that. If it had been, perhaps I might have risked the libel suits. Would any man who had been the lover of this sharp-eyed and cynical writer have been foolish enough to identify himself?

Sir John was a proud man and he hated being under any obligation to me. Before the year was out, he had succeeded in doing me a service which was of great value to me at the time. He bore me no grudge for having done him a good turn, since he had been able to reciprocate it. Level once more, we were able to remain as friendly as we had been before, each of us rejoicing at our good luck in having so useful a friend.

* * *

The secret history of publishing will never be written and perhaps would not be worth writing. Yet I have in this book torn aside a few veils from the inner sanctums of the trade, and shown how one not entirely untypical publisher has dealt with problems which are usually obscure to an outsider. The following story links together two well-known books, each a first novel, Günter Grass's *The Tin Drum* and Joseph Heller's *Catch 22*, which at first sight have absolutely nothing in common except that they are both first novels and well known.

The Tin Drum was published in Germany in 1959 under the title of *Die Blechtrommel*, and was received there with the utmost enthusiasm. Soon it became a best-seller, and its author was hailed as the rightful heir to Thomas Mann and a kind of emperor of German letters. Of all this, I am ashamed to say, I was ignorant. But there was in England a young man, whose father had left Germany in the days of Hitler, whose knowledge of and interest in modern German literature was considerable. He was a publisher, who hoped to find a job with Secker & Warburg, a firm he warmly admired. His name was Tom Maschler, and he knew my colleague Farrer fairly well from meetings at the Frankfurt Bookfair and elsewhere. Maschler approached Farrer and tipped him off about Grass's novel. Farrer told me, and I promptly wrote off for a copy from Luchterhand, a German publisher hitherto unknown to me. Soon afterwards Farrer told me of Maschler's hope of an editorial post with us, but after consideration I rejected him on the grounds that we were already overstaffed. In chess terms Maschler had advanced a German knight (black) which had been captured by an English king (white), and appeared to have gained no compensating positional advantage in the game of publishing. Soon after he found an editorial job with the house of Jonathan Cape, but the game was not yet over. The white king (myself) was soon to make a serious blunder, and the black knight (Maschler) was able in the end to achieve at least a draw. It was Maschler, as will be seen, who linked the two novels I have mentioned in the chess game of publishing.

When the book, soon to be known as *The Tin Drum*, arrived in my office, I sent it to our top German reader, Countess von Wiedenbruch. It was the last work she did for us, and perhaps the most important, for six weeks later she died. Her report is lost, but I remember the gist of it well enough. The novel was, she wrote, a fine satirical picture of lower middle-class Germany under the Nazis, a loathsome and uninhibited account which certainly ought to be translated, although the translation would present almost insuperable difficulties to even the finest translator. Another reader, Mrs. Eva Wilson, said much the same. The firm decided to accept the challenge. We would publish, but only if we could obtain the support of an American publishing house. *The Tin Drum* was of immense length, some 280,000 words making 592 full pages in the English printing, nearly four times as long as the normal novel of commerce. The translator would have to be paid not less than £1,000, and this would increase the publishing price by about £1 per copy on a 3,000 printing, and this was simply not viable.

It did not take me long to decide which American publisher to approach first. Kurt Wolff, the head of Pantheon Books, New York, who had made it, with the help of his wife Helen, perhaps the most distinguished mini-firm in the U.S. But Wolff was not just another American publisher. Forced to flee Nazi Germany, he had been one of the great German publishers of his time. Probably he had read Grass's book already.

I wrote Wolff, suggesting a collaboration, and two days later he rang me from Zürich. Yes, he had read *Die Blechtrommel*, yes, it was indeed a fine novel, perhaps a great one. But I sensed there was a doubt. 'It can never be translated,' said Wolff sadly, 'I've already seen it and turned it down. The German is too difficult, too outrageous, there are words that no one has used before.' But I refused to admit defeat. If Wolff rejected it, it seemed altogether unlikely that I would ever find a more sympathetic publisher. 'There is no text which cannot be translated,' I asserted brashly, 'if you find the right translator for it.' Wolff promised to reconsider and phoned Luchterhand immediately. A few days later he had agreed terms. So did we. The search for a translator began.

We asked at least half a dozen of our best translators for a sample translation of a difficult passage, so did Wolff, and at last we chose one in whom each of us had great confidence, Ralph Manheim, an American living in Paris. Of his translation the *Times Literary Supplement* was to write in its one-page review on October 5, 1962 'Deserves very special praise because of the extreme difficulties presented by the text . . . great ingenuity in finding English counterparts for some of Herr Grass's typical juxtaposition of the familiar and the surrealist, of folklore and private fantasy.'

The Tin Drum is the autobiography of Oskar Matzerath, 30 years old, detained in a mental hospital after conviction for a murder he has not committed. At the age of three he has staged a fall down the steps to the cellar, and thereafter remains three foot high and a child in appearance. It is then that his mother gives him his first tin drum, which becomes the chosen symbol of his way of life and enables him to recall the story of his past, for he has had from birth the mind of an adult. Beating the drum he breaks up Nazi mass meetings and other religious, political and social activities, for Oskar is an anarchist, an artist, certainly an individualist. His legal father is a German grocer who becomes a plain S.A. man, but his true father he believes to be his mother's lover, Jan Bronski, a Pole, whom Oskar loves the better. Pole or German, Oskar (like Grass) is a child of Danzig. Oskar's themes are sadistic, sexual, political, social, blasphemous, infinitely strange and varied. In the German invasion of Poland, both Oskar's fathers are killed. At the funeral he flings his drum on the grave . . . and starts to grow. Soon he develops a hump. When the war is over, he goes on a nightmare journey through battle-scarred Europe.

Even in this brief description it is possible to grasp some of the symbolic brilliance of Grass's novel, a supreme creation of the German and perhaps of the European imagination. In Germany a critic described it as 'a barbaric counterpart to Mann's *Felix Krull*', and another as 'Goethe's *Wolhelm Meister* on a tin drum' – the literary evolution is obvious from Goethe to Mann to Grass, but the critics' words suggest a certain degree of shock. In Puritan England the shock was even greater. Some of the reviewers were bitterly hostile, including Stephen Spender. But the *Times Literary Supplement* of October 5, 1962 was generous in praise – 'Only the monstrous innocence of an Oskar could respond with such immediacy to [the Nazi] world, only his inhuman eye register such humanity as survived in it. If Oskar had been a responsible adult he would not have got away with half of it and lived to tell the whole story, and we should be greatly the poorer for that.' Several stunned reviewers recovered enough to write favourably, and the general impression was that, in spite of its apparent moral neutrality, the book was a masterpiece. Though the sales fell far short of my hopes, they were not insubstantial. The book paid its way, and we had once again acquired a major European writer. Maschler's advice had been well worth following, but it had taken considerable audacity to do so.

In 1958 I made my seventh publishing trip to New York, accompanied for the first time by my wife, and was offered by a remarkable young agent, Candida Donadio, the first 150 pages of a first novel by an unknown writer, Joseph Heller, titled *Catch 18*, later to become famous as *Catch 22*. Pamela read it first and with enthusiasm. As soon as I could in the whirl of a New York trip I read it, and found that I had enjoyed it as much as she had, something of a surprise, for she had an extremely individual taste. With husband and wife agreed about its merits, I made a contract to publish.

For three long years I had waited for the complete manuscript, and when it arrived, I saw that it had grown from about 40,000 words to around 200,000. Flabbergasted by this monstrous inflation, I sent it to Paul Scott, a major novelist, for whom we had published three novels; for a report. 'Three years ago, believe it or not,' I wrote, 'I bought on the basis of what seemed to me then 150 brilliant pages

. . . a novel by an American writer, called *Catch 22*. The years have passed, the leaves have fallen, my hair has grown grey, though not much, and now the novel is complete and I dare not read it until I have your report.' 'Dare not,' of course, because what had seemed comic at 40,000 words, and might still seem comic at 70,000 words, could hardly remain comic at 200,000 words.

Catch 22 is about a combat bombing squadron stationed in Corsica during 1943, the crews' morale is low and their somewhat callous superior officers have to urge them on. The central character is a pilot, Yossarian, of whom the author writes (page 28) 'Colonel Cathcart wanted fifty missions, and he was dead serious about them. Yossarian had one mission, and he was dead serious about that. His mission was to keep alive as long as he could, for he had decided to live forever or die in the attempt. Yossarian was a towering 192 pounds of firm bone and tender flesh, and he worshipped the whole bloody mess so much that he would have lain down his life to preserve it. Yossarian . . . had courage, as much courage as anyone else he'd ever met. He had courage enough to be a coward, and that's exactly what he was, a hero.'

In a week back came Scott's report. 'In isolation it very nearly works, but there are pages and pages and pages all written in exactly that tone and eventually I lost patience because so much of it reminded me how easy this turning-reality-inside-out-for-comic-effect is. So easy that you can do it for 200,000 words . . . a pity because, buried under this weight of words is a sharp mind and eye and a genuine concern to reveal truth through idiocy. In other words, Heller isn't being just clever. But, as he might put it himself, he isn't just being clever for too long.'

To my mind Scott's report seemed bang on target. It had knocked out that lunatic fictional bombing squadron which all the same was about to give so much pleasure to so many. 'Better admit defeat early,' he continued, 'than plough through all the 800 (nearly) pages and pretend afterwards that I can write an intelligent report.' Concluding he remarked that 'it is always possible that a reader who goes for this zany-epigram stuff will think it is a work of genius, and of course he may be right. But from your long publishing experience you will know that it is less disastrous to turn down a work of genius than to turn down talented mediocrities.'

Soon I felt bound to tell my wife that I had decided to reject the book. She wasn't pleased at all. 'I think you're being a bloody fool,' she remarked acidly. In desperation I passed the typescript to Farrer, who handed it back to me two days later with a cheerful smile and the simple comment 'I don't think it's funny, Fred, and it's far too long.' That was the end. Next day I returned the book to the agent, asking him to allow me to cancel our contract. Gossip had it that Tom Maschler, tipped off by the novelist Graham Greene, was hungry to buy the rights for Cape. So we come full circle back to Maschler, to whom consciously or otherwise I was returning the knight he had sacrificed so many months ago. It turned out to be a valuable piece indeed. Backed by a brilliant promotion campaign, *Catch 22* became a bestseller and was made into a film. It received an almost uniformly favourable press. Maschler's coup established him inside Cape as a formidable book-getter. From then on he never looked back. Today he is, with Graham C. Greene, son of an ex-Director-General of the B.B.C., joint head of his distinguished firm. Since it was I who gave Greene his start and training as a publisher in my own firm, then foolishly let him go because I thought he was too young to be given the directorship he wanted, I may be said to have given Cape its two powerful top leaders. Had I acted otherwise, Maschler and Greene might have been today the leaders of Secker & Warburg. The history of publishing would have been different. And as a result, would the development of English and foreign literature have changed either for the better or the worse? I don't really know.

Was my rejection of *Catch 22* a blunder? From the viewpoint of profit it most certainly was. Yet I do not mourn overmuch. Had I rejected *The Tin Drum*, forty days and nights of wailing would hardly have been sufficient. Recently I re-read as much of *Catch 22* as I could endure, about 100 pages. Talented though it is, it is too long, too monotonous, and basically too absurd. And I re-read *The Tin Drum* also. It is long but not too long, never monotonous, and stands up as the masterpiece it most certainly is. Grass has written a series of important books since *The Tin Drum*, and continues in full spate. Heller has not. From the viewpoint of literature at least, I owe Maschler far more than he owes me. It is strange to realize that, though we have met, we have never had even one long or important conversation in our lives.

15
The Great Lama Mystery

It's a long way from Peru to Tibet, across the rolling breakers of the Pacific Ocean, yet these two countries make use of the same sound to stand for two very different objects. The etymologists write it as '*lahma*'. In Peruvian, spelt *llama*, it indicated a ruminant animal allied to the camels, but having no hump, with a thick woolly coat. This beast stands about three feet high, is domesticated and is used for load-carrying. In Tibet it is spelt *blama*, but the b is silent and the word means 'priest'. In English the word loses its silent b and becomes lama, and by it we refer to a buddhist priest of Tibet. A grand lama is the chief priest, normally referred to as the Dalai Lama, and lamaism is the form of Buddhist religion practised in Tibet among the lamas. It was a Tibetan lama or his alter ego with whom I became mixed up in 1955.

The affair began about 11 a.m. on April 15, when the telephone operator rang to ask whether I would speak with Cyrus Brooks of the Heath literary agency. The ensuing conversation set off a train of events that was to have repercussions all over the world. Brooks' first words to me were drama. 'Would you be interested,' he inquired, 'in a book with a four-figure advance?' 'Of course,' I replied, as calmly as possible, 'but what is the subject?' 'The autobiography of a Tibetan lama,' Brooks said, with a justifiable hint of pride in his news.

At that time, an advance of £1,000 was a sizeable amount for us, requiring rather careful consideration. 'The autobiography of a Tibetan lama,' I said to Brooks, 'you're surely not serious. There's never been such a thing before. Lamas don't write them. They're not allowed to. How do you know it's genuine?'

How do you know it's genuine? This crucial question was to din in my ears a great many times before I was much older. In a few minutes Brooks conveyed to me the gist of the matter, pricking the little bubble of scepticism already forming in my mind. The author's name was Dr. Kuan-suo, normally shortened to Dr. Kuan. This was the Chinese name he had found it convenient to adopt, but he intended to sign his book with a Tibetan pseudonym, T. Lobsang Rampa. Dr. Kuan or K., as I propose to call him – for indeed he was involved in mysteries as complex as though rather less transcendental than Kafka's hero, K. – had left Tibet some twenty years before, and after a series of adventures and wanderings which would have done credit to Ulysses himself, landed up in London. Finding himself hard up, he had called on Charles Gibbs-Smith, an official of the Victoria and Albert Museum, who impressed by K's personality had sent him to Brooks. K. wanted Brooks to find him work writing advertising material for medical supplies. Why *medical* supplies, Brooks had inquired? At this point K. had taken from his briefcase a certificate of considerable elaboration, stating that he held degrees both in medicine and surgery from the University of Chunking, but that he could not practise in Britain without British qualifications. The certificate described him as a lama of the Potala Monastery in Lhasa.

Visits by lamas to literary agents' offices in London are, to put it mildly, infrequent. Brooks, riveted by this information, began to smell a success of gigantic proportions, the publication of a lama's autobiography, the first, he believed, ever to be published in the Western (and perhaps also the Eastern) world.

Reluctant at first to speak about this period of his life, which K. said he found painful to recall, he yielded at last to Brooks' persistent questioning. He told him of his adventures after leaving the Lamasery and how eventually he had managed to reach England. Having heard, the experienced agent had no doubts whatever. K's problems could be solved, if only he would agree to write his autobiography. Only after severe pressure on a number of occasions did Dr. Kuan finally consent to attempt this task. This was the project which Brooks detailed to me on that April morning. 'Tell me,' I said to Brooks, 'is the autobiography already written?' 'Only in part,' Brooks told me, 'I have about 30,000 words of typescript here, and most extraordinary material it is.' 'When can I see it?' I asked excitedly. 'It shall be in your office tomorrow afternoon.'

So began the great lama mystery.

The manuscript arrived as promised. It was typed rather efficiently on about 100 flimsy canary-yellow sheets of paper. A casual glance at a few pages was enough to tell me at least that it was an unusual book. I placed it in my despatch case and took it home to read over the week-end. When I had finished, I had no doubts about my view. If the author succeeded in completing it with the same degree of skill as he had shown in the sections before me, and if the material could be authenticated, then there could be no question that I had in my hands one of the biggest sellers of all time. If, on the other hand, the material was not authentic, we had a fascinating work with a strong if limited appeal, which my firm might or might not publish.

From the beginning there emanated from Dr. Kuan's masterpiece a magical aroma of enchantment. The book, even in its partial and provisional form, was literally bewitching. It cast a spell over me. In the months and years to come it was to cast this spell with an equal potency over millions of readers.

For those who have not passed under the lama's spell, it is necessary to provide a brief sketch of the book's contents.

About half a century ago a son was born in Lhasa, capital of Tibet, to one of the top officials of the theocracy. That boy was to become the writer of the book I had just read. For the first six years of his life, he lived in the family household with its pomp and wealth, its retinue of servants, its complicated organization. At the age of seven, in the course of a magnificent reception for the notables of the country from near and far, his future is decreed by two famous astrologers – he is to enter a lamasery to be trained as a surgeon-monk. A week later, alone, the little boy sets out for the Chakpori lamasery on the outskirts of Lhasa. For the next ten years he serves his apprenticeship, cut off from his family and subject to incredible hardships. Soon he shows such unusual progress in his peculiar studies that the Dalai Lama decides that his already exceptional powers of clairvoyance shall be enhanced still further by a surgical operation on his forehead known as the opening of 'the third eye'. The operation is performed and the boy continues his studies in memory training, herb medicine and Tibetan philosophy under the guidance of the Lama Mingyar Dondup.

It was at about this point that the original manuscript on yellow paper came to a stop. But it will be as well to set down the rest here and now, although it was in fact many weeks before I was able to read the second part of this fabulous story. The boy, now a youth, Lobsang Rampa, becomes a confidant of the Dalai Lama, and in the volcanic caves beneath the Potala Monastery submits to the astonishing mystical experience known as 'the living death'. There are also chapters dealing with his flights in a man-carrying kite, journeys across country on stilts, a trip to collect rare herbs on the mysterious Chang-Tang highland, 24,000 feet above sea level. The story ends with the young man's departure in his early twenties on a special mission to China, about which the reader is promised a second volume.

On the following Monday I returned to my office raving like a lunatic. I told my directors with a profusion of superlatives what I thought of Dr. K's book. One after the other, with one exception, they read it and were bowled over by its mysterious appeal. Speed replaced the traditional lethargy which publishers are presumed to show when faced with the need for a decision. Within a bare ten days terms had been agreed. I had kept my sang-froid, up to a point. Instead of the £1,000 advance proposed by Brooks, I had negotiated one of £800, £250 to be paid on signature, £260 to be paid at the rate of £20 a week for thirteen weeks to support the author while he completed the remainder of the text, and the balance of £290, dangling like a carrot before the donkey, to be presented to him 'on delivery of the complete typescript ready for press' in the time-worn phraseology of publishers' agreements. Everyone seemed delighted, author, agent and publisher. There were no dissentient voices. Morale was at a peak, and a meeting had been arranged for 3 p.m. on April 26th in my office, at which the four directors were to come together with Cyrus Brooks and the man out of Tibet, the man perhaps rather a long time out of Tibet, the representative of a dying theocracy whose inner secrets he carried within him. The moment was magical, the rendezvous one to which all looked forward with anxious excitement.

Before the meeting took place I had received a rather discouraging letter from Brooks, disclosing information about the history of the manuscript before it had come into my hands. It had been offered first to the firm of Gollancz, and accepted, but the advance proved too great for his colleagues to accept while Victor Gollancz himself was away on a trip to Europe. It was next offered to Robert Hale who accepted it with enthusiasm, but before long personal differences arose between the lama and Hale's editor which proved insurmountable, and reluctantly the author was released from his contract. A third publishing house, William Collins, was next given it, but their director, Mark Bonham-Carter, showed what seemed to the agent an unimaginative scepticism of the author's credentials, and the deal fell through. It is not uncommon in my experience for another publisher to reject a work which I have subsequently published with success. So I was not unduly depressed by these rather tepid reactions. My enthusiasm carried me forward, and I was encouraged still further by the knowledge that the President of the well-known American publishing house of E. P. Dutton had accepted the book for publication after an interesting talk with the author in London, and signed an agreement for it with a big advance. The president of Dutton was an old friend of mine, Elliott Macrae, and I had worked with him and his father on many projects over a period of thirty years. The house of Dutton had recently published a number of well-known books about Tibet, including works by André Migot, Heinrich Harrer, Colonel Younghusband and Sven Hedin. Since Dutton felt confident that this was a venture of unusual importance, who was I to have doubts?

As the hour of the meeting drew nearer, my colleagues and I felt a growing apprehension. It was not merely that we were about to meet the author of a book with tremendous sales possibilities, nor that our caller came from a far-distant and mysterious land which few had visited, nor even that he was a religious personage of high degree. Our apprehension was based on a starker fact. Dr. K. had clairvoyant power of which he had given proof already to his agent, and about which he had written in the manuscript in our possession. With this power, we felt uneasily, he might penetrate the superficial layers of our beings, and look deep into our hearts. What might not he discern there? What auras were ours? Were we in fact the kindly, generous, sympathetic, intelligent, modest, alert characters we hoped we were and pretended to be, or were we . . . something rather different?

Dr. K. had described in his book the strange operation by which his natural powers of clairvoyance had been increased. 'The aura which surrounds the body, and which anyone can be taught to see under suitable conditions, is merely a reflection of the life force within. We Tibetans believe that this force is electric, the same as lightning . . .,' he had written. On his eighth birthday, at dusk, 'into the room came three lamas of high degree. They put a herbal compress to my head and bound it tightly in place.' This was to make aseptic the place for the incision. Later an instrument of shining steel – it resembled a bradawl – was sterilized in the flame of a lamp, pressed to the centre of the young man's forehead and the handle rotated.

The needle was pressed home. 'Suddenly there was a little scrunch and the instrument penetrated the bone. Instantly its motion was arrested by the very alert operator.' Into the hole was passed 'a very hard clean sliver of wood which had been treated by fire and herbs to make it as hard as steel,' and so the operation proceeded until it was complete. Then 'the lama Mingyar Dondup turned to me and said "you are now one of us, Lobsang. For the rest of your life you will see people as they are and not as they pretend to be." It was a strange experience to see these men apparently enveloped in a golden flame. Not until later did I realize that their auras were golden because of the pure life they led, and that most people would look very different indeed.'

The language of mysticism is strange. Some may interpret this crudely in physical terms, others as metaphor. However interpreted, it is clear that the opening of this 'third eye' stands for the final stage of an awareness of reality, when the illusions of youth and the senses have given place, after years of study and training and hardship, to the sliver-sharp perception of truth. To this perception the lama, Lobsang Rampa, had advanced, so my directors and I were inclined to believe. Small wonder then that we who were about to greet him looked forward to the occasion with a certain degree of humility. For a quarter of an hour before our visitor was due to arrive, my colleagues were busy in the washroom, like soldiers before an inspection by a commanding officer. They straightened their ties, cleaned their shoes, brushed their hair. Since they did not know how to brush up their auras, it was the best they could do. As for myself, I made no special preparation. My aura, I felt certain, was in a spotty condition – let the lama see it, spots and all. At my age it was too late to start any aura-reconditioning process.

The meeting went well. The lama's entrancc was unobtrusive, he was at the door, then he was sitting in a chair. I do not suggest that he passed from one to the other by a process of levitation. I looked at him closely. Slightly below the medium height, well-shaped head with a domed forehead, hair rather scanty, cut tonsure-like round the crown of his skull, a long nose and full mouth, a swarthy face with prominent ears. Nothing remarkable, nothing which I could wholly associate with what I knew of Tibetan physiognomy. But the eyes were strange, large, luminous, penetrating, under heavy lids and heavy bushy eyebrows. Between the eyes, slightly to the left of centre, a small purplish-red mark could be seen, almost the size of a collar button, the scar no doubt of that remarkable incision. Dr. K.

looked like a monk. He seemed a man not to be trifled with. He appeared composed, relaxed, indifferent, with a tendency to jest. From the beginning I took a liking to him.

The discussion lasted an hour. It covered the questions of title, illustrations, maps and of course the actual contents of the book. The title, suggested by my wife, was to be *The Third Eye*, not as originally proposed either *Passionate Priest* or the tame but straightforward *Autobiography of a Tibetan Lama*. Dr. K. agreed to confine himself to the period before he left Tibet and to keep his later adventures in and out of Japanese prison camps for a second volume. It was agreed that the book should run to between 70,000 and 80,000 words. To achieve this it would be necessary for Dr. K. to enlarge some of the earlier chapters as well as to add new chapters bringing the story down to the agreed date.

What was my state of mind at this point? It seemed to me, I must admit, almost (but not absolutely) certain that what we had in our possession was an authentic account of the early life of a lama from Tibet, touched up maybe a bit here and there, as is not uncommon with autobiographies. Against the charge of credulity, which it is only too easy to level against me, I assemble the following pleadings:

1) of those who had read the manuscript, only one was doubtful of its authenticity, Mark Bonham-Carter of Collins. The others – and there must have been over a dozen by this time – believed that it was what it purported to be.

2) the account given by Dr. K. of his adventures and wanderings *since* he had left Tibet some twenty years ago was so odd that it was hard not to accept it. An impersonator could have invented a vastly more believable story in five minutes.

3) I was naturally impressed by the attitude of Cyrus Brooks, a man in whom I had confidence as a sensible and critical person. Brooks after all had known Dr. K. for some months, had seen him from time to time, and was convinced that he was writing a truthful book. He had given me at least two examples of K's ability to read character and diagnose disease with considerable accuracy.

4) the introduction of Dr. K. to Brooks by a reputable and learned member of the staff of the Victoria and Albert Museum illuminated the affair right from the beginning with an aura (what other word can I use?) of scholarship.

5) I had discussed with Ram Gopal, the great Indian dancer whose book we were soon to publish, the existence of auras and the

possibility of viewing them, to discover that he himself claimed the ability to see them and read character from them.

6) my two colleagues, David Farrer, who had lived for a year or two in India, and John Pattisson, who had not, seemed certain of the lama's genuineness. These two had never appeared to me as men given to foolish credulity.

7) the contract given Dr. K. by Elliott Macrae of Dutton, the publisher of Tibetan works of indubitable value, strengthened my feeling that we had the experts on our side.

8) I liked Dr. K. He had an attractive personality and a lively wit, allied to a mind of his own. He was not a man of vague or misty views. A genuine mystic, so I supposed, must have a sharp outlook based on a blinding and immediate revelation of the ultimate reality.

9) Lastly and above all, there was the book itself. The account I have given of it above may appear somewhat overblown when read in cold blood, too bizarre to permit credence. Yet the life of the young boy growing up to manhood in a distant land was set down with such simplicity, naturalness and candour that it blew my doubts away. In particular, I was impressed by the portrait drawn by Dr. K. of his teacher, the lama Mingyar Dondup, a man tender, wise and at times stern, who helped the boy through the difficulties of a harsh curriculum. I found it impossible to imagine that this portrait was not drawn from life.

This view was shared, at least in part, by the anonymous reviewer of *The Third Eye* in the *Times Literary Supplement* eighteen months later. He (or she) was to write:

'No doubt that this book was worth publishing, since though it would be a matter of extraordinary difficulty to say whether it is a work of truth, it comes near to being a work of art. . . . If one can suspend judgment upon where the boy was being made to go, he is real and recognizable as such, the universal unruly and hungry imp of London or Lhasa, expanding against the pressures of family, schooling, teachers and moral precepts. Everything is strange in this progress except the familiar outline of its moving core.'

Steadily during the next three months the typescript accumulated at the rate of about a chapter per week. Farrer, a knowledgeable editor, was in charge, giving advice, asking for expansion here, cutting there. He was delighted with what he was getting and passed it on to me. I read it with equal enthusiasm. A map of Lhasa was prepared by the author 'accurate, although done entirely from memory. There is NO map of Lhasa in the British Museum, to their astonishment and mine.' So wrote Dr. K. on May 12. On June 6, addressing me by the Tibetan equivalent of my name, he wrote, 'Our Scriptures say: "I teach only two things, O disciples, suffering and release from suffering." It will ease mine if you tell me how many words you want in this wretched book, 70,000 or more?' This comparatively halcyon period was disturbed by a letter from Macrae of May 31. 'Our editors have raised a number of questions which we sent to Dr. Kuan,' he wrote, 'the good doctor was rather sarcastic in answering them, and dismissed most of them with a wave of his hand. . . . I think we may have a very good book here, but it is important that we establish beyond a shadow of doubt Dr. Kuan's background, the year he graduated, the names of several important people that he knew or worked with, etc.'

'We think,' I wrote in answer, 'that this book is going to be a fascinating best-seller. . . . When it is complete, we will take account of the numerous points raised in your letters. We have no doubts about the author's authenticity, and even if the book were a fake, which it is not, it would be one of the greatest fakes of our time. . . .' The words quoted make three distinct points; the future was to prove that only two of them were fully justified.

The time has now come to reveal that the doubts of Macrae were as nothing to the full-blooded scepticism of my wife. She held from the beginning of the affair that *The Third Eye* was a splendid work of the imagination, and that its author was bogus. On this subject many violent clashes occurred between us. 'How can you tell that Dr. K. is a fake?' I inquired, 'you haven't seen him or heard his arguments or experienced the full impact of his personality. Those who do know him are certain that he is genuine.' But Pamela was adamant. 'You don't have to take my word for it,' she retorted, 'ask to see his passport.' Ask to see his passport. It was a simple solution and one which naturally was far too obvious ever to have occurred to me. As I turned the idea over in my mind, I found an increasing distaste for it. I told Pamela as much. But her response was blunt, even brutal. 'I don't believe he's ever been out of England at all,' she replied. This answer went too far – it impugned my commonsense, attacked my pride, hurt my feelings. My attitude stiffened. 'You're preposterous,' I said, 'jumping to conclusions for which you have no shred of evidence.' It is a hard thing for a husband to nurse in his bosom a viper of doubt with a forked tongue. I felt uneasy and unhappy. But soon I was to lunch with Dr. K. Then I would have the chance of questioning him yet more fully.

Dr. K. arrived on the dot, and we took our seats at table. But almost immediately he bent forward and seized my left hand in his, peering at it meaningfully. 'You are 57 years of age,' he began, 'and recently you entered a vast building associated with the Law. You have been twice married, and your second wife . . .' but at this point I snatched my hand away. I was furious. 'Excuse me,' I said, 'but I don't like my palm read. I have no wish to know my future. If it's a good one, I can wait for it cheerfully, and if it's bad, I'd just as soon not know.' Taking up the menu, I asked him whether he would have scampi with rice, an excellent dish at the M. 'Certainly not,' Dr. K. said, with loathing in his voice. 'I can't stand rice, I had too much of the horrible stuff in Japanese prison camps.' 'What would you like then?' I asked politely. 'I'll have fish and chips,' Dr. K. replied.

I called the waiter and ordered fish and French fried potatoes for my guest. Not a muscle of my face twitched, at least I hope not. My demeanour remained unaltered, at least I hope so. But in my heart was alarm – I could not bring myself to accept that an honest-to-goodness Tibetan lama of high degree would order fish and chips.

From this poor start the lunch never wholly recovered. The lama was in an aggressive mood with a tendency to boast. When I congratulated him on the fascinating nature of the chapters already delivered, he replied 'all these commonplace descriptions of life in the country of my boyhood may fascinate you, but they bore me. I know it all too well. You want to call the book *The Third Eye* but my name for it isn't printable.' Unfortunately I forbore to ask him what it was. Later, when I questioned him about the possibility of a second volume on the philosophy of lamaism, he displayed an intense irritation. 'I'm not interested in philosophy at all,' he said, 'nor in theology. There are far too many lamas in Tibet. Why do you suppose I never returned there? Because there's no freedom. One is never permitted to do as one wishes.' This cavalier assessment of Tibet as a theocratic dictatorship, although it has since been repeated by Chinese communist propagandists, disturbed me. How, I wondered, could a man so highly trained in lamaistic studies as Dr. K. speak in so derogatory a manner of what had made him the man he was?

After lunch I sped back to the office and confided my fears to Farrer. He was sympathetic but not unduly concerned. '*Gurus*,' he said, 'the wise men of the East, I met quite a few *gurus* when I was in India. They're not cultured, you know, rather crude, awfully dirty. Don't worry about it all.'

Early in August, the manuscript was complete and delivered, the large advance paid, and the first descriptive note was written. There could hardly be any going back now. The die was cast. The pages shone with movement and colour. Already the news had got out that an extraordinary book was in the press and orders were coming in steadily from all over the world, although no proofs had yet been showed to booksellers. On the publishing front hopes were buoyant, but September proved to be a month of crisis. At its beginning, though wracked with doubt, I still entertained the hope that the manuscript possessed a certain amount of authenticity. There were five possible explanations of the affair, as I saw it then.

1) The manuscript was authentic, though touched up here and there by flights of fancy and slips of memory.

2) The manuscript, though authentic, was not written by the man I knew as Dr. Kuan, but by another who was himself an authentic lama screening himself behind Dr. K.

3) The manuscript was part true, part false. The author had been born and bred in Tibet, or in the neighbouring province of Sikkim and had experienced some of the events described and learned about others from a genuine Tibetan or Tibetans.

4) The manuscript was the work of a brilliant psychopath who had thought himself thoroughly into the mind of a lama, after studying the history of Tibet and the theory and practice of lamaism.

5) The manuscript was a fake, written to deceive.

Between September 15 and October 6, the persona so painstakingly built up by Dr. K. for the benefit of his agent and publisher, British and American, was shattered. The rot started when we received a long letter dated September 15 from Macrae. 'I have now had three outside reports,' he wrote, 'and all three readers agree that there are many inaccuracies in the manuscript . . . serious questions have been raised as to the author's accurate knowledge of Lhasa – both in the geographical sense and from the standpoint of customs, traditions and monasteries, as well as his knowledge of Buddhist and Tibetan religious belief and the Tibetan language. . . . One of these readers believes that the author may have been in Lhasa, but that he came there from one of the outlying provinces, possibly in China, and may have read up books about Tibet and presented some of the material from them as personal experiences and observations.' The other reader, whose report Macrae forwarded, stated bluntly, 'Having read it, I can say that the English construction, grammar, idiom and vocabulary are most unlikely to have been achieved by any Tibetan.' Macrae in his letter added, most reasonably, 'I think that both we and Secker & Warburg would be in a very embarrassing position if we cannot authenticate the material we publish.' The same thought was present in the minds of my colleagues and myself. The situation demanded instant action. We sent Macrae's material to Dr. K. for his comments, and arranged that he should meet my directors with his agent three days later.

The meeting took place in the morning, and in the afternoon I wrote a three-page account of it to Macrae. 'K. brought to the meeting a long comment on all, or practically all, the points raised by your readers. Some of your readers' criticisms are accepted, and the author admits he made a mistake, but those which virtually involve doubts about the author's authenticity are denied. We were looking for any sign of fraud, prevarication or lying. Possibly on one or two occasions something suspicious occurred, but I am not certain. The most fantastic thing is Kuan's statement, made in writing, 'Pema Choki (Macrae's Reader One) is particularly virulent. Rather a pity, because she used to be quite a nice girl. Perhaps she wants to get her book published first.' Was your reader one Pema Choki? . . . Kuan claims that she knows him well and could recognize a photograph of him if one was sent to her. . . . We propose to submit the typescript to the Lecturer of Tibetan in the School of Oriental Studies, Dr. Snellgrove. It is probable that Kuan will agree to meet this distinguished scholar. Kuan behaved with patience. . . . I think it is fair to say that we feel tolerably certain that despite the criticisms of your readers we incline to the opinion that Kuan is either authentic or part authentic.'

As I re-read fifteen years later this still over-optimistic letter, I smile a somewhat wry smile at human credulity. Clearly I was still bewitched by the resolute charm of a very clever man, whose audacity knew no limit. So I pinned my faith or what was left of it on Dr. K's identification of Reader One as Pema Choki. Three days later a cable came from Macrae, 'Pema Choki not one of our readers, completely unknown to us.'

I stopped all further payments to Dr. K. He had already received £500 from us. This not unnaturally provoked a complaint from him. 'It is really insulting how this affair has been managed,' wrote the angry man to his agent. 'Before the cancelled cheque arrived I was willing to do anything possible to help. Now I am not. Mr. Warburg, of course, acted under pressure from others. I do not blame him; he is a man after my own heart and I like him. He will agree with me when I state that I am not going to be led around like a condemned animal who is an unusual specimen.'

By now Brooks also was at the end of his tether, but he attempted one final effort. 'Mr Warburg is a man of honour and discretion,' he wrote to his author. 'The best thing would be for you to see him alone and tell him, if necessary under pledge of secrecy, the many matters you have hitherto concealed. If he is then personally satisfied, the book could proceed to publication.' A meeting was arranged, but it did not prevent us from sending the manuscript to Dr. Snellgrove, who had just returned from holiday. The age of faith was over.

What did I expect from the confrontation, as I prepared a list of searching questions, like a barrister with a dubious witness to examine? A show of innocence or an admission of guilt? More and more complex prevarication or a confession? I started off with a brutal attack. 'You are not a Tibetan lama,' I told him grimly, 'and you have no real knowledge of the Tibetan language. Our reports demonstrate that elementary mistakes have been made in the Tibetan script, most if not all of which has been copied, sometimes very clumsily, from readily available sources.' I opened a learned work at a marked page and pushed the book towards him, so that he might see the script for himself. 'That has been copied by you into your manuscript,' I told him. A look of horror passed over Dr. K's swarthy face and he covered his eyes with his right hand as if suffering from a violent spasm of migraine. Then he pushed the book away from him. 'Part of what you say is true,' he said finally. 'I have told no one before, but you I must tell because you have always been honest with me. I *am* a lama and I *have* been trained at the Chakpori Monastery. When I left Tibet, I served, as you know, as a medical aide with the Chinese armies fighting the Japanese invaders. The Nipponese captured and tortured me. They wanted me to tell them the dispositions of the Chinese armies. They had seized Tibetan documents and plans, and now they wished me to translate and explain them.'

'Well, but what has that to do with your mistakes in Tibetan?' I asked.

'Do you think I would reveal important secrets to the bloodthirsty Japanese?' he said.

'Why, of course not,' I replied with seeming seriousness. After all, this game had to be played in accordance with some set of rules. 'What did you do?'

'I knew my weakness under torture,' Dr. K. went on, 'my peculiar voice is due to the introduction of water into the mouth through a hosepipe. They did it to me after tearing off my nails.'

I shuddered. Even to hear about tortures, real or imaginary, makes me feel sick. Dr. K. looked at me. 'I had my resources,' he said quietly. 'My teacher, Mingyar Dondup, had prepared me well. To prevent myself telling what was forbidden me to tell, I imposed a hypnotic block on my knowledge of the Tibetan language. After that, I couldn't read or write or understand Tibetan. The secrets were safe.'

'And did your knowledge not come back to you later on?' I inquired.

'In part,' he said, 'only in part. My present knowledge of Tibetan is faulty. That is why I got a friend to copy the script for me. Even to look at a passage of Tibetan writing makes my head ache.' He paused and pushed away the learned work still opened on the desk between us. I closed the book politely. 'I can read Tibetan,' he went on, 'but slowly. I can write down simple words – like bread, mother, carpet – but it produces a violent migraine, so that I cannot see things in front of me but only those at the side.'

I stared at him with admiration The performance had been magnificent, but hardly convincing.

'You are *not* a Tibetan lama,' I said, 'though you appear to know a great deal about Tibet. How you have acquired this information I don't know, but it has impressed some of the experts. Speaking as a publisher, I tell you that you have a great gift for writing – narrative power, characterization, local colour. Why not come clean and tell me the truth? It will help you and help me. If the book is fiction, confess it. We can then publish it as fiction or as an imaginative autobiography. In a year's time or two, you can have mastered another subject, and you can produce another fictional work which will be a success. But . . . *I must know the truth.*'

The lama didn't even hesitate. 'I have told you the truth from the beginning,' he said. 'I am a lama. Everything in my book is true, with a few trifling mistakes. The shock of your disbelief is terrible.'

I stood up. 'And that is your final word?' I said. Dr. K. stood up too. He looked pale and depressed. 'For six years,' he said, 'I have been suffering from an incurable disease. I was examined at Guy's

Hospital and the Rotunda in Dublin. But already it was too late. In less than two years it will make no difference to me what anyone thinks of *The Third Eye*. I wish I had never started it.' Across the gap of mistrust, bridging it momentarily, we shook hands. Even now I could not bring myself to dislike him. Whoever he was, whatever game he was playing, he was resolved to see it through to the finish.

A few days later, Snellgrove sent in his report. It was damning. 'The book is a complete fantasy,' he wrote, 'culled from the writings of others. Nowhere does he demonstrate personal acquaintance with his subject. Just note how he deals with the Potala. He writes chiefly of telescopes and the imaginary underground lake. Note the imagined conversation with the Dalai Lama, who admonishes him not to speak of the ego or soul in the west. There is no ego or soul in Buddhism and his thought is just confused. . . . The fellow is a complete impostor, and has probably never been to Tibet. . . . He should be properly unmasked, as such men may be dangerous.' There followed a detailed criticism of Dr. K's use of the Tibetan language. Sadly I read the report. Only one thought gave me a slight encouragement – the well-known dislike of experts for each other.

A couple of days after that a long letter arrived from Macrae, dated October 7. His Reader Two had written 'our impression is that the author has been in Lhasa at some time and has fairly intimate knowledge of life there, though we doubt his parentage. The author has been given as much latitude as possible on the assumption that some of the customs and incidents which he writes about occurred in, and that he comes from, one of the distant Provinces of Tibet, some of which were lost to China.'

So the puzzle continued. Snellgrove (and my wife) said Dr. K. had never been to Tibet; Macrae's Reader Two thought he had. Snellgrove did not 'find even half-truths'; Reader Two believed he 'has a fairly intimate knowledge of life in Tibet.' But it was the murderous and authoritative report of Snellgrove which weighed most heavily with me, taken in conjunction with the odd goings-on at the 'secret' conclave with Dr. K. On October 17 I wrote to Macrae, 'In my opinion, we and you have been the victims of one of the most remarkable and interesting fakes in modern times.'

The well-known 'I've been robbed' syndrome now took possession of me, and I started being nasty to everyone around. I cancelled our contract with Dr. K, and demanded the return of the advance, which naturally I did not get. I was nasty to my colleagues for discouraging my scepticism by their own credulity. I was nasty, so far as practicable, with my wife for revealing the truth weeks before I was ready to receive it. But it was, of course, to myself that I was nastiest of all – for being duped. The New Year came in, and Dr. K. wrote me a farewell letter. 'I am leaving England today – a very sick man indeed. What any of you think of the book does not matter to me now. I wrote the TRUTH.' This letter remained unanswered.

But soon I became possessed by a feeling of intense sadness. My lama and his book had become dear to me. The thought that we were never to publish it was detestable. Like a pregnant woman who has been advised an abortion and loves her unborn child, I prayed for a happier outcome. Could we not publish it after all, while warning the reader that we had been unable to authenticate it? After so many discrepant reports we decided to send the manuscript to a new reader, a fine Orientalist, John Morris, who had travelled widely in the East. It was this report that proved decisive. 'This is a curious mixture of fact and fancy,' he wrote, 'the descriptions of Lhasa and of Tibetan family life are completely authentic. Whatever the author's real nationality may be, there is not the slightest doubt that he was brought up in Tibet from an early age. . . . There is nothing unusual in the boy being sent away from home to a lamasery at the age of seven. I have known many cases of it. What I cannot believe is the treatment he received as an incarnation. I have never before heard of a boy being recognized as an incarnation *after* he has entered a lamasery for education. It is always the other way round.' My spirits rose, though the second half of the report was less satisfactory. 'I think this story goes completely off the rails,' he continued, 'as soon as the author ceases to write of ordinary everyday life in Tibet. I think the whole business of the so-called 'third eye' is absolute nonsense. The operation on the skull as here described could only have resulted in death from sepsis. Nor can I believe that the author was on the friendly terms he describes with the late Dalai Lama. . . . I also find the human kite incident very hard to swallow, and I am sure the account of the yeti (abominable snowman) is a fantasy. I think there is, however, an element of truth about the author's life in the lamasery, but I feel he has embroidered it. . . . *My own opinion is that the author is some sort of psychopath living in a private neurotic world of his own. It is even likely that he has persuaded himself that all this occult nonsense is true. . . .*'

This viewpoint came close to my own. Dr. K. *had* been in Tibet, I surmised, *had* fantasticated his life story, *had* now become psychopathic and swallowed his own fantasies. This was the truth as I saw it at the time. I would reject the other experts whose views contradicted each other. We should publish *The Third Eye* with a 'beware' notice, but without suggesting that it was a complete fabrication. It would, I felt certain, become a best-seller. As a publisher, I could not reject it. The decision was made. Publish! At least then, I thought, the truth will somehow emerge.

Early in February the preparations for manufacture began. I drafted a Foreword. 'To believe or not to believe, that is the question we have pondered long and earnestly,' I wrote. 'For the autobiography of a Tibetan lama is a unique book and like a roc's egg hard to authenticate.' I might have added 'hard also to hatch'. It was hard also to persuade the author to agree to what I had written, and in the end it appeared somewhat mangled in the first and early editions of the book. But for those who had eyes to see, without the necessity to make use of a third eye, we put the matter clearly enough. 'For these reasons,' the Foreword stated, 'the author must bear – and willingly bears – a sole responsibility for the statements made in this book. We may feel that here and there he exceeds the bounds of Western credulity. . . . None the less the publishers believe that *The Third Eye* is in its essence an authentic account of the upbringing and training of a Tibetan boy in his family and in a lamasery. Anyone who differs from us will, we believe, at least agree that the author is endowed to an exceptional degree with narrative skill and the power to evoke scenes and characters of absorbing and unique interest.'

Since publishing is the pursuit of the possible rather than the perfect, the Foreword is perhaps adequate. In the light of what happened afterwards, I wish it had been nearer my original, blunter draft. Our lawyers advised, not unexpectedly, 'that the risk of action for libel at the suit of Dr. Kuan is extremely remote in all the circumstances.' They suggested sending a duplicate to Dr. K. which we did. His reply came in a letter to Brooks of March 29, and datelined Canada. Canada? How on earth, I wondered, had he got to Canada?

> I confess that I am most surprised that you now want to publish the book. This is against my own wishes and I believe I have the law on my side as the contract was broken by you people.
>
> Mr. Warburg is the only one among you who has been at all decent or fair to me, and I would like him to recover his losses. My book is TRUE and provided that it is published as I wrote it (with my last alterations) . . . I will raise no objection.

I have suffered very greatly over this and have lost everything. . . . However that is finished with. If you had sent me the copy manuscript [sic] when I asked for it, I could have obtained the proof or verification requested. Now – I care less than I did before!

On April 11, Dr. K. wrote Brooks that he was returning to England at once! 'If the book is to be a success now, there will have to be some amity between us. I am prepared to forget the past. . . .' By April 21, Dr. K. was back in England – if indeed he had ever moved from his London address (Monomark BM/KEK, London, W.C.1) expressing indignation at our Foreword, 'a very spiteful affair, I simply cannot imagine Mr. Warburg permitting it. I understood that in English law a person was innocent until proved guilty. The Foreword implies in a biased way that no one can prove me innocent or guilty.' It is strange, though, how throughout the correspondence, it is Mr. Warburg who is always honest and sympathetic, the others who are spiteful and pettifogging. But the explanation is easy to come by. Since I was head of the firm, it was I who had the power ultimately to publish or to reject *The Third Eye*. Since Dr. K. with quiet desperation wanted it published, he was careful never to say anything derogatory about myself, and assumed that I would have no grumble about rude remarks on my colleagues. Cynical as was Dr. K's intuition, it was not lacking in perception.

In November, 1956, *The Third Eye* was published at a price of 18s. Right from the start it looked to be a best-seller. The advance sale was 10,000 copies out of a first printing of 15,000. Reprint after reprint followed. By the end of 1957 we had sold over 45,000 copies. Translated editions were published in France, Germany, Italy, Sweden, Finland and elsewhere. In the U.S. too it was published, though not by the sceptical Macrae. The reviews were far more favourable than I had dared to hope, though two at least described it roundly as a fake. I was interviewed on television where I had some difficult questions to answer. On the whole, however, all went well. Another gamble had succeeded. Or had it?

On January 29, 1958, fourteen months after publication, my cosy world of Tibetan delights blew up. At 11 a.m. of that day, a call came through from Dublin. Hugh Medlicott of the *Daily Mail* was on the wire. 'Would it surprise you to know,' he asked, 'that your Tibetan lama is a hoaxer?' He paused and waited. My heart missed a beat. My mind raced over the complex series of events I have described, as a drowning man reviews his life in the moment before he sinks for the last time. Then, unexpectedly, I heard a voice, my own voice, saying firmly, 'It is no surprise to me at all.' 'Did you know,' pursued Medlicott, 'that he's the son of a master plumber from Devon, and that his name is Hoskins?' 'Of course I didn't know all that,' I said. 'What do you take me for?'

For half an hour the long-range conversational battle raged, while Medlicott tried to trap me into embarrassing admissions and I strove to obtain all the information I could. 'It'll all be in tomorrow's *Mail*,' he said finally, 'bang on the front page, a scoop, if ever I saw one.' 'I'll buy it,' I said, 'don't you worry.'

The next day I received a telegram from Dr. K., who knew by then of the storm that was about to break. It contained only fifteen words, but they will be forever engraved on my memory. 'HI FREDDIE STOP BOOK IS STILL TRUE STOP BEEN FRAMED BUT NO OIL PAINTING RAMPA.'

This was the first time that the aloof Dr. K. had addressed me by my Christian name, and it was surely significant, the hurried attempt of a cornered man to be on familiar terms of friendship with a man he has duped, who he fears may seek to exact revenge now that the incredible facts of his gigantic deception are to be revealed.

On the same day, about a quarter of an hour before midnight, as I was deciding to go to bed, the telephone rang. 'Is that Mr. Warburg, the publisher?' a voice said.

'Yes.'

'*Daily Express* speaking. We've just seen the proofs of tomorrow's *Mail*. Do you know that the Tibetan lama in your book, *The Third Eye*, is a fraud?'

'I know he is.'

'Then why did you attempt to defraud the reading public by publishing a hoax?'

'We made no attempt to defraud the public,' I said sharply, 'obviously you haven't read the Foreword to the book.' 'What Foreword? There's no Foreword in the copy I have here.'

'There *was* a Foreword in the first editions,' I said, 'which made it crystal clear that we as publishers had doubts about this book. We took great care not to authenticate it. Let me read you the relevant passage.' I got the book off my shelf and read it to him, clearly, slowly, emphatically. Disappointed at being unable to write a scathing report on our behaviour, he started plying me with questions. 'Stop asking me all these damn-fool questions,' I said irritably, 'the affair's quite a complicated one. I'm perfectly ready to write you a piece on it.'

'You are? Hold on a minute while I talk to my night editor.'

'Tell your editor I'm not a complete amateur as a writer. I've had a couple of pieces in the *New Yorker* magazine.'

'Good gracious, do you mean you want to be paid real money?'

'Take it any way you like,' I said.

He went away for a few minutes, then came back. 'My editor wants you to go to Dublin with me tomorrow morning. The lama is barricaded in his place at Howth – he's asked for police protection – and we want to get in to see him and take a statement. But he won't see anyone unless you're there.'

'I can't go to Dublin tomorrow,' I said. 'I've got a busy weekend. I have to be in Birmingham on Sunday morning to debate with the secretary of the Public Morality Council on television.'

'What in heaven's name are you debating with him?' he asked.

'Dirty books,' I said. 'I'm the man they put in the dock on an obscenity charge two years ago.'

'Dirty books! Fake Lamas! A gay life you publishers lead,' he remarked.

'My firm is a reasonably respectable one,' I told him, 'considering the temptations.'

But now it was half an hour after midnight, and I cut the conversation short. Nothing was finally fixed. The *Express* had half offered to buy a 1,000 word article at a stiff price. I had half promised either to go to Dublin myself or send Eric Newby, then my promotion manager.* I rang off, swallowed a stiff sedative, and retired to bed. But sleep did not come. I visualized Dr. K. in Howth with the world's press baying him like hounds for the kill. What would he say? What could he say? How had he been unmasked? Who had unmasked him? I got out of bed and sat down at my desk. It was 1.30 a.m. By 3 a.m. a 1,000 word article was completed.

In it I sketched briefly the story as I have told it here. 'And the lama himself,' I concluded, 'I hope it's not true that he's ill. Though we had our quarrels, I liked him. I admired his pluck. It is no mean feat to have hoodwinked the world for fourteen months. As a writer, I think he's first-rate, and no publisher can grant higher praise than this.' Five minutes later, my need for self-expression and perhaps

*Newby, a friend of David Holt, had already published with us a lively and highly successful narrative, *The Last Grain Race*, describing his own experiences as a hand on a sailing ship from Australia to Liverpool. Later we were to publish his amusing account of another adventure, *A Short Walk on the Hindu Kush*. Since then he has written other books and has a distinguished career on the *Observer*.

self-justification satisfied, I got into bed and fell asleep instantly.

The phone woke me up five hours later and kept ringing intermittently throughout the day as the drama continued its erratic course. I rushed to the door for the *Daily Mail*. There on the front page was Medlicott's story. My best-selling author was no Tibetan lama. His name was neither T. Lobsang Rampa, nor Dr. Kuan-Suo, it was Cyril Henry Hoskins. Born in 1911, the son of Joseph Henry Hoskins, a plumber of Plympton, Devon, he had been to a simple local school and later worked as his father's assistant till the latter's death in 1937. He then went with his mother to live in Nottinghamshire. There he worked for a firm of surgical instrument makers. In 1940 he married a state registered nurse at a Richmond hospital. Later, he left and became a clerk with a correspondence school in Weybridge, Surrey. Here, in the early days of the war, he shaved his head, grew a beard and changed his name to Ku'an Suo. Hoskins had never been to Tibet, indeed he had never been out of England till he went to Howth, Dublin. As I sat there, stunned, the pieces of the jigsaw began to fall into place. What a fool I had been! How neatly I had been duped! How strong the power of wishful thinking! The Tibetan lama's autobiography was such stuff as dreams are made on.

But there was more to Medlicott's story than this, there was the clue to how Dr. K. had been exposed. A number of eminent Tibetan scholars, including, I believe, Heinrich Harrer, author of *Seven Years in Tibet*, and Marco Pallis, writer and Himalayan explorer, enraged at the hoax played on the world of Oriental scholarship and literature, had engaged a detective to unmask the bogus lama. A Liverpool private detective, Clifford Burgess, had been instructed to make inquiries. Aided by a nineteen-year-old assistant, Miss Sheila Bryant, described as 'pretty', of Hoylake, Cheshire, they travelled 3,000 miles in three weeks, interviewed scores of people and took statements running into thousands of words. 'It has been a long and difficult job,' Burgess is reported as saying, 'but I am glad I have been able to help in the exposure of this man.' The statement is colourless, like any police report, and one could have wished for more illuminating detail about so extraordinary a person.

But there was little time for reflection on that busy Saturday morning, as I clinched my deal with the *Daily Express* for the article at a price beyond my wildest dreams in return for a promise to send Newby to Dublin. There was not a moment to lose. Mrs Kuan had called up from Howth and wept over the phone, begging me to relieve the pressure on her husband who was, she said, gravely ill, in case he should be driven mad or destroyed. Newby came to my apartment for briefing. He had entered wholeheartedly into the spirit of the melodrama and was dressed in a costume more suitable, it seemed to me, for an arctic voyage than a trip to Dublin. I handed him a letter for Dr. K. 'Thank you for your cable, but how can I believe it in the light of the *Daily Mail* exposure? I am sending the bearer of this letter, my friend and colleague, to see if you can give him a statement with which the bona fides of your book and your own person can be maintained.' Armed with this document, Newby sallied forth on his peculiar mission.

The atmosphere at Howth, as pieced together from the newspaper accounts and Newby's report, was fantastic. In and around a green and white villa at the top of a cliff overlooking a small island, Ireland's Eye, in the Bay of Dublin, a considerable group of people were milling around. Dr. K. lay on his bed, suffering, according to his wife, from a severe coronary thrombosis; he was refusing to see anyone, because, as he remarked, their auras made him ill. It may also have been, it seemed to me, that he was cooking up a story to extricate himself from the mess with the least loss of face. Certainly, from time to time, he released a statement. An early one is as good an example as any. 'This story is true, but for very good reasons the identity of the Tibetan author cannot be revealed. I have never bedraggled anyone in my life, no matter what the cost. I have almost no chance of life. This shock is reducing it even more. . . . My life had been hard and bitter, and in this other (?) blow of publicity, I am doing what is right.'

His wife, plump and with greying hair tied in a bun and an Eastern medallion hanging round her neck, was bearing the brunt of the assaults from the outer world, as wives are so often forced to do. She was fending off a wide selection of the world's press, who were attempting to make an entry through front or back door, window or even down the chimney. She was issuing communiqués about her husband's health. She was calling me up in London for aid. No doubt, she was also cooking, cleaning and making the beds. A woman's work is never done. At one time, in a moment of weakness, to which she was surely entitled, she appears to have phoned the *Mail* reporter, and said, 'I've got to tell you. This will hurt him very much. He is not a Tibetan. That is his photograph on the cover of the book.' But from this lapse she was soon to recover and declared, 'he was asked to write the book. At first he didn't want to do it. He did what he thought was right. He's trying to do some good in the world. He's a very wonderful man. He's willing to have the book investigated. Anyone can analyse it.' At least Dr. K. had a loyal wife.

The third member of this unusual household was a 27-year-old woman, Mrs. L., once, according to the detective, 'a gay member of West End society, one of his many followers who believe in his celestial and clairvoyant powers.' She was helping Dr. K. answer the 'world-wide flood of letters from people seeking advice' from him. But now, of course, it was the lama who required advice. Mrs. L., blonde and attractive, had stated aggressively 'we were prepared for snoopers to come and pry out the facts. I have seen the real Dr. Kuan but I will not tell you where he is.' In the confusion of the moment, the versions did not always tally. Round and about, at the door, in the pubs, on the roads, in the phone-boxes and even grubbing in the dustbins for 'documents', reporters and strong-arm men from British, Irish, European and United States newspapers struggled to get the story. Among them members of the Irish police force attempted to keep order and see fair play.

Into this maelstrom from the calm of a winter weekend in London came Newby. He was received in an incense-laden room with a wooden statuette of Buddha on the mantelpiece and an Oriental brass table from Birmingham in the corner. After a brief talk he was shown into Dr. K's room, alone, the first outsider to see K. that day. The lama lay on the bed, groaning from time to time. Soon Newby was permitted to bring the reporter from the *Express* into the room, and a photograph of the sick man was taken and duly reproduced in Monday's paper at the head of my own article. An interview of sorts took place. From time to time Dr. K. rested between sentences to gain strength to continue. He said that he had never taken money for advising people about their health and spiritual problems. In this matter he was probably telling the truth, no one ever wrote to his agent or to me complaining of being charged or overcharged. He said of Mrs. L., 'I saw this girl's marriage breaking up. I wanted to help.' But it was obvious that in this case at least he had not been successful. Indeed Mrs. L. announced later, 'there is no hope of a reconciliation. It is all over. Someone employed a private detective to discredit the lama and win me back.' This may well have been true, though the eminent scholars, concerned to rehabilitate the integrity of Tibetan studies, must have collaborated. Later the room was cleared, and Newby settled down to record on tape the long and detailed statement which Dr. K. gave him for posterity. With this he flew back to London to report.

What this statement lacked in plausibility, it made up for by a bizarre quality which must always rank high in the history of psychopathology. 'I, a Tibetan lama, now occupy what was originally the body of a Western man, and I occupy it to the permanent and total exclusion of the former occupant. He gave his willing consent, being glad to escape from life on this earth in view of my urgent need. In the East, it is acknowledged that the stronger mind can take possession of another body.'

The possession of Hoskins' body by the Tibetan took place, according to Dr. K's statement, on June 13, 1949, after a 'slight accident', though advance warning by telepathy had been sent to the Englishman eighteen months before. The doomed man fell in rather quickly with the plan for his own demise, surely a fate worse than death, and 'to make the change-over easier he altered his addresses a number of times and lost contact with all friends and relations', though not with his wife. Finally, on that fatal June day, Hoskins, apparently unheedful that his final hour had come, climbed up an oak tree with his camera – he was a keen amateur photographer – to snap an owl which, blinded by the sunlight, had perched there. An unfortunate fall onto the grass below resulted in a mild concussion 'which knocked me out of myself'. As he recovered consciousness, across the lawn towards him floated the figure of a lama in blue and saffron robes and entered into his body. That was the effective end of the Englishman.

There are an astonishing number of people all over the world who do believe it, though I am not among them. Many of them wrote to me or Brooks, and Dr. K. himself must have received whole sackfuls of letters. Some of my correspondents themselves claimed possession of a third eye. A few claimed that they thought the lama an even greater man to have overcome (so ingeniously?) the many difficulties facing him before he could acquire a new body. One woman wanted to know what had happened to the old and presumably useless Tibetan husk. Another wished to subject him to 'psychometric' tests, whatever they may be. There were surprisingly few indignant letters.

For me the lama's statement was frankly a disappointment. Perhaps it was composed too hurriedly. But I felt that I could have done a better job myself. Dr. K., I thought, had been crude, and even worse, sadistic. The conception of the stronger mind driving out the weaker has an air of brutality to it, a Darwinian flavour out of key with the milder and more altruistic teachings of any of the higher religions. It was materialistic rather than spiritual. At least some effort should have been made to give Hoskins' side of the case, some explanation of his wish to leave this world of sorrows for ever.

By February 9, Dr. K's coronary attack must have abated, for on that day, little more than a week after his exposure, he wrote to me in his old jaunty style which I knew by now so well. 'Dear Mr. Warburg, I am polite and put "Mr." but that is not why I write. So you like me, eh? To the extent of getting £250 plus a few extras out of my misfortune.* No plumber's son, Mr. Warburg, no bogus lama either, but no doubt you have read about that now. I still like you – though goodness knows why, in view of the above (the only one in your firm that I do like!). How about taking my new book, *Medical Lama*, or can't you face up to it? Yours sincerely, C. Ku'an, GENUINE LAMA.' Alas, we couldn't 'face up to it', but it was duly published elsewhere in London, not without success, as well as several others.

The rate of sale of *The Third Eye* increased enormously for months after the exposure, and we sold nearly 10,000 copies before the end of 1959. Even today, so many years later, we continue to sell it remarkably well. It was put into paperback by Corgi Books in 1959, and has sold no less than 250,000 copies since publication. It was one of the most profitable books we ever published.

Two women, Mrs. Ablett and Mrs. Boxall, had been neighbours of Dr. K. at Weybridge, Surrey, during the war. Two days after my piece on the lama had appeared in the *Express*, Mrs. Boxall rang my wife, to congratulate her on her 'womanly intuition' in seeing so swiftly through Dr. K's pretensions. In 1960 I went to see them. They had not, they said, liked Dr. K. overmuch, but they knew him reasonably well. It was in 1942 that he told them he proposed to revert to his 'real' name of Kuan Suo in place of Cyril Henry Hoskins. He had cards printed in this style and insisted he be called by his 'proper' name. His mother, he said, was Chinese and, though he detested English children because they were so badly brought up, he loved Chinese ones. He demanded to be treated with the greatest respect, and could not endure to be told off by anyone, even in a

*The fee paid me by the *Express* for my article.

superior position to himself. He loved cats, and had a collar and lead for his own which he took driving in his car at night hanging round the back of his neck. He took many snaps of her, for he loved photography – and trick mirrors. He was also interested in numerology and palmistry. He showed little interest in women. but was married to an ex-nurse or hospital sister. He was not much interested in men either, for he was solitary and secretive. He was, however, these two women informed me, a marvellous teller of tales.

Here, in fact, is a striking portrait of a counterfeiter and impersonator in the making, but it took more than ten years before he was ready to attempt his successful coup, persuading first his experienced agent and then my colleagues and myself to accept him, if only briefly, as a Tibetan lama. But, though our belief was brief, it lasted long enough to make it intolerable for us *not* to publish *The Third Eye*.

Why should Dr. K., who had declared himself Chinese, pose to us as Tibetan? Simply that too much was known about China and so little about Tibet. I believe too that, during Dr. K's years of study and apprenticeship and planning for his supreme achievement, he had heard of George Psalmanazer, studied his life, and read his successful *Description of Formosa*, 1704 (it ran to three editions) with admiration and care. The two men have much in common. K's Tibet is much the livelier and more lifelike book of the two. It has the characteristics and the characters of a novel, and might well have succeeded even if it had been published as straight fiction. K. could have had a great future as a writer of historical fictions or fictional histories, as I had told him at our 'secret' confrontation. But he refused to take my advice, and the works he wrote after *The Third Eye* must have been a disappointment to his numerous admirers.

There is one last point, an important one. Psalmanazer never believed for one moment that he was a Formosan. His book was a concoction, while K's was a brilliant counterfeit. For K., I feel tolerably sure, believed in some sense in his lamahood, believed he was in fact the lama who had entered the body of Cyril Henry Hoskins. Pathological, perhaps, but it was this belief that made his book one of the most readable and successful of any I have published. *The Third Eye* was the product of faith, of love for Buddhism as he understood it, a religion as far away from the sordid materialism he sensed around him, as the lowland counties of southern England from the sparkling peaks and glittering domes and palaces of holy Lhasa. All the best counterfeiters surely loved their work.

It must be agreed that the counterfeiter's work can gravely harm his dupe or dupes. In the case of money or banknotes or share-certificates, the loss is financial and can be tremendous. In the field of artistic or scientific forgeries, there can also be large or not so large financial damage, though in my own case the possible financial damage was turned into a substantial profit. But there is also a damage to the reputation of the dupe and to the particular branch of art or science (or publishing) to which the forged article belongs. The damage to the reputation of Secker & Warburg might have been considerable, had we not refused to authenticate *The Third Eye*. Even as it was, the damage to Tibetan and Oriental Studies generally was considered serious enough by some experts in this field to induce them to employ a private detective to investigate the affair. For it is a sad fact of life that the ignorant (that is, most of us) cannot help laughing when the experts are deceived. Their credulity is a balm to the knowledge that we know so little about so much.

* * *

A few months after the Lama Rampa had been exposed, we received a typescript from a woman in South Africa. Its title was *Brides of the Third Reich*. It didn't take me long to read, because once begun it was compulsive reading. Having finished, I knew we had another best-seller in our hands, *if it was true*. But was it?

Brides was an autobiography, the story of a young German girl of lower middle-class parentage, selected by a department of the S.S. dealing with Eugenics and Population Growth, for an unusual service to Hitler and the Third Reich. She and 49 similar girls had been chosen to become the brides of 50 young S.S. men, to mate with them and bear pure Aryan babies for a future upper-class meritocracy when Germany had become master of Europe. The girl was taken from her parents, who were handsomely compensated, and given a thorough training for six months in manners, general education, the history of Germany, and last but not least, in sexual behaviour and hygiene. They were then transported to a large and magnificent castle in Central Germany and informed of the glamorous and exciting adventure that lay before them. Fifty young Aryan males, blond, physically fit and virile, were to visit them in the castle, staying about a month for a honeymoon period, during which, after the couples had paired off, they would pursue those pleasurable activities intended to lead to the production of babies. At the end of the allotted time, the S.S. men were despatched to the Russian front, where no doubt most of them died in defence of the Fatherland, while the Hitler maidens, virgins no longer and all with luck pregnant, stayed on to bear their children and prepare for a second honeymoon with a new batch of S.S. men about fifteen months later.

All this was described with gusto and a realism which made it almost impossible not be believe that the author was describing what had actually happened to her. After that, however, the narrative becomes a good deal less plausible. I made inquiries of experts on Nazi Germany about the likelihood of such a mass mating. The experts took the line that such events had probably taken place, and one of them thought he knew where he could find evidence. I remained in doubt, encouraging myself with the thought that an ex-Hitler bride might well have settled ultimately in such a place as South Africa. At last, I wrote Mrs. L. and inquired whether *Brides of the Third Reich* was indeed a true record. A bogus lama and a bogus Hitler maiden in close proximity would be altogether too much for the reputation of Secker & Warburg. The answer from Mrs. L. came quickly. The letter is lost, but the gist was on the following lines. 'Dear Mr. W., My book is not a true narrative of events. I have noticed recently the vogue for fictional autobiography, several have appeared, including your own excellent one, *The Third Eye*. I thought I'd try one myself. Sincerely. . . .' It was all over! Honour had been saved, a potential best-seller had been lost. We returned the manuscript with a polite note. I have often thought since then that the field of fictional autobiography might be worth tilling. Perhaps, though we know it not, it is.

16

Robert Musil and Thomas Mann

IF you were to list the ten major prose writers now no longer living of the period 1910–50, particularly those who practised fiction, a possible list might be made up as follows – Proust, Mann, Joyce, Kafka, Svevo, Orwell, Gide, Colette, Musil and Mishima. Of these, my firm and I have been concerned with all except Proust and Joyce, an extraordinary record. In considering this list it is noteworthy that no American writer appears – I have omitted Henry James on the ground that he belongs to an earlier epoch. The great American writers of the past – Whitman, Melville, Hawthorne and others – do not appear to have had major descendants in spite of the wealth of talent in modern American writing. The great Russian literary tradition has been stifled by the Soviet censorship – Gorky died, Pasternak has emerged. The rest struggle so far in vain. Of the South Americans I know too little to speak, but I am aware that several writers have most definitely made their mark as major figures. The world of letters is not dead, nor specifically is the world of the novel, still the most significant and important literary form of the age. In Europe, Asia (Japan), Russia and America there is an international literary society of the highest quality, which has to contend with the problems of form and content in a world notable for changes that are all too swift and for a constantly growing chaos. To bring form into the chaos, to establish that not all means justify the ends which must be pursued, to maintain that man, the individual man and the individual woman, is the measure of all things, these are the tasks of writers today. If the old traditions are dead, new traditions must be created. Surely such tasks have been the concern of writers in the past and is their concern today, as Musil said himself, 'writing is the attempt to create a higher moral species.' It is not, of course, the concern of writers alone, but of all who have the ability to create and recreate myths and symbols by which we may steer a course through the storms to come.

Of the three major authors writing in German, all have been published by my firm – Kafka from the Sudetenland in Czechoslovakia, Mann from Lübeck in East Germany, and Musil from Vienna in Austria. Of these three I knew only Mann personally. But it is of Robert Musil I wish to write first, since he is less well-known to the English-reading public than the other two and a man of a most unusual character. For him I performed as a publisher a service of some importance, taking him on while he was regarded everywhere as unsaleable, and establishing him as a major writer with the English-speaking public, indeed actually reviving his reputation in Germany and in his native Austria, where his books languished out of print, forgotten and with further chapters of his major work posthumously and privately printed in Switzerland during the war, and so virtually unpublished.

Robert Musil was born on November 6, 1880, in Klagenfurt, in Carinthia, the son of Hofrat von Musil, a professor of engineering, a keen horseman and an amateur portrait painter. His mother, Hermine, was a lively woman who tended to put her husband in the shade.* Educated in the military academy where Rilke had suffered such agonies, Musil coped readily with its rigours and used it as the background of his first novel, *Young Törless* (1906).† Before he was commissioned, Musil changed his career and switched to study civil engineering, but after gaining his diploma in Brno in 1901 and after his military service, he switched again, this time to philosophy and experimental psychology and took his degree in 1908. He also invented the Musil chromometer, of which he was inordinately proud.

At the age of 30 Musil married and, having now to support a wife, took a 10 a.m. to 2 p.m. job in the Technical Library, Vienna. In 1911 he published two long short stories,‡ but gave up his job at the library, because he preferred to do his writing in the mornings and

*Throughout this chapter I have made great use of Mrs. Kaiser's letters to me of November 1972 and of her introductions to volumes of the English edition of *The Man Without Qualities*.

†Published by Secker & Warburg, 1955.

‡Both included in *Tonka and Other Stories*, Secker & Warburg, 1965.

to take a walk after lunch. So he became an editor of the *Neue Rundschau*, and wrote reviews and criticism. This had an even more damaging effect on his creative energies than the library. However, in 1914 he went into the army and fought right through the war with distinction until his demobilization in 1918. In 1919 he was working in the Austrian Foreign Ministry, and two years later acting as scientific adviser to the War Ministry. He was now 41, with a growing reputation as a writer in Austrian and German literary circles. This wealth and variety of experience was to stand him in good stead when he came to write *The Man Without Qualities* (Der Mann Ohne Eigenschaften). Except for the military art it is said that he lacked certain practical skills, including even the ability to make a pot of tea. However, his wife provided what he lacked – buying his ticket for him on trams, calming him down when he got over-excited in argument, dosing him with a bromide when he had smoked too much or drunk more coffee than was good for him.

In 1921 he published a play, *Die Schwärmer* (Dreamers), described at the time as 'a peak in dramatic art' and in 1923 *Drei Frauen*, a group of novellas.* It was at this period that he was preparing to begin *The Man Without Qualities*. In 1925 Musil signed a contract for it with the German publisher Ernst Rowohlt, who began to pay him advances month by month and year by year. The novel, then titled *The Twin Sister*, was to have been ready for publication in autumn 1925. However, it was not till 1930 that the first volume appeared (translated as the first two volumes of the English edition). But during 1931–2 his publisher's finances became strained to near breaking point by the onset of the world economic crisis at the time, leading to pressure by Rowohlt on his author to complete the much heralded second volume of this gigantic work. The first volume contained over 1,000 pages in 123 chapters, the second, published in 1933 (translated as the third volume of the English edition), contained a mere 600 pages in 38 chapters. Well before 1935, therefore, Musil had a grave problem to solve – what was he going to live on, since his main source of income came from his advances on royalties, and his publisher was hard up and in no mood to continue paying out indefinitely.

Foreseeing this, Musil was not unwilling, indeed it might well be said that he was delighted, to accept a regular income from patrons, first the Musil Society in Berlin, founded by the art historian, Ernst Glaeser, which 'dissolved under the pressure of events', as Musil

*Also included in *Tonka*.

caustically put it, when the Nazis seized power in 1933. Early in 1934 he was approached by the art-historian, Bruno Fürst, an admiring reader, who asked him what on earth he could be living on now. Musil replied, untruthfully in my opinion, that he was considering suicide. As a result the Vienna Society was formed, supported by a number of distinguished cultural personages, many of them Jewish.

Happily Musil settled down to work at his leisure on Book Two from chapter 39 onwards. In 1936, Frau Fürst, wife of the founder and treasurer of the Society, bought back from Rowohlt with her own money the rights and the stocks of Musil's books. This enabled him to make a contract with a new German publisher, Bermann-Fischer, a refugee from Germany to Vienna, and to start once again the not unpleasing routine by which he received regular royalties from a reliable source. But as the royalties mounted ever higher, Bermann was naturally anxious to receive something in return for his money, in fact the completion of *The Man Without Qualities.* His anxiety would have been even greater had he known how confused were Musil's plans.

The transaction of business between publishers and authors in respect of advances is veiled, and is likely to remain veiled, in mystery, but it is on a scale which may well surprise the reader. Forty years ago Alfred Knopf had told me to publish only those writers who were rich or at least fairly well-off. Wise advice, indeed, and utterly impossible even then to follow. Ten years ago Sir Allen Lane confessed that Penguin books had no less than £780,000 out in advances to authors. It would be no surprise to me to learn that by now this figure had doubled. My own moderate-sized firm, at a guess, will have advances running well into six figures on which to pay interest. Interest on advances to authors is an item of publishing overheads often forgotten by writers.

From time to time to Bermann's inquiries Musil would answer that he had just one more chapter to complete, and Bermann would believe him, as I would have done in that situation. After all, what else is there for a publisher to do? But the stress imposed on Musil by all this, though it resulted in the completion of 20 more chapters in the next two years (nos. 39 to 58), had an unforeseen side-effect – in 1936 the author had a stroke while swimming with Dr. Fürst and would have drowned had not Fürst been there to rescue him. On the plea of ill health he persuaded the abashed publisher to postpone delivery of the completion of the book from spring 1937 to spring 1938. In the spring of 1938 Musil was happily correcting his proofs –

in practice he was as usual largely rewriting them – when the Nazis occupied Austria. Bermann escaped from Austria at the last moment. His firm being Jewish property was instantly sequestered by the Gestapo. Musil was left with two sets of galley proofs, heavily corrected, and precious little else. Most of the Musil Society members being Jewish (though not Frau Fürst) were also forced into exile. Musil, whose wife was Jewish, remained till August and then left for Switzerland where he remained until his death in 1942.

Such was the experience of many writers, great and not so great, during the second quarter of this murderous twentieth century. Mann also was forced into becoming a refugee. A tribute should be paid to such authors for their ability to complete masterpieces (in itself a task demanding the most intense concentration by men of the highest sensibility) while harried from pillar to post by the enemies of civilization. Musil, however, did not complete *The Man Without Qualities*. For one reason – there were others more important – he dared not, because his livelihood, the subscriptions from Swiss and American patrons, depended on his being able to state that he would not be able to continue working on the novel without financial support. To some patrons he wrote that he was making rapid progress, to others that he had still another 190 chapters to compose. To Hermann Broch, himself as I know a talented leg-puller, who inquired why he did not write a new book, he remarked plaintively that there was now nothing else he was still fitted to do except go on with what he had begun twenty years earlier.

In 1942 Musil died after four years of comfortable living in good Swiss lodgings. He had spent the morning as usual at his writing table in the garden. Before lunch he had gone upstairs to take a bath. 'When he was satisfied with the way work was going – not often the case – he was cheerful. I have rarely seen him so cheerful five minutes before his death. He had written some sentences that were to stand.' So wrote his widow. The expression on his face was said to be one of mockery and mild astonishment. He had had nothing of substance published since 1933. The third volume, the second part, or part of a part, of Book Two, was privately printed in Lausanne soon after his death. Otherwise Musil's books were out of print.

Almost unknown outside the German-speaking countries, he now became equally unremembered inside them. In 1940 he had written in a letter 'In spite of the reputation as an artist that I undoubtedly have in Germany and abroad, I have always kept some slight distance from the main road of success. I am not the kind of author who tells his readers what they want to hear because they know it anyway. My attitude and my work tend rather more towards the severe. . . .' Yet year by year *The Man Without Qualities* is being read by more and more readers. What seemed strange and irrelevant in the 1930's strikes a deep and resonant chord for readers today. But it might have happened that the spirit of Musil would never, or at least not so soon, have risen from the grave, had it not been 'for the efforts of three men – Ernst Kaiser, Alan Pryce-Jones and Fredric Warburg. The names are placed chronologically, each man in his place', as Mrs. Ernst Kaiser wrote me on November 20, 1972. 'In each case,' she continued 'it was a remarkable act of faith in quality, in the thing for its own sake, and an involuntary tribute to each man's intuition, regardless of material consequences.' She concludes with a sentence of delightful sagacity 'that is not to say that none of us (perhaps including Musil, who didn't do all that badly out of publishers) didn't want to live tolerably – why shouldn't we, why shouldn't everyone?' As applied to myself as a publisher, the words express part of my attitude to publishing in the neatest way possible.

* * *

What was the nature of this novel in which the three men had faith? The scene is Vienna, the time 1913–14, the hero Ulrich, the man who, because he had all the qualities, had none, as all the colours of the spectrum blend together in a pure white light. To Vienna Ulrich returns after a long absence, an unattached man in every sense of the word. Soon he is immersed in the highest society, and is elected Honorary Secretary to the imperial Liege Count Leinsdorf's Collateral Campaign Committee to celebrate the jubilee of the Emperor's long reign of peace. For one feckless year, the campaign, a gigantic symbol of human foolishness, ambles like a blind dinosaur to the war, the destruction of Austria and the end of a great if imperfect civilization.

The novel is peopled with characters not larger, nor yet smaller, than life – Diotima, the influential lady of ineffable intellectual charm, waiting in readiness to devour her cousin Ulrich; Arnheim, the Prussian millionaire industrialist who tempts Ulrich with the offer of temporal power in exchange for renunciation of what he stands for; the Jewish bank-manager, Fischel, who believes in the guidelines of reason and progress, and gives ten minutes each day to philosophizing in a world turning to racialist theories and the slogans of the gutter; Ulrich's friends from his youth, Walter and Clarisse, he the intellectual and artistic Jack-of-all-trades rather than the genius his wife requires him to be; General Stumm, perhaps the most lovable general in literature, who with his friend Leinsdorf is possessed of a modicum of commonsense, a distrust of overdoing it, leading to a political system of weights and balances, a régime of compromises all too akin for comfort to the dangerous English habit of 'muddling through'. Pre-war Austria, Musil's Austria, a pleasant and ageing imperial power, may fruitfully be compared with the English imperial power whose final disintegration began in 1940.

Many of Musil's characters, drawn with a satirical realism, are from life – Feuermaul the poet, Maingast the master of prophecy, and the Superman of letters, a hostile portrait of his rival, Thomas Mann, who in 1929 won the Nobel prize for literature for which, I fear, Musil was never even considered.

But to attempt to summarize or describe so long and complex a novel is impractical in a book of this kind. There is barely space to mention even the sombre and terrible portrait of the sexual maniac, Moosbrugger on trial for murder, a threat to the existence of society, yet also strangely moving, a sad animal who has spent so much of his life behind bars.

* * *

It is interesting, at least to me, to uncover the infinitely complex, highly unlikely and utterly unplanned manner in which Musil was rescued from almost complete obscurity to take his proper place as an author of world significance. It had started early in 1940 and took ten years to run its full course.

During the phoney war a series of remarkable coincidences brought together the two people who deserve by far the most credit – Ernst Kaiser and Eithne Wilkins. He was a political refugee from Vienna, a Jew and member of a resistance group, who reached England just before the outbreak of the War, possessing nothing but the clothes he wore and a small sheaf of his own poems and stories. She was a former Scholar of Somerville College, Oxford, a distinguished poet of Anglo-Irish extraction, at that period what would now be called a literary layabout. No two people could have been more unlike – he dark-haired, swarthy, with rugged features, and stocky, she pale-skinned, fair and tall for a woman, afflicted with a most painful limp. While visiting the home of the Swedish cultural attaché in Hampstead together, Wilkins met Kaiser, who spoke little English, and explored their host's library. Suddenly, Kaiser pulled out the first volume of *The Man Without Qualities* and exclaimed 'that's a book that ought to be translated.'*

During the war Kaiser saw active service with the British Army and later served as interpreter for Military Government in Germany. As a result he acquired a thorough knowledge of English which he spoke with a strong accent. By chance during the war his wife, as Eithne Wilkins had now become, found and bought a copy of *The Man Without Qualities* in Charing Cross Road, home of the London second-hand book-trade. Soon after the war ended they teamed up, to translate from the German (Wilkins had previously translated only from the French, Italian and Dutch). This partnership was to prove one of the most productive in the history of translations, comparable in difficulty with C. K. Scott-Moncrieff's rendering of Proust's *A La Recherche du Temps Perdu*, and not all that much shorter. For this onerous task their financial reward was much too small. The payment to translators by publishers is not adequate to persuade the best qualified to undertake it, unless like the Kaisers and some others they are fanatics. With the rest of the publishers I plead guilty, though it is true that in the case of my firm and a few others the rate has increased since 1946 by considerably more than is required to cover the postwar inflation.

Late in 1946 Kaiser got a friend in Germany to write Musil's pre-war publishers, Rowohlt, who replied that in the mid-thirties he had ceded the rights to the Bermann-Fischer Verlag (then in Stockholm), since Musil's wife was Jewish 'and his works might therefore no longer be published in Germany', something of a half-truth since only two of Musil's works were officially proscribed by the Nazis, and then not till December 1938. Kaiser now determined to find, if he could, a German publisher for Musil, since he had discovered that Bermann had sold the rights to Musil's wife, Martha. He learnt also from her, in 1949, of the printing in Lausanne by private subscription of a small edition of the twenty chapters, 39–58, on which Musil had been working before his death. Many of the Lausanne copies were unsold, and Kaiser had them imported into England by a foreign books merchant, Barmerlea. Musil's fame at this time, 1949, was at its lowest point.

In London in the summer of 1949 Kaiser and Wilkins were very hard up indeed, to the point of enduring at times the pain of hunger.

*Although the pages which follow are based on Mrs. Kaiser's (Eithne Wilkins') material, much of the comment and the responsibility for what is said is entirely my own.

Their sole means of livelihood was translation of novels from the German and French, but Wilkins had refused to continue with work on one she considered as anti-semitic, and endured a tremendous dust-up both with the author and the publishers. She was suffering from a long-term undiagnosed illness. Kaiser had worn out several pairs of shoes walking from one publishing office in London to another in the vain attempt to persuade one of them to get to grips with Musil's massive work.

Meantime, he had reviewed a remarkable short novel, *Die Grössere Hoffnung* (The Greater Hope) by Ilsa Aichinger for the *Times Literary Supplement*. It was a book I had long been interested in, and I hastened to find out from the editor who had reviewed it. Alan Pryce-Jones informed me, whereupon I wrote asking Kaiser to come and see me. He set out on foot from Eton Road, Hampstead to walk the four miles to my office in central London. Eithne Wilkins now continues the story. 'On his return from Warburg Kaiser was exuberant. "*That*" he said with intensity, "is a publisher of a different kind." ' After rejecting Aichinger's novel, which either Senhouse or I disliked – I can't remember which – I went on to decline several German-language writers, including the mystical-occult Gustav Meyrink – I was never one for occultism – and Ernst Kreuder, author of *Die Gesellschaft vom Dachboden* (The Crowd in the Attic).

After this discussion, which must have occupied all of half-an-hour, I asked him whether there was any other writer whose work he'd like to suggest to me. It may be that I hoped to end the conference by this question, but more likely I was still searching for a German writer of distinction after the empty years since 1933, when Hitler had barred self-expression to almost every civilized German-speaking writer. Wilkins takes up the story again. 'At this point Kaiser produced what he must have considered his most unlikely card, the one which in fact was the ace of trumps, "Well, there is one writer," he said, "but I don't think there is any point in talking about anyone reckoned so difficult – nobody's interested." "Whereupon," Kaiser reported to his wife, "this Lorenzo de' Medici figure, very tall, sitting there in a carved chair, all Renaissance grandeur and knowing his own mind, *barked* that he wanted to be told about it. So I told him. And, damn it, he took it! It was difficult, and so he actually wanted to know about it." '

This interview in fact marked the turn of the tide for Kaiser and Wilkins and also of course for Musil's reputation. It might reasonably be described in the vernacular as 'a turn-up for the book'. Only a few weeks earlier two leading German publishers had refused Kaiser's suggestion that they reissue Musil's works, in terms which Kaiser, writing to Martha Musil, described as 'boring and typical'. Herbert Read, a director of Routledge, had failed to interest his colleagues in *The Man Without Qualities*, though he 'regarded the work with respect'. Other English publishers had also refused. But now Kaiser had found a publisher brave or foolish enough to give him hope. Forthwith he managed to persuade Alan Pryce-Jones to publish a long front-page article in the *Times Literary Supplement* on *The Man Without Qualities*, using the Lausanne private publication as a pretext. It was quite a bold step for the editor since Musil was virtually unknown in England – in fact, a Cambridge don went to the University library on reading the article to check whether a Robert Musil actually existed. He suspected the piece to be a hoax.

On August 2, 1949, I wrote to the Kaisers 'I am prepared to take an interest, however provisional and hesitant, in Musil's great book. It is obvious that to bring this out in English would be a Herculean task, but it cannot hurt us to take a look at the first volume.' For the Kaisers this was enough, I was already *their* publisher, all others were warned off the course. In the U.S. too the American publishers began to make inquiries. It was not till January 5, 1950, however, that the die was cast, I had been waiting for the support of an American publisher to make the translation costs bearable. Who would it be, I wondered – Knopf, Viking, Harcourt Brace, Harper? It was to be none of these great houses. It was in fact to be published by Coward McCann, a firm whose imprint indicated to the cognoscenti that they were almost exclusively concerned with books for the popular taste. Tom Coward, the head of the firm, arrived in London and came straight to see me. 'Why on earth have you taken the Musil, Tom?' I asked him, 'it's not your sort of book at all.' He smiled at me. 'The fact is, Fred, I haven't published a good book in twenty years,' he replied, 'and I thought it was high time I did.' There was nothing I could say or do. I gave what advice I could – and he did not follow it. When sending out the review copies, he wrote a letter to the literary editors virtually demanding a favourable review. Editors are rightly proud of their independence, and the results were shocking. *The Man Without Qualities* made a very poor start indeed in the U.S., so poor that only with difficulty could Coward be persuaded to continue with the second volume. The third appeared under another imprint. Since then, I believe, the excellence of *The Man Without Qualities* has at last begun to be realized in the U.S.

There is not much more to say. The English reviews were excellent, the sales satisfactory, after a longish period reprints were required. Profits have been made, not large ones but not altogether negligible. I have never understood why *The Man Without Qualities* was regarded before its translation as intolerably difficult. To me it is a delight all the way through. Even the 'boring' passages pleased me – to be bored by Musil is a tremendously exciting reaction compared to being interested in most modern novels.

In conclusion, an elegy. During 1972 Ernst Kaiser, the prime mover in the Musil affair, died. It might be said of him, as of Robert Musil, that he died with his work unfinished – the fourth and final volume of his translation of *The Man Without Qualities* is not yet done. It must be hoped that his widow, with such assistance as she may require, will perform this final task and complete for English-speaking readers the revival of so important and sparkling a novelist.

* * *

Many books have been, and many more will be, written about Thomas Mann. Nor is this at all difficult to understand, for Mann was not only a magnificent novelist but also the last survivor of that great literary tradition of humanism and liberalism which was dealt a body-blow by World War One and received its quietus from World War Two and the horrors which preceded and followed it. We live today in an age of barbarism, barely concealed by double-talk and hypocrisy.

It hardly needs to be said that Mann was a powerful enemy of the Nazis. When the Rector of Bonn University wrote to him on December 19, 1936, sensibly signing his letter with a wholly illegible signature, that 'the Philosophical Faculty finds itself obliged to strike your name off its roll of honorary doctors,' Mann replied in one of the noblest political utterances any writer has ever put on record 'Certainly I challenged the wrath of these despots . . . but not merely in the last four years. Long before I had been driven to do so – earlier than my now desperate fellow-countrymen – I saw who and what would be the result. But when Germany had actually fallen into those hands, I thought to keep silence. . . . Such were my precepts. They could not be carried out, I should have suffocated. . . . That challenge perturbed all the free-flowing creative fancies to which I would so gladly have yielded. . . . The mystery of the Word is great, it has by no means only an artistic but also a general ethical significance. . . . In the Word is involved the unity of humanity, the wholeness of the human problem which permits nobody, today less than ever, to take refuge in the Ivory Tower of the cultural.' These words from nearly 40 years back should be heeded by every serious writer today, each in his own country, to denounce the crimes committed daily in his name.

These words to the Rector give a clue to one side of Mann's genius, the need to unify, that aspect of his chameleon-like character pictured mischievously by Musil when he named him 'the Superman of Letters'. But there were many sides to his character, and of some of them I personally became aware.

Mann had been on Martin Secker's list from the middle twenties, and I had inherited him when I took the firm over in 1936. At that time his collected *Stories of Three Decades* was under offer to us, which naturally we accepted. No doubt becoming Mann's publisher was the greatest single asset I inherited from Secker, though it did not appear quite that way at the time. Mann's reputation was undoubted. Secker had published *Buddenbrooks* in 1924 and *The Magic Mountain* in 1927, also some of the individual stories now collected in one volume. In 1929 he had won the Nobel Prize. The two novels had had fair sales and continued selling a few hundred a year, but *Stories* proved a poor seller and actually made a loss. It seems difficult to credit this lamentable fact, but the reception of Mann's work in England has been shoddy. He had his admirers, of course, of whom J. B. Priestley was the best known. It was Priestley who did more than any other writer to make the public interested in him. But the critics were persistently hostile. Adjectives like Germanic, long-winded, tedious, difficult to understand, punctuated their reviews. Of this Mann was well aware. In 1945, for instance, we got some paper on which to reprint his *Joseph the Provider*. I informed Mann of this and he wrote me on October 15, 1945, 'it has made me very happy, particularly in view of the rather lukewarm and perfunctory English reviews which I have seen. It goes to show that the public does not care much about them. . . .' But it was not till the publication of *Dr. Faustus* in 1949 that Mann's sales took a strong upward turn, although *Faustus* must be regarded as the most 'difficult' of all his novels. With the appearance of *Felix Krull* in 1955 we had for the first time a really substantial sale right from the start.

In a letter from Mann's wife, Katya, of January 9, 1971, she wrote, after receiving our two-volume edition of Mann's *Letters*, 'I think it astonishing that so much attention is immediately given to such kind of publication, the more so, as Tommy always worried about he was so little popular in the country he most valued. In the last years of his life fortunately the situation improved.'

It would not have been surprising had Mann become dissatisfied with us as his publishers between 1938 and 1948. It says much for the tranquillity of his temperament that he did not, even though in this decade his American sales far outstripped the English ones. There was never a critical or harsh sentence in any of his letters to me. We had no trouble in agreeing advances satisfactory to both parties. Our relationship as author and publisher was so harmonious and so uneventful that it provides little material for a full chapter. After the war he came to London more than once, and he met me and my 'Florentine cinque cento wife' as he described Pamela. He admired immensely what the firm stood for, not least the steadfast anti-Fascist attitude we had maintained from our foundation in 1936 onwards. But he knew also how quickly I read his books when the English translation was available, how rapidly I wrote him to comment on them and praise them.* The intelligent interest of a publisher in his author's books is a powerful cement binding them together in times of stress or relative failure.

The first news I had of *Dr. Faustus* was contained in Mann's letter to me of September 27, 1944 – 'I started it soon after the completion of the Joseph novel and approximately 300 pages are written. But it is a difficult, delicate and complicated topic on which I should by no means proceed hastily . . . it will be a modern novel, dealing with the fictitious biography of a German composer, whose life passes tragically, and stands in certain symbolic relations to the fate of Germany.' His final paragraph speaks of his sadness at 'the suffering which this terrible war has inflicted upon your country, and I find no words for the damnable nonsense this robot bombardment presents in its senselessness.'

On February 22, 1945 he writes again 'thank you for your kind inquiries as to the progress of my new novel. . . . I believe that two thirds have been born. . . . However, the subject matter is so difficult that I cannot rush it . . . so you don't have to worry about paper for this book yet. . . . I believe I have already mentioned to you what the book is about, the fictitious biography of a modern musician, written by a surviving friend. The artist shares the fate of, let us say, Nietzsche

*My letters to Thomas Mann have annoyingly disappeared from our files, which makes it impossible for me to provide documentary evidence for this statement.

and Hugo Wolf which, however, in my representation becomes less a clinical than a moral and theological affair . . . the book contains a long conversation of the infected artist with the devil.' Mann then refers to a relationship between the fate of the composer and that of Germany. 'That this fate is now on the verge of being fulfilled,' he concludes, 'and in the most gruesome manner, nobody can doubt. Oh, that everything was already over! Never before did a people have more cruel masters, who relentlessly insist that it perish with them.'

Faustus was published on April 28, 1949, and Mann and his wife came to London for ten days. The firm gave a lunch party at the Carlton Hotel for 24 people to celebrate the occasion. It was a distinguished company, including the great music critic, Ernest Newman, author of a standard *Life of Wagner*. The table was a round one, at which Mann had my wife on his left side and Newman on his right. I sat across the broad table from him with Frau Mann on my right. All seemed to go well. After lunch we got up and I walked across to my wife. 'How did things go?' I inquired. Pamela smiled a trifle enigmatically. 'Things went well,' she said, 'really very well indeed. Mann talked to Newman most of the time about Schönberg and atonal music. Of course, I didn't understand one word of what they said.' She paused. 'Sounds a bit dull for you,' I suggested. 'No, not dull at all,' Pamela replied, 'about half way through, while he was chatting away with Newman, I felt his hand on my bare thigh just above my nylons.' My 'fifteenth century Florentine wife' is certainly a most attractive woman, but all the same I was surprised. 'What did you do?' I asked her. 'Nothing,' Pamela said, 'nothing for a few minutes. I thought the old man was paying me a compliment. But soon, when he took his hand away to hold his fork, I moved my chair a bit further away from him.'

The affair had been well handled, I thought, by both parties. And how revealing it was of the man, then aged 74, behind the writer, the man of feeling behind the superman of literature. Here was the duality of spirit and flesh, the theme of so many of Mann's stories, made manifest. Later I recalled a scene in one of Mann's novels, where an 80-year-old artist wakes one morning in bed and finds to his manifest delight that between his thighs his sex is hard. In his *Sunday Times* review of *Faustus* Newman called it 'the greatest achievement of the greatest living man of letters.' Yes, certainly Mann was still alive.

On October 31, 1955, came the first volume of *The Confessions of Felix Krull, Confidence Man*, a longish novel of 110,000 words. It had been announced to me by the author on October 11, 1954. 'Unfortunately,' Mann wrote, 'I have not terminated yet the Felix Krull Memoirs. The volume published by S. Fischer on September 20 is still a fragment, though it has about 450 pages. . . . The reception of the book in Germany is unusually friendly, I have however no illusions about the possibilities in England. . . . I am really sorry that the country nearest to my heart from all European countries is the least responsive to my work.' But at last the English public were going to demonstrate their appreciation of the great German writer in the only way open to them, by buying and reading his book. *Krull* sold nearly 12,000 copies in the first few months. It was perhaps the supreme irony for the man described by Professor Erich Heller in his book of that title as *The Ironic German*, for about ten weeks before publication Mann was dead. He had just passed his 80th birthday. Broadcasting on the B.B.C. in celebration of his fourscore years, Heller said 'With *Felix Krull* the world receives the gift which German literature has almost withheld from it, the great comic novel.'

To those who have never read a Mann novel, I would recommend *Krull* as the book to begin with and *Buddenbrooks*, the last and the first of his major novels.

The critics had at last greeted a Mann novel with enthusiasm. But Mann unwittingly had made it easy for them, he had written a *comic* novel, a contemporary novel without too much 'philosophizing', a novel of Paris rather than of the German heartland which the English so deeply suspect, a novel about a rogue – forger, procurer, evader of military service, seducer, impersonator, and con man. The English above all nations can appreciate a rogue. Their own literature is full of them from Falstaff onwards. So now, after 25 years as Mann's English publisher, I could forget my indignation at English neglect of 'a genius more universal, yet more intimately representative of his age, than any other novelist in the last half-century,' as Philip Toynbee wrote in the *Observer*, and be at peace. But, irony yet again, Thomas Mann was now himself at peace.

One should be prepared for the death of a man of 80 years, yet the news, when I received it, hit me hard. I had seen Mann, spoken with him, lunched with him, only a short year or two before. Well-dressed in the English style, scrupulously neat, calm, full of vitality, he resembled some great English surgeon. He had talked easily to me and I had talked easily to him. There was no showing-off, no assertion of superiority. Conversation was pleasant.

A publisher who does not mourn the death of an author is a heartless fool. Yet with Mann there was another factor. He had told me that what he had written was only 'a fragment'. Clearly he had intended another volume, indeed more than one. Krull at the end of the book is posing in Lisbon as the Marquis of Venosta, and is on the point of departure for a further career of rascality in South America. That was a book I was looking forward to reading, not merely as a publisher but as a private person. Indeed, I had begun to imagine a work like the *Casanova Memoirs*, a social history of the twentieth century as Casanova's of the eighteenth. In *Krull* Mann, the great bourgeois, I thought, had found the ideal medium for the release of the inhibitions and repressions within which his real life had had to be lived. At 9.30 every morning after breakfast, Frau Mann said to her husband, so she told me, 'now, Tommy, you'll go into your study and work till lunchtime.' While he worked on *Krull* at his desk, he could have lived in imagination the life of his character, crook, seducer of women, the scoundrel who lives in all of us. But, alas, he had left it too late. Dubious of the reception his German public would accord his con man, he had spent the last year or more of his life in study of Martin Luther, planning to write a play about him. So *The Confessions of Felix Krull* remains one of the greatest unfinished books in European literature. It is a loss I shall always regret.

17

John Prebble, Professional Writer

The deeper feelings of publishers are not often revealed to their authors while the publishing relationship exists. The publisher tends to be wary, diplomatic, reserved, rather hopeful, slightly pessimistic, laudatory, jolly, critical, or so diverse a mixture of all these as to end up more or less blank. Praise is dangerous – it might give an author ideas. Blame is perilous – the author may stop writing or even seek another publisher. To tell an author the unvarnished truth, as the publisher sees it, is no doubt hazardous, but it is a policy I have always tried to follow as far as possible, and with that policy I have had more successes than failures.

What about the feelings of an author towards his publisher? Since authors are undoubtedly more capable of self-expression in print than publishers, a good deal must be known on the subject, apart from Lord Byron's notorious statement that 'Barabbas was a publisher.' The great Victorian novelists must have referred to such matters in their letters with a certain amount of sincerity, so must many of the later writers, Wells and Bennett, Maugham and James, Galsworthy and Conrad. But there is a gap in my knowledge here which it is now too late for me to fill. In this book I have been able to produce some evidence of what a few of my authors have thought of me, since they have freely told me. One author, John Prebble, however, has gone further and sent me a substantial account of his attitude to me and my firm, intertwined with an analysis of his own writing career from its beginning. This has seemed to me of unusual interest on both counts, and it forms the basic material of this chapter. It is a more favourable report on my actions than I would have written myself, and lays me wide open to a charge of boastfulness. But this is a risk I have decided to take.

John Prebble is a good example of the professional writer. He has written novels, novellas, Westerns, short stories, history and reportage. He has been a journalist of unusual skill. He has written film scripts. He has written plays and features for radio and television. If some new medium were invented, I have no doubt that he could and would contribute to it. Prebble in fact is an all-rounder. He may never win a Nobel Prize for literature, but he is always interesting, accurate, original and compassionate, a writer of good English prose.

We met first in July 1943 at the office while he was on a week-end pass from his unit in Wales, serving in the army as a radar mechanic. These specialists were given more freedom than the rest, which enabled them to live in a permanent state of revolt, running a wall newspaper on the Soviet model started by Prebble, the first of its kind in the British Army; conduct debates of a seditious nature; and pleasurably plan post-war Britain. In this wild and hilly countryside Prebble's talents emerged.

After having short pieces accepted by *Penguin New Writing* and a leftist magazine, *Our Time*, Prebble decided to try something longer as an escape from the boredom of army life. He wangled himself onto the duty roster as the permanent orderly lance-corporal on night duty and wrote his first book (quite quickly) in the night hours. The theme was taken from a newspaper story about a Japanese bomber that had crashed on a small Pacific island and taken it over by force instead of surrendering. Its title was *Where The Sea Breaks*. Once complete, the problem was where to send it. Jack Lindsay of *Our Time* recommended two small publishing firms, Frederick Muller and Secker & Warburg. Fortunately it came back from Muller by return. Who had the paper in those days of strict rationing to publish a novel which was not a novel, which was too short, and anyway on an absurd and improbable theme? Next it went to Secker & Warburg – who also had no paper in those days of strict rationing – and I expressed a wish to see the author. It was the first tottering step towards a partnership that has lasted thirty years and still continues.

'I have a fairly vivid recollection of our meeting,' Prebble wrote to me on January 15, 1972,* 'not of what was said, apart from the fact that the tone was encouraging. But I remember a small sunny

*All quotations are from this letter and another of January 24, 1972.

room,* white paint and books everywhere, and this tall urbane man moving gently in a swivel chair, occasionally fastening his eyes on me as if he were waiting for me to make some earth-shattering comment on life, literature and the pursuit of happiness. It must have been a very hot day, for I remember how uncomfortable my battle-dress was, how heavy my ammunition boots. . . . When I left it was with an intensely moving feeling, not just that I had a publisher or that I had written a book that was to be published, but a grateful awareness of your kindness. This is odd, for I was also greatly awed by you.'

Though Prebble on his return to Wales could not bring himself to believe that he had actually written a book and that it was about to be published, his friends in camp had no doubts on that score. They escorted him for four miles over the hills to the Dolben Arms, where they all got happily drunk, returning unsteady along country lanes smelling of meadow-sweet, singing at the top of their voices.

When the book came out in July 1944, Prebble was overseas, billeted in a shell-wrecked house in France. Publication, an event of such vast significance to most writers, was a non-event, and remained so even when I sent him later some excellent reviews and 'a most encouraging letter', which he received in the Dutch corridor near the ill-fated town of Arnhem. The book had done well. Priced at 6s. (30p) the first printing of 3,750 copies had been sold within a few days of publication, a second impression of 3,500 copies lasted only four months, and a third of 3,000 copies in February 1946 also went rapidly. In all, we sold over 10,000 copies, a fine result even in those days of easy sales. But none of this registered on Prebble. 'I have never had the experience, which I imagine most writers have on publication of their first novel, of waking up to an entirely new world. My world was precisely the same as it had been the day before, and not very pleasant at that.'

When the war ended, Prebble started writing his second novel, *The Edge of Darkness*. He was then working on *Soldier* magazine in Hamburg. He continued to do so after demobilization, but made no effort to contact me, partly, he writes, because he still held me in awe, partly because he still could not believe in himself as a writer of books, indeed he regards *The Edge of Darkness* as 'most truly my first novel'. In December 1946 I wrote to his wife, Gail, to ask where he was and why on earth I hadn't heard from him, and soon

*At 22, Essex Street, Strand, looking out over the Thames. This office was completely destroyed by a bomb a year later. See Chapter 2.

after we lunched together. I demanded the 60,000 words written of the new novel, and he very reluctantly sent them, waiting sadly for the news that the end of his career was approaching. Instead, he was astounded to discover that we were accepting the book. 'You were critical of many things in the book,' he recalls, 'but you had a way, as you still have, of making suggestions for improvements as if you were picking them out of my brain rather than discovering them in your own. Over the following years, the awe melted slowly and was followed by admiration, affection and respect. There was also something more, something essential to a good author-publisher relationship. That is your loyalty to my work even where your doubts about it were very strong.'

The Edge of Darkness, published on April 8, 1948, was a study of a group of men, fortuitously assembled in a Searchlight Troop, through the fighting in Holland, across the Rhine and in Germany. It ends with an account of the first winter of occupation in Hamburg. It is one of Prebble's best novels. It was followed on May 25, 1950, by *Age Without Pity* and on January 15, 1954, by *The Mather Story*, written in 'a fit of passion after John Gordon fired me from the *Express*. The first version was very bad, and if I hadn't been in a state of near-panic I would not have sent it.' At this time Prebble was receiving a substantial salary from the Beaverbrook Press, which no doubt got spent with ease since he had a lively young wife and three growing children. What his books were earning him at that time would not have kept him for a month. About *The Mather Story* I was in no doubt. It wouldn't do.

The task of rejecting a writer's fourth novel after success with the first three is a horrible task, but one that has to be done, for two reasons – first, a bad novel will go far to destroy the writer's good reputation built up over years, second, the novel is likely to lose the publisher quite a bit of money. The first of these reasons is the more important. Since I had a high opinion of Prebble's work and potential and since I felt an affection and regard for him which I have not invariably felt with all my authors – this sentence is understated – I decided to break the bad news face to face rather than through the cold medium of a letter, however subtly phrased. 'You invited me to a publishers' lunch at Kettner's,' Prebble relates, 'perhaps you believed that if I were flanked by publishers I would not break down. Between courses you explained, with exquisite politeness and more by expression than words, why it was a very bad book, and since I agreed with you there was no argument. . . . I did not enjoy the lunch or the speeches.' Farrer, however, more merciful or perhaps less critical than me, speaking as an ex-journalist to Prebble, expressed the view that a newspaperman should not give up too easily, in consequence of which Prebble completed an entirely new version and delivered it to me a year later in summer 1952.

But then yet more trouble broke out. 'Your loyalty came under stronger pressures,' Prebble records, 'you may remember the circumstances. When I was running the diary column for the *Sunday Express*, an art dealer approached me. . . . He was totally deaf, which made interviewing next to impossible. He had acquired some pencil drawings by Stanley Spenser of a pornographic nature and had shown them to Alfred Munnings who proposed to place them before Scotland Yard, Church House and the Athenaeum.' This incident was the mainspring of the plot of *The Mather Story*. Off it went to our solicitors to vet for libel. Their report suggested that publication would have to be abandoned unless we got a clearance from the two warring artists. So Prebble dispatched it first to Spenser who unwrapped it, rewrapped it and returned it without comment. This was taken by us as indifference. Munnings replied from his home near Dedham on January 6, 1953. I quote from his letter as Prebble has recorded it for me.

Dear Mr. Prebble,

Here's your precious MS and may you make a fortune as a Best Seller. You've put a lot of work into it and I wish you well – I'm a queer fellow I suppose, to others – and to you!! Your idea is having a cut at the Press... but you yourself in a far more endless style are doing the very same thing. All's forgotten . . . but you now try out a reminder of a distant event and have made, so to speak, a Mountain out of a Molehill . . . Yours sincerely, Alfred Munnings.

Remarks –

The mere fact of you – in one page – speaking of *horses* and *horse quarters* spots me as Lovat. . . . You have covered up Spenser to a certain extent . . . still he never had a mistress like your goddess. You veil the real matter, you should describe the paintings!! Pornographic and poor. A pity a writer with your qualities couldn't find a more exciting story.

There is some excellent passages.

A.M.

Thanks for sending it.

Jan 6, 53

Please Mr. Prebble – For the Lords sake don't send me another MS – It has all but killed me – packing this – and the P.O. is nearly a mile away. Spare me.

Alfred Munnings.

MS posted today. Deep snow. Cold as hell.

This delightful letter made it possible for us to publish the book, and by that time we had the MS of his next, *The Brute Streets*. But this too gave us a libel problem, since one of the central characters was based upon Mrs. Van der Elst. Prebble sent her the typescript which after many weeks was returned with a great tea-stain across the cover and early pages. 'I telephoned her,' Prebble relates, 'and had a bizarre conversation. . . . "I'm sorry the cover's marked," she said, "have they accepted your novel?" Yes, I said, did she object to any of it. "No, I don't see how it could be connected with me," she replied, "I'm not old for one thing. I don't look old. And when I'm on a platform I'm alone. I speak alone. I've nothing to do with the Russians, I don't interfere with Communism, but I'm against Kings, taking this fabulous wealth when most of our poor people live in sheds. . . . There's a lot of truth in your book. A lot of things may be fiction, but there's truth in them." Later that year the novel came out without trouble.' It was the last novel of Prebble's to appear with an English setting. Their sales must have seemed too discouraging to him. But there were many and varied arrows in this writer's quiver.

John Prebble was born in 1915 and spent his early boyhood in a Scottish township in Saskatchewan, Canada, called Sutherland, since it was largely peopled by descendants of Scots forced out of their homelands by the cruelty of the Highland clearances. These Canadian Scots, Prebble records, 'were fiercely nationalistic, and their emotional nostalgia dominated my boyhood. I was impressed by images of blue mountains and black lochs, by all that Caledonia-stern-and-wild-fever of the Scots exile. Despite my parents' staunch Anglo-Saxon patriotism, I began to believe in Scotland as my homeland. I promised myself that I would visit Scotland some day, and Scotland in this sense was always the Highlands. I did not do so until I was 22, and by a happy accident . . . it turned out to be all and more of what I had dreamed.'

But the years in Canada had given Prebble a second interest, the American West. There were Cree Indians in his class at Sutherland Public School No. 1 – there *was* only one – built of red brick by someone obsessed with the Tower of London. 'I remember seeing some of the Indians who had taken part in the Louis Riel Rebellion of 1885,' Prebble continues, 'also an old man produced every year at the Saskatoon Rodeo as "the man who captured Louis Riel." In fact, Riel surrendered himself. I saw cowboys roping steers before I ever saw an aeroplane, and I knew the names of the Plains Tribes before I knew the names of the Kings of England. I saw Red River carts [over 50 years old] parked alongside Model-T Fords. Once I saw a Mounted Police Corporal ride into town to arrest the Chinese laundryman for murder. I dug arrow-heads out of slough-holes and traded them for apple-cores like Huck Finn. And after all that romantic nostalgia, it must be admitted that all I really wanted to do was to return to England.'

It was not till 1955 that Prebble turned as a writer to the deepest sources that fed his imagination, the American West and the fate of the Indians, the Scottish Highlands and the tragedies of their history. Here perhaps may be an explanation of the relative failure of his early novels, not *Where The Sea Breaks*, an allegorical tale, but those with an English background. In his recent letters to me, Prebble has said, 'I have a feeling that I never became what you expected of me after *Where The Sea Breaks*.' The accusation, if such it is, is true. I never saw him as a traditional English novelist, banging out a goodish novel every year or two on his typewriter. He was meant for better and more important work than that, and he has already achieved some of it, but not yet all. At the very heart of Prebble's character lies compassion and his intense feeling for the underdog – the Red Indians, the Highland Scots, the poor bloody Tommies of World War Two, the Germans in defeat with a hostile army billeted on them. It was not for nothing that in those grim years before the War his sympathies lay with the underpaid worker and the unemployed, a feeling which at times drew him near to the Communist Party. His sympathies lay with those in travail, the oppressed. It is no accident that among the authors on my list who attended my trial at the Old Bailey was Prebble. A man can well be considered oppressed, when he is accused of a criminal charge of which he is not guilty. 'I sat through your case,' he writes me, 'saw you first in the dock from which the judge compassionately removed you, and shared your triumph when it was over. I realized that your loyalty to any individual author comes from a deeper loyalty to man's inalienable freedom to write, publish and read.' Note the two words – compassion and loyalty. Here lie those feelings which have made Prebble unique among those who have written about the history of the Highlands. From these feelings, it is my hope and belief that a greater novel than any he has yet written will spring, a worthy successor to his first and not negligible attempt, *Where The Sea Breaks*.

Since being fired from the *Express*, Prebble had worked as a freelance with a growing success. Freed from subjection to a single boss, he thrived and laid firm foundations for successful careers in several professions based on writing. It was the editor of *Lilliput* who set him going on books by suggesting a long Western story. Recalling an old tale told him by his father years before about his true great-aunt, Prebble wrote *My Great-Aunt Appearing Day*, which we published in 1958.* Against the background of the treaty talks with the Sioux and Cheyenne nations, it tells how Josh Tanner wooed and won the Indian girl from two young braves. In 1959 *The Buffalo Soldiers* followed. This sprang from Prebble's urge to record in one book material spread among many, in this case, Negro cavalrymen in the American West, and so is placed on or near the Texan border where men living on the outposts of civilization are beset by the insoluble problems resulting from the Civil War.

But as early as 1954 came the first stirrings of the deep inspiration that led to the composition of what may be called Prebble's four Scottish symphonies – *Culloden*, *The Highland Clearances*, *Glencoe* and *The Darien Disaster*, followed by his massive *The Lion in the North*, giving a personal view of 1,000 years of Scottish history, with 32 colour plates, 152 black-and-white illustrations and 7 maps. *The Lion* does not count in my terms as a 'symphony', but I feel sure Prebble will return to that form before long.

Once again it was journalistic activity that launched Prebble into the rôle of a Scottish historian. He was looking as a freelance for a piece in a magazine to celebrate an anniversary, and suggested to his agent, Curtis Brown, the train disaster on the Tay Bridge, which happened (just happened?) to be in Scotland. Colin Young, son-in-law of Curtis Brown himself, said it would make a book.† Prebble agreed. The book, titled *The High Girders*, was published in 1956. It was the first non-fiction book Prebble had written. In it he showed the same qualities which mark his novels – narrative power, scrupulous research, and compassion for those who suffer misfortune. *The High Girders* enjoyed an excellent sale, and it led directly into the

*Reissued in 1973 with four shorter stories and retitled, to my regret, *Spanish Stirrup*, a good title, but how inferior to the original.

†Colin Young died tragically at a very early age, a considerable loss to the book world.

next phase of his career, the decade from 1961 to 1971 devoted to aspects of the history of Scotland after the Union of 1707, mainly the Highlands, with which his name will always be associated.

In 1958–9 Prebble had gone to the Highlands to do some research on tartans. There he returned to the Culloden battlefield and wandered among the graves. 'I had long since lost my romantic Jacobitism,' he writes me, 'but I was curious about the men under those well-mown mounds and about those who got away from the battle. . . . I told Graham Watson [a Curtis Brown director] that I wanted to write about Culloden and its aftermath.' When the idea was put to us, we asked for a synopsis and then commissioned it. There is no doubt in my mind that we expected a limited sale and no direct successors. Nor did Prebble. 'I believed it would be one book and an end to my writing on Scotland,' he writes, 'but before it was finished I knew it would be only a part of the whole, the destruction of the Highlands and the clans.'

The success of these Scottish books has surprised the author. 'Where they are original,' he writes, 'they are not something a Scots author could not have done. The material has been there all the time in Record Offices and archives.' Though Scotland must be considered now as Prebble's second homeland, he is careful to preserve its appeal by visiting it only, like a man living happily with his English wife, but taking infinite pleasure in visiting occasionally his dearly loved and beautiful Scottish mistress. Prebble's roots lie in the south-eastern corner of Britain, in Kent where his ancestors have lived for centuries. 'Kent has always been the cradle of revolt,' writes Prebble, 'it never had a true system of serfdom, a man had only to prove himself a Man of Kent to be treated as a free man.' It is no surprise to me that Prebble too is a Man of Kent.

18

Three English Novelists

'EVERY publisher knows' that short stories don't sell. 'Every publisher knows' that a first book of short stories doesn't sell at all. Every publisher with sense will ignore such folk wisdom, though not without peril. We read Angus Wilson's short stories in December 1947 when he sent a few of them to his old school-friend, John Pattisson. We told the author that, if he would write a few more, we would publish them in book form. He wrote several others, three more in fact than we had room for in the allotted space. The book appeared on March 24, 1949, and was immediately acclaimed. It was titled *The Wrong Set*, and sold just over 5,000 copies in the first year, an unheard-of triumph for short stories by a new writer. So began one of the most extraordinary success stories of my time in the book world.

Angus Wilson was born in 1913 on the south coast of England, the youngest of six sons. The nearest to him in age was thirteen years older. His father's family came from Dumfriesshire, his mother's came from Durban in South Africa, which he visited when he was nine. Both had been well off. His early life was spent mainly in hotels and even boarding houses, since the family income tended to shrink, partly because his father refrained from doing any paid work and so had no career, partly because he spent freely on women and gambling. There was also, of course, the post-World War One inflation which must have reduced the real value of the family income by half or even more. However, there was enough money to send Wilson to Westminster School and Oxford, after which in 1936 he took a rather routine job in the library of the British Museum. The war service which followed was in an ultra-secret department of the Foreign Office, which made good use of his knowledge of languages. Returning to the Museum after the war, he became deputy to the

Superintendent of the Reading Room, where he made many friends in and outside the Museum. Conversation with them barely postponed the confrontation with his own character which was to lead to a severe nervous breakdown. 'Bathed in the glow of the cosiness of my earlier life,' he wrote,* 'I had always thought of myself as a person of unusual gentleness and a natural liking for other human beings. I now learnt that I could hate intensely . . . and that I was capable of cruelty . . . particularly towards those who attracted me most strongly. Finally I was forced to think that my sophistication, easy sociability and worldly tolerance had been a form of carefully protected ignorance of life that had fooled myself. . . . The panic that had been packed beneath the lid since childhood at last broke loose. . . .'

At the museum they said of him respectfully 'he's writing a life of Charles Dickens.' But he wasn't, not then. When the rumour that he was writing stories began to circulate, they said 'he's taken up writing as a hobby.' That too was far from the truth. In fact, the breakdown which had stopped him working had given him the freedom and the leisure to undertake a task necessary for his preservation. 'A man thirty-three years old, whose emotional *ad hoc* plan of living had broken down,' wrote Wilson, 'had had to cope with solitude and self-knowledge – and these with that intensity of emotion . . . that country surroundings bring to those who have lived most of their life in towns.' It was in the country that he found the secret springs that were to fertilize the rich soil of Wilson's imagination. He analysed his problem as having three headings – an impossibility of worthwhile communication with society, a failure in love, and a lack of response to nature in the form of fields, farms, plants and animals, wild and tame. Self-discovery began in November 1946 when he wrote his first story, *Raspberry Jam.*

But, of course, nervous breakdowns do not inevitably lead to great literature – or painting or music or any other fine art. If they did, the world would be full of great artists. A man or a woman, well-adjusted to reality after a breakdown, may and usually does settle down to a satisfactory if humdrum relationship to the world. The sources of art lie deeper and are as scarce as food at the end of a long siege. Can we name them? I rather doubt it. Sharper perceptions than the normal, perhaps? Vanity? A tendency to be bored by the usual or by the actuality? A love of solitude or at least of a high

*In *The Wild Garden*, page 22, an analysis of the sources of his creative achievements.

degree of privacy? Curiosity? A facility to speak in one of the languages which art must employ, words, notes, pigments? Such qualities develop early in an individual, some inborn, some acquired from the environment at a very early age. To Wilson and to other great artists, a gift has been given. They, and we who enjoy their creations, can only be grateful.

This gift, this creative energy (which already spans a quarter century without sign of exhaustion) burst out in November 1946 in an orgasmic release. The evidence is in the breathless sentences of the early stories, written without much punctuation. Subconsciously Wilson must have felt that he had delayed too long – he was 33 before he started writing. Hence perhaps the breakdown. Hence the fact that in his first three years of writing two volumes of short stories (*The Wrong Set* and *Such Darling Dodos*), one novel (*Hemlock and After*) and a critical study of Emile Zola came from his pen. Here was a not-so-young man in the hell of a hurry. What is amazing is that even the earliest work is of the finest quality – many critics today still regard the short stories as his best work. So far as I was concerned, I had little doubt after *The Wrong Set* that we had 'discovered' a major writer. But the test was to come when the first novel was delivered.

Certainly it had an explosive effect on arrival at the office. Certainly I admired it. But I was worried about possible libel and about the frankness, as it seemed to me then, of some scenes. Would the Public Prosecutor intervene? Farrer wrote a long report on it. 'Structurally this is a bad novel,' he wrote, and went on at length to give his reasons, 'faultily constructed, yet it is often brilliantly written . . . in fact, an ambitious failure which may well be a commercial success. But it's going to be savaged by the critics – and rightly.' Nevertheless Farrer, only four years old as a publisher, had the sense to make a positive recommendation. 'Yet since it is crammed with evidence of what Angus Wilson *could* do, and it's on the censorship borderline, I regard it as a likely candidate for big sales. The author has a remarkable gift for depicting unpleasant characters. . . .' For Pattisson, the author's friend, this report was akin to blasphemy. For K. W. Gransden in *Angus Wilson*, a booklet in the series, Writers and Their Work, '*Hemlock* remains arguably his best [novel] because it is the most passionately written.'

We made a contract without hesitation, and the book was published on July 17, 1951. Farrer was wrong about the critics, it had an excellent press. He was right about the sales, which were substantial, nearly 12,000 copies in its first year. But there was an element in this first novel which angered many. A leading London bookseller, for instance, wrote to our sales-manager 'I do not like it at all. A miasma of unpleasantness pervades it which patches of wit and good dialogue do little to disperse. The chief character is an insubstantial creation . . . the emphasis laid on homosexual elements will ensure it some market, but I regret I cannot see it either a literary or a commercial success.'

In the U.S., where *The Wrong Set* had been rejected by Viking, Knopf and Simon and Schuster, *Hemlock* failed to impress Wilson's publisher, William Morrow, a house with a powerful 'middlebrow' novel list. They rejected it, and it was bought by Viking who have published him ever since. If this makes no sense to the reader, it makes no sense to me either.

By 1955 the urge to become a full-time professional writer overwhelmed Wilson, but he had no resources apart from what he earned. To assist him we guaranteed him a salary of £600 a year for three years, worth more than double today, while the *Observer* guaranteed him the same amount for three or four full-length reviews each month of important books. Backed in this way Wilson resigned from the British Museum, not without regret. This, to my mind, was an extremely courageous decision, because the number of writers who have been able to support themselves by writing alone, without hackwork, is pitiably small. I admired it all the more because Wilson's anxiety about money, after a childhood where financial disaster was always waiting round the corner as a result of his father's imprudent habits, was acute and remained so for many years.

Over three years went by before Wilson's first post-museum novel, *Anglo-Saxon Attitudes*, was ready, but when it came, I told him that I was 'quite bowled over by its qualities. . . .' I wrote to him three days later on October 7, 1955, after finishing it, 'I have developed an admiration for it of great strength. Compared to *Hemlock* it makes a tremendous advance in the closely knit fabric of plot and character, in the authoritative interpretation of human strength and weakness. All these . . . indicate the hand of a master of his craft, and to be truthful I cannot think of any English writer today who can hold a candle to you.

'When a publisher reads a novel for the first time . . . he is forced into the position of making judgments about it without anyone to hold his hand. Since he is not a literary critic, and since he is perpetually forced to judge things on two levels at once, literary and commercial, he feels diffidence in coming to a firm conclusion, but I have nevertheless come to one and do not expect to have to alter my mind whatever the critics say. [My belief] is that it is a novel which marks a new birth of fiction in this country, and that it is now again possible to answer distinguished foreigners when they ask "what important writers have you in England today?" ' A few months after *The Wrong Set* had been published, Orwell had died. After *Anglo-Saxon Attitudes* I felt as if the torch had been handed over from the older to the younger man, and it seemed miraculous that my firm had been privileged to publish both of them.

On Wilson my words must have had a tonic effect, for in those days, as I well remember, he was fully conscious of the difficulties he had in constructing a novel. He was still the learner. *Attitudes* was a full-length book. Since then every novel of his has been full-length, and indeed far longer than average. He puts it clearly himself in *The Wild Garden* (page 32) 'Having left the British Museum, I had more time to develop Gerald Middleton [the hero] . . . I was able for the first time to expand the canvas of the novel, to give it a setting of an imaginary world broad enough in social scale to make Middleton's personal problem seem no abstraction but the centre of "life" which expands beyond the novel, beyond the reader's view, into "reality". It is this that prevents a moral theme from seeming a "set piece" or a formal pattern. . . . This is the real challenge and triumph of the novel and, however excellent, thematic novels seem to evade it.'

Here is Wilson's philosophy of novel-writing in a nutshell, and for him it worked to perfection. Any doubts he had on this score must have been swept away when *Anglo-Saxon Attitudes* appeared. 'Brilliant and ambitious' wrote V. S. Pritchett in the *New Statesman* of May 12, 1956, '. . . one of its great pleasures is in its construction. But he is a personal novelist, filling out his characters by opinionating. . . . In that he is like D. H. Lawrence and not like George Eliot, our great duty-monger.' Most of the reviewers were equally appreciative, but one reviewer, he or she of the *Times Literary Supplement* (May 18, 1956) had reservations – addressing the author in the tone of a schoolmaster admonishing a promising pupil, more in sorrow than in anger. In the final sentence, the suggestion is that young Mr. Wilson may yet win a prize if only he will try harder.

But the grudging praise of such reviewers did little to injure the sales, which were massive. Starting with an advance sale of 10,000 copies, it reached an overall sale of nearly 33,000 copies within a year. There could be no doubt after *Anglo-Saxon Attitudes* that the future of Wilson was assured. This was the major and complex novel he had to write in order to satisfy himself that he could 'do it' and so to open the way for the sequence of five long novels which have appeared since then.

The Middle Age of Mrs. Eliot was Wilson's next novel, published on November 17, 1958. Once again the *Times Literary Supplement* on November 21, 1958 honoured it with a full-page review. Although critical, this review had a more positive and good-natured approach than its predecessor. 'In the past ten years the art of Angus Wilson has been gaining more and more upon the centre of the common reader's experience. Of the eight or nine genuine creative talents that have emerged since the war, he is the writer who has grown most. . . .' A little later the review remarks 'it must be said at the outset that [it] is a brave and very worth-while failure for two reasons: first, in terms of his own development as a novelist, secondly in terms of the reader's enjoyment, because of its supremely smooth readability.' The plot is basically simple – Meg Eliot married to a brilliant barrister takes her on a round-the-world air-trip, when he is briefed at an astronomical fee to appear in Singapore in a case involving Malayan rubber. During the journey he is killed accidentally in a shooting affair at an airport. The rest of the novel is concerned with Meg's efforts to rebuild her life. Here the reviewer remarks 'there is little point in chronicling the interminable ins and outs of Meg's attempts to regain her hold on life and sanity' and refers to 'a long – for the reader an all too long – recuperation at a strange establishment that her brother runs in the country, a nursery garden community established on quietist lines and staffed by a team of oddities who are perhaps meant to endear themselves to us, but who only succeed in irritating.' Another critic, K. W. Gransden, in a British Council pamphlet, stresses the importance of gardening in Wilson's life since he left the Museum and lived in an East Anglian cottage. Gransden remarks drily 'I do not think he makes this subject interesting [in Mrs. Eliot]. Perhaps it is something one has to do, not write about.' This was indeed my own view, and it led to the one major conflict in my 24 years of publishing Angus Wilson. The conflict is of some interest, since it involves the sensitive point between a publisher and a writer – Is criticism from the publisher allowable, and if so how far?

In the U.S. the editor is king. With few exceptions novelists will expect their novels to be edited, substantially. Indeed, many of them do not actually finish their books, but present a great pile of typescript for the editor to cut and shape. When an editor leaves a publisher to take up a new appointment, it is virtually certain that all or most of that editor's 'stable' – to use a racing term – will follow him, since they rely on him to finish or polish their books. All this happens quite frequently and gives American publishing a very different appearance to British. It may be true that British publishers edit too little – editing is a costly affair and British publishers tend to be thrifty – but I am certain that American publishers edit too much. Often the basic structure of a novel will be shaped, not by the author but by the editor.

Now no real editorial work had been done by us on Wilson's work up to the publication of *Mrs. Eliot*, and I for one had never till then considered it necessary. But with *Mrs. Eliot* it occurred to me that a good editor could have measurably improved the flow of the narrative, if only by suggesting drastic cuts in the nursery garden section. My opinion was strengthened by the impression I had formed, not so much that the novel had not sold as well as its predecessor, but that it had not sold as well as could have been expected. I thought also, wrongly, that Wilson had been disappointed with our sales, and that a disappointed author can become a lost author.

About three months after publication I took Wilson, whom I regarded as by far the most important English novelist on our or indeed any list, to lunch for the purpose of a frank *tour d'horizon*. All seemed to me to go well, or at least fairly well, but in coming to this opinion I was seriously mistaken. A letter of December 18, 1958, arrived from Wilson which indicated that he had been grievously wounded by what I had said or by what he thought I had said. He referred to 'the tactless way you have handled me'. He continued 'I know that you have always been a staunch friend to me as the world goes – it was only that I felt you voiced your criticisms of *Mrs. E.* and your belief that I should get down to the next book and seek expert advice on writing it, at a strange moment. I was, of course, dead tired and on edge, though I tried not to show it – I think you too were tired and worried.' This letter I read with dismay. How could he, I reflected, have misunderstood me so completely? I decided to write him a long and considered letter, from which I quote.

'On the question of seeking expert advice from another writer,' I began, 'I had in mind that Orwell always discussed new projects with Koestler.* I assume he found this helpful. It occurred to me that a literary confidant might be equally helpful to you. Probably I was

*I believed this statement to be true at the time, but today I think it false.

wrong about this, but it does not seem to me in any way insulting. At lunch you mentioned the name of [a very distinguished woman novelist] in this connexion. . . .

'As to "getting down to the next book," I feel not guilty, because I did not suggest that . . . I could not have done so, because I have always held that a real writer, who puts himself and his energies into his books, as you do, needs time to fill up, like a well after a drought . . . I seem too to remember refusing to discuss the idea for a next novel on the ground that "there was plenty of time for that later on". . . .

'As to the utility of editing I do not feel so happy, yet when a novelist has finished a book, especially a long one, he is perhaps too near it to see precisely how this book will strike a sympathetic reader. It is here that a good editor can sometimes (not always) help by making suggestions which the writer should accept *only if* he absolutely agrees with them. Farrer is such an editor. . . .'

As a result of this letter and the healing of injured vanities on both sides, peace was established between us and has lasted unbroken to this day. When Wilson sent me his next novel, *The Old Men at the Zoo* (1961) he indicated that he wanted Farrer 'to look at it' before we sent it to press.

With hindsight I can see today what a sensitive part of Wilson's unconscious was touched by my probing criticism of the nursery garden section of *Mrs. Eliot*. In *The Wild Garden* (pages 52–75) Wilson discusses at length the symbolic importance of gardens in his work, wild gardens and the garden in the wild. 'The two symbols,' he writes (page 62) 'have become so powerful for me because they really do have a prelapsarian association for me. They lie in the very earliest conception I ever received of happiness, not even in my own infant happiness, but in the childhood happiness of my mother and my father, unhappy people both, who looked back from lives of broken-down urbanism to real rural childhood paradises.' How well I can understand the force of this symbol myself who have known it in the person nearest to me in my life. And indeed the Garden of Eden, from which we have so irreversibly been expelled by the nature of our own humanity, is a symbol of which few are not consciously or otherwise aware. In my criticism of Wilson's nursery garden I was attacking unwittingly the most powerful generator of his work, his unconscious. How lucky I was to have escaped so lightly! How forgiving of Wilson to have accepted me so soon into his circle of friends! As a matter of fact it was I who had given the novel its title,

The Middle Age of Mrs. Eliot. Wilson's original title was *Change of Life*, 'a dubious title which would, you thought, put off a lot of readers,' Wilson wrote me early in 1973, adding, 'it was a salutary lesson to me not to be too clever.'

After *Zoo*, which I believe is Wilson's favourite novel, came *Late Call* (1964), which takes place in one of England's 'New Towns', followed by the longest and most complex of all his books, *No Laughing Matter* (1967), which follows the Matthews family through three generations from 1912 to the present. In the blurb I hinted that this perhaps was Wilson's *Forsyte Saga* or at least a serious attempt, no laughing matter in fact, to explore the possibilities of this form and discover whether the family saga can be used to write a novel that is not merely sociology but actually literature.

It was six years before his next and latest novel was ready, *As If By Magic*. But in the meantime he had written the book he was said to be contemplating at the British Museum in 1949. *The World of Dickens* came out in 1970. It was a wonderful book, splendidly illustrated in colour and black-and-white, produced for us by the well-known production unit of George Rainbird. It had an enthusiastic press and an enormous sale. At last Wilson had paid tribute to the great English novelist whom he has acknowledged as a major influence on his work.

Wilson is a man of many parts. For me one of his most sensational performances was displayed in the lectures he delivered at the University of London on Evil in the English Novel. I listened to all four of them, and when the course was concluded, I asked him to send me the typescript of the lectures with a view to making a book of them. He looked at me blankly. 'Typescript?' he said, 'What typescript? I had no typescript.' He had delivered an hour-long lecture at the rate of at least 150 words per minute (that is, very fast), in all some 9,000 words, with the aid of nothing but three or four sentences scrawled on a sheet of note paper. No wonder he is sought after as a lecturer and as a speaker. My prophecy is that, unlike Orwell or Mishima, but in the tradition of Mann and Dickens, Wilson will continue his extraordinary career into a mature old age, and his later books will excel those that have gone before them.

* * *

Among the talented younger English novelists on the Secker & Warburg list I have chosen two whose books generate in me a special sense of excitement – Melvyn Bragg and Julian Gloag. No two writers could be less alike. Bragg sprang from the fells and farms of Cumberland, a working-class boy who proceeded upwards in the social scale by means of scholarships to Wigton Grammar School, Cumberland, thence to Wadham College, Oxford, thence to the B.B.C. where he has already done much fine work in television. But from the very first day I met him he has made it clear that what he wanted above all was to be a novelist, to write novels. The need to do this was so strong in him that it led him to abandon good positions and highly paid jobs for the desk with the blank paper and the typewriter, the lonely business of writing. And in this he has most certainly succeeded. Seven books in eight years from *For Want of a Nail* in 1965 to *Josh Lawton* in 1972, makes an output almost unheard of today among serious writers. Some critics may regard this as an indication of superficiality, but for me it appears as creative vitality, a characteristic of many of the greatest literary talents.

Bragg came from a home without books, in which to read books was unusual and to write them unheard of. Yet soon after coming down from Oxford, while he was making his mark on B.B.C. television, he switched and began the task which can never really be completed until age has dispersed the energies required and weakened the urge to achievement. After three or four hours work on a novel, Bragg feels free – 'the rest of the day can take care of itself,' something which does not happen with any other type of occupation.

Bragg sees himself as a 'graft' from his non-literary background onto the tree of literature. It is this, I think, which makes him feel so powerfully the need to be appreciated, to be read, for he has nothing in his past to build on apart from his own success. 'I need to know,' he writes me, 'that what I already do is in some way laying a foundation for what I want to do. That is one of the reasons why I write so much.'

For a writer driven by so powerful a compulsion the attitude of his publisher is of crucial importance. He needs sympathy and criticism in proper amounts at the proper times. He has to feel confidence in his publisher, not only as the editor of his books, but as the successful seller of them. Our first meeting, often the most important meeting of all, went well. 'You told me stories about Mann, Orwell, Mishima, Grass which almost resulted in death by choking as the buttered skylarks at the Epicure Restaurant dropped into my gaping mouth. You impressed me unforgettably. . . .' For Bragg, the new writer, to be associated by implication with four such great names made him feel that he was already living, if only in the suburbs, as a citizen of the world of literature. My wife too played a part, as Bragg relates – 'Pamela brought a sense of mischief and even – dare I say it? – delicious and fertile corruption into the world of letters. She is one of those who *invented* the London literary scene in her lifetime. By equating haute couture with high culture* she introduced a feeling of demi-monde to the literary world, and made the whole business of writing much more exciting than it had any right to be. Most misleading!' Spurred on by his publisher and gently mocked by his publisher's wife, Bragg has certainly made a successful leap into that new world he dreamed about ten years ago in the Cumberland countryside. It must have been difficult, and it has not been often achieved.

* * *

When I read Julian Gloag's first novel, *Our Mother's House*, for the first time in 1961, I thought it was one of the most powerful and the most extraordinary first novels I had ever read. I think the same today. In my report I wrote 'this novel I rate as in the very top class, and if the author is only 26, he must have a brilliant future before him – barring accidents.' We accepted it immediately. Proof copies were sent before publication to a number of distinguished people, and the reactions were strong. The late Evelyn Waugh wrote 'I read it with keen pleasure and admiration . . . I preferred it to William Golding's *The Lord of the Flies* with which it can be compared.' Carol Reid, the film director, described it as 'a quite remarkable book'. The late Robert Henriques, a powerful writer himself, wrote 'it illuminates one's own personal experience and makes one comprehend something new, not only about childhood, but also about being alive.' He adds that he is 'still suffering from the very considerable ordeal' that reading it entails.

In the U.S., where it was published by Simon & Schuster, it was acclaimed on publication. It sold nearly 20,000 copies. Film rights were bought by Twentieth Century Fox for $75,000, paperback rights by Pocket Books for $28,000, and translation rights were sold to France, Germany, Italy and Holland. It was in fact a smash hit. Even *Time* honoured it with a review. *Time* noted an aspect of the novel referred to in Henriques' letter as 'a considerable ordeal'. It commented that 'the writer who can breathe fictional health into a

*My wife has spent an important part of her life as a dress designer in London, under her unmarried name of de Bayou.

story as sick as this must be credited with a minor miracle. Genuine magicianship must be conceded to Julian Gloag who has made a memorable fable about his seven motherless moppets.' When we published in London on October 21, 1963, I had hopes of big sales, not less than 10,000 or even 20,000 copies. We sold in the first three months about 5,800 copies, then put on a very expensive advertising campaign but sold only a few hundred more. *Our Mother's House* had done better than the average first novel, but its sales were not commensurate with the good reviews and the heavy promotion. The fact was that there was an element in the novel which disturbed its English readers. They did not recommend it to their friends. Without mouth to mouth recommendations it is virtually impossible for a novel to enjoy big sales.

Three years later Gloag's second novel, *A Sentence of Life*, appeared. In 1968 came *Maundy*, and in the course of 1973 his fourth novel, *A Woman of Character*, is due for publication. The first two are written in a fairly conventional manner, but the last two, composed with a very conscious understanding by the writer of his own motives and of his main objective, read strangely at first. What is this objective? Nothing less than a ruthless and destructive analysis of a broad section of English middle-class society, which Gloag, himself born into it, appears to hate with a savage intensity. Gloag, in fact, might well be described as the Ignatius Loyola of the bourgeoisie and of the social, business and sexual society which they have constructed.

What is Gloag's view of a healthy society? It is one where the individual is constantly acting and reacting with the society of which he is a part. But in fact, Gloag is asserting, this society is so hidebound by stale conventions, so lacking in any worthwhile set of values, so dominated by greed for money and the power that money brings, so riddled with hypocrisy, that only an exceptional person, virtually a saint, can remain free and uncorrupted. In each of his four novels, but especially in the last two, the hero or heroine is shown, either to disintegrate, as Maundy does, or to acquire the ugly character pattern which this society demands of those who are to flourish in it.

It was not until I read *Maundy* that I became fully aware of the black underlying pessimism which informed Gloag's work. Maundy is a well-to-do, handsome young banker who goes through the motions of his utterly conventional existence with an almost neurotic correctness. He has no thought that life could or should be other than the one he is leading. Utterly controlled by the conformist platitudes of his upbringing and education, completely repressed by the unnatural commandments of society, he is unable to release the vital passions of his body or his mind. One morning he is unable to find a pair of his socks, which he has left to soak the evening before. They have disappeared, an event as inexplicable to him as the failure of the sun to rise. Against this tiny crack in the tenuous fabric of his life, he has no adequate protection. There is a flaw in his artificial and abstract world which he cannot disregard. Instead, he seeks refuge in archaic rituals to ward off the evil spirits that seem to have invaded him. Eating, drinking, washing, sex, money, sacrifices, he tries them all, but in vain. Instead of guarding him, the rituals evoke the very passions of life which the dictates of 'common-sense' refuse to accept. Maundy's nightmare journey to escape from the deadness of his past, to discover the life-giving source of a new life which he is no longer fitted to live, has come too late. Step by step, using all the resources of his lyrical imagination, Gloag traces this twentieth century man of good will, this paradigm of our middle-class society, this Everyman, to his dissolution and union in some sort with nature or with the Godhead. In all modern literature it would be difficult to find a novel so unrelenting and so powerful in its attack on the way we live now.

Of course, on reading *Maundy* I became aware that it was a 'difficult' novel, and I worked hard to make it a success. Never before have I tried so desperately to convey my own enthusiasm, first to my colleagues, then to the literary editors and the potential reviewers. But, as I see now, this task was almost impossible, for the very people to whom *Maundy* is addressed, readers and reviewers alike, are the people who are accused in it. So the defendants became the judges, and the verdict was 'guilty of failure but with mitigating circumstances'. The sentence could be taken to be 'don't do it again'. For Farrer the book was obscene; for Julian Symon a mystery novel gone wrong; for Philip Toynbee a flawed case-history of a psychotic; for the *Times Literary Supplement* a symbolic poetic hotch-potch that didn't come off. Other reviewers were harsher still. Yet the book was not a complete flop. It sold nearly 3,000 copies. One day, if my judgment of this work is a true one, it will sell ten times as many.

And the author? What does a writer feel when his work is so totally misunderstood? Recently Gloag wrote me, 'the virtue of this book is that it comes close home, that very virtue explains why it must be beaten off – we do not want this sort of thing in our home. . . .

'Then how can I write? I wondered, after *Maundy*, whether I could write novels any more, because after all a novel, in whatever privacy it is received, is a serious and public matter. *Our Mother's House* was acceptable because the vagaries of children can be touching but easily dismissed on grounds of innocence. *A Sentence of Life* bows with a long agonized sigh to the absolute quality of the way things are. The threshold of disturbance is reached, but not breached.'

No doubt, Gloag was encouraged by the fine reviews *Maundy* received in France, particularly Françoise Wagner in *Le Monde* and Raymond las Vergnas in *La Nouvelle Litteraire*. Mlle. Wagner calls it 'an excellent novel by one of the most promising writers of his generation', which she says should find many readers among those who were admirers of Joseph Losey's film, *The Servant*. This comparison I find most illuminating. The utter collapse of the hero in the film when his valet introduces to him the alluring girl who seduces and overpowers him does indeed provide a remarkable parallel to Maundy's collapse. M. Vergnas refers to 'the lively conversations, the almost poetic lyricism which appear in the grotesque parody of the most tormenting themes of the contemporary conscience. For, and it is this which gives force to this very fascinating work, Maundy is a spokesman (porte-parole) for today's man suspicious of the tangible elements which he no longer trusts because they have let him down.'

Bravely Gloag fought on against misunderstanding and incomprehension. He wrote his fourth novel, *A Woman of Character*. What will be the fate of this book in which the unformed and naturally pleasant character of a girl is moulded by the corrupt standards of Gloag's (and our) world into a deadly succuba? According to the dictionary, a succuba is a demon having sexual intercourse with sleeping men. In the novel the men can be considered as 'sleeping' because they are unaware of the risks they run. It is none of my doing that this novel will not appear on the Secker & Warburg list. Can Gloag succeed or will he be driven into a stifling silence or perhaps have recourse to another medium, the cinema, for which his talents fit him? A film of *Maundy*, directed by a Losey or one of the great Italian directors, would be an experience worth having.

19
The Sixties

TOWARDS the end of the fifties the Heinemann Group became short of capital and made a deal with the important financial group of Thomson Tilling. In return for more capital, Tilling acquired control of the Heinemann Group. Tilling's chairman then was Lionel Fraser and their managing director was Peter Ryder. Soon Tilling began to feel doubts about their ability to run a publishing group which had serious problems to overcome, not only in the field of liquidity and profits, but also in the organizational field where tendencies prevailed that appeared to them anarchic. Fraser, a self-made man, the son of Gordon Selfridge's butler, as he relates in his memoirs, had a passion for books, and he most certainly regarded the business of publishing them as important. But from the business aspect the Heinemann Group seemed to him to have many failings. These misgivings were unknown to me at first.

But the sixties were not yet seven months old when I heard, quite by chance, from a close American publishing friend that a plan existed and was well advanced to sell the Heinemann Group of Publishers, of whom of course we were a not unimportant part, to an American house. The news seemed to me at first incredible, but if it were true I had no doubt that it would be a bad, perhaps even a disastrous, day for the whole British publishing trade. It was not that the Americans were inefficient – far from it – nor that they were harsh taskmasters – we have plenty of them over here – it was much simpler. The trouble with the Americans was . . . that they were Americans. It was my view then, and it is my view now, as I have expressed it more than once in these pages, that the publication of English books and of English newspapers should be with few exceptions in English hands. A month later, in August 1960, confirmation came to hand. The deal was on, terms were virtually agreed, a top executive of the Heinemann Group was flying to New York. The buyer to be was the McGraw Hill Company.

McGraw Hill was a huge organization, housed in its own massive skyscraper on West 42 Street, N.Y.C. Much of the firm was occupied with the publication of trade papers with large circulations, but it had also a substantial books section. No more unsuitable owner of the Heinemann Group, so it seemed to me, could have been chosen. There was, of course, nothing to be said against its reputation or that of its directors, those were of the highest. But it was too big, too American, too insensitive to British susceptibilities, too involved with scientific and technical books to become involved with the delicate susceptibilities of certain members of the Heinemann Group, not least myself and Rupert Hart-Davis, whose list was of undeniable distinction.

But the stakes were high. At this period the American Stock Exchange was bullish, new equity shares were being taken up on the day of issue and their quotation soared upwards. It was something of a bonanza. The money men and bankers had done their sums and discovered that the big upsurge in births immediately following the war, as the soldiers returned from overseas to the welcoming arms of their wives and fiancées, was leading inevitably to a big increase in children at school and university. The children would need books. The books would be provided by those curious old-fashioned characters known as publishers. Clearly publishing was a growth industry. That magic phrase 'we must get into publishing' was the word round Wall Street. Soon it became known to some of us in London that a massive coup was in preparation, the banking house of Lehmann Brothers would make a multi-million-dollar loan to the McGraw Hill Co. who would purchase with it control of the Heinemann Group in London and the substantial publishing house of Farrar, Straus in New York. So we believed. Shares would accordingly be issued on Wall Street, would be snapped up by eager buyers and go to a premium. Everyone would be pleased. It was an example of constructive industrialization, modern capitalism at its best, rationalizing the untidy, unplanned, higgledy-piggledy mess which publishers had got themselves into (so it was believed), in the name of greater efficiency and higher profits. I hated it.

But there was another reason, not less powerful, which appealed more perhaps to the American publishers themselves than to the money men. This prize was what used to be known as the British Empire market, the English-speaking countries of the world, Australia, New Zealand, South Africa and other not negligible centres where English books were read. This overseas market was of supreme importance to the British publisher. The U.K. market with a population of, say, 50 million was out of balance with the U.S. market of, say, 200 million. Without the Commonwealth, British publishing would be a very junior partner indeed in the provision of English-language books to the world. There was not one British publisher who did not accept the truth of this assessment, indeed all had signed an agreement (which would have been illegal under the American anti-trust legislation) not to buy any title from an American publisher or agent without gaining exclusive rights in all the Commonwealth territories, an agreement which was honoured to the full.*

The inside story of the deal that never was did not get told in 1960, the utmost secrecy was demanded by its champions. There were no leaks, the consequences might have been disastrous to those who blabbed. The battle, and a mighty battle it was, was fought behind closed doors. A key representative of Lehmann Bros and of McGraw Hill flew over from New York to convince the doubters of their folly. On October 16, a Sunday morning at 11.0 we all arrived at the Tilling offices in Curzon Street one by one, to avoid the exposure of so many important persons to the press. Eight or ten of us lunched in a private room at the Dorchester Hotel, and I had an instinctive feeling that I was about to be bribed. From 11.0 that day till tea-time we were at it hammer-and-tongs. Around 4 p.m. the banker addressed me in memorable words. 'My dear Warburg,' he declared bluntly, 'you seem to me like a man born into the wrong century, obstinate and almost wholly irrational.' Even at the time I felt he had enunciated at least a half-truth. But I knew then that we had won. The great takeover bid had crashed. Thereafter things in the Heinemann Group began to improve. Soon the substantial losses of the past – surely the basic reason why the bid was ever entertained by Thomas Tilling – were made good and transformed into even more substantial profits. How did we, the small battalions, turn the tide of battle against the big? By using our brains, the only weapon the weak had against the strong. By talk, phone, letter and cable we convinced Tilling that the deal would be against the national interest and that they would be blamed for it, in the press, on television and radio, and even in the House of Commons. Publishing, as Frere had written me years before, has a mystique of its own. Its

*Canada was sometimes an exception. The long mutual frontier made policing impossible.

importance cannot be estimated entirely by a survey of profit-and-loss accounts.

The McGraw Hill affair had been an insurrection, and it had given me some insight into the mind of the revolutionary. I realized that my publishing life till then had been concerned with financial rather than 'political' problems. It had been calm. My colleagues inside the firm had accepted my rule as an autocrat, even if as I hoped a benevolent one. Clashes had always been capable of resolution. But in the McGraw Hill affair it was make or break, victory or most probably the sack. This was shown significantly by what happened when we had won. Tilling's chairman, the late Lionel Fraser, whose services to the Heinemann Group and to my own firm within it were beyond praise, thanked me 'for my great service to the Group', while Tilling's managing director, Peter Ryder, read me a long and impressive lecture on the wickedness of my behaviour in going over the heads of my superiors to the top. It is true that Ryder had difficulty in restraining a smile while he delivered his oration.

Meantime, the processes of publishing continued. On September 12, 1960 we issued in two large volumes David Daiches's *A Critical History of English Literature*, covering in 1,000 pages the whole field of English and Scottish literature from Beowulf to modern times. In an age of specialist studies, when more and more is being written and even published on less and less, the attempt was unusual and even rash. Perhaps that is why it was rejected by an important educational house before it was offered to me, and why I decided that 2,000 copies was the largest number I dared order from the Ronald Press, New York. But my caution was out of place, the reviews were excellent, the first edition was sold out in a few weeks. Our re-order of 1,000 copies came rapidly across the Atlantic into the London docks . . . and stayed there for weeks while the dockers fought the good fight for higher pay. Rapidly we manufactured a big new impression by photo-offset, the situation was saved and, since then, the work, now revised and issued in four volumes, has sold many more thousands of copies, particularly overseas, where many students gain their knowledge of the subject from Professor Daiches's work.

It is an astonishing feat for one man to have dealt with so massive and so significant a subject as the thousand years stretch of English literature, where such writers as Shakespeare and Milton are given space enough for their sections to rank as independent critical studies. The author remarks in his preface that the work is intended less as a work of reference, a book to be looked up, than as one to be read. Hence no doubt its success. It is astonishing also that it could have been composed so rapidly, I believe in less than three years. But the author had need of the advance of £3,000 promised by Ronald Press to help pay for his return. Without it he could not have paid for his return to England with his wife, family, furniture and belongings, no small undertaking.

Another massive work appeared on November 7, 1960, William Shirer's *The Rise and Fall of the Third Reich*, running to 1,260 pages. It must have been one of the dozen biggest profit-makers we ever issued. Shirer and Daiches, American journalist and English academic, provided a solid foundation to our turnover through the sixties. Yet no one, I am certain, could have prophesied the enormous success of either of them with assurance, and to bet on the double with odds at less than fifty to one would have been foolhardy.

The book we commissioned from Shirer soon after the American firm of Simon & Schuster had made their contract was not precisely what was to emerge some five years later. Farrer on his first brief trip to the U.S. for the firm was offered it by a well-known agent, Paul Reynolds, as a study of Germany under Hitler from 1933 to 1945, planned to be about 100,000 words. It turned out to be well over six times as long. Instead of paying 80p for every thousand words of text, we were paying about 12p. A real bargain for the publisher it might be said. Yet, more truly it might be described as a disaster for the publisher, for how could he possibly sell a work of this enormous length, with a subject on which by 1960 many excellent books had already appeared at a price the public would pay. Priced on publication at £3·15 (63s.), equivalent to a price in 1972–3 of at least £8, the margin of profit was low, but . . . we sold 50,000 copies in the first six months, with many thousands more to follow.

Shirer must rank as one of the greatest of all American foreign correspondents. Stationed in Germany for the *Chicago Tribune* and later for the Columbia Broadcasting Company from 1926 to 1941, he was one of the last Americans to leave Berlin when Hitler declared war on the United States. Soon he published *Berlin Diary* which had an immense sale in English-speaking countries. Nevertheless, it was not these experiences that decided Shirer the journalist to become Shirer the historian, a transition rarely made successfully, for the qualities required of the one differ from the qualities required of the other. The reason was simple, powerful and convincing – 'at the end of World War II there occurred an event unique in history,' Shirer wrote in his Foreword, 'this was the capture of most of the confidential archives of the German government and all its branches,' together with a vast quantity of other secret material normally available, if at all, only many years after the affairs with which they are concerned. To this material Shirer was one of the few who had access in 1955, when the American authorities made it available for a limited period of time. 'I lived through the whole war, old enough to understand what had gone on and keen enough to study the events in order to discover the truth behind so many lies.' So wrote . . . not William Shirer, but Thucydides in his *History of the Peloponnesian War*, the terrible conflict between Athens and Sparta, which led to the virtual ruin of the Greek world. My translation is rough and ready, but not too far from the original.

Thucydides's book was one of the greatest historical works ever written. It is far too early after only 12 years to make the same claim for Shirer's. Yet there can be no doubt that *Rise and Fall* has held a unique place with the millions who have now read it, enjoyed it and been impressed by it. In spite of some critical reviews on publication by historians jealous of the attention it was receiving, it remains to my mind the most successful narrative of one of the darkest periods in human history.

* * *

In 1966 I was sitting in my office after lunch, feeling for once at leisure, when my desk-buzzer rang. It was Jeremy Hadfield, then my promotion manager, later a director of Weidenfeld & Nicolson. 'I have Barley Alison with me,' he said. 'I'd like to bring her up to see you.' In a minute they entered my room. I looked at Miss Alison with interest. I had never met her, but I knew she had a great reputation as a senior editor, and had been with Weidenfeld for ten years. Why was she leaving the firm? Miss Alison related her troubles at some length. She was clearly devoted to George Weidenfeld personally and had helped him over the years to overcome the dangerous problems, financial, social and technical, which often bedevil the early years of a new publishing house. But now, so it seemed to me, she was the victim of a raw deal, which she was accepting with a Christian charity I found difficult to understand. 'Why doesn't the woman fight back?' I asked myself.

Miss Alison wanted to stay in publishing. After a distinguished career in the Foreign Office, it had become her addiction, as powerful as the smoking of cigarettes, which were piling up in one of my ashtrays. She liked looking after her authors as a mother her children. She liked seeing, feeding, entertaining, supporting, encouraging them, and rejoicing with them when they had a success. She was, in my view, God's gift to a needy author struggling to gain a reputation without starving to death. While she talked, I pondered. It was not possible to engage her as an editor. We had already three editors and could certainly not afford another. Yet I felt great sympathy for her. Outside publishing she would, I thought, be like a fish out of water. Publishing was her life. Suddenly, out of these muddied or muddled elements which we like to describe as our thought-processes, a plan emerged.

The proposal was in certain respects a revolutionary one. Put briefly, we demanded of Miss Alison that she find, edit and lovingly cosset the authors to be published; that we should accept her choice of books, unless we felt overwhelmingly pessimistic about their prospects; that we should pay all costs of production and publishing, including the author's advance and royalties; that Miss Alison should receive no salary or expenses, but a substantial share of the profits as and when there were profits to share.

'The idea attracted me immediately,' Miss Alison wrote to me in December, 1972, 'since, if it worked out, it seemed to offer all the things I wanted. It would depend on whether I found your ideas about books and publishing similar to my own. . . . I never considered any other idea after our initial conversation. . . . Three weeks later I returned with the classic publishers' nightmare, a very short novel by an American (John Hopkins) with a South American background and no plot to speak of. But it was marvellously well written and I had faith in the author. To my delight you shared my enthusiasm.* Five years later I am still delighted with my set-up and grateful to you for having dreamed it up.' The new imprint was called The Alison Press, and it has made its mark. Obviously a plan of this type will be acceptable only to a person with sufficient means to wait for the profits which, after all, may never come. Such means were available to Miss Alison.

Fortunately the next novelist to arrive was less 'difficult' than Hopkins. He was Piers Read, son of Sir Herbert Read, who had published a first novel of exceptional unsaleability with Weidenfeld.

**The Attempt*, by John Hopkins has made £43 after only two years, even allowing for the cost of overheads. Hopkins' second novel, *Tangier Buzzless Flies* has recently appeared.

Read has published six novels since his debut in 1965, and won a number of literary awards. I regard him as one of the younger generation most likely to make his mark in the world of fiction.

Read was born in 1941. His second novel, *The Junkers*, published of course by the Alison Press, was one of the most ambitious for a man then only 25 to have composed. Read has expressed his views on novel-writing in an article in the *Evening Standard* of September 14, 1971. 'Already I find my interest in the world narrower than it was. I have had enough of travelling. The pleasures of Katmandu can now never be greater than those of my own study and garden. I emphatically prefer repairing stone walls in Yorkshire to walking around ruins and art galleries in Italy and Greece. I admit all this with slight shame. It is decrepit to prefer comfort to travel and adventure, and hard on my wife who is only 22.

'My justification is that a writer of 30 needs peace and solitude in which to unravel the experiences of his earlier years: yet I foresee a time when this peace and solitude will provide me with nothing to write about, and I shall be forced either to imitate my former books or go out in search of new experience at an age when it will be harder and less dignified.'

I suspect that many novelists have had such thoughts, but few have expressed them with such an awful clarity.

* * *

Le Prix Goncourt brings more prestige to its lucky winner than any other French prize. Worth in cash only a trivial amount, owing to the depreciation of the franc, it assures the winner a minimum sale of 100,000 copies of his novel in France as well as translations into many foreign languages. The Goncourt novel in 1959 was *Le Dernier des Justes* (The Last of the Just), the work of young Jew of 31, born in Metz to a family of Polish Jews who had fled the pogroms to arrive in France in 1924. By 1941 at the age of 13 he was alone in the world, since his parents had been seized by the Nazis and deported to an extermination camp. André Schwarz-Bart joined the Resistance at the age of 15, he was arrested, escaped, rejoined the maquis, then transferred to the army where he fought throughout the campaign for the liberation of France, 1944–5.

After demobilization, still in his teens, without any formal education, Schwarz-Bart worked in many jobs, including that of market porter in Les Halles, teaching himself as best he could and studying for a time at the Sorbonne. He had become a voracious reader of crime stories and detective novels. One day he bought a new one for a few francs to read over the weekend. It was Dostoievsky's *Le Crime et le Châtiment.* It opened his eyes to the possibility of writing about matters of importance. By 1950, at the age of 22, he began writing short pieces in his spare time. In the course of years these pieces fused into the novel which became a best-seller on our list at the end of 1960 with sales in excess of 25,000 copies. No novel had had such a powerful emotional effect on me since Orwell's *1984* just ten years earlier. Bouleversé is the word a French critic used to describe his feelings on reading the book. It certainly applied to me.

According to the legend, in each generation of Jews one man, a descendant of the Rabbi, survived to become 'the Just', marked out by God to become the symbol and sometimes the scapegoat for Jewish suffering. From the year 1190 when the Jews of York chose suicide rather than massacre by the mob, the procession of the Just continues down to Ernie Levy, born in Germany in the 1920's, the last of the Just. This is his life story, a strange, eventful and ultimately a tragic one.

Anxious to meet this extraordinary young man, I made a trip to Paris in the autumn to persuade him to visit London for the launching, which was to be elaborate, since our advance promotion had been highly successful. He was good-looking with a fine aquiline nose, wide mouth and pointed chin. His eyes were dark brown and looked very calmly at you when he spoke. He seemed to me like a latter-day saint, but fortunately with a sense of humour. I asked him whether he would come, and he told me that, on the urgent representation of his publisher, Paul Flammand of Editions du Seuil, he had agreed to stay in Paris for publication day and the two following days. After that he had fled to his hide-out on the Swiss-French border. 'Est-ce qu'il est vraiment necessaire que je me rends à Londres?' he asked me. I looked at him carefully before I spoke, but I knew already what I would have to say. 'Not really, your book will be a best seller whether you come to London or not.' He smiled, and we talked of other matters, including his future plans.

It appeared that he intended next to write a novel about the plight of negroes, parallel in some sense to the plight of the Jews in his first. He asked me to send him a list of books on the subject.

WARBURG: 'Novels, histories, or biographies?'
SCHWARZ-BART: 'Ah, tous les trois.'
WARBURG: 'In English, French or German?'

SCHWARZ-BART: 'Ah, tous les trois'.
WARBURG: 'That will make a very long list of books, indeed.'
SCHWARZ-BART: 'Mais j'ai beaucoup de temps.'

What a wonderful and comic sentence to come from a writer's mouth – an expression of hope, of devotion to an important task. I sent him a list of nearly 100 volumes, and he thanked me. Some years later he sent me a brief announcement of his marriage to a girl from Guadeloupe. A year or two later an exquisite printed card, about one inch by three-quarters, arrived to tell me of the birth of a son. Only recently has his book arrived at the office, titled *La Négresse Solitude*. A West African woman, fleeing from a massacre in her village, is forced aboard a slave ship bound for the New World. Solitude, her mulatto daughter, is conceived on this nightmare voyage. Born into slavery in Guadeloupe, she is bought at public auction by a plantation family, typical of the corrupt and parasitic society of the island. Once again, Schwarz-Bart has revealed the hateful mechanics of repression and painted a moving portrait of a woman and a race.

So Schwarz-Bart has carried out the task he discussed with me in Paris twelve years ago. Did he learn more from the lovely Guadeloupian girl he married or from that dusty list of books I prepared for him? The reader must judge for himself. But one thing is certain – this writer has ranged himself with Orwell, with Prebble, with so many of the other writers on my list and the lists of others, as an indefatigable campaigner in the never-ending war against the inhumanity of man to man.

A factor in publishing which has received little, if any, attention, is that of luck. Is it possible for luck to play a big part in a book's success? I have no doubt that it can, but on one basic condition – the lucky book must have real merit, the writer must have considerable talent. Without these a book can benefit from luck on the rarest occasions. Dennis Bloodworth had luck, so much luck that his friends should, and maybe do, call him Lucky Bloodworth.

It was luck too for me that brought me into touch with him in the summer of 1965, for I knew him vaguely only as the Far Eastern correspondent of the *Observer*. The introduction was effected by Anthony Verrier for whom I had recently published a not very successful book on the British army. Bloodworth came to see me on leave from Singapore where he lived. Verrier was certain he 'had a book to write'. In June, 1965 he came into my room. I stared up at him. He was a giant, six foot six inches tall, broad and good-looking.

Bloodworth tells of our meeting. 'He rose from behind an extensive desk to shake hands – one firm, decisive shake – a long stiff man with a long stiff face, whose even tan added to a quick first impression that he could have been a cigar-store publisher* elegantly carved in teak. . . . In focus, the immobility resoved itself into a stylish composure, a practised old-world calm which forbade any unnecessary movement. His speech matched his manner, his laugh was a drawing-room chuckle. But his eyes were as lively as his dry wit and it dawned on me that I was trying to sell a book about the Chinese way of life to a man of almost Confucian calm. The Confucian poise was combined with a severely professional attitude to publishing, and I was soon given an almost clinical account of the facts of life in the book world.'

That was how a first-rate journalist saw me in 1965, and bears little resemblance to my own picture of myself, any more than Prebble's picture of me in the last chapter. To both I seem to have appeared as an all-knowing and all-powerful god who held in his confident hands the key to the publishing door through which, if I could be placated, they would pass to enjoy fame and riches abundant. Both appear to have held me in awe but, reading between the lines, I sense a mischievous appreciation of the fact that an idol may have feet of clay. It was, of course, the feet of clay of which I have been most keenly aware – the knowledge of authors to whom I had paid too much, or too little; the excellent books I had rejected and the poor books I had published.

There were two possible subjects suggested by Bloodworth, the memoirs of his life as a journalist in the Far East and a book on the Chinese. 'When I babbled about my reminiscences,' Bloodworth writes, 'I was politely but briefly informed that memoirs of journalists had not been marketable for thirty years. I might have my pretensions, but . . . my ego should only be expressed in terms of pounds, shillings and pence. It was not a rebuke, just a statement of accounts. A book on the Chinese, however, might go. Would I like to submit a synopsis?'

A contract was signed for a book which was called *The Chinese Looking-Glass*. The advance was £500. Bloodworth asked me what would happen if he departed far from the synopsis. According to Bloodworth, I replied, 'I will never hold you rigidly to a synopsis, because authors frequently go off and write something quite different. It is better for you to write what you want to write than to write

*A type of publisher hitherto unknown to me.

what I think you ought to write. Of course,' I added with a small smile, 'what I agree to publish is another matter.' A bit cruel on my part perhaps, if I really said it.

But now Chinese Bloodworth has become Lucky Bloodworth. The book came out on August 21, 1967. It was well received and had an excellent sale, but in the U.S. the heavens opened and poured a rain of gold on to the delighted head of the astonished author. I had sold the book to Farrar, Straus soon after signing the British contract for an advance of$2,000. When the proofs reached their office, Roger Straus sent it shrewdly and promptly to the Book of the Month Club. Bingo! For some reason the Club lacked a selection for a month in the coming season. *Looking-Glass* gave them precisely what they needed. They made it their Choice, and printed something over 100,000 copies, which were absorbed rapidly by the members eager to read a book lively enough for non-experts about their Great Antagonist, the mysterious race of people lurking behind the bamboo curtain. Indeed, it is widely believed that President Nixon regarded it as essential reading before his meeting with Mao Tse-tung in 1972. Soon a lot more copies were called for. Both the British and the American publishers made small fortunes (say £10,000), while the author must have made about five times as much. Lucky Bloodworth! For it is rare for an unknown writer, English, to make a killing with a non-fiction book on a subject not obviously saleable, especially when the book is his first.

Three years later Bloodworth wrote and published with me that book of journalistic memoirs which I had so resolutely refused to commission. *An Eye for the Dragon* appeared on October 5, 1970, and – surprise on surprise – it had a success exactly parallel to that of its predecessor, Book of the Month Choice and all. The heavens once again let down their golden rain. The author rallied quite quickly from the shock of success, and in 1970 confessed to me that he wanted next to do a novel. 'You were doubtful,' writes Bloodworth, 'you said, with a slight shrug of those massive, almost immovable shoulders, "I suppose you've made enough money for us all round to be entitled to make a fool of yourself." So I did.'

The novel, *Any Number Can Play*, was published on October 30, 1972. In its review the *Sunday Times* wrote 'Few areas of the world are as absurdly but richly extraordinary as Indo-China. . . . Mr. Bloodworth understands better than most the unfathomable darknesses of the American "serving his country" abroad, he understands even more clearly (and ironically) the tragedy of Indo-China as big powers, utterly ignorant of the area, have thrust themselves upon it. His book is as macabre and as exciting, as sad and as complex and as alluring as Indo-China itself. More instructive than most text-books, infinitely more enjoyable than most novels. . . .'

That was Lucky Bloodworth having an excellent press, and having also an excellent sale for his first novel, 3,500 copies sold in the first few weeks. And in the U.S.? We wait for the day of publication to dawn. Surely it's inconceivable that he should become Thrice-lucky Bloodworth?

20

Goodbye to Publishing

IN *The Times* of November 16, 1968, on the verge of my 70th birthday, Pooter (Alex Hamilton) interviewed me.* Clearly it was time for me to prepare my exit from the publishing stage. Yet, as I remarked to Pooter, 'the problem of succession is not at all an easy one. It's all right for the dynasties like Macmillan and Longman, but otherwise it's a tricky business.' Many firms have collapsed on the death or retirement of their founder. Of those that have survived, few are run by a son or an heir of the man who gave the firm its name. As my own publisher, the shrewd Sir Robert Lusty, deputy chairman of Hutchinson has recently pointed out, 'When I went to Hutchinson, there was a Stanley Paul. There is no Stanley Paul now, (nor) a Hurst or a Blackett, a Skeffington, a Jarrold. And there is no Heinemann, no Constable, no Chatto, no Hutchinson, no Cassell.' For publishing is not only a speculative, it is equally a personal business. Except perhaps in the monster firms, the character of the executive head is decisive. For the success of a publishing house depends ultimately on its choice of books to publish, and this rests squarely on the chief executive, whether he exercises it by reading the books himself, accepting the reports of colleagues and readers, or by gazing into the clouded crystal ball. The man who chooses the books is the man of destiny or of disaster.

In 1966 I had appointed Maurice Temple Smith as my successor. He had been willing to leave the firm he was running, which was part of a group, because the well-known process of centralization was

*He was himself an attractive novelist, with a special interest in the book world. In 1968 he was contributing a weekly piece of considerable length to *The Times*, dealing with notable individuals in the book trade, and had selected me for his next one on account of the recent change of plan for my retirement which had attracted attention in the press.

driving him, as it has driven so many, to desperation. For two years I worked with him happily enough, but the profit position did not improve and it became only too obvious that the overheads must be reduced and the character of the list changed to a considerable extent. A complex battle developed inside the firm, brief but bloody, as a result of which Temple Smith resigned, 'having apparently miscalculated,' as Pooter puts it, 'the mood and strength of the forces opposed to his personal view of the right course for the imprint.' In just this fashion had I been forced to resign as managing director of Routledge over thirty years earlier.* Since then Temple Smith has set up his own firm, yet another example of the fission process for the creation of new publishing houses. He seems to have made an excellent start.

The failure of my attempt to find an heir apparent weakened my position in the firm. I was five years beyond the normal retiring age, and I couldn't or at least hadn't found a successor. The heads of Heinemann and Tilling became desperate. There was talk of bringing the firm directly under Heinemann management. Naturally and inevitably I fought hard against this policy, which would have destroyed the independence I had guarded so zealously since my 1952 deal with Frere. The news got out, the grapevine buzzed with rumours. A letter appeared in the *Times Literary Supplement* with the theme, 'Warburg must stay, this important firm is in danger.' Savagely I cut the overheads, a painful process for those who lose their jobs and for the man who makes it happen. Drastically I pruned the advertising budget. To the surprise of all, we crept in 1968 into the black.

Before this welcome news was known to anyone – for our accounts took three months in the making – in December the house of Jonathan Cape took action. It was headed by Graham C. Greene and Tom Maschler, with Michael Howard as chairman. They came to see me, as I reported on December 12 to Dwye Evans, then managing director of the Heinemann Group. 'They said,' I reported to Evans, 'that they thought the future of Secker & Warburg was seriously threatened and they wished to save it, that they had the money to buy the necessary shares and finance the firm, and that they wished to do so. . . . I pointed out that the top management, Farrer and myself, were the age we were and that the firm had made losses during the last five years. These remarks in no way deterred them.'

No doubt there was a personal element about this approach, based

*See *An Occupation for Gentlemen*, Chapter 6.

on the fact that I had trained Greene for the first five years of his publishing life – a deep mutual affection and admiration existed between us. But there was another and more fundamental reason, which Greene explained to me. In the field of speculative publishing, the number of firms devoted to quality books was small, and the loss of one of them as well-known and important as ours would seriously weaken the whole of that branch of the trade, in many ways the most vital and significant of all, to a dangerous extent. Greene's argument, if it is correct, as well it may be, has obviously wide application outside publishing. The reasoning behind it would appear to be similar to that of those who criticized the action of the British government in not 'saving' Rolls Royce. A quality firm must be preserved at almost any cost.

Obviously the Cape affair strengthened my position. The firm and I were wanted for our own sake by a reputable house with money. As I wrote to a friend at the time, 'I am being treated like a rare Etruscan vase recently dug up.' Negotiations began, balance sheets were examined, an offer was made . . . a rift appeared inside Heinemann between those who wanted to accept the offer and be rid of a firm whose profits were unsatisfactory and on the other side those who believed that Secker & Warburg was much too valuable a prestige asset to part with. The uncertainty got me down and I said irritably in the columns of *The Times* Diary, February 24, 1969, 'I am not a principal in these discussions . . . I am only a commodity being thrown about in the middle.' Cape fought hard, but there was a limit to the amount they could borrow from their bank and therefore offer to Heinemann, owing to the squeeze and credit control policy of the Labour government while sterling was under pressure. In the end, for better or for worse, Heinemann rejected the Cape bid and retained control. To the astonishment of nearly all save myself, the 1969 profit figure was an extremely healthy one. The overhead cuts and the basic strength of the new books had prevailed. The 1970 profit and that of 1971 were the biggest the firm had ever had. So it goes, sometimes, in publishing. By 1971 a new executive head for the firm had been found – Tom Rosenthal from Thames & Hudson. He was almost exactly half my age. On April 30, 1971, I retired.

The last two years of my life in publishing had brought with them yet again danger, a crisis and a final resolution. But I no longer enjoyed them, as perhaps I had done in the past. Pooter had written of me in his interview as 'the Grandee who feels that the stars alter their courses when a great manuscript comes into the office' and he contrasts the Grandee with 'Fred (who was never that silly)'. At the end of our interview, Pooter asked me the customary question addressed to a notable or a Grandee – to what do you attribute your success? I cannot think of a better way of ending my book than by quoting Pooter's final paragraph: 'In a climate which has caused so many general publishers to founder, Warburg has survived through the strength of his nerve. He is one of those who do not succumb to stress: apart from the crisis in his business, his wife, expressionist painter Pamela de Bayou, has been seriously ill this summer, and it was she whose temperament might be said to have defrosted him into the publisher he became. How, I wondered, had he come by his reputation as a subtly dominant publishing figure? "By knowing what I want to publish," said Fred, "what I can give my heart and mind to, and by not whoring after what would be, for me, false gods. But the answer to your question", continued the Grandee, "is that I've lived a long time. The mere fact that you exist gives you a certain strength".'

'A certain strength.' It was a fine ambiguous phrase, and I cannot better it now. This strength I still possess and will always possess so long as my wife is there to sustain me. Her serious illness in 1968 passed, and Pamela remains at my side as vigorous as when I first married her so many years ago.

Index